A Century of Revolution

AMERICAN ENCOUNTERS/GLOBAL INTERACTIONS
A series edited by Gilbert M. Joseph and Emily S. Rosenberg

This series aims to stimulate critical perspectives and fresh interpretive frameworks for scholarship on the history of the imposing global presence of the United States. Its primary concerns include the deployment and contestation of power, the construction and deconstruction of cultural and political borders, the fluid meanings of intercultural encounters, and the complex interplay between the global and the local. American Encounters seeks to strengthen dialogue and collaboration between historians of U.S. international relations and area studies specialists.

The series encourages scholarship based on multiarchival historical research. At the same time, it supports a recognition of the representational character of all stories about the past and promotes critical inquiry into issues of subjectivity and narrative. In the process, American Encounters strives to understand the context in which meanings related to nations, cultures, and political economy are continually produced, challenged, and reshaped.

A Century of Revolution

Insurgent and Counterinsurgent Violence

During Latin America's Long Cold War

GREG GRANDIN & GILBERT M. JOSEPH, *editors*

DUKE UNIVERSITY PRESS

DURHAM & LONDON

2010

© 2010 *Duke University Press*
All rights reserved
Printed in the United States of America
on acid-free paper ∞
Designed by Katy Clove
Typeset in Galliard by Achorn International, Inc.
Library of Congress Cataloging-in-Publication Data
appear on the last printed page of this book.

THIS BOOK WAS PUBLISHED WITH THE ASSISTANCE OF THE
FREDERICK W. HILLES PUBLICATION FUND OF YALE UNIVERSITY.

In a revolution, the revolution comes first.

—C. L. R. JAMES

Contents

Acknowledgments

This volume took root during a three-day international conference, "Rethinking Latin America's Century of Revolutionary Violence," which we organized at Yale University in May 2003. The conference, which was sponsored by Yale's Council on Latin American and Iberian Studies and the MacMillan Center for International and Area Studies, was generously funded by the Andrew W. Mellon Foundation and the Poynter Fellowship in Journalism at Yale. The event represented the second of two conferences that Yale staged in 2002–2003 in an attempt to expand conceptual frameworks for studying the Latin American cold war; the initial conference, held in Mexico City, resulted in *In from the Cold: Latin America's New Encounter with the Cold War* (2008), which was also published by Duke University Press in the American Encounters/Global Interactions Series. We thank Arno J. Mayer for graciously participating in the May 2003 conference and for continuing conversations.

We are grateful to Beatriz Riefkohl, then assistant chair of Yale's Latin American and Iberian Council, and to members of her staff for their assistance in staging our lively 2003 event, at which earlier versions of many of this collection's essays were first presented. We are greatly indebted to several other colleagues who shared ideas and insights that substantially enriched this volume—particularly Christopher Browning, Emilia Viotti da Costa, Mark Danner, Laurent Dubois, Sinclair Thomson, Piero Gleijeses, Alan Knight, Deborah Levenson, Barbara Weinstein, Stuart Schwartz, Ada Ferrer, Rebecca Scott, Peter Hallward, Kristin Ross, Harry Harootunian, Manu Goswami, Elisabeth Wood, Molly Nolan, Marilyn Young, Patricia Pessar, and Michael Zeuske. We thank Matthew Vitz for helping with translation. Greg Grandin is grateful to Gary Gerstle and other members of Vanderbilt University's History Seminar, as well as attendees at a Yale University Latin America and Iberian Council presentation, for comments on earlier drafts of this book's introduction. We are indebted to the anonymous reviewers whose helpful comments improved the manuscript, and to Tim Elfenbein, the managing editor who helped shepherd the project to its conclusion. Finally, we take pleasure in thanking (yet again) our editor at Duke, Valerie Millholland, and her assistant, Miriam Angress, for their attention and encouragement at every stage of the editorial process.

Living in Revolutionary Time

Coming to Terms with the Violence of Latin America's Long Cold War

GREG GRANDIN

Over the course of the last century, millions of Latin Americans have lived some part of their lives in revolutionary time. From the Mexican Revolution of 1910, through the uprisings and massacres in Argentina, Chile, Cuba, the Dominican Republic, Mexico, and El Salvador of the 1920s and 1930s, into the heightened period of mobilization and terror in the Southern Cone in the 1960s and 1970s, and Central America and the Andes from the 1970s through the 1980s, Latin America has experienced an epochal cycle of revolutionary upheavals and insurgencies. What was it like to live through any one of the many insurgent chapters of such a momentous century? What does it feel like to live in revolutionary times?

The essayist George Steiner tried to answer this question as it pertained to the transformative force of the French Revolution and Napoleonic Wars.[1] "No string of quotations, no statistics can recapture for us what must have been the inner excitement, the passionate adventure of spirit and emotion unleashed by the events of 1789," he wrote. To pass through such insurrectionary moments was to experience "great storms of being" that "literally quickened the pace of felt time," to believe that justice and renovation would be achieved not with the glacial pace of patrician prudence but immediately. The mobilization of revolutionary war likewise superseded provincial dangers associated with the agricultural calendar, natural disasters, and everyday exploitation, with each day bringing news of political conflict and breaks with the "pastoral silences and uniformities" that ruled the rhythms of rural life. "Whenever ordinary men and women looked across the garden hedge, they saw bayonets passing," was how Steiner described how the intrusion of warfare into everyday life changed notions of historical time. "As Hegel completed the *Phenomenology*, which is the master statement of the new density of being," he wrote, "he heard the hoofbeats of Napoleon's escort passing through the nocturnal street on the way to the battle of Jena."[2]

In Latin America, at least since the early nineteenth century, peasants have marched and countermarched in independence wars, national levees, and rural insurgencies, and not since then could politics, and the terror that often accompanies it, be experienced as the property of the privileged few. Pick up any one of the many *testimonios* of twentieth-century Latin American activists and you will find a similar exhilaration and hurrying to what we see described by Steiner, and a similar belief that the old dispensations no longer reigned and that "ancient time was at an end."[3] As Jeffrey Gould recounts in this volume, in the days and hours moving toward El Salvador's 1932 La Matanza, peasant Communist militants reacted to increasing repression by shortening the horizon of justice: "They killed my compañero," said one indigenous widow, "but here are my sons and they will see the revolution."[4] During the cold war, terror expanded into an almost inconceivable scale, confirming for "ordinary" Latin Americans that the terms of history had changed. One morning in 1962, for instance, Cuban peasants stepped out of their houses, looked across their gardens, and saw ballistic missiles rolling past. "I saw these weird weapons," said an unnamed interviewee, who appeared in an episode of CNN's cold war documentary series; "I said to my friend Pablo, 'Pablo, how powerful are these weird weapons?' and he answered, 'These are nuclear missiles.' So I thought, 'Oh, really powerful.'" "And they just put them here," said the campesino pointing to his field, "out in the open."[5]

The speeding up of felt time corresponded to, and was driven by, an acceleration of the state's capacity to repress. For untold numbers of Latin Americans, living through revolutionary times meant living part of a life in which political violence and terror were the stuff of everyday existence. First, in the nineteenth and early twentieth centuries, telegraphs, telephones, railroads, cars, wireless radios, repeating rifles, and automatic weapons allowed the state to respond more thoroughly and rapidly to threats. Then, during the cold war, tape recorders, fingerprint and surveillance equipment, cattle prods, filing cabinets, typewriters, carbon paper, radio and other communication technologies, binoculars, cameras, cars, and helicopters contributed to the creation of an omnipresent counterinsurgent infrastructure. But more than stemming from advances in technology, counterinsurgency, above all else, is choreography: starting in the 1950s much of Washington's "public safety" aid was directed at synchronizing the work of military and police forces to better their reaction time—to gather raw information quickly, transform it into serviceable intelligence swiftly, store it effectively, and act on it promptly.

The extension of counterinsurgent violence also entailed a sequential jumping of scale, from the regional to the national, and then to the transnational. At different times in different places, but generally running from the last decades of the nineteenth to the first decades of the twentieth century, local private armies and part-time militias, often headed by regional strongmen, were consolidated into government institutions, be they armies, police agencies, or national guards. During this stage, in southern South America, European countries did the training—Prussia in Chile and Germany in Bolivia, for example, or France in Peru, as Gerardo Rénique discusses below.[6] Further north, in the greater Caribbean basin, where the United States after 1898 engaged in a series of "nation-building" counterinsurgencies, Washington learned it could project its influence and ensure stability through the strengthening of local constabularies. Most infamously, Marines created Nicaragua's National Guard in 1927 and installed Anastasio Somoza as its head. And as the sociologist Martha Huggins documents in her *Political Policing: The United States and Latin America*, the United States either established or trained police agencies and national and civic guards in Haiti, the Dominican Republic, Panama, Guatemala, Cuba, and El Salvador.[7] Washington soon came to displace Europe as the primary provider of security aid and training throughout the whole of the continent, leveraging first the Second World War and then the cold war to win a near monopoly, helping to either create or fortify centralized intelligence agencies in one country after another: Argentina's Secretaria de Inteligencia del Estado, Chile's Dirección Nacional de Inteligencia, Brazil's Sistema Nacional de Informações, Uruguay's Dirección Nacional de Información e Inteligencia, El Salvador's Agencia Nacional de Servicios Especiales, Haiti's Sécurité Intelligence Nationale, Venezuela's Dirección de Servicios de Inteligencia y Prevención, to name a few examples.[8] Once lethargic units of limited range were transformed into effective national agencies, the next step was to coordinate their work on a supranational level. By the mid-1960s in Central America, the U.S. Central Command had set up the Sistema Militar Centroamericano de Telecomunicaciones, along with other coordinating bodies, to synchronize the work of individual intelligence agencies.[9] In the

1970s, the United States helped facilitate a similar counterinsurgent consortium in South America with Operation Condor, which carried out operations in multiple continents.[10]

The learning curve of state repression has steadily increased throughout the twentieth century and, except in the cases of Cuba in the late 1950s and Nicaragua in the 1970s, was always a step ahead of movements seeking social and political transformation. But it took a radical and great leap forward in the 1960s. Elsewhere I've described the political and experiential effect the progressive foreshortening of the time it took the state to repress dissent had on a generation of Guatemalan activists.[11] In 1966, reformers trying to recreate the domestic political coalition that generated Guatemala's 1944 October Revolution ran headlong into a new international anticommunist alliance committed and equipped to prevent that from happening. Within the course of three days in a series of sequential raids executed in multiple regions throughout the country—each yielding information that provided intelligence to carry out follow-up raids—a paramilitary unit established and trained by U.S. advisors kidnapped, tortured, interrogated, and assassinated thirty-three activists, and then threw their bodies into the sea from U.S.-supplied helicopters.[12] This exemplary act of compressed repression achieved in three days what just a decade earlier would have taken three months, forcing domestic crisis to keep pace with international polarization: the disappearances occurred less than two months after the six hundred delegates from more than one hundred countries, including Guatemala, at the Havana-hosted Tri-Continental Conference endorsed, over the opposition of the Soviet Union, armed struggle in Latin America and elsewhere in the third world. Many in the Guatemalan Left, though, decided to hold to an electoral strategy. That would soon change, as the most persuasive proponents of moderation were disappeared in the March raid.[13]

Escalating political repression was made possible by the provision, coordination, and enthusiasm provide by the United States. Yet its animal spirit was driven by a domestic reaction against the democratization of the region's status hierarchy that had steadily advanced since the decades prior to independence. Expectations of historical progress notwithstanding, the political conflicts that erupted as a result of democracy's march led to the experience of revolutionary time as suspended time, as a "hiatus between the no-longer and the not-yet."[14] During this pause, contrasting visions of where in time justice and redress were to be found vied for dominance. For those who wanted change, the future summoned: in Chile, as Peter Winn writes in his contribution to this collection, the leaders of Salvador Allende's Popular Unity coalition believed they could buck historical precedent and lead Chile through the world's first socialist revolution without violence. For those threatened by change, the past beckoned: "Let Chile continue being Chile" was a rallying cry for many who refused such a precedent. But more commonly, political actors embraced not temporal consistency but bricolage, where the past exists simultaneously with the future. To take Chile again as an example, in the early 1930s on the country's southern frontier, as Thomas Klubock's essay discusses, the vanguardist, modernist Communist Party championed Mapuche peasant demands to establish an independent "Auracarian Republic," which would entail not only the return of dispossessed lands but a restoration of indigenous language, culture, and religious practices. "Let's struggle for the constitution of soviets of workers, peasants, and indios," proclaimed Communist pamphlets. That many of Latin America's revolutionary actors had either experienced firsthand the violence used to break up common land and force them into a labor market, or had second- or third-generation memories of what it meant to live in a community that was not as commodified or bureaucratized as the one they lived in, gave force to the presence of the past in such visions of the future. It was exactly in these disputed moments when political violence became most incandescent, promising to light the way to either the no-longer or the not-yet, when its executors, in either the name of change or the name of order, became more verbal in justifying its use.

Political Violence as a Category of Analysis

In recent years, accounts of the acceleration and diffusion of twentieth-century Latin American political violence have drifted from explanation to interpretation. In the first instance, scholars working in the 1960s and 1970s—whether influenced by Marx, Weber, New Left critiques of imperialism and dependency, or modernization theory—took violence not so much as a primary focus of research but as a byproduct of either social transformation or the dynamics of domination and resistance, depending on their perspective. The Marxist tradition tends to explain violence as a condition of class relations, while modernization theorists take conflict as an indicator of an immature polity. Attempts starting in the early 1970s to sketch out the structural causes of bureaucratic authoritarianism that drew from Marx and Weber often ignored close inquiries into not only the cultural, ideological, and psychological dimensions of terror but also its contingent political dynamics. *State repression*, therefore, was taken as a reflex of crisis (caused either by class struggle or by an inability to modernize properly) and an instrument of class power, a repeating divisor in the algorithms of state formation and capital accumulation. *Social violence* was understood, especially by those scholars broadly working in the modernization paradigm, as perpetuated by weak or arbitrarily applied government laws and institutions, which bestowed on a majority of a given country's inhabitants what Guillermo O'Donnell called "low-intensity citizenship"—a phrase that implies the dependent relationship between structural and overt political repression.[15]

Recently, in the cold war's recession, scholars have offered more interpretative, subjectively sensitive descriptions of political violence. Such studies include those that focus on testimonials, memory, as well as a wave of ethnographies exploring the psychic slashes and cuts of daily counterinsurgent life, how protagonists and victims lived through and recollect experiences of heightened mobilization and terror. Much of the work in this vein rests on the sociological foundations provided by earlier, more macro-level approaches. Yet paralleling the general scholarly turn toward culture and retreat from metanarration, recent efforts to come to terms with the extremity of cold war terror in Latin America have operated within the hermeneutic rather than the analytical wing of the humanities and social sciences.[16] Some postmodern-inflected studies of violence exist in tension between these two branches, interpreting culture or linguistic structures while at the same time offering ambitious explanatory claims. Michael Taussig's *Shamanism, Colonialism, and the Wildman: A Study in Terror and Healing* (1987), for instance, while still deploying categories such as "primitive capital accumulation," argues that the totalizing power of colonial reason produced "spaces of death" and "cultures of terror" that persisted well after formal Spanish rule ended and can account for *both* the enslavement and murder of early twentieth-century native Americans in the Putumayo region of the Amazon *and* the torture of Jacobo Timmerman at the hands of the Argentine junta.[17]

In other regions that have been plagued by mass violence and terror, particularly those outside of Europe and the United States, there has been a more explicit shift away from trying to understand the historical causes and social consequences of violence to an almost exclusive focus on how violence is experienced. Scholars do not necessarily dispute the function or instrumentality of violence, which is often taken as a symbolic enactment of power or an essential element in creating fractured, wounded subjectivities that correspond to the rules of domination, particularly along gender, race, or ethnic lines.[18] Yet they often do so in a flat, historically static manner, which, for all the celebration of contingency, ambiguity, and rupture, results in a leaden account of social power. Gone are attempts to examine the relational formation of political subjectivity, the transformation of economic relations and state forms, and the evolution of competing ideologies vying for common-sense status. Studies of third world violence increasingly replace analytical categories with metaphysical ones: "exploitation," for instance, has given way to "social suffering" as the basic condition of human interconnectivity: "Suffering," runs the opening sentence of an edited volume titled *Social Suffering*, "is one of the existential grounds of human experience; it is a defining quality, a limiting experience in human conditions."[19]

One important polestar in much of this writing is Elaine Scarry's *Body in Pain*, which has not only provided a template to explore the visceral, up-close dynamics that take place in the torture cell but a reference for those scholars who emphasize the "unspeakable," or "incommunicable"—and thus unanalyzable—nature of violence.[20] What makes violence, particularly acts of political violence such as torture, a singular, untranslatable human experience is, according to this perspective, its immunity to human understanding. Extreme pain stands outside the world, writes Scarry: "To acknowledge the radical subjectivity of pain is to acknowledge the simple and absolute incompatibility of pain and the world."[21] Pain, she writes, is a human sensation that defies conveyance. It can't be rendered into verse, music, or art. It is inexpressible. Since pain and the world are absolutely incompatible, the infliction of pain through torture has the effect of, in Scarry's famous formulation, "unmaking" the victim's world. Extreme pain destroys the world by radically reducing the victim's conscious experience to his or her body, dissolving all other worldly claims. The only remedy to this reduction is to inform on comrades, furthering the severance of the victim from his or her world, in this case, his or her political and ethical world. Moreover, torture cannot be explained through a search for political motives. The primary point of torture, Scarry contends, is rarely to garner information. Whatever intelligence that is culled from pain is secondary to torture's structural logic. The relationship between the tortured and the torturer—which for Scarry stands proxy for a dictatorial regime (for others who tend to reduce history to an undifferentiated drive for power, such as Giorgio Agamben, this dyadic relationship encapsulates modern life itself)—locks the sentience of the victim and the sentience of the tormentor in a zero-sum metaphysical game: "the larger the prisoner's pain, the larger the torturer's world."[22] Implicit in Scarry's argument is the idea that the specifics of political violence—interests, motives, ends—matter less than the function (albeit prepolitical function) of violence.

E. Valentine Daniel's *Charred Lullabies: Chapters in an Anthropography of Violence* makes the point more explicit, drawing on Scarry to argue that the political terror inflicted on Sri Lankan Tamils, particularly torture, belongs not to the realm of politics or even ethics but to aesthetics, since it shares with the concept of beauty both an unpurposiveness and an untranslatability that precedes the predicates of language.[23] The difference between the two, however, is that beauty depletes language by opening up the world, by calling forth an inexhaustible parade of unsatisfying metaphors, while pain closes the world. Pain can burst into language through memorialization—through the kinds of postviolence memory projects familiar to Latin Americanists, such as poetry, music, art, writing, theater, and museums—yet the breakthrough is always partial. According to Daniel—who spends very little time discussing Sri Lanka's plantation economy or the subordinate position of Tamils as disenfranchised plantation workers—most Tamils experience power not as either Foucault or Gramsci would explain it, but as unmediated and brutal, which confirms for him the epistemological limits of social analysis, where "understandings abound, explanations appease, reason holds court, and concordance is king," yet meaning remains elusive.[24] Rather than considering the possibility that brute force could have a more prosaic end—having, say, to do with the distribution of power and resources in a highly exploitative society—Daniel instead waxes on the limits of representation: "Violence is such a reality that a theory which purports to inform it with significance" must make an "open admission to its inadequacy to measure up to its task."[25] Taking violence itself—not its effects or causes—as the subject of analysis, theorists of violence such as Daniel void the possibility of analysis, approaching terror not by examining its productive function but by stressing its epistemological mystery, its literal senselessness.[26]

For the most part, Latin Americanists have not, either through soft ethnographies or sharp-edged theoretics, challenged the explanatory claims of social analysis by embedding political violence deep in prepolitical sentience or in transhistorical linguistic syntaxes of culture. The one notable exception is, again, the anthropologist Michael Taussig, who in his *Shamanism, Colonialism, and the Wildman* uses the term "epistemic murk" to capture what, for him, was the irrationality of rubber traders killing needed laborers. Transposing his own confessed fascination with terror—Taussig once described himself to the *New York Times* as a "violence junkie"—onto the rubber barons, Taussig argued that violence can't be explained but only, through fevered experimental prose, experienced by trying it "out for yourself, feeling your way deeper and deeper into the heart of darkness until you feel what is at stake, the madness of the passion."[27] Taussig's leap into experience seems to have less to do with the actual legibility of terror than it does with a reified definition of "rationality"—reduced, in his account, to the economic logic of labor and profit—that he pronounces not up to the task. But between economism and postmodern swoon, there exists a world of politics, ideology, and even emotion and psychology, that mediates rationality. Often presented as a radical assailant of disciplinary practices and Western epistemologies, Taussig here, and in subsequent writings, reveals himself not unlike more conventional guides to third world violence, like Michael Ignatieff and Philip Gourevitch, who put themselves at the center of their chronicles of dehistoricized horror, trapped in a trope as old as colonialism itself: tales about specific violence inflicted on colonized or previously colonized peoples become transformed into universal parables about "all times and places," mirrors used to cultivate first world sensibilities.[28] "Perhaps, in examining the extremity with me," Gourevitch writes of his tour through the Rwandan genocide, "you hope for some insight, some flicker of self-knowledge—a moral, or a lesson, or a clue about how to behave in this world."[29] "What is it in me? Am I a bad person?" asked Taussig about his interest in the violence that attended the Amazon rubber trade.

Historians and other scholars of Latin America have also largely avoided the impulse (driven by a reaction to an alleged tendency of the Old Left to justify, and the New Left to romanticize, revolutionary terror) to abstract political violence from its larger context of provocative social violence and to equate, both in analytical and moral terms, left- and right-wing repression.[30] One exception of course is the controversy a while back surrounding the facts of Rigoberta Menchú's life. The debate was sparked by the argument put forward by the anthropologist David Stoll that political terror in Guatemala during the 1980s was caused not by the country's oppressive social system but by the romanticism of its revolutionary Left, whose decision to abandon electoral politics and embark on a strategy of armed struggle aborted the possibility of peaceful reform and provoked the military to commit genocide.[31] It is an argument that parallels, undoubtedly unwittingly, revisions of the French Revolution. Since according to these revisions, feudalism was already on the wane prior to 1789, revolutionary violence did not advance liberalization but rather represented what François Furet describes as a ghastly *dérapage*, a slide into chaos (in later work, Furet revises himself, rejecting the contingent implications of the word *dérapage* to stress that the terror of the Jacobins is generated by the "very idea of revolution").[32] Yet subsequent research in Guatemala and elsewhere in Central America, including that produced by the United Nations Truth Commission on Guatemala, which explores the centrality of violence in the formation of the region's states, institutions, and social classes, has demonstrated Stoll's provocative thesis to be unsustainable.[33]

Within Latin America, the way scholars have come to terms with prolonged periods of political terror has been conditioned by their country's particular experience of violence, as well as by the political alliances that emerged in its wake. In Peru, which ended more than a decade of military dictatorship in 1980 with a strong, politically ambitious Left, only to be plunged into the nightmare of Sendero Luminoso's "people's war," scholars, including many progressive scholars, have embraced the *teoría de los dos demonios* to explain the origins of political violence, a perspective that Gerardo Rénique below contests. But in Chile in 1999, a number of that country's most prominent scholars signed the Manifiesto de historiadores, strongly rejecting attempts to blame political polarization and terror on the "spell of Guevarismo."[34] And in Argentina, the "theory of two demons" is used not as an analytical category but a political slur, to criticize politicians, journalists, or scholars who try to establish a moral equivalency between junta repression and insurgent violence.[35]

The history of twentieth-century revolutionary and counterrevolutionary violence provides a sociologically nuanced view of the chronological unfolding of ideological hardening and polarization, one that refuses a tautological positing of ideological radicalism as the cause of radicalization. It forces an appreciation of the catalytic power of political reaction to breed ever more accelerating rhythms of frustration, fear, and extremism. Far from being unfathomable, terror in Latin America is so politically recognizable—in relation to enforcing domination, to generating and maintaining social exclusion, and to propelling historical change—that historians, with a few notable exceptions such as Steve Stern in his anthology on Peru's Shining Path, have mostly taken it for granted, leaving unexamined important questions regarding its form, dynamics, and meaning.[36] Well-versed in political economy and anti-imperialist struggles, yet attuned to insights provided by new social and cultural history, Latin Americanist historians, perhaps better than in any comparable area studies division, have produced finely crafted monographs that have successfully bridged explanation and interpretation, infusing larger structural assumptions about the economy and international relations with the contingency of politics, the imperatives of ideology, and the subjectivity of experience.[37] Deborah Levenson's *Trade Unionists against Terror: Guatemala City, 1954–1985*, to cite one example, fully articulates terror as both a structural determinant and an existential reality with symbolic import in the lives of union organizers.[38] Yet social historians have largely forsaken sociology, ceding to other disciplines—literary studies, political science, psychology, law, and sociology—the task of assessing and defining the larger historical meaning of twentieth-century Latin American political violence.[39] Of the many volumes produced over the last two decades addressing Latin America's recently concluded so-called authoritarian cycle and transition to democracy, few if any were written or edited by historians. This volume hopes to provoke historians to start thinking about Latin America's "Century of Revolution" as a distinct historical period.

The Dynamics of Revolutionary and Counterrevolutionary Violence

In considering the dynamics of Latin American revolutionary and counterrevolutionary violence, Arno Mayer's *The Furies: Violence and Terror in the French and Russian Revolutions*, published in 2000, provides a useful comparative study. Over the course of his career, Mayer, a diplomatic historian, has written a series of books dedicated to presenting an alternative account of European history, one that stands askew to liberal and orthodox Marxist approaches alike.[40] The major focus of his work has been that of containment, not of the Soviet Union but, starting in the nineteenth century, of the contagions of, first, political liberalism and then, socialism.

The Marxist New Left of the 1960s comprised three broad currents. There was much overlap, yet each was defined by distinct understandings of capitalism's relationship to "modernity," with implications for how subsequent generations of scholars thought about issues of power and rule. One current indexed modern times to the development of capitalism as an economic form, focusing on modes of accumulation, relations of production, and commodity circulation. A second current, associated with the Frankfurt school and French structuralism, defined modernity by its abstractions, emphasizing the importance of reification and alienation, along with subjectification and internal regulation of the self as structuring forms of power in modern society.[41] Mayer worked more fully within a third tradition, which stressed the importance of ideology but avoided diffusing power into the mystifications of bureaucratic alienation, commodity fetishism, cultural hegemony, or similar abstractions that others identified as the keystones of modern life. The emphasis was placed on clash, conflict, and coalitions; the template here was not chapter 1 of *Capital*, volume 1, but rather "The Eighteenth Brumaire of Louis Napoleon," with its close attention to factional politics, potentially autonomous expressions of state power, and the force of the past in producing vital and mobilizing ideologies. Mayer also sought to exorcize functionalism from Marxism. The social order was primed for "system maintenance," he argued. Yet ideology, sentiment, and the dynamics of elite alliances, once activated, often proved difficult to contain, throwing reaction into "overdrive," and resulting in a destabilization of rule that pushed European society over the edge into total war. Like Walter LaFeber in his 1963 study, *The New Empire: An Interpretation of American Expansion, 1860–1898*, Mayer has been consistently concerned with linking war and expansion to domestic crisis. Militarism and international conflict, Mayer wrote, are located in "over-reaction to over-perceived revolutionary dangers," which generates "organic crises that often spin out of control."[42]

At roughly the same time that Mayer was working out the conceptual framework that would scaffold his best known work, *The Persistence of the Old Regime: Europe to the Great War*, a group of Argentine social scientists in the late 1960s, among them José Nun and Juan Carlos Portantiero, were independently applying many of the same concerns to explain the persistence of militarism in Latin America, in particular to account for the cycle of postwar coups in Brazil and Argentina.[43] In a pioneering 1966 essay, Nun drew from many of the same intellectual sources as did Mayer, including Antonio Gramsci and Joseph Schumpeter, to explain why the Southern Cone's middle class consistently refused to leverage popular mobilization to confront and overcome the landed oligarchy. Like Mayer, Nun used Gramsci's distinction between, on the one hand, the hegemonic blocs of civil and class society and, on the other, coercive state institutions, like the military, to explain the resilience of the governing order even during moments of intense political and economic stress. Yet where Nun presented the middle class as a fairly homogenous social formation and centers the weight of his analysis on its social weakness, Mayer instead emphasizes what he calls feudalism's "interpenetration" of both the bourgeois order's "steel cage"—that is, its political, judicial, and military bureaucracies—and civil society. Building on the historical sociology of Schumpeter, Mayer has been especially attentive to the ongoing political and cultural power of a manorial ruling class, and that class's ability to fuse premodern or, better, preliberal sentiments, values, relations and institutions to new populist politics in order to mobilize counterrevolutionary opposition. "All this was more than atavism," Mayer quotes Schumpeter as saying; "it was an active symbiosis of two social strata," in which the state, while taking "account of bourgeois interests," relied on the aristocracy to staff high policy and military offices and the church to maintain hegemonic authority.[44]

Rather than serving as the ideology of a fully realized bourgeoisie, liberalism, then, along with the concomitant liberalization of social relations, in Mayer's work became by default the historical project of a militant labor and socialist movement. To the degree that Europe became liberal in the years after the Second World War, it was, according to Mayer, a result of a cataclysm of violence and terror, the roots of which Mayer, pace postmodernist and revisionist critiques, locates not within modernity but in the reaction against modernity. It took the "two World Wars and the Holocaust to dislodge and exorcise feudal and aristocratic power," he writes, which entailed not only breaking its class structures, political institutions, and economic foundations, but also deactivating the incantations, rituals, and myths that authorized that power.[45] In *The Furies*, Mayer takes up a variant of this argument to counter those who believe that the terror associated with the French and Russian Revolutions sprung not from social conflict between old and the new orders but from the revolutions themselves, from the unyielding utopian paranoia, language, and vision of their leaders.

Mayer, in contrast, emphasizes the sociological dynamics of political terror, paying close attention to the chronological unfolding of radicalization as it takes place within a hierarchy of overlapping fields of power.

Mayer's framework triangulates between three conceptual coordinates. The *first* is the violence generated by the clash between, on the one hand, an established, centralized, and relatively sovereign state and society representing incumbent elites, institutions, status and class relations, values, ritualized symbols and mythologies and, on the other hand, insurgent classes and groups driven by leaders with a more or less coherent opposing worldview based on innovation and not restoration. The degree to which such a clash breaks and recasts political and social relations and conventions is the degree to which it is a political and social revolution. The *second* coordinate focuses on the essentially contingent, indeterminate, and decidedly not inevitable nature of politics and history. It is this open contingency, and not a fixed ideological template, that propels militants to act in an unfamiliar present. Mayer here draws from Marxist existentialism to argue that political actors operate in "an open, not closed history," in a social system that is not unilaterally determinant but something to be transformed through political action.[46] As emerging historical actors on the political stage faced with apparently archaic obstacles and opposition, Mayer writes, "revolutionaries accelerate their lunge into an imperative but uncontrollable and hazardous future." He cites Maurice Merleau-Ponty to argue that during revolutionary moments, "history is suspended and institutions verging on extinction demand that men make fundamental decisions which are fraught with enormous risk by virtue of their final outcome being contingent on a largely unforeseeable conjuncture." "History," Merleau-Ponty writes, "is terror because there is contingency."[47] Readers of *The Black Jacobins* may recognize a similar relationship between terror and contingency in C. L. R. James's observation that "in a revolution the revolution comes first"—meaning that it is the imperative of maneuvering through the intricacies of immediate insurgent politics and confronting real opposition that determines action, rather than an insistence on holding true to ideological dogma.[48]

Third, this clash and contingency is passionately experienced and interpreted. The revolutionary breakdown of state sovereignty creates a vacuum filled not just by political and ideological conflict but by parochial antagonisms, hatred of elite pretensions, desire for vengeance, religious rivalries, base interests, and ambitions. Revolutions are simultaneously compressed and exploded moments of intense hope and dread—hope of release and liberation, dread of either the coming of the new or the return of the old. In short, revolutions are "hothouses" of "wish fulfillment."[49] Historians, insist Mayer, need to pay careful attention to the chronological unfolding of these ecstasies, to the real or imagined tit for tats that mark the contours of polarization. Revolutionaries, both successful and aspiring, have to harness these furies, linking the local to the national in a novel system of sovereignty. Counterrevolutionaries, for their part, need to mobilize them to their own ends in order to draw the curtains on the future.

Clash, contingency, and passion play out within two overlapping and interdependent fields of political and social power. The first is national, where the assault on the previous regime's centralized rule—in terms of political authority and worldview—leaves multiple zones of unstable, fractured sovereignty. This national field is largely refracted in the rural/urban divide. The fact that the countryside often is actually a formidable bastion of the institutions, mores, and social relations of the possessing classes is multiplied by the cosmopolitan condescension of urban militants. The second field is the interstate system. On the one hand, the universal, ecumenical, and world-historical claims of revolutionaries spill over national borders and, as such, pose a challenge to the international order's ruling states and classes, themselves inflamed by émigrés warning of apocalypse. In his early work, Mayer insisted on the importance of studying domestic crisis politics to understand the origins of war. In this later work, he maintains that international variables are critical in accounting for the course revolutions take. The French Revolution, though threatened by foreign reaction, could take advantage of a divided interstate system to "externalize" the revolution through the Napoleonic wars. The Bolsheviks, on the other hand, following the end of the First World War and their victory in their civil war, consolidated their authority at a moment when external opposition was united against it, which led to their revolution's "internalization" in the shape of Stalinist terror. (The "deeply subversive success" of the Haitian Revolution, as Peter Hallward describes, begs to be added to this comparison, having provoked "both at home and abroad a counter-revolution that in many ways continues to this day," with the "slave-owning world immediately" closing ranks and locking the "island in a state of economic isolation from which it has never recovered."[50])

The social and ideological conflicts produced by the clash between the old and the new, heightened by the contingency of politics and aggravated by the fervent defense of interests, status, and values, takes place within these two realms of power—national and international—where, feeding off each other, they become inflamed. Both civil war, usually unfolding along the rural/urban divide, and international war (or siege) are potent radicalizing agents, which, depending on the specifics of any given case study, condition both the nature of revolutionary and counterrevolutionary violence and the pace of internal social transformation. As politics polarize, coalitions form. Revolutionaries seek to establish sovereignty over a social terrain that they themselves shattered. Violence and terror is often part of this centralization, as leaders attempt not only to neutralize opposition but incorporate popular demands for justice and revenge into new state structures. This is one reason why red terror—which is driven by an attempt to create a new order and value system—is often public and incessantly theorized, while white terror—which operates to defend or restore the status quo—can usually do its work quietly and covertly. Yet revolutionary leaders often take the natural resistance engendered by their program of modernization, liberalization, secularization, and centralization to be more coherent than it often is, leading to an ever-intensifying friend-enemy schism. Revolutionary contretemps deepen schisms, charging every act with political meaning, transforming every event into a provocation, and winning new adherents to either side.

Counterrevolution is not an apparition, writes Mayer, conjured to validate a Manichean worldview: "Old regimes are not easily destabilized and brought down, above all because the privileged orders fight back rather than vacate the stage, negotiate their demise, or lie down to die."[51] In fact, since both chronology and ideology, which shape the way individuals and groups interpret danger, are central categories in Mayer's work, it is more often than not a preemptive counterrevolution or diversionary war launched in reaction to an overestimated threat that kicks off a revolutionary "organic crisis." "Whatever the extent and intensity of crisis," Mayer writes of Europe on the eve of the First World War, "it rarely took the form of prerevolution rooted in popular discontent and protest. In fact, the essence of the crisis was the opposite: a drive by aggressive ultra-conservatives to harden the established order."[52] One of the many strengths of Mayer's work is not only his insistence on the inseparable nature of revolution and counterrevolution but his analysis of the dynamics specific to the latter. Counterrevolution is presented neither as a mechanistic reaction to, nor a mimetic reproduction of, revolution. It is vital in its own right. Mayer distinguishes between "traditionalists" and "counterrevolutionaries." The first group is threatened by the dislocations of economic change and social liberalization, yet as members of the political and economic elite they position themselves not in opposition to modern life but as a needed bulwark to its excesses. The second group, which draws from the anxious middle strata of society, tends to be more doctrinal than conservatives and more comfortable with the "populist politics" of "mass mobilization and manipulation."[53]

The distinction is more heuristic than actual, with broad overlap between the two. Yet the typology is key to understanding how, for Mayer, social actors invested in preserving the status quo become prime agents in pushing it to the precipice of destruction. In the case of conservatives, resistance is not theorized or conceptualized but based more on a pessimistic view of human nature and an exaltation of order, along with disgust with new times and new politics. During periods of political repose, conservative politics is rooted in an underthought celebration of family, religion, property, and a minimal state. Counterrevolutionaries, in contrast, emerge from the "anxious" middle classes and possess both an ideology and a program, and are more vocally critical of the rot and degeneration of the existing society, even going as far as to call for its destruction to bring about its purification, clarification, and regeneration. Conservatives and counterrevolutions might be opposed during periods of equilibrium but cleave together during moments of threat. Crisis forces a loss of self-confidence and a more self-reflective conservatism, yet it still tends to remain in the realm of affective feelings, spiritual evocations, and celebrations of communitarian and patriarchal values and national glories. But in the face of the revolutionary threat, conservatives shift their support from freedom to order, change to stability, and preventive repression to exemplary terror.

In addition to this transformation of conservative politics, for the counterrevolution to gain full steam, two other steps need to take place. It has to look outward, attracting the attention and support, in the form of either invasion or siege, of foreign powers; it also has to look downward, connecting with grassroots discontent. As rural populations use the breakdown of sovereignty to press their own interests, multiple points of divergence and convergence between elite and popular opposition to revolution emerge. On the one hand, antagonism toward centralizing rule may lead peasants to ally with local religious and secular elites, who in order to ward off the nationalization of provincial patron-client hierarchies claim to defend local cultures, folkways, and autonomy. On the other hand, peasants can break with those elites and side with revolutionaries over issues of land, rent, and labor. Oftentimes the balance one way or another is tipped by a sober assessment of the local correlation of forces, as the inability of new authorities to effectively establish control makes it easier for the disenfranchised to "live inside" the counterrevolution than the revolution.

There are a number of points where Mayer's conceptual scaffold is obviously not applicable to Latin America's revolutionary twentieth century. Most of the region's major insurrectionary thrusts of the last century, for instance, emanated not from the city but rather from the countryside—and Mayer displays an unreconstructed urban disdain for peasant traditions. In Latin America after the 1960s, the Catholic Church, while in many places a pillar of the old regime, could also, especially at the grassroots, function as an agent of liberalization—and Mayer is an unreconstructed secularist. Likewise, as Peter Winn argues for the case of Chile and which can be extended—with a few important exceptions such as the Shining Path in Peru and the Revolutionary Armed Forces of Colombia (FARC)—to Latin America as a whole, the furies were decidedly nondialectical. The Left, owing largely to its deep humanist tradition, generally refused to respond in kind to the torment inflicted on it by the Right, to enter into the swirl of retribution and reaction outlined by Mayer. Yet there is much in Mayer's work that speaks to Latin America's revolutionary history: to the chronological unfolding of political polarization; to the transformation of the Right and the intensification of elite repression; to the distinct forms violence and terror took when it was put to either defend established orders or forge new forms of sovereignty; and to the fundamental inseparability of national and international politics, as manifested in the response of the United States to successive revolutions from Mexico to Nicaragua, along with the role played by émigrés and right-wing authoritarian states like Argentina and others who made up the Condor bloc, in inflaming international relations. The essays in this book, combined with recent scholarship on political mobilization and terror in Latin America, support Mayer's call for a socially embedded approach to diverse expressions of political violence. Taken together, they point to a number of programmatic suggestions that could help historians rethink Latin America's revolutionary and counterrevolutionary twentieth century.

Five Suggestions

The first suggestion concerns the need to historicize political violence. This means not just understanding its relationship to both institutions of dominance and exploitation and to the instigating social violence those structures generate. It also means examining the specific chronology of crisis: how actions taken during moments of extreme volatility are interpreted though ideology and sentiment; how this interpretation both propels and hardens polarization; and how this propulsion multiplies through overlapping fields of power, ranging from local land, labor, and family conflicts, to national and international efforts to establish legitimacy and control dissent. Friedrich Katz's opening essay measures Mexican revolutionary violence in light of the Russian Revolution, examining how Mexico's destructive initial "revolution from below" gave way to a stable and relatively peaceful "revolution from above" headed by Lázaro Cárdenas—in contrast to Stalin's contemporaneous top-down repression. Katz posits two variables to account for this outcome: the first is the ongoing economic power of Mexico's landed class, which didn't so much moderate revolutionary elites as force them to make real concessions to workers and peasants in order to prevent a neo-Porfirian restoration; the second is the relative weakness of the United States during the Great Depression, which meant the absence of a serious and sustained external threat that could have provoked ideological hardening and militancy.

A similar attention to chronology, which brings local provocations more into play, is present in Jeffrey Gould's essay on El Salvador's 1932 La Matanza, and in Thomas Klubock's study of a 1934 massacre of Mapuche rebels in southern Chile. Both review how the steady accretion of state and planter agrarian violence to unbearable levels, combined with an aborted period of anticipated political reform on the national level, pushed peasants to revolt (thus these two cases are closely homologous to Mayer's notion of elite "over-reaction" inducing an "organic crisis"). In El Salvador, far from being propelled by utopian rapture, the Communist Party was practically paralyzed by events that had long since escaped its control. Compare Gould's description of Salvadoran Communists who were aware of, but unable to halt, their plunge into catastrophe with Georg Lukács's account from 1921 of Rosa Luxemburg's participation in the 1919 Spartacist uprising in Berlin. According to Lukács, Luxemberg approached history with "clear-eyed certainty;" knowing the revolt was doomed to fail "years before it took place," she supported in it anyway.[54] Thus, for Lukács, Luxemberg's resulting execution, one among hundreds, consecrated an unwavering commitment to dialectical totality, to living a life that unified theory and action to drive history forward toward its final reconciliation. In El Salvador, in contrast, the Communists Miguel Mármol and Farabundo Martí were driven by historical contingency and not fantasies of necessity; they reached their decision to issue a call to insurrection in clear-eyed agony. Driven by a rural social base that was moving toward open rebellion, demanding retribution both for escalating repression as well as for stolen municipal elections, they knew that no matter what strategy they opted for, the government would respond with murderous violence.

A common theme running through a number of essays is the tension between an after-the-fact insistence of historical inevitability and the in-fact indeterminacy that marked any particular conjuncture. This tension is pronounced in cases such as those studied by Gould and Carlota McAllister, in which insurgent leaders invoke historical analysis to account for decisions and actions that resulted in horrific consequences. But the constant reiteration of the catastrophe in historical terms provides little consolation, for it ratifies the failure of would-be revolutionaries to have "read" history correctly. McAllister breaks out of this cycle by examining incongruities in the way the military, revolutionary leaders, and indigenous peasants narrate the coming of the "war" to one western highland Guatemalan community devastated by counterinsurgent terror in late 1981. Both the military and Ladino revolutionaries describe events with a sense of predetermination, as if no other outcome but ruin was possible. Peasants, in contrast, recount their participation in the revolution with more flexibility, allowing, according to McAllister, an appreciation not only of peasant agency but of the experience of revolution as an open process. Local interpretations of violence, she argues, inhere not in the morality of revolution—that is, in its supposed tragic inevitability—but in its undetermined historicity.

But the essays in this volume also suggest that contingency is not enough to account for the degree of violence any given revolution or insurrection experiences. As a number of cases under consideration here demonstrate, the Latin American Left has more often than not tried to live outside of rather than within history: it has repeatedly refused to accept the precedents set by previous revolutions, either in terms of their cruelty or their outcomes. This refusal can only partially be explained by the indeterminacy of the revolutionary moment, the sense that the future was not preordained, for ideology—and not just the kind of reactive, immediate interpretation of threats that plays a large role in Mayer's work on crisis—did loom large in determining courses of action. The Popular Unity coalition, as Peter Winn's essay shows, consciously debated its response to escalating counterrevolutionary violence in the light of historical antecedents provided by a larger international radical history. Influenced by Chile's deep democratic tradition, the leadership deliberately refused to launch a *levée en masse*, pursue Soviet terror, or embark on Guevarist armed struggle, instead modeling itself on the antifascist popular front struggle of the Second World War. Nicaragua's Sandinistas, writes Gould, rejected repressive revolutionary justice, instead attempting to articulate a new radical Christian ethos of forgiveness based on the prominent role that Liberation Theology played in their movement. In at least one notable exception, accounted for in this volume by Gerardo Rénique, a refusal to live "within" history (as Steve Stern elsewhere has described the Shining Path's unbending rejection of the Peruvian Left's history of compromise and conciliation) has led to an escalation of revolutionary brutality.[55]

A second suggestion concerns the need to explore the active relation between revolutionary and counterrevolutionary violence, particularly as it pertains to how competing political actors vie to fill the vacuum of sovereignty that arises during moments of crisis. It is not enough to acknowledge that the two forms of violence feed off each other; they do so in distinct ways. As Michelle Chase points out in her essay, Cuban revolutionaries staged public executions not only to prevent the kind of popular vengeance against old regime repressors that took place during the 1933 overthrow of Gerardo Machado, but also to tame that rage, to channel it into new institutions of revolutionary sovereignty and thus win for the new regime a legitimate monopoly of force. The trials were incorporated into the massive demonstrations that overwhelmed Havana during the first years of the revolution and were meant to openly contrast the transparency and morality of revolutionary justice with the covert and corrupt repression of the Batista regime. At the local level, Gould describes how during the 1932 insurrection, rebels who took over municipalities executed around twenty "political and class targets," many of whom were linked to recent electoral fraud. These killings, writes Gould, were part of a "calculus less guided by vengeance than by political design," after which Communists who were robbed of their victory at the polls were ceremoniously placed in their rightful office. McAllister documents a similar phenomenon whereby guerrilla leaders conducted public *ajusticiamientos* (a term that literally means "bringing to justice" but has been understood to mean "execution") against counterrevolutionaries as a way to establish their community authority. Jocelyn Olcott, in her essay on the struggle over how to represent a massacre of Communists that took place in Matamoros, Mexico, in 1930, highlights how struggles over the legitimacy of violence—who had the right to use it and when—continued well into, and beyond, the Mexican Revolution's second decade.

During moments of crisis, the burden of defending the status quo is considerably lighter than that of creating an innovative political, economic, and cultural order. Hence counterrevolutionary violence, while no less instructive than the forms of revolutionary violence described above, tended to be less vocal and less historically self-referential. On the whole throughout the last century in Latin America, the lesson offered by counterrevolutionary violence was by example, as opposed to exegesis. Gould, Klubock, and Olcott chart the progress of how everyday forms of diffuse social coercion and violence, associated with an exploitative agrarian order, exploded into concentrated terror when that order was threatened. In the case of El Salvador, the retribution was so immediate and all-encompassing that there was little effort made to justify it, even in terms of racism. Augusto Pinochet, in contrast to Cuban revolutionaries, carried out his postcoup executions with considerably less fanfare.[56] The mutilated and raped bodies that appeared most mornings on city streets in Guatemala and El Salvador, or washed ashore along the banks of the Rio Plata in Argentina or the Rio Mapocho in downtown Santiago Chile, said what they needed to say.[57]

But throughout the cold war, as the revolutionary threat refused to abate, white terror did become more historically self-aware of itself as an agent of both containment and change. By the late 1970s, the increasingly loquacious Argentine junta believed itself to be waging a "Third World War" between "dialectic materialism and idealistic humanism." "We who believe in a pluralistic democracy are fighting a war against the idolators of totalitarianism," declared Admiral Emilio Massera, "a war for freedom and against tyranny."[58] Such a vision of modernity included eradicating the influence of "Karl Marx, because he tried to destroy the Christian concept of society; Sigmund Freud, because he tried to destroy the Christian concept of the family; and Albert Einstein, because he tried to destroy the Christian concept of time and space."[59] For his part, Pinochet presented himself both as a stern defender of the status hierarchy *and* a "pioneer in the world trend toward forms of government based on a free social order."[60] In some places, as efforts to restore a world of unquestioned deference and subservience proved futile, the function of terror moved from instruction to catharsis. In the 1980s, the U.S. ambassador to El Salvador, Robert White, admitted the preternaturally violent nature of the military and the oligarchy, reporting that their ideal solution to the civil war was not simply the defeat of the Farabundo Martí National Liberation Front (FMLN) but apocalypse: they wanted the country to be "destroyed totally, the economy must be wrecked, unemployment must be massive" and a "cleansing" of some "3 or 4 or 500,000 people" must be carried out.[61]

In their drive to create new national cultures and carry out either capitalist or socialist economic modernization, it has been the fortune of many revolutions to generate opposition, particularly in the countryside where the reach of the previous regime was often weak and the private relations of domination of the old order were strong. While largely not as retributive or vengeful as white terror, revolutionary attempts to counter this opposition and extend centralized sovereignty, such as what occurred in Mexico during the Cristero revolt or Nicaragua during the Contra war became as discreet as the kinds of violence that defended the old regime. In this volume, Lillian Guerra's excavation of the largely silenced history of the Cuban revolutionary government's counterinsurgency against peasant opponents in El Escambray, which lasted five years, took thousands of lives on both sides, and led to the forced relocation of thousands of surviving rebels, starkly contrasts with the public displays of revolutionary justice documented by Chase.

A third suggestion of the volume, then, signals the need to acknowledge the dynamic nature of counterrevolution, both in terms of its ability to draw new political actors into its orbit and its ability to revitalize its worldview in order to meet the challenge of revolutionary times. In his pioneering work in the 1960s, José Nun, while positing the urban middle class in Argentina and Brazil as a fairly homogenous social formation—as opposed to Mayer's notion of a governing class "interpenetrated" by both modernizing elites and landed reactionaries—nonetheless emphasized its susceptibility to manorialism. Unable to develop a universalizing ideology, the middle class, he wrote, "merely adopted that of the oligarchy. It accepted its heroes, its symbols, its culture and its laws."[62] Borrowing from Gramsci, Nun argued that "civil society" functioned something like "trench systems in modern warfare," providing the middle class a place to hunker down during moments of crisis—such as, in Nun's example, Juan Perón's confrontation with Argentina's oligarchy—to cultivate their conservative impulses.[63] But Nun's early efforts to grapple with the issue of ideology and its dynamic relation to class and politics in order to explain the coups of the early 1960s were not taken up by historians, at least not in the kind of comparative perspective he was attempting, and they were sidelined by social scientists.

By insisting on the relative autonomy of military as an institution, Nun foreshadowed much of the "bureaucratic authoritarianism" scholarship that would soon become the dominant framework for explaining the region's revision to militarism. Yet where Nun's work was dynamic, much of this subsequent literature tended to be economistic. Sociologists such as Guillermo O'Donnell argued that by the early 1960s the region's import substitution model of development had reached exhaustion.[64] Not only could countries not attract or generate enough capital to move beyond light industrialization but the governments implementing import substitution were increasingly incapable of containing popular mobilization, ensuring political stability, and protecting capital investment—thereby paving the way for the military regimes of the 1970s. While often positing the state as a venue of class conflict, most work operating in this tradition tends to mute the political and ideological dimensions of that conflict. While emphasizing the weakness of industrialists, it ignores the rejuvenating power of the world represented and defended by the rural order. Such analyses usually focus on the inability of the new to be born but downplay the violent ideological and institutional resurgence of the old.

Recently, scholars such as Sandra McGee Deutsch and Margaret Power have begun to examine in detail the origins and composition of what could be called Latin America's New Right.[65] While more needs to be done on how Latin America's old regime, after the Second World War, recomposed itself in the face of modernizing pressures, taken as a whole this new work testifies to the ability of the landed class to coopt new bureaucratic structures, civil society, political cultures, interest groups, and party politics, to infuse them with its values and conventions. It also speaks to its ability to pull into its ideological and cultural orbit emerging middle groups, either drawn from the ranks of the military, the clergy, or the urban economy.[66] As I've argued elsewhere in the case of Guatemala, the affective investment of socially aspiring middle-class soldiers and anticommunist students in, yet structural autonomy from, incumbent elites, traditions, and hierarchies allowed them to breathe new life into the old order. In many countries, the military embodied many of the values and traditions of the upper class while serving as a transmission belt that allowed lower- and middle-class outsiders, more ideologically committed to defend a patriarchal vision of nationalism, entry into that order. In the process, conservativism as a worldview moved from an instinctual defense of the status hierarchy to a more contrived, self-conscious ideology, confected from component parts of ultramontane Catholicism, martial nationalism, and patriarchal allegiance. Guatemala's Movimiento de Liberación Nacional, for example, was modeled on the Spanish Phalange and organized by urban-based, university-educated sons of middling planters. Declaring itself to be "the party of organized violence," a "vanguard of terror," the MLN launched a relentlessly vicious campaign in defense of the agrarian oligarchy, unnerved by Jacobo Arbenz's land reform. The MLN's campaign was built on an urban-rural coalition that in many ways matched the diversity and vitality of its left opponents.[67]

A number of this volume's essays—including Corey Robin's final reflections on the deep strain of revolutionary counterrevolution that runs through U.S. history—document the emergence of anticommunism as a spreading global ideology capable of absorbing isolated local conflicts and projecting them into an international movement with universal pretensions. Gould and Olcott describe how in the 1920s and 1930s landed interests both mobilized protofascist shock troops to protect their interests and used the new political vocabulary provided by the Russian Revolution to label peasant organizers as "subversives" and "Bolsheviks." In Mexico, groups that tended to disdain mass action—the landed elite, U.S. investors, and at least a few members of the U.S. diplomatic corps (even as the U.S. New Deal diplomacy was increasingly focused on the threat of fascism)—united in their support for the fascist Camisas Doradas, which served as the shock troops against local agrarian organizing. In El Salvador, both the Communist-led insurrection and the repression that followed baptized by fire the component parts of what would become the death squad regime's social base in that country. Ladino smallholders, urban middle classes, plantation owners, and security forces all came together in defense not only of the agrarian elite but of the quasi-fascistic military government of General Maximiliano Hernández Martínez.

The process by which the Latin American Right grew more ideological entailed rendering explicit the violence of state and elite power that during moments of stasis tended to remain implicit and undertheorized. Winn's essay here charts this surfacing in Pinochet's rehabilitation of the "pessimistic conservative" Diego Portales, credited as the founder of the Chilean state. "The social order in Chile," Portales wrote in 1832, "is maintained by the weight of the night." If this should fail to be the case, if the passivity of the "ignorant" masses should begin to stir, Portales warned, "we will find ourselves in darkness and without any power to contain the rebellious aside from the methods dictated by commonsense or those which experience has proven useful." Throughout most of the twentieth century, those methods, Winn writes, included limited reforms punctuated by repression, such as the 1934 Ránquil slaughter documented here by Klubock. By the early 1970s, though, as the Popular Unity coalition and its supporters tried to force the dawn, intermittent repression was replaced by systemic terror.

A fourth methodological challenge posed by many of this volume's contributors is to examine how the dynamics of conflict outlined above played out on in an international field of power. The outbreak of the Mexican Revolution in 1910 not only brought down the Porfiriato but shattered nearly a half-century of assumptions and practices that governed the United States' political and economic diplomacy in Latin America. In this case, the possibility of reaction posed by the United States was relatively weak, especially during the critical juncture of the Great Depression and compared with the preponderance of power the United States would bring to bear on post–Second World War revolutions. Yet Katz, here in passing and elsewhere in more depth, discusses how the constant threat, and occasional realization, of North American military intervention, along with economic and political pressure, shaped the rhythms of Mexico's initial uprising and subsequent civil war, as well as the program of reform early revolutionary governments embarked on.[68] While not "world-historical" in the way, say, the leaders of the Russian Revolution understood themselves, *agraristas* who had gained experience in Mexico did head south to organize on plantations in Guatemala, Nicaragua, and El Salvador.[69]

In the years after the Second World War, Washington abandoned the multilateralism that it had embraced in the 1930s—an embrace partly spurred by the Mexican Revolution, as well as by other instances of Latin American opposition to U.S. militarism. By the early 1950s, Washington had swung back, according to the State Department's Division of the American Republics, "toward a policy of general cooperation [with dictators] that gives only secondary importance to the degree of democracy manifested by [Latin America's] respective governments."[70] Technical and financial aid provided to security forces was stepped up, now part of a more systemic policy of containment, which included the support and orchestration of coups and destabilization programs (Guatemala, Honduras, Brazil, Uruguay, Chile, Argentina), the patronage of counterrevolutionary expeditionary forces (Cuba and Nicaragua), and, when all else failed, invasion (the Dominican Republic and Grenada). Increasingly after the Second World War, reaction "ran in transnational veins," with foreign intervention in turn proving to be a powerfully radicalizing catalyst, as Michelle Chase's essay on Cuba's revolutionary tribunals demonstrates.[71] Chase focuses on an especially consequential conjuncture not just for Cuba but for Latin America as a whole. She shows how before economic or geopolitical issues came to the fore, the issue of "law" quickly became a flashpoint of hostility between Washington and Havana, as U.S. policy and opinion makers pushed the revolutionary regime to conform to international standards. In response, Cuba's new leaders mobilized popular demands for retribution, not only in favor of new state forms of national sovereignty but also against U.S. criticism, deemed to be both a violation of sovereignty and hypocritical, given Washington's long silence in the face of Batista's well-known atrocities. Such contretemps between the hemisphere's dominant power and an insurgent upstart produced an ever widening radius of radicalization. Since "ideas always come in pairs and they contradict one another," wrote Jean-Paul Sartre—following a visit to Cuba that coincided with the March 1960 bombing of the merchant ship La Coubre in Havana harbor, which left scores dead and hundreds wounded—the U.S. backed counterrevolution allowed the ideologically indistinct Cuban Revolution "to convert itself into what it was" (an observation that cuts many ways with the hindsight of five decades).[72]

Outside Cuba, throughout Latin America, a young generation of nationalists in nearly every country formed militant organizations and armed guerrilla groups that sought to follow Cuba's model. Meanwhile, anti-Castro exiles fleeing to the United States revitalized networks of anticommunist paramilitarism that would spread throughout South America and Southeast Asia and, in the 1980s, Central America (in the process, another constituency was added to the United States' gathering conservative movement: indeed, it was Florida's right-wing Cuban American community that supplied the shock troops to shut down the 2000 presidential recount vote).[73] For its part, the United States both laid siege to the island and fully reoriented its hemispheric policy away from defense against external threats to internal security, creating an infrastructure for the death squads that would preside over much of Central and South America. In tandem, the expulsion of Cuba from the Organization of American States had the added effect of binding Latin American nations closer to Washington, extending the cold war divide even deeper into regional politics and allowing domestic elites to harden the internal order.

Much more so than in Guatemala in 1954, Cuba in the 1960s, or Chile in 1973, Washington executed its most fully realized counterrevolution in Nicaragua in the 1980s, bringing together a diverse foreign and domestic coalition to besiege and contain the Sandinistas. In the country's interior, the U.S.-funded, -trained, and -equipped Contra rebels were able to build momentum by mobilizing rural folkways and clientelistic relations. In so doing, Washington transformed diffuse regional resistance to the Sandinistas' modernizing project into an ever-sharper and more polarized ideological conflict.[74] The Contras destroyed cooperatives, schools, health clinics, and other government projects, and murdered civilians to demonstrate to a wavering rural population that the Sandinistas could not establish effective sovereignty—that is, protect against counterrevolutionary violence. Again, white terror found its effectiveness in stealth and unpredictability, while revolutionaries had the liability of establishing public and comprehensive rule and security.

A final suggestion points to defining Latin America's revolutionary twentieth century as a distinct historical period. In its broadest sense, the period, defined here as running from the Mexican Revolution to the Central American conflicts of the 1980s, was marked by sequential attempts to transcend what by the early twentieth century had become an unsustainable model of exclusionary nationalism, restricted political institutions, persisting rural clientelism, and dependent, export-based development. By the early twentieth century, the model had entered into crisis, unable to absorb the demands of mass politics—made urgent by an economic system that generated displacement and poverty—and entirely incapable of making room for new, would-be manufacturing or industrializing elites. As noted above, Nun and other Argentine "Gramscianos" of the 1960s had begun to chart out a comparative sociology of this period, particularly of the more economically developed societies of the Southern Cone, which, having experienced a process of "industrialization without an industrial revolution," had therefore developed a weak middle class too structurally and ideologically dependent on the oligarchy to lead this bid at transcendence.[75] Much of their comparative framework was developed by subsequent sociologists, and some historians have addressed similar concerns to examine the "problem of persistence."[76] Yet there has been little attention in Latin American historiography to how sequential crises rooted in specific national conflicts generated waves of radicalization that extended spatially, that is, across the region, and temporally, from the first cycle of post–Second World War coups, through the rise of the New Left and New Right of the 1960s and 1970s, through to the Central American civil wars of the 1980s. More recently, Charles Bergquist has pointed out that nowhere in Latin America was there a "North," a region with a free-labor system from which political liberalism could gestate.[77] In the four years of the U.S. Civil War, union troops demolished the slaveholder's pretense to national governance. In Latin America, that assault would be dispersed across centuries, and would come not from a region but from below. Every step in liberalization's march was driven by violent social conflict, dispersed across Latin America's revolutionary century. Each country's experience with, and contribution to, this cycle of insurgent politics was distinct, though many shared broadly homologous patterns of polarization and radicalization, followed by revolution, civil war, or state terror. Yet what most joined Latin America's insurgencies, revolutions, and counterrevolutions into an amalgamated and definable historical event was the shared structural position of subordination each nation in the region had to the United States.

From the Mexican Revolution forward to the Central American insurgencies, the progress of both Latin America's attempt to transcend its "feudal" past *and* the United States' ascension to, first, hemispheric and then, global hegemon proceeded on parallel tracks, with each greatly informing the shape the other took.[78] And as the anti-imperial content of revolutionary politics gained force, Washington's post–Second World War containment policy, as discussed above, became a common dominant variable shaping each nation's revolutionary history. The massive infusion of counterinsurgent aid in the decades after the Second World War had the effect of simultaneously hastening and staying the disaggregation of domestic politics, eroding the compromise-seeking center—which in pre–cold war Latin American politics was already narrowly circumscribed and only tenuously able to incorporate the strains of modern politics. The preponderance of influence exercised by the United States over the hemispheric system ensured that the crisis politics of any given country didn't spill over into external war—except in the case of the Argentine junta's attempt to retake the Malvinas in 1982, a case that conforms closely to Mayer's understanding of reactionary "over-reaction." In other words, where Mayer believed the domestic problems of European mass society tended to be deflected in external war (save for the exceptional cases of the French and Russian Revolutions), and where Mayer's contemporary William Appleman Williams contended that the United States was able to avoid a direct confrontation with the motor contradictions of Anglo liberalism by expansion, Latin American nations, denied those two options, turned inward.

Charles Tilly has argued that the modern European state was forged through warfare. In Latin America, where the bloodletting was largely internal, state formation was confected through domestic counterinsurgency, which, once any given crisis passed and quasi-independent death squads were reigned in, allowed national governments to establish an effective monopoly on violence.[79] Yet counterinsurgent terror, by eliminating alternative developmental programs, did more than just ensure that most countries emerged at the end of the cold war subordinate to the economic and political neoliberal protocols of what became known as the Washington Consensus. In many countries, the turmoil associated with sustained periods of state terror and civil war broke down the patronage bonds that had had long structured the Latin American countryside and forced a modernization of productive relations.[80] Though as Forrest Hylton describes in this volume's last case study, the persistence of a cold war counterinsurgent apparatus combined with the economic liberalization that gained speed in the 1980s often led to a "refeudalization" of social relations—though with intimidation largely displacing the kind of patron-client relations often associated with manoralism. In Colombia, the institution building held up by political scientists as the basic requisite of successful state consolidation was brought about by an alliance of paramilitaries, organized crime linked to the narcotics economy, neoliberals, and a political class looking for a way out of a four-decade civil war impasse. In fact, Colombia's recent president Álvaro Uribe functioned much like Joseph Schumpeter's "warlord . . . sovereign" (as described in the same essay Mayer draws on to emphasize the survival of atavistic elements in the modern state), whose "war machine" allows divergent constituencies—in the case of Colombia, economic elites, *paras*, *narcos*, soldiers, and politicians—to become "statized."[81]

The ideological and tactical evolution of Latin America's revolutionary century is strikingly coherent, with each bid to transform society generating experiences that shaped subsequent attempts. In 1910, Mexico's revolution signaled the first sustained assault on nineteenth-century authoritarian liberalism, putting agrarian reform and social rights fully on the policy agenda.[82] In the 1930s and 1940s, populism, in Brazil and Argentina for example, sought to extend rights, supersede caudillo patronage relations with national institutions, and articulate a more inclusive national-popular identity; in the 1940s, socialists, nationalists, and social liberals tried to make good on the promise of antifascist social democracy. In the 1950s, a sharper nationalism gained ground, with a defined program of import substitution, particularly in Guatemala and Bolivia. By the late 1950s, the frustrations and radicalization that produced the Cuban Revolution could have, in fact, come to fruition in a similar upheaval in any number of other countries: in Guatemala, Colombia, or, as Gerardo Rénique points out below, in Peru, where a mass peasant and worker movement anticipated Fidel Castro's triumphant march into Havana.

An overdetermined event in the fullest sense of the term, the Cuban Revolution both crystallized decades of regional experience and linked that experience to a broader, global crisis of legitimacy that by 1958 had threatened to overwhelm both West and East alike. The revolution was consequential not just in that it was the first in Latin America to fully understand itself as "world historical" and thus try to "externalize" itself, fracturing Latin America's already debilitated Old Left and spawning and supporting imitators throughout the Andes and Central America in the 1960s and the Southern Cone in the 1970s. It was also consequential because, especially after the disaster of *foco* theory in Venezuela, Peru, Bolivia, and Guatemala, it quickly gave rise to movements that tried to transcend the theory's limitations. Liberation theology; new social movements organized around nascent political identities that resisted vertical integration into reformist parties or bureaucratic corporatist states; Chile's Popular Unity coalition, which sought to achieve socialism without sacrificing political pluralism; and even new guerrilla organizations that hoped to avoid *foquismo's* errors and build mass support through a New Left attention to consciousness raising—all were as much reactions to the Cuban Revolution as they were products of it.[83] These elements came together in their fullest expression in Central America in the 1980s, where it seemed like something new and vital was taking place, in terms of the political alliances being formed between urban workers and peasants, the fusion of radical Christianity and socialism, and, in Guatemala, the incorporation of indigenous communities as such into the struggle. Yet in retrospect, the killing unleashed to contain the threat turned the region into one of the cold war's endgames, and the place where Latin America's revolutionary century broke and rolled back.

Notes

1. George Steiner, *In Bluebeard's Castle: Some Notes towards the Redefinition of Culture* (New Haven: Yale University Press, 1971), 11–13.

2. Ibid., 12. See also the work of William H. Sewell Jr. for the emergence of a modern political language of revolution and sovereignty, including *Logics of History: Social Theory and Social Transformation*, Chicago: University of Chicago Press, 2005, particularly the essay "Historical Events as Transformations of Structure: Inventing Revolution at the Bastille." See also his debate with Theda Skopol, reprinted in Skopol's *Social Revolutions and the Modern World*, Cambridge: Cambridge University Press, 1994.

3. Cf. Rigoberta Menchú's autobiography, *Me llamo Rigoberta Menchú y así me nació la conciencia*, (Mexico City: Siglo XXI Editores, 1985); Roque Dalton, ed., *Miguel Marmol*, trans. Kathleen Ross and Richard Shaaf (Willimantic, Conn.: Curbstone Press, 1987); Claribel Claribel (with D. J. Flakoll), *No me agarran viva: la mujer salvadoreña en la lucha* (Mexico City: Ediciones Era, 1983); Chico Mendes, *Chico Mendes in His Own Words: Fight for the Forest* (London: Latin American Bureau, 1989); Rosa Isolde Reuque Paillalef, *When a Flower Is Reborn: The Life and Times of a Mapuche Feminist*, ed. and trans. Florencia Mallon (Durham: Duke University Press, 2002); Daniel James, *Doña María's Story: Life History, Memory, and Political Identity* (Durham: Duke University Press, 2000); Gioconda Belli, *The Country under My Skin: A Memoir of Love and War*, trans. Krotina Cordero (New York: Knopf, 2002); Domicilia Barrios de Chungara, *Si me permiten hablar: Testimonio de Domitila, una mujer de las minas de Bolivia* (Mexico City: Siglo XXI, 1977); Elvia Alvarado, *Don't Be Afraid Gringo: A Honduran Woman Speaks from the Heart*, ed. and trans. Medea Benjamin (New York: Harper and Row, 1987).

4. See a similar comment in Allen Wells and Gilbert M. Joseph, *Summer of Discontent, Seasons of Upheaval: Elite Politics and Rural Insurgency in Yucatán, 1876–1915* (Palo Alto: Stanford University Press, 1996), 202; for the transformative effect that participation in revolutionary struggles had on politically marginalized individuals, see Elisabeth Jean Wood, *Insurgent Collective Action and Civil War in El Salvador* (Cambridge: Cambridge University Press, 2003).

5. CNN, *Cold War* (documentary series), episode 10 (1999), "Cuba, 1959–1962."

6. William F. Sater and Holger H. Herwig, *The Grand Illusion: The Prussianization of the Chilean Army*, Studies in War, Society, and the Military (Lincoln: University of Nebraska Press, 1999); Emily O. Goldman and Leslie C. Eliason, *The Diffusion of Military Technology and Ideas* (Palo Alto: Stanford University Press, 2003), 239; Brian Loveman and Thomas M. Davies Jr., eds., *The Politics of Antipolitics: The Military in Latin America* (Wilmington, Del.: Scholarly Resources, 1997).

7. Martha Huggins, *Political Policing: The United States and Latin America* (Durham: Duke University Press, 1998). See especially chap. 2, "Gunboat Policing: The First Twenty-Five Years," and chap. 3, "Good Neighbor Policing," 25–47.

8. For El Salvador, see National Security Archive, *El Salvador: The Making of US Policy, 1977–1984* (Alexandria, Va.: Chadwick-Healey, 1989), 73; for Uruguay, see the declassified U.S. documents located on the National Security Archive Web page, http://www.gwu.edu/~nsarchiv. Although the military turned Uruguay into a prison state in 1973, U.S. counterinsurgency aid to the country continued until 1977. For Chile, likewise see the documents on the NSA Web page. For Operation Condor, see Dinges, *The Condor Years: How Pinochet and His Allies Brought Terrorism to Three Continents* (New York: New Press, 2005); and J. Patrice McSheery, *Predatory States: Operation Condor and Covert War in Latin America* (Boulder, Colo.: Rowman Littlefield, 2005). For training manuals used at the U.S. School of the Americas, see "SOA Manuals Index" on the School of America Watch website: http://soaw.org (accessed December 18, 2009). For a list of Latin American officers who graduated from the School of the Americas, see "SOA Graduates" (accessed December 18, 2009). For Brazil, see Huggins, *Political Policing*, which also provides the most detailed historical description of U.S. involvement with a Latin American security force. For the United States' role in creating Colombia's modern death squad intelligence system, see Dennis Rempe, "The Past as Prologue: A History of U.S. Counterinsurgent Policy in Colombia, 1958–1963," Strategic Studies Institute of the U.S. Army War College, 2002. Available at http://www.strategicstudiesinstitute.army.mil/; see also John Childs, *Unequal Alliance: The Inter-American Military System, 1938–1978* (Boulder, Colo.: Westview Press, 1980), and Michael McClintock, *Instruments of Statecraft: U.S. Guerilla Warfare, Counterinsurgency, and Counterterrorism, 1940–1990* (New York: Pantheon Books, 1992). See also Brian Loveman, *No Higher Law: American Foreign Policy in the Western Hemisphere since 1776* (Chapel Hill: University of North Carolina Press, 2010), for an excellent survey of U.S. militarism—and the legal formulations that justify that militarism—in the Western Hemisphere.

9. Robert Holden, "Securing Central America against Communism: The United States and the Modernization of Surveillance in the Cold War," *Journal of Interamerican Studies and World Affairs* 41, no. 1 (Spring 1999): 1–30.

10. McSheery, *Predatory States*; also Alfred McCoy, *A Question of Torture: CIA Interrogation, from the Cold War to the War on Terror* (New York: Metropolitan, 2006), and Lesley Gill, *The School of the Americas—Military Training and Political Violence in the Americas* (Durham: Duke University Press, 2004).

11. Greg Grandin, *The Last Colonial Massacre: Latin America in the Cold War* (Chicago: University of Chicago Press, 2004), 73–74, 94–104.

12. In *Last Colonial Massacre*, I argue that the practice of "disappearances" in its cold war form began in Guatemala, with this episode. But the former Venezuelan vice president José Vicente Rangel argues that the technique started in Venezuela, around the same time. See his comments made in *Chamosaurio*, June 9, 2008 ("Rangel asegura que desapariciones forzosas de América Latina comenzaron en Venezuela," http://chamosaurio.com/ [accessed December 18, 2009]) in reference to Agustin Arzola Castellanos's *La desaparición forzada en Venezuela, 1960–1969* (Caracas: Tropykos, 2005). See also Rangel's *Expediente Negro*, first published by Ediciones La Muralla in 1967 but repeatedly reissued in multiple editions. Interestingly, John Longan, the U.S. security advisor who set up the unit that carried out the disappearances in Guatemala, had previously been stationed in Venezuela. See Grandin, *Last Colonial Massacre*, 74.

13. See also Gabriel Aguilera Peralta, *La violencia en Guatemala como fenómeno político* (Cuernavaca, Mexico: Centro Interdisciplinario de Documentación, 1971).

14. Miriam Revault D'Allonnes, *Ce que l'homme fait à l'homme* (Paris: Seuil, 1995), 15, quoted in Arno J. Mayer, *The Furies: Violence and Terror in the French and Russian Revolutions* (Princeton: Princeton University Press, 2000), 37.

15. Guillermo A. O'Donnell, *Modernization and Bureaucratic-Authoritarianism: Studies in South American Politics* (Berkeley: University of California Press, 1973), and *Counterpoints: Selected Essays on Authoritarianism and Democratization* (Notre Dame, Ind.: University of Notre Dame Press, 1999), 143.

16. For historians, the first two volumes of Steve J. Stern's trilogy on memory politics in Chile are the standard: *Remembering Pinochet's Chile: On the Eve of London 1998. The Memory Box of Pinochet's Chile* (Durham: Duke University Press, 2004), and *Battling for Hearts and Minds: Memory Struggles in Pinochet's Chile, 1973–1988* (Durham: Duke University Press, 2006). See also Frank Afflitto, "The Homogenizing Effects of State-Sponsored Terrorism: The Case of Guatemala"; Antonious Robben, "State Terror in the Netherworld: Disappearance and Reburial in Argentina"; and Kay Warren, "Death Squads and Wider Complicities: Dilemmas for an Anthropology of Violence," all in *Death Squad: The Anthropology of State Terror*, ed. Jeffrey A. Sluka (Philadelphia: University of Pennsylvania Press, 1999). For ethnographic considerations, see Leigh Binford, *The El Mozote Massacre: Anthropology and Human Rights* (Tucson: University of Arizona Press, 1996), as well as the exchange between Binford and Philippe Bourgois regarding the relationship between political

and everyday violence: Bourgois, "The Power of Violence in War and Peace: Post-Cold War Lessons from El Salvador," *Ethnography* 2, no. 1 (2001): 5–34; Binford, "Violence in El Salvador: A Rejoinder," *Ethnography* 3, no. 2 (2002): 201–19; and Bourgois, "The Violence of Moral Binaries: Response to Leigh Binford," *Ethnography* 3, no. 2 (2002): 221–31. For an anthology of recent ethnographic considerations of violence that does not include a Latin American case study, see Pamela J. Stewart and Andrew Strathern, *Violence: Theory and Ethnography* (London: Continuum International, 2002).

17. Michael Taussig, *Shamanism, Colonialism and the Wildman: A Study in Terror and Healing* (Chicago: University of Chicago Press, 1987). See also Lesley Gill's review of Taussig's *My Cocaine Museum,* in "My Cocaine Museum," *American Anthropologist* 106, no. 4 (2004): 780–81.

18. Of course, much postmodern thought celebrates fractured subjectivity—unlike social theorists working in the Marxist or Hegelian tradition, there is no "there" there to repress—and sees attempts to impose a false unity on it resulting in what Gayatri Chakravorty Spivak, following Foucault, calls "epistemic violence." See Spivak, "Can the Subaltern Speak?" in *Imperialism: Critical Concepts in Historical Studies,* ed. P. J. Cain and Mark Harrison (New York: Routledge, 2001), 182.

19. Arthur Kleinman and Joan Kleinman, "The Appeal of Experience," in *Social Suffering,* ed. Arthur Kleinman, Veena Das, and Margaret Lock (Berkeley: University of California Press, 1997), 1. An important exception to this trend is the work of Jean Comaroff and John L. Comaroff, which does embed different forms of violence in large-scale economic shifts. See their "Occult Economies and the Violence of Abstraction: Notes from the South African Postcolony," *American Ethnologist* 26, no. 2 (1999): 279–301, and "Millennial Capitalism: First Thoughts on a Second Coming," in their edited collection *Millennial Capitalism and the Culture of Neoliberalism* (Durham: Duke University Press, 2001).

20. See Bibi Bakare Yusuf, "Economies of Violence: Black Bodies and the Unspeakable Terror," in *Feminist Theory and the Body,* ed. Janet Price and Margrit Shildrik (London: Taylor and Francis, 1999). Another touchstone is, of course, Michel Foucault, as well as subsequent political theorists who likewise emphasize the diffuse, totalizing nature of power, and violence and terror, in modern society, such as Georgio Agamben. See Beatrice Hanssen, *Critique of Violence: Between Poststructuralism and Critical Theory* (London: Routledge, 2000), and Pasquale Pasquino, "Political Theory of War and Peace: Foucault and the History of Modern Political Theory," *Economy and Society* 22, no. 1 (1993): 77–88.

21. Elaine Scarry, *The Body in Pain: The Making and Unmaking of the World* (New York: Oxford University Press, 1985), 50.

22. Ibid., 37.

23. E. Valentine Daniel, *Charred Lullabies: Chapters in an Anthropography of Violence* (Princeton: Princeton University Press, 1996).

24. Ibid., 120.

25. Ibid., 6.

26. See Gyanendra Pandey, *Violence: Nations, Fragments, Histories* (Palo Alto: Stanford University Press, 2005) for a work that makes like arguments questioning the ability to analyze or represent violence. A similar move has been made by some scholars of the Holocaust, where claims to the event's unknowability have less to do with the experience of terror than with coming to terms with Nazi intent. For some scholars, the Jewish genocide's singularity is rooted not just in the extremity of Nazi violence toward Jews, but in its epic quality, religious dimension, and technoindustrial scope and precision. See Richard L. Rubenstein, "Religion and the Uniqueness of the Holocaust," in *Is the Holocaust Unique? Perspectives on Comparative Genocide,* ed. Alan Rosenbaum (Boulder, Colo.: Westview Press, 1998), as well as Rosenbaum's "Introduction."

27. "Anthropology's Alternative Radical," *New York Times*, April 21, 2001.

28. Adam Hochschild, *King Leopold's Ghost: A Story of Greed, Terror and Heroism in Colonial Africa* (Wilmington, Mass.: Mariner Books, 1999), 143, discusses the way scholars have drained the historical specificity out of Joseph Conrad's *Heart of Darkness.* See Corey Robin, *Fear: The History of a Political Idea* (New York: Oxford University Press, 2004), 147–48 for a discussion of Ignatieff and Gourevitch.

29. Philip Gourevitch, *We Wish to Inform You That Tomorrow We Will Be Killed with Our Families: Stories from Rwanda* (New York: Farrar, Staus, and Giroux, 1998), 19.

30. See, for example, Eric D. Weitz, "The Modernity of Genocide: War, Race, and Revolution in the Twentieth Century," in *The Specter of Genocide: Mass Murder in Historical Perspective*, ed. Robert Gellately and Ben Kiernan (Cambridge: Cambridge University Press, 2003).

31. Stoll advances his argument concerning the Left in two books: *Between Two Armies in the Ixil Towns of Guatemala* (New York: Colombia University Press, 1993), and *Rigoberta Menchú and the Story of All Poor Guatemalans* (Boulder, Colo.: Westview Press, 1998). See also Jorge Castañeda, *Utopia Unarmed: The Latin American Left after the Cold War* (New York: Knopf, 1993), which offers a similar argument for the hemisphere as a whole.

32. See the discussion in Steven Laurence Kaplan, *Farewell Revolution: The Historian's Feud, France, 1789/1989* (Ithaca: Cornell University Press, 1996), 140–42. For a strained attempt to apply Furet's approach to the civil war in El Salvador, see Yvon Greiner, *The Emergence of Insurgency in El Salvador: Ideology and Political Will*, Pittsburgh: University of Pittsburgh Press, 1999, along with his follow-up, "The Rise and Fall of Revolutionary Passions in El Salvador, *3*, no. 3 (September 2004): 313–29.

For an important corrective, see Joaquín Mauricio Chávez Aguilar, "The Pedagogy of Revolution: Popular Intellectuals and the Origins of the Salvadoran Insurgency, 1960–1980," Ph.D. dissertation, New York University, 2010.

33. Robert H. Holden, *Armies without Nations: Public Violence and State Formation in Central America, 1821–1960* (New York: Oxford University Press, 2004); Jeffrey Gould and Aldo Lauria-Santiago, *To Rise Up in Darkness: Revolution, Repression, and Memory in El Salvador, 1920–1932* (Durham: Duke University Press, 2008); Carlota McAllister, *The Good Road: Conscience and Consciousness in a Post-Revolutionary Maya Village* (Durham: Duke University Press, forthcoming); Elizabeth Oglesby, "Politics at Work: Elites, Labor and Agrarian Modernization in Guatemala, 1980–2000," Ph.D. diss., University of California, Berkeley. For the Guatemalan truth commission, see Comisión para el Esclarecimiento Histórico, *Guatemala: Memoria del silencio*, 12 vols. (Guatemala City: CEH, 1999); see also Greg Grandin, "The Instruction of Great Catastrophe: Truth Commissions, National History, and State Formation in Argentina, Chile, and Guatemala," *American Historical Review* 110, no. 1 (2005): 46–67, and Greg Grandin, "History, Motive, Law, Intent: Combining Historical and Legal Methods in Understanding Guatemala's 1981–1983 Genocide," in Gellately and Kiernan, *The Specter of Genocide*.

34. Sergio Grez Toso and Gabriel Salazar Vergara, eds., *Manifiesto de historiadores* (Santiago: LOM Ediciones, 1999).

35. In 2006, the government of Néstor Kirchner inserted a new prologue into a new edition of *Nunca más* by the Comisión Nacional sobre la Desaparición de Personas, which explicitly rejected the "two demons" thesis that had been prominently featured in the prologue, written by Ernesto Sábato, to the original 1984 version. A government spokesman said that the "prólogo original no reproducía la filosofía política que hoy anima al Estado en la persecución de los crímenes de lesa humanidad." The new one reads: "Es preciso dejar claramente establecido, porque lo requiere la construcción del futuro sobre bases firmes, que es inaceptable pretender justificar el terrorismo de Estado como una suerte de juego de violencias contrapuestas como si fuera posible buscar una simetría justificatoria en la acción de particulares frente al apartamiento de los fines propios de la Nación y del Estado, que son irrenunciables." Defending the change, the president of the Asociación Madres de Plaza de Mayo, Hebe de Bonafini said, "Nuestros hijos no eran demonios. Eran revolucionarios, guerrilleros, maravillosos y únicos que defendieron a la Patria."

36. Steve J. Stern, ed., *Shining and Other Paths: War and Society in Peru, 1980–1995* (Durham: Duke University Press, 1998). Of works published in English the one that comes closest to the historian Christopher Browning's *Ordinary Men: Reserve Police Battalion 101 and the Final Solution in Poland* (New York: Harper Perennial, 1993)—a thick, yet historically grounded description of the mutation of ideology and psychology during

wartime—is by Martha Huggins, a sociologist, and Mika Haritos-Fatouros and Philip G. Zimbardo, both psychologists. See their *Violence Workers: Police Torturers and Murderers Reconstruct Brazilian Atrocities* (Berkeley: University of California Press, 2002). Outside of history, see also Nancy Schepre-Hughes, *Death without Weeping: The Violence of Everyday Life in Brazil* (Berkeley: University of California Press, 1993).

37. For some examples, see Ada Ferrer, *Insurgent Cuba: Race, Nation, and Revolution, 1868–1898* (Chapel Hill: University of North Carolina Press, 1999); Florencia Mallon, *The Defense of Community in Peru's Central Highlands: Peasant Struggle and Capitalist Transition, 1860–1940* (Princeton: Princeton University Press, 1983); Thomas Miller Klubock, *Contested Communities: Class, Gender, and Politics in Chile's El Teniente Copper Mine, 1904–1951* (Durham: Duke University Press, 1998); Jeffrey Gould, *To Lead as Equals: Rural Protest and Political Consciousness in Chinandega, Nicaragua, 1912–1979* (Chapel Hill: University of North Carolina Press, 1990); Heidi Tinsman, *Partners in Conflict: The Politics of Gender, Sexuality, and Labor in the Chilean Agrarian Reform, 1950–1973* (Durham: Duke University Press, 2002); Daniel James, *Resistance and Integration: Peronism and the Argentine Working Class, 1946–1976* (Cambridge: Cambridge University Press, 1988); Gilbert M. Joseph, *Revolution from Without: Yucatan, Mexico, and the United States, 1880–1924* (New York: Cambridge University Press, 1982); Gilbert M. Joseph and Allen Wells, *Summer of Discontent, Seasons of Upheaval: Elite Politics and Rural Insurgency in Yucatan, 1876–1915* (Stanford: Stanford University Press, 1996); and Gilbert M. Joseph and Daniel Nugent, eds., *Everyday Forms of State Formation: Revolution and the Negotiation of Rule in Modern Mexico* (Durham: Duke University Press, 1994).

38. Deborah Levenson, *Trade Unionists against Terror: Guatemala City, 1954–1985* (Chapel Hill: University of North Carolina Press, 1994).

39. For some examples of works that identify, in different ways, the postwar period as a defined historical juncture, see Kees Koonings and Dirk Kruijt, eds., *Societies of Fear: The Legacy of Civil War, Violence and Terror in Latin America* (London: Zed Books, 1999); Idelber Avelar, *The Untimely Present: Postdictatorial Latin American Fiction and the Task of Mourning* (Durham: Duke University Press, 1999); Jorge Castañeda, *Utopia Unarmed: The Latin American Left after the Cold War* (New York: Vintage Books, 1994); Jean Franco, *The Decline and Fall of the Lettered City: Latin America in the Cold War* (Cambridge, Mass.: Harvard University Press, 2002).

40. See Arno J. Mayer, *Politics and the Origins of the New Diplomacy, 1917–1918* (New Haven: Yale University Press, 1959); *Politics and Diplomacy of Peacemaking: Containment and Counterrevolution at Versailles, 1918–1919* (New York: Knopf, 1967); *Dynamics of Counterrevolution in Europe, 1870–1956: An Analytic Framework* (New York: Harper and Row, 1971); *The Persistence of the Old Regime: Europe to the Great War* (New York: Pantheon Books, 1981); and *Why Did the Heavens Not Darken?: The "Final Solution" in History* (New York: Pantheon Books, 1988).

41. Taussig uses Marx's brief comments on "commodity fetishism" as his take-off point not only to question the historical intelligibility of violence and terror but also to attack Marxists, such as Eric Wolf and Sidney Mintz, who analyze the production and circulation of commodities. See Taussig, "History as Commodity: In Some Recent American (Anthropological) Literature," *Critique of Anthropology* 9, no. 1 (1989): 7–23, as well as Wolf and Mintz's reply, "Reply to Michael Taussig," in the same issue of *Critique of Anthropology*, 25–31.

42. Mayer, "Internal Causes of War in Europe, 1870–1956: A Research Assignment," *Journal of Modern History* 41, no. 3 (1969): 291–303; Mayer, "Internal Crises and War since 1870," in *Revolutionary Situations in Europe, 1917–1922: Germany, Italy, Austria-Hungary*, ed. Charles L. Bertrand (Montreal: Interuniversity Centre for European Studies, 1977); Mayer, "Domestic Causes of the First World War," in *The Responsibility of Power*, ed. Leonard Krieger and Fritz Stern (Garden City, N.Y.: Doubleday, 1967), 286–300.

43. José Nun, "América Latina: la crisis hegemónica y el golpe militar," *Desarrollo Económico* (Buenos Aires) 6 (July 1966); Juan Carlos Portantiero, "Clases dominantes y crisis política en la Argentina actual," in *El capitalismo argentino en crisis*, ed. Oscar Braun (Buenos Aires: Siglo XXI Editores, 1973). For the early influence of Gramsci among Argentine New Left scholars and activists, see Raúl Burgos, *Los gramscianos argentinos: cultura y política en la experiencia de pasado y presente* (Buenos Aires: Siglo XXI Editores, 2004). Like Mayer, Argentine social scientists were drawn to what could be called the "sociological Gramsci," with his attention to crisis, alliances, blocs, and political and civil society, in contrast to the "ethnographic Gramsci," a polestar for those concerned with the cultural sedimentation—the "infinity of traces" inherited from the past—that layer popular "common sense." See also Atilio Baron, "El fascismo como categoría histórica: en torno al problema de las dictaduras en América Latina," *Revista Mexicana de Sociología*. 39, no. 2 (April–June 1977): 481–528.

44. For the Joseph Schumpeter passage cited by Mayer, see *Capitalism, Socialism, and Democracy* (New York: Harper and Row, 1950), 136. See also Schumpeter, *Imperialism and Social Classes* (New York: Meridian, 1955).

45. Mayer, *The Persistence of the Old Regime*, 329.

46. Mayer, *The Furies*, 111.

47. Maurice Merleau-Ponty, *Humanism and Terror*, trans. John O'Neill (Boston: Beacon Press, 1969), quoted in Mayer, *The Furies*, 37, 110.

48. C. L. R. James, *The Black Jacobins: Toussaint L'Ouverture and the San Domingo Revolution* (New York: Vintage Books, 1989), 111.

49. Mayer, *The Furies*, 53.

50. Peter Hallward, *Damming the Flood: Haiti, Aristide, and the Politics of Containment* (London: Verso, 2007), 12. William Appleman Williams once remarked that

the threat of the Haitian and French revolutions to the U.S. was that they spawned an "idealism that was so broad as to question the uniqueness and mission of America," in reaction to the U.S.'s all-embracing "imperial anticolonialism" (*America Confronts a Revolutionary World, 1776–1976* [New York: Morrow, 1976], 60).

51. Ibid., 47

52. Mayer, "Internal Crisis and War since 1870," in Bertrand, *Revolutionary Situations in Europe, 1917–1922*, 201.

53. Mayer develops this anatomy of counterrevolution more thoroughly in his earlier *Dynamics of Counterrevolution in Europe, 1870–1956*. See also Mayer, "Internal Causes and Purposes of War in Europe, 1870–1956," 299.

54. Georg Lukács, "The Marxism of Rosa Luxemburg," in *History and Class Consciousness: Studies in Marxist Dialectics*, trans. Rodney Livingston (Cambridge: MIT Press, 1972), 44.

55. Stern, *Shining and Other Paths*, 13–21.

56. Three hundred and twenty Chileans were condemned and executed by military tribunals within two months of the September 11, 1973, coup against Allende. This figure does not include other forms of state-administered "extrajudicial" killings; in Department of State, Briefing Memorandum, "Chilean Executions," November 16, 1973. Available at the website for the National Security Archive, The George Washington University, http://www.gwu.edu/~nsarchiv/.

57. For bodies washing ashore along the Rio Plata, see Martin Edwin Andersen, *Dossier Secreto: Argentina's Desaparecidos and the Myth of the "Dirty War"* (Boulder, Colo.: Westview Press, 1993); For the Mapocho, see Peter Winn's essay below.

58. For "Third World War," see Department of State, "ARA Monthly Report (July): The 'Third World War' and South America," August 2, 1976; available at http://foia .state.gov/, For "consciousness," see Marguerite Feitlowitz, *A Lexicon of Terror: Argentina and the Legacies of Torture* (New York: Oxford University Press, 1998), 25.

59. Feitlowitz, *A Lexicon of Terror*, 42–43, discusses the public relations campaign; see Nancy Caro Hollander, *Love in the Time of Hate: Liberation Psychology in Latin America* (New Brunswick, N.J.: Rutgers University Press, 1997), 93, for the anti-Semitic quote.

60. Cristián Larroulet, ed., *Public Solutions to Public Problems: The Chilean Experience* (Santiago: Fundación Libertad y Desarrollo, 1993), 7.

61. Quoted in *The Central American Crisis Reader*, ed. Robert S. Leiken and Barry Rubin (New York: Summit Books, 1987), 563.

62. José Nun, "The Middle-Class Military Coup," in *The Poltiics of Conformity in Latin America*, ed. Claudio Veliz (London: Oxford University Press, 1967), 85.

63. Nun, "América Latina," 393.

64. See, for two classic studies of the rise of postwar authoritarianism, Fernando Henrique Cardoso, *Autoritarismo e democratização* (Rio de Janeiro: Paz e Terra, 1975), and Guillermo O'Donnell, *Modernization and Bureaucratic-Authoritarianism* (Berkeley: University of California Press, 1973).

65. For an earlier study of the roots of what could be called Latin America's cold war New Right, see Frederick B. Pike, *Hispanismo, 1898–1936: Spanish Conservatives and Liberals and Their Relations with Spanish America* (Notre Dame, Ind.: University of Notre Dame Press, 1971). For more recent work, see Margaret Power, *Right-Wing Women in Chile: Feminine Power and the Struggle against Allende, 1964–1973* (University Park: Pennsylvania State University Press, 2002); Sandra McGee Deutsch, *Counterrevolution in Argentina, 1900–1932: The Argentine Patriotic League* (Lincoln: University of Nebraska Press, 1986), and *Las Derechas: The Extreme Right in Argentina, Brazil, and Chile, 1890–1939* (Stanford: Stanford University Press, 1999), as well as Sandra McGee Deutsch and Ronald H. Dolkart, eds., *The Argentine Right: Its History and Intellectual Origins, 1910 to the Present* (Wilmington, Del.: Scholarly Resources, 1993). Also see Federico Finchelstein, *Transatlantic Fascism: Ideology, Violence, and the Sacred in Argentina and Italy, 1919–1945* (Durham: Duke University Press, 2010).

66. Steve Stern discusses the reconstitution of the Peru's old regime in the midtwentieth century, followed by its exhaustion, leading to the rise of the Shining Path; see "Introduction to Part One," *Shining and Other Paths*, 14–15.

67. Norman Gall, *Correo de Guatemala*, September 1971, no. 13; Carlos Cáceres, *Aproximación a Guatemala* (Culiacán, Mexico: Universidad Autónoma de Sinaloa, 1980), 112; *El Día* (Mexico), March 6, 1982. Cf. Grandin, *Last Colonial Massacre*.

68. Friedrich Katz, *The Secret War in Mexico: Europe, the United States, and the Mexican Revolution* (Chicago: University of Chicago Press, 1981), and *The Life and Times of Pancho Villa* (Stanford: Stanford University Press, 1998).

69. John Dwyer, *Agrarian Dispute: The Expropriation of American-Owned Rural Land in Postrevolutionary Mexico* (Durham: Duke University Press, 2008).

70. David Schmitz, *Thank God They're on Our Side: The United States and Right-Wing Dictatorships, 1921–1965* (Chapel Hill: University of North Carolina Press, 1999), 145; See also Gilbert M. Joseph and Daniela Spenser, *In from the Cold: Latin America's New Encounter with the Cold War* (Durham: Duke University Press, 2007).

71. Mayer, "Internal Crisis and War since 1870," 211.

72. Jean-Paul Sartre, "Ideology and Revolution," *Studies on the Left* 1, no. 3 (1960), 7–16: p. 9.

73. Allan Lichtman, *White Protestant Nation: The Rise of the American Conservative Movement* (New York: Atlantic Monthly Press, 2008), 1; "Miami Heat: A Burgher Rebellion in Dade County," *Wall Street Journal*, November 24, 2000.

74. Lynn Horton, *Peasants in Arms: War and Peace in the Mountains of Nicaragua, 1979–1994* (Athens: Ohio University Center for International Studies, 1998).

75. Nun, "América Latina: la crisis hegemónica y el golpe militar," 363.

76. Jeremy Adelman, *Colonial Legacies: The Problem of Persistence in Latin American History* (New York: Routledge, 1999).

77. Charles W. Bergquist, *Labor and the Course of American Democracy: U.S. History in Latin American Perspective* (New York: Verso, 1996).

78. Greg Grandin, *Empire's Workshop: Latin America, the United States, and the Rise of the New Imperialism* (New York: Metropolitan Books, 2005).

79. Though as Jeremy Adelman points out, the extent of this process varied by region, as the central and northern Andean countries of Venezuela, Peru, and Colombia—having not experienced the kind of mid-century populist movements that occurred in other Latin American nations and being spared the "wave of brutal military dictatorships that swept the rest of the continent"—emerged out of the cold war with considerably more shaky governmental institutions than did countries in southern South America; Adelman, "Andean Impasses," *New Left Review* 18 (November–December 2002): 52.

80. Elizabeth Oglesby shows how labor unrest and political violence forced the Guatemalan sugar industry to modernize labor relations and production techniques, which made it highly competitive on the world market: "Politics at Work: Elites, Labor, and Agrarian Modernization in Guatemala, 1980–2000," Ph.D. diss., University of California, Berkeley. The sociologist Jeffrey Paige contends that Central America's armed revolutionary movements acted as a battering ram to crack the unity of the old landed order (which was needed because there existed no autonomous industrial bourgeoisie which could have served as an agent of representative democracy); his view is similar to Mayer's on the role that Europe's working-class and socialist movements played in bringing liberal modernity to capitalism's heartland. Paige, *Coffee and Power: Revolution and the Rise of Democracy in Central America* (Cambridge, Mass.: Harvard University Press, 1997).

81. Schumpeter, *Imperialism and Social Classes*, 123.

82. But as Ada Ferrer shows in *Insurgent Cuba*, Cuban revolutionaries—who, starting in 1868, fashioned a democratic, antiracist anticolonial movement that harked back to a Jacobean patriotism defined by virtuous action in defense of liberty—could be considered to have waged the first ideological assault on the exclusionary positivism that dominated Latin America at the time.

83. For different "waves" of insurgencies, see Timothy P. Wickham-Crowley, *Guerrillas and Revolution: A Comparative Study of Insurgents and Regimes since 1956* (Princeton: Princeton University Press, 1993).

PART ONE   *The First Cold War*

Violence and Terror in the
Mexican and Russian Revolutions

FRIEDRICH KATZ

A defining characteristic of twentieth-century social revolutions is that they comprise two distinct phases. The first might be called the revolution from below, movements to overthrow old authoritarian regimes that have strong support from popular classes: peasants, workers, and members of the middle classes. In many cases, this phase did not end with the downfall of the old order but devolved into a bloody civil war among competing revolutionary and counterrevolutionary factions. During this first phase there is significant violence, repression, and frequently mass terror, not only against the participants in the fighting and their active supporters but against, at times, uninvolved, or collateral, segments of the civilian population as well. This was certainly the case in Mexico, Russia, China, and Iran. It was also true in Cuba after 1959 and Nicaragua after 1979. Though in the former case, the civil war was contained to a regional, largely underreported, conflict, as Lillian Guerra's essay in this volume documents, and in the latter case, the terror was decidedly disproportionate, directed primarily by counterinsurgents at civilians with the goal of preventing the new Sandinista regime from stabilizing and legitimizing its rule.

In all the examples mentioned above, once a new revolutionary state had consolidated itself, there was a profound, systematic attempt to change both society and the individual through a revolution from above. Such attempts took place in the Soviet Union during the 1930s, in China during the Cultural Revolution, in Iran after the victory of the revolutionary faction and the overthrow of the shah, and in Mexico in the 1930s. In all cases except the Mexican one, these revolutions from above were linked to mass terror, frequently, as in the case of Russia and China, affecting millions of people and bringing about the elimination of democratic elements of the first phase of the revolution and the emergence of a semidivine cult of the leader.

The revolution from above that took place in Mexico in the 1930s under the presidency of Lázaro Cárdenas did seek to profoundly transform both society and the individual in Mexico and institute major social and economic changes. Yet it took place in a climate of minimal repression. Strong opposition forces continued to exist legally, and the leader of the country not only was not considered an infallible leader but also did not attempt to perpetuate himself in power as Stalin or Mao did in Russia and China respectively. It is these differences that first sparked my interest to examine the very different role that repression and terror played in the Mexican and Russian revolutions.

There are critical differences between the two countries and between the origins and aims of their two revolutions. Unlike Mexico, Russia was a world power, and its revolution took place in the context of the enormous ravages and weakening of the state that resulted from Russia's involvement in the First World War. Nothing similar took place in Mexico. The triumphant faction in the Russian Revolution, the Bolsheviks, was a utopian party that saw itself as an agent of world-historical change. They wanted to completely transform society and the individual and saw themselves as the vanguard of a global revolution, which they sought to achieve by forming the Communist International and fomenting revolutions in many parts of the world. In Mexico, there likewise existed groups with utopian objectives. In central Mexico, the Zapatistas hoped to recreate a rural society entirely constituted by communal villages, a society that in fact had never existed. In northern Mexico, the Villistas envisioned the recreation of an old frontier institution: military colonies. In the words of one American observer, they also believed "that the property of the rich ought to be administered by the government for the benefit of the masses, and even if not clearly articulated, the socialist ideal appeared to dominate the movement."[1] But these quasi-utopian, or backward-looking millenarian movements, were ultimately defeated by a victorious faction that was decidedly not utopian, one that rejected meaningful land reform and firmly believed in capitalism, albeit a national capitalism that would be dominated by Mexicans. In general, the aims of the Mexican revolutionaries were more limited than those of their Soviet counterparts, and no official, systemic attempts were made in the initial phase, either ideologically or practically, to export the Mexican revolution. Nevertheless there are valid points of comparison between the two. Both can be called "social revolutions," a term I use not to impose a fixed typological definition on either historical event but rather to look at certain characteristics that all movements that have generally been called social revolutions in the twentieth century have in common.

One point of comparison is the massive participation of popular classes, above all the peasantry, in the initial phase of both the Mexican and Russian Revolutions. A second similarity is the destruction of the old state that took place in both countries. Another is the profound transformation in land tenure patterns and in the countries' relations with foreign capital and foreign countries that both revolutions engendered.

In Mexico, during the revolution's first phase, these changes were far more limited than what occurred in Russia. While in Russia the land-owning class was either killed or exiled and peasants seized most of the lands that belonged to these classes, in Mexico such land seizures occurred only in a limited part of the country. By 1920 a significant part of the Mexican old land-owning class, after having fled during the violence of the early revolution, had returned to assume control of their properties (though they never fully regained the political power that had been theirs on the eve of the revolution). In Russia, foreign capital had been expropriated during the first phase of the revolution, while in Mexico only the legal basis of such expropriation had been established.

In both Mexico and Russia, foreign powers tried to influence the course of the Revolution by armed intervention. In Russia foreigners actively supported counterrevolutionaries, helping to launch and execute a sustained civil war that lasted from 1917 to 1921. In Mexico armed intervention by the United States also occurred, but it was much more contradictory in nature, with Washington offering hesitant, sporadic support to some revolutionary factions. In Russia, the direction of and eventual victory against a defined counterrevolution in a protracted civil war allowed the Bolsheviks to consolidate their legitimacy and rule. In Mexico, the civil war remained fractious and multidimensional, and the party that would eventually come to dominate the revolution only emerged many years after the armed phase of the revolution. In Russia the old ruling class was either exterminated or exiled. In Mexico it was seriously weakened, but after the first phase of the revolution it still held on to much of the country's economy, even though it had lost its hold on political power.

Traditions of Repression

In order to compare counterrevolutionary and revolutionary terror in Mexico and Russia, one needs to examine the tradition of repression and violence in both. Russia's massive prerevolutionary tradition of state repression is well documented, reaching back all the way to Ivan the Terrible and Peter the Great, and including the bloody persecutions that took place during the reign of its last czar, Nicholas I—namely, the pogroms against Jews and the intensive repression against the revolutionaries of 1905. There was also a well-established tradition of terror directed at individuals on the part of revolutionaries, that is, the assassination of high-level personalities of the Russian regime including Czar Alexander II.

In one respect there was a stronger tradition of violence in nineteenth-century Mexico than in Russia, since no stable regime had existed in that country up to the dictatorship of Porfirio Díaz in 1876. Yet for the most part, the violence inherent in nineteenth-century state formation threatened the properties of civilians much more often than their lives. For the most part, massacres throughout Mexico's prerevolutionary period were perpetrated by foreigners rather than by Mexicans. It was the Spaniards during the War of Independence and the French during Maximilian's empire who carried out some of the worst massacres of civilians in Mexican history. And even after the consolidation of the Porfiriato, the Díaz regime was far less repressive than that of Nicholas I in Russia. The massacres of strikers at Río Blanco and Cananea were the exception rather than the rule, as was the suppression of a dissident, millenarian religious community in Tomochic, Chihuahua, in the early 1890s.[2]

Where the prerevolutionary Mexican state did deploy lethal, inhumane terror, conducted with ferocity comparable to its Russian counterpart, was in its policy toward indigenous populations. Even just a suspicion of an indigenous uprising could provoke a deadly government response. In the 1830s, the state government of Chihuahua established bounties for anyone bringing in scalps not only of Apache males but of Apache women and children as well. After the uprising of Maya Indians in Yucatán was crushed in the 1850s, thousands of Mayas were sold into slavery to Cuba. Thousands of rebellious as well as peaceful Yaqui Indians were either killed or deported to Yucatán, in the same way that the czar exiled his enemies to Siberia.

As in Russia, Mexico had a tradition of revolutionary violence. "Death to the Gauchupines" was a rallying cry during the Hidalgo rebellion of 1810, and after rebels captured the city of Guanajuato they did indeed execute large numbers of Spanish civilians. During the "Guerra de Castas" in 1847, Mayan insurgents likewise slaughtered many non-Indians. But unlike Russia's violent anarchists, Mexican anarcho-syndicalists who organized in the Partido Liberal Mexicano did not believe in individual terror and assassinations, focusing their energies on building mass union movements rather than conducting isolated acts of violence.

Revolutions from Below

Both in Russia and in Mexico, the initial stages of their revolutions were not characterized by massive killings, massacres, or terror against the civilian population. One cannot speak of any kind of mass terror either by the revolutionaries or the Díaz government during the first phase of the Mexican Revolution. There was no mass extermination or killing of landowners, tenants, or other supporters of the old regime. Nothing comparable to the jacqueries in France or to the Boxer Rebellion in China took place. Some in the Díaz government did advocate mass terror: in a memorandum written by Jorge Vera Estañol, Díaz's minister of education, to the secretary of foreign affairs, the minister called the peasant revolts that were proliferating in many parts of Mexico "anarchy." These, he stated, "cannot be destroyed through proclamations, reforms or government plans; anarchy can only be dealt with by force, using the most radical means of annihilation."[3] But Díaz was forced to resign before he had time to implement it. The transitional Francisco León de la Barra administration, and then Francisco Madero's government (1911–13) did take some actions against Emiliano Zapata and his peasant followers in Morelos, but these were relatively low-level compared to the anti-Zapatista campaigns led by Victoriano Huerta's neo-Porfirista dictatorship (1913–14) and Venustiano Carranza's (1914–20) Constitucionalista administration.

Likewise in Russia, the early stages of both the February and October Revolutions were relatively unbloody affairs. Yet during the early years of civil war between 1917 and 1922, violence quickly escalated into massive terror perpetrated by all sides. The counterrevolutionary whites killed not only their prisoners but also many suspected of Bolshevik sympathies and organized massive pogroms against Jews. The "red terror" established by the Bolsheviks was no less violent. In the early days of the civil war, revolutionary violence was mainly directed against the old upper classes as well as members and sympathizers of revolutionary factions opposed to the Bolsheviks, such as Mensheviks and socialist revolutionaries. As the war dragged on, it concentrated more and more on peasants who were resisting requisitions of food by the Red Army for the cities, as well as the draft of their young men into that army. Repression was even more ferocious against peasant revolutionaries such as the anarchist Nestor Makhno, who tried to establish independent peasant republics. In the process the Bolsheviks used mass executions, the taking of hostages, and the establishment of concentration camps. The white armies and the anti-Bolshevik peasants in turn tortured captured Bolsheviks and buried many of them alive.

On the whole such terror was less pronounced in Mexico. Nevertheless, the treatment of the Zapatistas and their supporters in Morelos by the early Madero administration, Victoriano Huerta's army, and the victorious Carrancista revolutionary faction was similar to the terror being exercised against peasants in Russia. Many villages in Morelos were burned; there were massive executions of civilians, and even more pillage of their properties. Still, revolutionary violence in Mexico directed against civilians was far milder than in Russia and it is questionable whether the term "revolutionary terror" is even applicable. When he began his revolutionary movement in 1913, Venustiano Carranza decreed that anyone caught fighting against the revolutionaries should be summarily executed. But in fact, captured rank-and-file counterrevolutionaries were often released or incorporated into the revolutionary armies, and only officers and former revolutionaries who had defected to Huerta's counterrevolutionary government were shot. When the armies of Emiliano Zapata and Pancho Villa occupied the city of Mexico, they executed about three hundred persons, many of them supporters of the old regime who had actively fought against the revolution. Others were revolutionaries with opinions that did not suit either Villa or Zapata. Nevertheless, their number was relatively small compared both to the victims of government terror in Mexico and to the huge number of executions that were carried out in Russia.

The difference in the scale of repression in the Mexican and Russian Revolutions goes well beyond the traditions of violence in both countries, and can be accounted for by a number of contextual factors specific to each event. One of the most important explanations for the tremendous amount of violence and terror in Russia was the First World War, which drastically brutalized society and embittered millions of people who felt that the enormous sacrifices that the war had demanded of them had been in vain. In Mexico as in Russia, once one faction was definitively triumphant in the civil wars that had engulfed both countries for many years (in Mexico, the forces of Venustiano Carranza and Álvaro Obregón; in Russia, the Bolsheviks), terror and repression tended to abate. At first glance the differences between the victors in the Russian and the Mexican Revolutions seem enormous: the Bolsheviks constituted a highly structured political party with a defined ideology, whereas Obregón and Carranza presided over a military organization; the Bolsheviks wanted to abolish capitalism and replace it by socialism, whereas Obregón, Carranza, and their supporters were firm believers in private property and capitalism.

Yet profound similarities do exist. Both the Bolsheviks and the victorious Mexican revolutionaries believed that the state should have ultimate control over natural resources and play a major role in the economic life of their countries. The Bolsheviks had in fact confiscated all foreign properties. The Mexican revolutionaries were too weak to do so, but the constitution that they had proclaimed in 1917 clearly stated that the Mexican nation was entitled to ultimate control over its natural resources. Carranza had in fact taken some first steps in that direction with regard to the foreign oil companies operating in Mexico. Moreover, both the Russian and the Mexican revolutionaries were profoundly anticlerical. And neither Lenin nor Obregón (president from 1920 to 1924) believed in democracy, any more than did Plutarco Elías Calles (who was president from 1924 to 1928, but remained the real power behind the throne until 1935, in a period known as the Maximato).

Both the Bolsheviks and the Obregonistas had established close ties to labor while their relations to the peasants were complex and ambiguous. While both had profound contempt for the peasantry and considered them a marker of their respective country's backwardness, they each made alliances with peasant revolutionaries in the earlier phases of their respective revolutions. Lenin had accepted the peasants' demands for land in 1917, and in 1920 Bolsheviks and Nestor Makhno's peasant anarchists made common cause against the counterrevolution. Two years later, however, the Bolsheviks were destroying Makhno's forces as well as those of other independent peasant revolutionaries. In Mexico a similar pattern of alliance and repression took place. Carranza, Obregón, Villa, and Zapata had all fought against the Huerta dictatorship, but then Carranza and Obregón had turned against their erstwhile peasant allies and defeated them in a long and bloody civil war.

Consolidations

Once they had achieved victory, triumphant Russian and Mexican revolutionaries faced a similar set of problems. Their economies had been devastated by long civil wars. New foreign investment did not emerge; foreign loans could not be obtained. In Russia this was the obvious result of the massive confiscation of all foreign holdings and the repudiation of all foreign debts by the Bolshevik government. In Mexico it was due more to the incapacity of the revolutionary government to repay foreign debts and to compensate foreigners for losses suffered during the revolution. In Russia as well as in Mexico agricultural production had fallen drastically. In both cases the old state had been destroyed and the new state had not yet been able to consolidate itself. In both cases the victorious revolutionaries felt that the moment had come to make peace with the peasants. In Russia this peace took the shape of Lenin's New Economic Policy. Forced requisitions of food from peasants stopped and were replaced by taxes. Peasants were allowed to sell their goods in free markets and peasant entrepreneurs could operate freely. In Mexico peace with the peasantry meant above all making concessions to those rural factions who had continued to fight the government. Obregón reconciled with the followers of the martyred Zapata and recognized the land division that Zapata had carried out in Morelos. A peace treaty was signed with Villa, though he too would soon be executed, which was soon followed by a massive land reform in Chihuahua. Land divisions carried out by the revolutionaries in San Luis Potosí and in Tlaxcala were also recognized. Land reform, however, was limited to those areas where revolutionary peasants had been fighting. Only when peasant pressure was very strong did Obregón accede to land division elsewhere. In many other parts of the country the landowners had recovered their properties and the Obregón and later Calles's administrations made no effort to dispossess them.

In both Russia and Mexico the period of peace with the peasantry was also a period of intellectual tolerance, though not of democracy. In Russia new forms of literary expression, theater, and the arts flourished. In Mexico, under the stewardship of the cultural minister José Vasconcelos, there was a brilliant development of muralist painting, literature, and art as well. But in the early twenties profound divisions among the victorious Mexican and Russian revolutionaries emerged, though in the case of Russia their resolution seemed more peaceful, at least at first, than in the case of Mexico. Stalin's enemies within the ruling party were at worst expelled from the party, and in the case of Trotsky exiled. In Mexico, by contrast, the conflict took the shape of armed confrontation among different revolutionary factions, which frequently led to executions of former revolutionary partners of Obregón and Calles.

By the late 1920s, this brief period of stability and cultural openness ended, and revolutionary violence returned both to Russia and to Mexico. In 1927 a dramatic change of policy took place in the Soviet Union. The Soviet leadership believed that an attack on their country might be imminent. These fears were triggered by events in Asia and in Europe. In China, Soviet policy suffered a disastrous defeat when Chiang Kai Shek put an end to his alliance with the communists and massacred thousands of them. In Britain, the government of Stanley Baldwin raided the Soviet trade mission, while in France the conservative administration of Raymond Poincaré attacked the French Communist Party. In December 1927, the Politburo of the Soviet Communist Party decided, "bearing in mind the possibility of a military attack . . . it is essential in elaborating the Five-Year Plan to devote maximum attention to a most rapid development of the economy in general and industry in particular on which the main role will fall in securing the defense and economic stability of the country in war-time."[4] In the views of the leadership, the new economic policy's "premise of trusting the future of military preparedness to gradual industrialization was abandoned."[5] One of the ways to obtain the means for such a policy was to exercise a tremendous amount of pressure on the peasantry. The wealthiest peasants, the Kulaks, were expropriated, and a hundred thousand of them were deported to Siberia. The rest of the peasantry, frequently against their will, were forced into collective farms, which were tightly controlled by the government and a large part of whose revenues were used by the state in its policy of forced industrialization. This policy led to unrest, and frequently to chaos in the countryside, which took the shape not so much of active armed resistance but rather of more passive opposition, including the wholesale slaughter of cattle and other domestic animals. Fear of an imminent imperialist attack was by no means the only motive for this change in policy. It was linked to the triumph of Stalin in the controversies within the Soviet Communist Party. Now in control of the party, Stalin wanted to destroy those sectors of the economy that had managed to maintain a certain independence from the state: the private enterprises of businessmen (the "Nepmen") who had emerged during the period of the new economic policy, and above all the peasants.

In 1924–25 a dramatic reversal of policy similarly took place in Mexico, likewise driven by international relations and likewise substantially affecting important segments of the peasantry. Throughout his presidency (1920–24), Álvaro Obregón had attempted to maintain a conciliatory policy toward both American business interests and the Catholic Church. In the 1923 Bucareli Treaty with Washington, Obregón agreed not to apply some of the most radical nationalistic provisions of Mexico's 1917 constitution, particularly those related to petroleum. He also limited the application of constitution's anticlerical provisions. That situation greatly changed under his successor Plutarco Elías Calles (1924–28), who attempted to apply the restrictions on the rights of foreign oil companies that the 1917 constitution had proclaimed. This led to tensions with the U.S. administration and at one point Secretary of State Frank Kellogg called the Calles government a Bolshevik instrument. In the eyes of the Mexican government, an armed American intervention or at the very least an occupation of the oil fields by the United States emerged as a real possibility. The reasons for these changes in policy are still a matter of debate among historians. They were certainly linked to the fact that Obregón's policy of conciliation with U.S. interests had brought no significant increase of U.S. investment into Mexico, even as Mexico's one significant resource, oil, was being pumped out of the country with very little benefit to Mexico's treasury. To make matters worse, U.S. petroleum companies had cut down on production and investments in Mexico because Venezuelan oil fields were more productive. Thus, Mexico's tax revenues were further eroded. Domestic considerations may have played a role as well: Calles lacked either the popularity or the military prestige of Obregón, and nationalism may well have been one of the means that he utilized to consolidate his regime.

At the same time that Calles turned against the United States he also began to attack what he considered the great bastion of conservatism in Mexico, the Catholic Church. The anticlericalism of Calles and other leaders of the victorious faction in the Mexican Revolution reflected in part the anticlericalism of the nineteenth-century liberals led by Benito Juárez. It may also have been due to the fact that the Catholic Church took a strong antirevolutionary stance in the years 1910 to 1920. The newly founded Catholic Party turned against Madero, and its leaders, along with important church officials, supported the Huerta dictatorship. In 1916–17 these same forces attempted to encourage an American military intervention in Mexico. The complex restrictions imposed on the church led to an uprising by many of its supporters in the countryside, especially in west-central Mexico, above all in Jalisco. Many of these armed supporters, known as Cristeros, were small independent peasants—*rancheros*—who not only believed they were defending the church but also their own autonomy from the encroachment of the state. Though to a far less degree than in the Soviet Union, the term "terror" can also be applied to the policies of both the government and the Cristeros during this armed conflict in Mexico. Government troops executed hostages as well as real and perceived supporters of the Cristeros, and frequently burnt rebellious villages to the ground. For their part, the Cristeros carried out executions of civilians who either opposed them or were believed to be potential opponents.

In both the Soviet Union and Mexico, fear of foreign aggression, along with increasing internal conflicts, led to a policy of supporting revolutions outside their borders. The sixth Congress of the Communist International declared that a revolutionary situation in the capitalist world was imminent and called on the communist parties to prepare for it. In Mexico, Calles supported revolutionaries in other parts of Latin America. This was especially reflected in Mexico's attempts to help the Nicaraguan revolutionaries and especially Augusto César Sandino. At the same time, Cuban exiles such as the founder of the Cuban Communist Party, Julio Antonio Mella, received asylum in Mexico and were allowed to campaign against the Cuban dictator Antonio Machado.

In the late 1920s Calles carried out a new dramatic shift in policy, which seemed to end any parallels between the evolution of the Soviet Union and that of revolutionary Mexico. In an agreement with the U.S. ambassador Dwight Morrow, Calles short-circuited his nationalist policy. He guaranteed oil companies all the rights they claimed as their due and signed a peace agreement with the church. This not only defused the foreign threat but won Washington's backing for Calles, who had left the presidency in 1928 yet continued to exercise power behind the scenes as *jefe máximo* of the revolution. When a military rebellion against Calles headed by General

José Gonzalo Escobar in 1929 took place, the United States threw its clear support to the Mexican government. Calles continued to reverse policy, declaring that the agrarian reform had been a failure and that land division should cease. He also ended the government's alliance with the Confederación Regional Obrera Mexicana and its president, Luis Morones, and cracked down on strikes. Significantly, it was in these years that diplomatic relations with the Soviet Union were broken.

Despite Calles's domestic reversals and rapprochement with Washington and foreign capital, significant similarities between the two revolutions continued. Stalin's policy to put an end to peasant autonomy continued unabated in the Soviet Union. In Mexico too, attempts to restrict the autonomy of the peasantry took place, though this time a very different group of peasants from those that had supported the Cristeros were affected. Now Calles targeted those radical agraristas who had helped him in his fight against the Catholic Church. In Veracruz, the government disarmed the peasant militias set up by Governor Adalberto Tejeda, and prosecuted the radical agraristas affiliated with the Communist Party.

Revolutions from Above

One of the greatest similarities between Mexico and Russia was the consolidation of revolutionary ruling parties. In the 1920s, opposing ideas and positions could still be aired within the Communist Party of the Soviet Union (CPSU), though debate was considerably reduced following the death of Lenin in 1924. After Trotsky's expulsion first from the party and then from the country, Stalin came to dominate the CPSU, which became increasingly militarized and vertical. In 1929, Calles created the Partido Nacional Revolucionario in Mexico, a move designed both to conciliate the different factions within the revolution and to create an organization that would be capable of controlling the popular forces. Both in the Soviet Union and in Mexico the ruling party attempted to exercise complete dominance over labor. In both countries, the global Great Depression shaped in distinct ways the evolution of their respective revolutions. In Mexico, the depression led to massive unemployment, which was compounded by the at-times forced return of hundreds of thousands of Mexicans who had worked in the United States. In Russia the effect of the depression took a very different shape. There was no unemployment; on the contrary the massive industrialization of the country created a huge demand for labor. The industrial goods that the Soviet Union imported were paid for by exports of agricultural products, above all of grain. As the price of these exports fell in the world market and Russia had to export more, the pressure on the peasantry increased.

In the early 1930s the Soviet Union faced a difficult situation. According to J. Arch Getty and Oleg Naumov, the country was in chaos:

> The collectivization and industrialization policies of the Stalin Revolution had uprooted society, destroyed formerly prominent social groups and classes, and abolished private property and markets in favor of a new, untested, and constantly changing form of socialism. Millions of peasants and urban proprietors were angry and confused; millions of others had been killed or had died of starvation. Nobody really understood how the economy was working or should work, not even its new directors. Nobody had a solid grasp of the shifting and reactive structure of state institutions, not even their new administrators. Nobody, including those specializing in intelligence gathering, had a very clear idea of what the population was thinking or who was organizing subversive activities. Across the country, political directives, juridical norms, and even ideology were being interpreted in a wide variety of ways that sometimes bore little relation to what Moscow was saying. Even though in 1932 the Stalinists had "won," insofar as they had in fact implemented collectivization, their victory was in many ways unsatisfying. Famine still stalked the land, and the regime had little doubt that despite its brave proclamations of victory and party unity there was desperate opposition to it at many levels. Peasants sang about Stalin chewing bones on top of a coffin. Student groups cranked out incendiary pamphlets, and well-known party members gathered in the night to write platforms calling for the overthrow of the leadership.[6]

Mexico too faced a difficult situation. When Calles gave in to Washington pressure and reversed the course of the revolution he had hoped that large foreign investments would pour into Mexico and bring about a new era of prosperity. But with the depression in full swing, no such investment took place, and disillusionment and opposition to the policies of the government grew by leaps and bounds.

The reactions in the Soviet Union and in Mexico to this situation were radically different. Stalin confronted increasing dissatisfaction in the country with a massive campaign of terror. Calles, on the other hand, carried out a limited policy of conciliation. Even if he had wanted to, Calles could not have carried out the kind of terrorist policy that Stalin implemented in the Soviet Union. Not only did both countries have very different traditions with regard to repression, the Mexican state was simply much too weak to implement a policy comparable to that of the Soviet Union. In addition it did not face the kind of foreign threat that confronted the Soviets.

But perhaps a more important factor was that unlike in the Soviet Union, where the old upper classes had been either killed or exiled, in Mexico they were still very much present and continued to hold economic if not political power. The revolutionary government thus needed to cultivate popular support to forestall a conservative restoration, and as such it returned to many of the social policies that Calles had just a few years earlier abandoned. The PNR's 1934 presidential candidate, therefore, represented the moderate *agrarista* faction, a man who had always been closely linked to and loyal to Calles: Lázaro Cárdenas. Calles was convinced that Cárdenas would carry out some limited reforms to appease the most radical peasant groups in the country but, beyond that, would be as loyal to him as his predecessors had been since 1928.

At a time when the utopia for which many of the Russian revolutionaries had fought in 1917–18 seemed to be drowned in a sea of blood in the Soviet Union, Cárdenas revived and applied many of the utopias of which Mexico's Zapatistas and Villistas had dreamed. He distributed millions of hectares of land to the peasantry in the form of communal property, thus securing a broad degree of popular consent. He implemented a system of social security for workers and passed legislation protecting labor rights, including their right to strike. The perennial conflict with the oil companies was finally ended when Cárdenas nationalized oil production in Mexico. All of these measures were carried out with very little violence, and a strong opposition press as well as powerful right-wing organizations continued to be tolerated in Mexico.

In 1937 and 1938, the differences between the role of terror in the Soviet Union and Mexico were further accentuated. In 1937 terror in the Soviet Union reached an unprecedented level. While violence in the preceding period had been directed at groups that either genuinely opposed the government or could be considered potential opponents—the Kulaks, members of the middle classes, remnants of the old political parties that had been opposed to the Bolsheviks, peasants who had lost the right to individual landownership even if they were not Kulaks, workers who objected to complete control of the trade unions by the party—the terror of 1937 was directed mainly against members of the Communist Party of the Soviet Union who could by no means be considered enemies of the government or even opponents of Stalin. By 1937 the former leaders of the opposition to Stalin—Kamenev, Zinoviev, Bukharin—had been purged; Trotsky was in exile. The Seventeenth Party Congress in 1934 had unanimously reelected Stalin as general secretary. He faced no opposition in the CPSU or in the army. Yet he unleashed a tremendous wave of terror. Hundreds of thousands of Bolsheviks were shot and 40 percent of the officer corps were either imprisoned or killed. Some historians attribute this slaughter to Stalin's pure paranoia, yet others believe he systematically set out to eliminate the generation of Bolsheviks who had carried out the 1917 Revolution, Communists who had lived through a very different climate of open discussion and debate within the party and might at some point renew attempts to create more democratic structures within it. Stalin's final aim was to perpetuate himself in power. Although he accused many of the old Bolsheviks of conspiring with Great Britain or with Nazi Germany, there is not the slightest evidence that this was the case, or that Stalin himself actually believed it. Thus the foreign threat that had been a genuine factor in influencing the terror of 1928–29 cannot be seen as an objective cause of the terror of 1937.

In contrast to what was going on in the Soviet Union, Cárdenas did in fact face a genuine threat in 1938, including an uprising led by General Saturnino Cedillo and a strengthening Right in the form of the quasi-fascist Sinarquista movement. That Right became even more dangerous after the nationalization of foreign oil companies, since American oil firms showed great sympathy toward Cárdenas's opposition. Yet no great wave of terror engulfed Mexico. In the course of the Cedillo uprising, he and a few of his supporters were shot, but on the whole the opposition to Cárdenas was left unscathed.

In 1938 Cárdenas was nearing the end of his term and was faced with three choices. He could attempt to perpetuate himself in power either by changing the constitution and having himself reelected or by naming a stooge to succeed him. Such attempts were by no means unprecedented in Mexico, as all revolutionary leaders from 1916 on had attempted to remain in power once their term in office expired. Carranza had sought to do so by naming Ignacio Bonillas as candidate for the presidency, a man who had no constituency of his own and who was completely dependent on Carranza. Obregón had amended the constitution to have himself reelected after Calles had been president for one term, and Calles had instituted the Maximato. But Cárdenas refused to replicate these precedents. He also could have selected as the candidate a man who essentially shared his political ideas, such as Francisco Múgica. Both of these alternatives would likely have led to civil war and required a massive terror to enforce. Instead Cárdenas chose Manuel Ávila Camacho as his successor, a man who in many ways did not share his views. With this measure he secured the support of the United States and prevented a wave of terror and violence from sweeping Mexico.

Two questions beg answers here. First, why did Mexico's upper classes, which still controlled a large part of the landed estates and wielded significant influence, wage so little resistance to Cárdenas's expropriation? Second, why did the United States not react forcefully to the greatest attack on American property to have taken place in the history of United States–Latin American relations? The lack of resistance of the landed upper class was certainly linked to the fact that the armed phase of the revolution had seriously weakened it both politically and economically. In many respects, too, this landed elite also found itself isolated. Mexico's industrialists were not profoundly affected by the Cárdenas reforms, although they disapproved of the power the president gave to labor. Yet Cárdenas made no efforts to implement socialism or expropriate their industries. Not surprisingly, then, many industrialists felt that Cárdenas's land reforms might create a national market for their products while his nationalization of oil would provide them with cheap fuel. In addition Cárdenas attempted to conciliate the church by reining in such fanatic anticlerical Callistas as the governor of Tabasco, Tomás Garrido Canabal. Likewise, right-wing forces in Mexico could not count on American support, since the United States also did not strongly react to the Cárdenas expropriations. As Nazi Germany became more and more aggressive, many Latin American military dictators showed strong sympathies for the Nazis. The Cárdenas administration in Mexico was one of the few Latin American countries that was strongly opposed to fascism and on which the United States could count in case of a war with Germany. In addition, the Roosevelt administration had very little sympathy for the oil companies that were its political enemies.

To return to the original question that was raised at the outset of this essay, why was terror necessary to implement Stalin's reforms while Cárdenas could implement his profound transformations of Mexico without resorting to it? Two fundamental differences played a major role in this regard. The first was that Stalin essentially reversed the reforms that had been carried out in the first phase of the Russian Revolution, when land had been given to the peasants and labor had been granted extensive rights. Thus, land was taken away from the peasants and the rights of labor were curtailed. In Cardenista Mexico, by contrast, the demands of the first phase of the revolution were now implemented on a massive scale for the first time, allowing the president to garner a tremendous base of popular support. In this situation terror was not only unnecessary but would have been counterproductive. The second great difference between the situation of Cárdenas and that of Stalin's Bolsheviks was that while the Bolsheviks faced a genuine and serious threat of outside attack, which had greatly increased when Hitler took power in Germany, no such threat confronted the Mexican government. Roosevelt had proclaimed the Good Neighbor Policy of not intervening militarily in Latin America and, as we have seen, had good reasons for not wanting to antagonize the Cárdenas administration.

The Cárdenas utopia did not last, for reasons that go beyond the scope of this essay. Still, Cardenismo was a unique movement in Latin American history, and it is no coincidence that among the region's leaders, Cárdenas is one of the few whose prestige outlasted his government and extended beyond his death.

Notes

1. Friedrich Katz, *The Life and Times of Pancho Villa* (Stanford: Stanford University Press, 1998), 430.

2. Paul Vanderwood, *The Power of God against the Guns of Government: Religious Upheaval in Mexico at the Turn of the Nineteenth Century* (Stanford: Stanford University Press, 1999).

3. Quoted in Katz, *The Life and Times of Pancho Villa,* 105.

4. Arno J. Mayer, *The Furies: Violence and Terror in the French and Russian Revolutions* (Princeton: Princeton University Press, 2000), 625

5. Ibid.

6. J. Arch Getty and Oleg V. Naumov, *The Road to Terror: Stalin and the Self-Destruction of the Bolsheviks, 1932–1939,* trans. Benjamin Sher (New Haven: Yale University Press, 1999), 573.

Mueras y matanza

Spectacles of Terror and Violence
in Postrevolutionary Mexico

JOCELYN OLCOTT

"There were twenty dead and eight wounded yesterday in a decisive battle that took place on the corner of Matamoros and Cuauhtémoc streets, in front of the Montecarlo cantina," began the article in the newspaper of nearby Torreón.[1] On June 29, 1930, a group of Communists affiliated with the Socorro Rojo Internacional (SRI) staged a demonstration near the Plaza de Armas in Matamoros, Coahuila, a town in Mexico's northern region of the Comarca Lagunera. When a standoff between SRI leaders and local authorities degenerated into an assault on the head of the rural guard, bullets rained down on the demonstrators. By late that afternoon, twenty Communists had been killed in what the Communist Party (PCM) newspaper *El Machete* called a massacre (*matanza*) and local authorities dubbed a riot (*zafarrancho*).

This divergent language—alternately dubbing the event a disorderly, disruptive riot or a senseless, terrorizing massacre—indicates competing narratives amid the high-stakes wrangling between rival factions that struggled to define the meaning of the violence and to claim the mantle of Mexico's 1910–17 revolution. "The founding myth of nearly every society or state," the historian Arno Mayer tells us, "romanticizes and celebrates its primal bloodshed."[2] This assertion certainly holds for 1930s Mexico, where the revolution's meaning remained very much unsettled and where efforts to memorialize conflicts such as the Matamoros incident raised questions about who claimed the legitimacy conferred by Mexico's bloody and protracted civil war as its original violence. Within the larger battle over which faction could claim the title of "revolutionary," the partisans in the June 29 confrontation sought to mark each other with the stain of terrorism. The characterization of each side's intervention—as a justifiable use of force, a disruptive episode of violence, or a wanton act of terror—became itself a realm of contestation in the struggle for legitimacy.[3] Analyzing violence and repression as part of the grammar of establishing and disrupting regime legitimacy, a process that dialectically links revolution and counterrevolution, Mayer describes repression as the victorious revolutionaries' effort "to institutionalize their own revolt at the expense of crushing all others in their drive to establish or impose their monopoly of centralized state power."[4] In the Mexican case examined here, while government officials had declared the revolutionary mission accomplished and dubbed challenges such as the Communists' as counterrevolutionary subversion, the Communists insisted upon the necessity of their resistance to prevent the revolution's betrayal.

The spectacular nature of the June 29 confrontation distinguished it from more private and quotidian encounters, rendering it simultaneously as both the atomizing intimidation of state terror and the founding bloodshed of revolutionary violence. From the public and staged nature of the episode itself to its contemporary newspaper coverage, and its subsequent memorialization over the following years and decades, the incident served didactic ends as competing factions sought, through its repeated representation, to offer a political education. These struggles over meaning both belied the regime's efforts to declare the revolution a settled matter and revealed the limits of its ascriptive powers vis-à-vis those of activists with longstanding political and affective ties to local communities. The Communists, while repeatedly insisting on their peaceful intentions in staging the protest, acknowledged that they had intended it as a provocation, a spectacle of a different sort than it became. More than a conflict over mere political power, these efforts to define who terrorized whom sought to determine who had a right to live and who had a right to kill.

"The Faith of a Revolutionary": Contextualizing Violence and Terror

Interpreting the spectacles and competing narratives that adhered to the protest and killing requires some local historical context. Although the Matamoros confrontation occurred twelve years after the postrevolutionary constitutional congress, a year after the creation of the Partido Nacional

Revolucionario (PNR), and during the Maximato (the period of domination of Mexican politics by the supreme leader [*jefe máximo*] Plutarco Elías
Calles), the governing regime's control over postrevolutionary society remained incomplete, particularly in areas far removed from Mexico City. An
opportunity still seemed to exist for alternative revolutionary programs to
have a hand in shaping the new regime. The Communist Party strove to
exploit that opening, making no effort to disguise its enmity toward the
Maximato and challenging the PNR's claims to the mantle of revolutionary
struggle. Communists consistently railed against the governing regime, at
least until the 1935 volte face of the Popular Front, regularly lambasting the
ruling PNR as "fascist" and "counterrevolutionary" and, as their prosecutors
repeatedly pointed out, shouting *mueras* (death) against the government,
recalling the independence-era rally cry, "death to bad government!" The
federal government, intent on establishing the ruling party's primacy as the
arbiter of postrevolutionary policies, had forced the Communist Party underground and launched a campaign of arrests and persecutions that would
last until 1934.

In the Comarca Lagunera, the federal government's hold was particularly
tenuous, and the Communists were not the only cause for concern. The
Escobarista rebellion, a barracks revolt involving an estimated thirty thousand militants led by nearly a third of the active officer corps, broke out on
March 3, 1929, demanding that Calles—still Mexico's political puppeteer,
although no longer president—relinquish political control. The uprising,
composed primarily of supporters of the slain president Álvaro Obregón,
would be the last sustained postrevolutionary rebellion.[5] Gonzalo Escobar,
the movement's leader, had served for several years as the chief of military
operations in the Laguna region and maintained close ties there. When
news of the revolt reached Torreón, a group of *torreonenses* reportedly stole
342,680 pesos from the Banco de la Laguna and joined the Torreón garrison
in supporting the Escobarista assault on the northern cities of Monterrey
(Nuevo León) and Saltillo (Coahuila). Federal forces, meanwhile, received
considerable support from the Herbert Hoover administration, which supplied arms through the U.S. army, authorized private arms sales, and secured
Mexico's northern border against arms shipments to the Escobaristas.[6]
On May 18, federal troops entered Torreón, where Calles, then serving as
the minister of war, established his military command to prosecute the re-
mainder of its campaign from Torreón.[7]

In basing his military operations in Torreón, rather than the center of the rebellion itself, Calles likely hoped to fight two pacification campaigns at once, one against the Escobaristas and the other against the Comarca Lagunera's growing Communist presence. Those executed following the Escobarista rebellion included José Guadalupe Rodríguez, a Communist militant who had traveled to the Soviet Union to celebrate the Bolshevik Revolution's tenth anniversary and by 1929 served on the PCM's central committee.[8] The historian María Vargas-Lobsinger contends that of the many parties and organizations that sought to organize Lagunero workers and peasants during this period, the PCM had emerged as the most active and successful.[9] While the Escobarista revolt paled in comparison to the more popular and widespread Cristero rebellion (1926–29) of the center-west district, it nonetheless marked the Comarca Lagunera as a dangerous region requiring discipline and control.

If the Comarca Lagunera distinguished itself as a trouble spot for the consolidating postrevolutionary regime, the municipality of Matamoros set itself apart as a site of particularly intense Communist activity. The historian Barry Carr has identified what he dubs the "Matamoros connection" in the PCM's regional success. One informant dated the party's presence in the Comarca Lagunera to the 1922 founding of the Matamoros cell, which claimed fifty members by the mid-twenties.[10] In 1924, PCM members, including several involved in the 1930 demonstration, led three hundred peasants from Matamoros and Torreón municipalities in a land occupation, landing some of the participants in the Matamoros prison.[11] By the end of 1929, Matamoros's municipal president informed President Emilio Portes Gil that Communist groups had infiltrated the cotton plantations, and local *hacendados* (land barons) demanded "guarantees" from the federal government. Federal troops arrived to disarm Communists, and the ensuing conflict resulted in the death of one Communist and the arrest of thirty-five others. Foreshadowing the June 1930 encounter, in late November 1929 the Communists staged a protest that occupied the Plaza de Armas. In response to the municipal president's urgent pleas for support, Portes Gil's *secretario particular* sent word that "orders have already been sent to put an end to this abnormal situation."[12] Thus, by the time of the 1930 confrontation between Communists and municipal authorities, previous clashes had already established the Plaza de Armas as a physical battleground of resistance and counterinsurgency—a stage for the spectacle of violence and terror.

These political conflicts reflected structural economic factors that heightened local tensions. An arid region of about six thousand hectares (14,820 acres), the Comarca Lagunera straddles the border between the northern states of Coahuila and Durango and is crisscrossed by two major rivers, the Nazas and the Aguanaval. The rivers remained uncontrolled until the mid-nineteenth century, when two prominent local families (reputed descendants of a Spanish marquis) constructed a vast irrigation network to render their properties suitable for cotton and wheat production. The families subsequently sold parts of their estates to pay debts, and the Juárez government distributed other parcels to veterans for service during the French intervention, creating an array of sizeable plantations that required a large supply of low-paid laborers and concentrations of capital to create and maintain the irrigation system. During the course of the Porfiriato, the Comarca Lagunera flourished with rising demand for cotton, and the capital and labor requirements of cotton cultivation encouraged the reconcentration of property holdings and the development of plantation systems of production.[13]

Still, as Barry Carr has pointed out, resident peonage and agricultural wage labor coexisted in the region with a small but important tradition of peasant smallholdings that offered Laguna's rural proletariat the possibility of security.[14] In a region where not only agricultural employment but also industrial and manufacturing employment depended upon highly unpredictable cotton crops and markets, cultivable land offered access to a subsistence other than through the company-run stores making it a top priority for *laguneros* seeking both security and dignity. The PCM initially denounced early land-reform grants of private property, rather than collectivization, as bourgeois concessions. Nonetheless, Comarca Lagunera's hybridity of occupations and unusual constellation of alliances—including peasant smallholders, laborers who moved seasonally between agricultural and nonagricultural work, and wage laborers in manufacturing, mining, and railroad sectors—resulted in a collaboration between syndicalists emphasizing wages and labor conditions and peasant radicals (*agraristas*) seeking land reform. Political parties and organizations aiming to secure popular loyalties—not only Communists but also anarchists, socialists, and the more conservative League of Agrarian Communities—combined syndicalist and agrarista strategies.[15]

Tensions over land reform intensified with the onset of the Great Depression. In late May 1930, the National Agricultural Chamber of the Comarca

Lagunera, representing the hardliners among the region's major landowners, demanded that the federal government definitively settle the agrarian question and then recognize the region as an agroindustrial zone exempt from land reform measures.[16] Then, on June 23, less than a week before the march on the Plaza de Armas, the Mexico City newspaper *El Universal* published Calles's declaration that land reform had run its course. "Thus I aspire, with all the love of a Mexican and all the faith of a revolutionary," Calles explained, "that the agrarian problem has reached its end. Not because of a regression in principles but rather to consolidate, once and for all, our national economy upon which rests, say what you will, the future of our country."[17] In the Comarca Lagunera, the revolution's birthplace, this declaration constituted a betrayal that sparked widespread discontent, deepening the ideological polarization not only between peasants and landowners but also between peasants and resident peons, who remained excluded from land reform efforts. Calles's statement raised the stakes of the region's political struggle, equating support for the PNR with the surrender of revolutionary aspirations for widespread land reform.

Thus, by June 29, the day of the massacre, economic and political factors combusted to release the Matamoros furies. The Escobarista revolt fueled concerns in Mexico City about the federal government's control over the economically critical region. The PCM's growing presence in the region, and specifically in Matamoros, compounded official apprehension. Despite ongoing persecution and its small size, the party exercised political and ideological influence well beyond its card-carrying membership, making it one of the alternative revolutions or rebellions that the PCM must squelch in order to establish its primacy and legitimacy. Finally, the economic conditions by mid-1930—rising unemployment, falling cotton prices, and a declared end to agrarian reform—exacerbated anxieties among rural workers and belied the postrevolutionary regime's egalitarian rhetoric.

Amid this economic and political instability, observers recounted the events of June 29 as a parable, deploying narrative devices of emphasis and framing to convey the tragedy's lessons. As in any parable, the narrators reduced the story to heroes and villains—to us-versus-them—to more easily elevate their own actions and vilify their opponents. Thus, the story emerged as a battle between Communists and their opponents, a narrative structure intended to amplify Communist influence and justify anticommunist repression. The two sides disagreed, of course, about who wore the heroes' white hats and who wore the villains' black.

Terrorists and Revolutionaries: Narrations of June 29, 1930

Over the weeks and years following the confrontation, Communists and their opponents shaped its meaning through competing narratives with different time frames, characterizations of the principal actors, and descriptions of central events. These narrative choices refracted the historical circumstances of not only the event itself but also its retelling. The first accounts of the June 29 confrontation appeared in its immediate aftermath, offering a textbook case for Hannah Arendt's explanation of the instrumental nature of violence and the need to examine the "speech and articulation" that give it meaning.[18] Newspapers, as extensions of opposing ideological camps, played a critical role in reiterating and redefining the confrontation and paid considerable attention to several specific issues that defined the parameters of legitimate violence: who initiated the violence and controlled weapons, whether one camp or the other enjoyed popular support, and whether the victims constituted acceptable targets. Partisans of each side portrayed themselves as disciplined and controlled, using only necessary, defensive violence, while their monstrous, inhuman opponents resorted to barbarism and terror. Each side claimed peaceful intentions, indicating that their adversaries had shot first, necessitating defensive action. And Communists and their assailants both pointed to popular support as evidence of their legitimacy. Disagreements over these matters implied a larger question about who could claim to speak for the revolution and where the boundary lay demarcating those inside and outside of the revolution.

In the Matamoros case, local authorities and civic leaders demonstrated a self-consciousness about how outsiders, including not only federal authorities but also U.S. officials and local popular sectors, viewed their response to the June 29 demonstration, consistently justifying their actions as a legitimate use of force rather than counterrevolutionary terror. The noncommunist press, especially *Siglo de Torreón*—a liberal paper nominally invested in the rule of law, akin to the *New York Times* in the United States—drew exclusively on local authorities for their narratives, justifying the violence by emphasizing the order of events and antecedents that rationalized their unfolding.[19] Authorities appeared, on the one hand, intent on demonstrating that they had remained in control of the situation and, on the other, concerned about seeming overzealous in their crackdown.

The newspaper bolstered the authorities' efforts by reproducing and defining the confrontation and dehumanizing the Communists, deploying a tactic reminiscent of Foucault's biopolitical concept of state racism.[20] Describing the episode as evidence of Soviet destabilization efforts branching out (*ramificándose*) into the Comarca Lagunera, *Siglo de Torreón* gave voice to official justifications to purge Communists, eliminating internal enemies to protect the political and social order. The legitimacy the editors accorded official statements, alongside the skepticism applied to Communist testimony, gives credence to historian Achille Mbembe's observation that "sovereignty means the capacity to define who matters and who does not, who is *disposable* and who is not."[21] The newspaper echoed government efforts to brand entire groups—in this instance, Communists—as threats to postrevolutionary society and, in a quasi-biological fashion, as homogeneous and categorically beyond redemption. According to this assessment, no amount of education would transform Communists into loyal revolutionaries; instead, like a disease, communism required quarantine and eradication.

Communists, for their part, recognized the authorities' goal, explaining, "The massacre in Matamoros, like all acts of repression, has the objective of destroying revolutionary organizations, demoralizing the working and campesino class, and decapitating the revolutionary movement by destroying its vanguard: the Communist Party."[22] Such efforts, *El Machete* exhorted its readership, called for renewed resolve against the "capitalist regime" to demonstrate that the structural roots of communism would sustain its struggle even in the face of tyranny. As part of this struggle, the PCM used the June 29 incident as the foundation of a counternarrative, one that celebrated the confrontation as the founding blood of authentic, forward-looking revolution opposing the tyranny of oligarchic repression.

Reports concur that the Communists had requested a demonstration permit to demand wage increases and an eight-hour workday and to protest their comrades' imprisonment in Mexico City and the deportation of several workers from the U.S.-owned El Boleo mine to the Islas Marías penitentiary off the Baja California coast. The police chief denied the permit request three times, explaining that previous demonstrations had culminated in "grave insults being hurled at high functionaries," an act he deemed "subversive."[23] *El Machete* indicated in its first full report on the attack that "the bourgeois press prepared the terrain for the June 29 carnage," noting that the Matamoros correspondent for the PNR newspaper, *El Nacional*, had reported that the local authorities would not permit any more demonstrations by Communists, pledging "to use all necessary force to teach respect for Institutions [*sic*] and, above all, for the principle of authority."[24]

The Communists recognized that to let such a threat pass unchallenged would annihilate the party's credibility as an opposition movement claiming revolutionary legitimacy. Citing their constitutional right to free expression and peaceful demonstration, they resolved to test the authorities' convictions, indicating that they would demonstrate with or without a permit. Their first mistake, the Communists later lamented, had been to warn the authorities by requesting a permit, "giving the henchmen [*esbirros*] time to prepare themselves."[25] The Communists' petition provided information about their planned route and timing, giving local authorities ample opportunity to ready their forces.

Police Inspector Arturo de la Peña consulted the municipal president, Tomás Rodríguez de la Fuente, about the impending protest. Rodríguez de la Fuente, having gone to the nearby city of Torreón for the day, instructed him to "break it up one way or another, since they have been taking advantage with their demonstrations."[26] He pointed out that just the previous Cinco de Mayo, the Communists had sat down during the national anthem and put on their hats "to the great disgust of those attending the civic events." Soon after the SRI's first request, Inspector de la Peña had ordered the quartering of rural guards, police, and *defensas rurales* (rural militia), putting them at the ready to break up the demonstration.[27] One Communist recalled that on the morning of June 29, the guards began patrolling the town and disarmed everyone entering it.[28] Marking the Communists as inherently lawless, the Torreón newspaper pointed out that "all the Communists, or at least the organizers, were the same ones who had been imprisoned in Mexico City a while back and since then have carried out acts of open hostility against the Federal Government, the Executive of Coahuila, and the administrative authorities." The only way to deal with such elements, the municipal president declared, was to "repress with an iron fist."

Almost immediately after the massacre, however, both local authorities and the mainstream media hastened to justify this "iron fist" and distance local authorities from the appearance of senseless repression. *Siglo de Torreón*'s first account explained Rodríguez de la Fuente's pledge to use an "iron fist" by reminding its readers of Communist offenses. "The demonstrations have been occurring until yesterday," the daily reported, "when

Señor Rodríguez de la Fuente, annoyed with putting up with the irritations [*inconsecuencias*] of the reds, gave the orders to repress with an iron hand the excesses of those individuals who are always agitated by their now-deceased leaders."[29] By this original account, Communists appear more nuisance than threat—a pest in need of extermination.

Newspapers consistently reminded readers that the municipal president, Rodríguez de la Fuente, had been away from Matamoros on June 29, implying that such a disaster could only occur without the community *paterfamilias* to impose order and discipline on unruly rabble. Rodríguez de la Fuente, whom one Communist account described as a *latifundista* (plantation owner) controlling nineteen thousand hectares of "the Comarca Lagunera's best land," explained to the governor that "the Communist leaders who had been taken to Mexico City [i.e., previously arrested], staged a demonstration by force, attacking the gendarmerie, resulting in twenty-two deaths between the Communists and the police."[30] (This description obscures the fact that only Communists had died as a result of the struggle, and confusion remained about whether any of the guards died. *Siglo de Torreón* reported that the rural guard chief Aniceto Cifuentes died of "numerous contusions produced by rocks and sticks with which the Communists hit him after he had already fallen" but two days later reported that his health seemed to be improving.)[31]

According to Communist accounts, *compañeros* began to arrive from the surrounding countryside at around nine that morning.[32] After negotiations with local authorities failed, a reduced number of demonstrators set out from the SRI offices around four in the afternoon, just as the searing summer heat abated slightly. A Matamoros peasant, Felipe Zárate, led the marchers along Avenida Hidalgo and toward the Plaza de Armas, carrying banners and signs and growing in number as the protest proceeded unchecked. They stopped in front of the market to listen to Zárate describe the demonstration's objectives and denounce government repression. Standing before the crowd, Zárate spotted Cifuentes accompanied by twelve well-armed men. Along other streets, Zárate could see the "so-called *defensa ejidal* (agricultural collective defense), also armed and with plenty of ammunition" led by Inspector de la Peña.[33] Discerning the social composition of these defensas ejidales remains difficult, but they appeared to consist of smallholding peasants. Zárate reportedly reassured the demonstrators that "those mounted men with carbines in hand are not our enemies; they have been pushed by hunger to make themselves servants of social injustice and therefore will not fire upon their starving brothers." Zárate would, unfortunately, be proven wrong.

Cifuentes approached Zárate and "in an arrogant manner" demanded to see a demonstration permit. Zárate instead offered him the letter denying the permit, explaining, "The authorities do not grant permits to protest their own abuses and crimes." According to Communist accounts, Cifuentes threatened to arrest Zárate, provoking an outcry from the demonstrators that he would have to detain all of them or no one. Cifuentes then reportedly unsheathed his saber and attacked the crowd, slicing his blade right and left from atop his horse. The two Communist accounts diverge slightly at this point, but both insist that the Communists did not fire upon their assailants. "Just as this thug was brought down from his horse and disarmed to control his aggression," the original *El Machete* report explained, "police, rural guards, and 'defensa ejidal,' conveniently located to avoid injuring one another, opened fire on the demonstrators. Trapped in the middle of the street, completely unarmed, they defended themselves by throwing rocks from the street itself." An account published over a year later recalled that when Cifuentes drew his saber, the crowd pulled him from his horse and kicked and stoned him, leaving him on the ground. When Cifuentes's rural guards fired into the air, the Communist Anastacio Adame's cry of "¡Viva el Partido Comunista!" precipitated a "rain of bullets from the other side and of stones from ours." This telling transformed the encounter into an uneven battle of parties and ideas rather than a defensive effort to "control aggression."

By all tellings, a bloodbath ensued. A Mexico City daily reported that the shooting lasted for "several minutes."[34] "The carnage was implacable," according to *El Machete*. Describing "the executioner" de la Peña as "drunk on alcohol and blood," the Communist newspaper said that he personally delivered a coup de grace to each of the injured demonstrators and then led the hunt for those who had taken refuge in the market and surrounding streets. "You, who are you with?" he reportedly asked. "Are you one of ours or with those *hijos de la* . . . Communists?" When a person "valiantly responded, 'I am a Communist,'" de la Peña shot the offending demonstrator point-blank. Those who survived had either feigned death or taken refuge in shops or private homes where owners, "horrified by the massacre, opened their doors and granted asylum."

Although not on the scene, Rodríguez de la Fuente reported to the governor—and anticommunist newspapers relayed as fact—that the Communists had fired the first shots. Police Inspector de la Peña, meanwhile, asserted that the demonstrators had planned their route along streets containing ample rocks suitable for throwing and, put on the defensive, had fired the first shots at the rural guards.[35] De la Peña sped to the cantina, where five Communists fought with him, resulting in the death of the Communist Gregorio de León and serious injury to de la Peña. "When the shooting became widespread and the police were reinforced with *vecinos* [residents] and agraristas," *Siglo de Torreón* reported, as if to trump Communist claims of taking refuge in neighboring homes, "the Communists retreated, including roughly 60 demonstrators," leaving behind the bodies of the dead.

The paper's later reports placed the blame even more squarely on the protestors, albeit eliding the question of who fired the first shots. "When the rurales arrived to break up the demonstration," the paper recounted two days after the incident,

> the reds resisted with stones, forcing the rurales to retreat a block. Everything was at the point of remaining in this state when somebody fired at the chief of the rurales [Cifuentes], bringing him down and setting off widespread shooting by the demonstrators at the rurales. At the same time a group of about thirty reds charged Señor Cifuentes with sticks, knives, and stones, and tried to finish him off. At this point, the rurales and the police arrived to shoot at the group that was on the verge of lynching Cifuentes.

As if in response to the obvious question of why only demonstrators had died if they had initiated the shooting, the paper explained that the rural guards and the police had superior aim, handling their weapons more ably than their barbaric, unmanly foes. Imbuing the Communists with spectral qualities, the paper described one Communist pursuing a policeman with a dagger. The "municipal employee" pulled out his .45-caliber pistol and fired seven shots at the demonstrator, "hitting his target every time," but his assailant persisted. Only when the police shot "at point-blank range in the head did the Communist tumble to the ground."[36]

The first substantive reports in Mexico City dailies appeared on July 1, 1930, and reiterated *Siglo de Torreón*'s language of Communist culpability. The *Excélsior* article began, "The only ones responsible for the tragic *zafarrancho* that occurred Sunday afternoon in Matamoros, Coahuila, were the region's Communist elements, who first staged a public demonstration without a permit and then attacked the rural police." *El Universal* headline blared, "Zafarrancho between Gendarmes and Offenders. Communists First to Fire." Both articles attributed this information to reports from the municipal president, Rodríguez, via the governor's office. In a front-page story about the incident, the *New York Times* repeated these accusations, attributing the information to cables received in Mexico City from Torreón.[37] By these accounts, Cifuentes and de la Peña, far from committing the monstrosities that appeared in *El Machete*, had done only what the maintenance of order required of them.

The Torreón correspondent from *El Universal* rendered the bodies of slain Communists as part of the spectacle, reporting the day after the confrontation that "in the streets of Matamoros there are dead and wounded that still have not been picked up."[38] The cadavers, *Siglo de Torreón* recounted, were carted off to the police headquarters and then "buried in a mass grave without sending them to family members."[39] The officials' decision to leave the bodies in the streets, literally occupying what Giorgio Agamben dubs the "no-man's-land between the home and the city," and then haul them off in an open, two-wheeled cart to bury them in an unmarked mass grave offered unmistakable warnings to those who would challenge their authority in the future.[40] The newspapers' emphasis on this display of bodies strewn in the Plaza de Armas—as bait to lure comrades and families to retrieve them and as threat against would-be demonstrators—extended its impact beyond Matamoros and beyond its specific moment in time. The unceremonious removal and burial of the Communists' bodies—dumped in a mass grave without informing their families—further branded them as "disposable" beings. *Siglo de Torreón* reinforced this impression by simply listing the names of fallen Communists (and often misidentifying them, since they listed among the dead Zárate, Negrete, and several men who later testified or were imprisoned), while it included the wounded guards' titles and precise descriptions of their injuries.

Racializing the Communists, marking them as biologically and essentially dangerous, also allowed officials to depict the conflict as cultural and personalist rather than structural. Authorities repeatedly indicated that the elimination of a few key Communist leaders would eradicate the plague of communism. *Siglo de Torreón* allowed that communism had "deep roots among the campesinos of the Matamoros region" but reassured readers that the "principal leaders under the red flag had fallen on the corner of Matamoros and Cuauhtémoc when they refused to obey the orders given by the chief of police."[41] For this newspaper, the story receded into the background once the remaining Communist leadership had been imprisoned.

War Is Peace: Bureaucratic and Judicial Reponses

In the aftermath of the slaughter, authorities from the local to the federal levels began a series of inquiries into the incident to restore the rule of law and enact a rational, bureaucratic response. The investigators appeared unconcerned with assigning culpability for the deaths and instead concentrated on arresting Communists. The chief of regional military operations, Jesús García Gutiérrez, dispatched one hundred infantry and cavalry to Matamoros to impose order. *Siglo de Torreón* speculated that many more injured had fled Matamoros to hide in the surrounding ranchos and that "many people had flowed out of Matamoros on burros and horses, presumably Communists who plan to continue taking up arms against the municipal authorities."[42] The authorities raided the SRI offices, collecting documents that they claimed proved the Matamoros Communists had acted on orders from Mexico City to bring down the federal government. Local authorities detained Communists in Matamoros as well as in the nearby cities of Torreón and Gómez Palacio, including José Refugio Aguilar, suspected of having fired on Cifuentes, the head of the rural guard. Aguilar later testified that he had come to Matamoros to sell sweets and had gone with friends to the SRI offices. When he realized that they planned to participate in an unauthorized demonstration, he went home. According to *Siglo de Torreón*, he explained to his interrogators that he was "respectful of the government and understood that what his compañeros were doing was improper."[43]

Despite claiming popular support for their efforts, the investigators apparently did not enjoy the townspeople's full cooperation. According to Colonel Domingo Cuevas, who led the military personnel in Matamoros, witnesses refused to offer evidence "for fear of Communist reprisals." Only after interrogating witnesses did Cuevas send personnel to "all the appropriate places" and authorize the municipal authorities to collect the bodies from the site of the massacre. In an effort to round up suspected Communists, the municipal president, Rodríguez de la Fuente, sent a circular to all local communities demanding that within ten hours they release the names of any injured men, all of whom should be detained and delivered to Matamoros authorities.[44] Municipal authorities in nearby Viesca turned over one wounded Communist and four other *ex-manifestantes*, and the Matamoros authorities reported finding a group of fifteen individuals in the Sierra de Hornos who displayed "a hostile attitude."[45]

The federal government declined to intervene directly, insisting that the incident did not result from a "political conflict," and Rodríguez de la Fuente placed authority for judicial proceedings in the hands of a local judge.[46] The case would focus on Zárate, a known Communist leader, who, according to *Siglo de Torreón*, "confessed to shouting *mueras* against the government, discrediting the current regime as reactionary and an enemy of the workers, forcing the inopportune response from the police."[47] Eight detained Communists attested that Zárate and Gregorio de León (among the first to die) had led the demonstration. Authorities planned to charge Zárate with obstructing investigations. The inquiry spread, however, to include Communists in Mexico City. Federal agents kept watch on five "known foreigners" to determine if they had "agitated the Mexican Communists"—a provocation that would justify their immediate deportation.[48] Concerned about a Communist response to this crackdown, authorities expressly prohibited any further demonstrations by "red" factions against the deportation of workers to Islas Marías or the events in Matamoros or "any disorderly act that attacks the established institutions."[49] Despite government proscriptions, demonstrators rallied in Guadalajara and Mexico City, encountering the threatened police repression.[50]

The case against the Communists apparently hit a snag when municipal authorities reported that the documents that military authorities had taken from the SRI office—documents that purportedly offered definitive proof of sedition—had gone missing. Undeterred by the loss of evidence, the municipality proceeded with its case against Zárate and another Communist, Manuel Negrete, asking that they be sent to Islas Marías. Police raided SRI offices in Mexico City and in towns surrounding Matamoros, allegedly finding more seditious materials. "Foreign elements mixed up in these activities," *Siglo de Torreón* reported, "have been detained and will be expelled from our country."[51] On November 2, federal authorities transported the Communists Dionisio Encina, Guadalupe Saucedo, Federico Reyes, and Aureliano Andrade to Mexico City, where they remained in prison for nearly three months.[52]

The PCM pointed to the official investigation as evidence of the hypocrisy and irrationality of the regime's rule of law. The party aggressively publicized the violence and persecution as a continuation of the revolutionary struggle and its demonstrated capacity to withstand official repression had become a centerpiece of its legitimating strategy. So, whereas officials at all levels cast the Communists as a menace to the revolutionary government, Communists sought—through repeated and often graphic descriptions of political violence against them—to depict the PCM as the revolution itself. By airing these atrocities, Communists hoped to make terror the foundation of solidarity rather than isolation, transforming a repressive spectacle into a prosthetic one to bind the party's wounds.[53] The Matamoros conflict and its aftermath, however, offered only a glimpse of both the persecution and mobilization still to come.

El Machete reported that imprisoned protestors endured beatings and torture but emphasized that Communists had faced these assaults with bravery and discipline.[54] Military police in Torreón detained four Communists, including Federico Reyes, a member of the Communist Youth, whose "fingernails were twisted until they drew blood, and, since they could not extract a single word from our *compañero*, they beat his face until it was disfigured, bringing only the same result."[55] Inspector de la Peña reportedly arrested SRI leader Narciso Reyes and "strung him up and beat him, leaving him for dead."[56] Felipe Zárate, having been released by November, allegedly became the target of police assassination attempts; other Communist leaders received death threats. The four Communists imprisoned in Mexico City remained incommunicado, raising speculation that they had been "disappeared" or executed.[57]

"A Trail of Blood and Dignity": Memorializing the Matanza

The PCM's memorialization of June 29 appropriated this spectacle of repression and persecution as part of Communist lore, rendering it a piece of the "usable past."[58] Judging by levels of PCM activity, it appears these efforts succeeded. The Comarca Lagunera—and Matamoros in particular—continued through the thirties as a hotbed of PCM militancy and labor unrest. Six months after the massacre, the PCM leader, Alejandro Adame, won the election for municipal president of Matamoros.[59] Several Communists arrested and tortured in the confrontation's aftermath went on to become prominent leaders during the successful PCM-orchestrated 1936 general strike, which resulted in a dramatic restructuring of power and resources. Dionisio Encina, a member of the Communist Youth arrested in the anticommunist sweeps that followed June 29, led the strike and later became the PCM's secretary general (1940–60).[60] Estación El Coyote, the site of some of the most aggressive anticommunist crackdowns in the Matamoros municipality, fostered not only Communist labor mobilizations but also some of the region's most organized and enduring women's activism.

Much like de la Peña, with his interrogation—"Are you one of ours or with those *hijos de la* . . . Communists?"—the PCM described their own boundary of revolutionary legitimacy by locating people on one side or the other of the confrontation. Pedro V. Rodríguez Triana, who stood in 1929 as the presidential candidate of the PCM-affiliated Bloque Obrero y Campesino, by the summer of 1930 had disavowed the Communist Party. *Siglo de Torreón* reported that rumors had circulated that he had planned a simultaneous protest on the Durango side of the Comarca Lagunera but "appropriately declared that he would not lead a rebel movement."[61] Describing Rodríguez Triana as "the cowardly general who betrayed the Bloque Obrero y Campesino when the repression intensified in the country," the PCM linked him with the massacre itself, indicating that in his "fascistic" plan to organize agrarian leagues he associated with one of the rural guards who had participated in the June 29 confrontation.[62] As the party planned memorial events to mark the massacre's first anniversary, it listed Rodríguez Triana alongside the *rurales* chief Cifuentes, Police Inspector de la Peña, the municipal president Rodríguez de la Fuente, and Governor Nazario Ortiz Garza, describing Rodríguez Triana as "complicit" in the massacre itself.[63] Within two years, Rodríguez Triana had gone from being the PCM's presidential candidate to finding himself listed among the party's most reviled enemies.[64]

If memorializing the massacre offered a means to define the party's boundaries (and therefore the authentic revolution), it also provided supporters a means to express their solidarity. *El Machete* repeatedly appealed for financial support for survivors and for the victims' families. An October issue described Felipe Zárate as being in very poor health, having lost an eye during the struggle; he risked blindness without proper treatment.[65] Zárate would die of heart failure less than two years later at the age of thirty-five. His obituary in *El Machete* described him as "literally exhausted by his hard life as an agrarista warrior [*guerrillero*]" and "a representative of that abnegated phalanx of laborers [*peones*] who, looking firmly into the future, have known to find the revolutionary path of our embattled and persecuted party."[66]

Just as the Matamoros authorities had deployed gender tropes of manly paternalism to situate their response as a legitimate use of force, the PCM used a different set to undermine these claims to legitimacy. Portraying themselves as disciplined and progressive, Communists depicted the authorities as inhabiting a barbaric, uncontrolled masculinity exemplified by Cifuentes unsheathing his saber and slicing it through the crowd.[67] The warrior Zárate, who struggled until his heart gave out, could hardly have offered a more striking contrast with the "cowardly" Rodríguez Triana, who turned coat under pressure.

It would oversimplify matters, however, to argue that the Communist memory of the 1930 massacre venerated a manly militant over an emasculated traitor. Those killed during the June 29 conflict included a woman named Martina Deras, an activist who had organized a PCM-linked women's league in Matamoros.[68] In the incident's immediate aftermath, her presence among the victims had attracted only passing notice. *El Machete* noted that she was pregnant and left behind six orphaned children.[69] *Siglo de Torreón* mentioned her among the dead but originally misspelled her name and identified her as "a woman who found herself among the demonstrators," implying she had accidentally ended up caught in the melee.[70] The paper only mentioned her again (although this time not by name) to indicate that hers was among the bodies taken to the police headquarters and then discarded in the mass grave.[71] At the time of the massacre, however, neither the PCM nor the anticommunist press made any further mention of her.

When an account appeared in *El Machete* in September 1931, it offered a few more details about Deras's death. "The executioner [Arturo de la] Peña came pistol in hand toward a group of six dying compañeros . . . [and] registered the bodies of the dead and wounded," the author recalled. "That was when he killed the compañera Martina Vera [*sic*], who was holding Macario Núñez (badly wounded). Then, Andrés Núñez, also wounded, tried to get up and scold Peña for his conduct, and the latter shot his gun and left him dead."[72] This narrative gave Deras, shot in cold blood while holding her dying compañero, a more central role in the events. The unsigned article cataloguing de la Peña's atrocities offers little sense of the perspective from which the seemingly omniscient author witnessed the events, but it transformed Deras into a heroic figure. The following month, a PCM flyer signed by the newly established PCM women's department exhorted readers,

We [*nosotras*] must be alert. We should learn from the experience of workers and peasants who, in 20 years of struggle, have received only promises from the Government. When they understood the deception and demanded improvement, the most ferocious repression was unchained upon them, as happened in Matamoros, Coahuila, in July 1929 [*sic*], in which 20 compañeros were assassinated when they staged a demonstration, among them a good and valiant compañera who was not even respected for being pregnant.[73]

Through the 1930s, as radical women's organizing exploded in the Laguna amid widespread PCM organizing in the region, a half-dozen women's leagues took Deras's name as a tribute.[74] A 1940 newsletter "March 8: Organizing Newsletter," published by the Confederation of Comarca Lagunera Women's Leagues and named after the Communist holiday International Workingwomen's Day, carried a story about the "martyrdom" of Martina Deras, incorrectly asserting that she had been killed during a May Day demonstration. The article mentioned that she had organized the Sindicato Femenil "Josefa Ortiz de Domínguez" (named after a heroine of the independence movement) but lauded her as a domestic woman (*mujer de hogar*) and the wife of an *ejidatario* (agricultural collective member).[75] By 1957, the June 29 massacre had become closely identified with Deras's death. An unsigned internal history of the PCM's historic role in the Comarca Lagunera described the repression by the rural guards and explained, "These police were the ones who massacred the demonstrators in an event organized by campesinos in Matamoros, Coahuila, on June 29, 1930, in which 21 compañeros died, among whom Martina Deras was prominent."[76] In a 1992 history of the region since the colonial era, Martina Deras was the only woman mentioned.[77]

The elevation of Deras as the figure most closely associated with June 29—rather than, for example, Felipe Zárate, who might have seemed a more obvious choice, or Gregorio de León, the first Communist killed during the massacre—seems curious and calls for a reconsideration of the motives and circumstances of remembering the incident.[78] Or, as Judith Butler would have us ask, why was the legacy of June 29 inscribed upon the body of the one woman killed on the scene?[79] At first gloss, the changing depictions of Martina Deras and her role in the Matamoros confrontation seem to reflect shifting gender ideologies underpinning women's organizing and Communist mobilizations more generally. In 1930, when the PCM celebrated the overall-clad workingwoman and studiously avoided depictions of the self-sacrificing mother (*madre abnegada*) that dominated mainstream press and popular culture, Martina Deras merited only passing mention among a list of victims.[80] In late 1931, as the PCM began to turn its attention toward the task of recruiting women members, she gained greater prominence in the narrative but as a victim who had not committed even the minor offenses of throwing stones or shouting *mueras* against the government and *vivas* for the Communist Party. The visual image conjured up by *El Machete*'s narrative portrayed the heartless killing of a grieving, pregnant woman cradling the dying body of the father of her children. The 1940 depiction of Deras as a mujer de hogar mirrors a turn within radical women's organizing toward more maternalist strategies that linked women's rights to their roles as mothers and caretakers; the apron had replaced the overalls as the icon of Communist womanhood. By 1992, Deras stood in for all women activists, obscuring the widespread, diverse popular women's organizing that occurred after her death.

However, elevating the martyred Deras also indicated the PCM's occlusion of its former defiance, depicting itself instead as a catalyst of the social peace that characterized Mexico's post–Second World War "miracle." The 1957 narrative linked regional development to the 1936 general strike and used the June 29 incident to contrast Communist solidarity with authorities' repression. The account exhorted party members to "remember the methods of terror applied by landowners and the government during the period leading up to the [strike], including jailings, firings, assassinations of many campesino militants. Confronting this, the agricultural laborers responded with a vigorous demonstration of unity." This strategy, the report continued, united a diverse array of workers under the leadership of a committee representing different federations but "remaining under the control of the party." This committee "put into practice the most varied forms of revolutionary struggle, principally the mobilization of masses, creating a situation that obliged the Federal Government to intervene [and implement land reform]."[81] The combat that played such a prominent, often romanticized role in the Communist self-representations of the 1930s had given way to an emphasis on healing the community through solidarity and mass organizing.

As indicated by the episode's continued memorialization, June 29 served as a cornerstone of the PCM's regional identity, the founding violence that legitimated its revolutionary credentials. The regional Communist narrative draws a direct line from the June 29 massacre to the 1936 general strike and its culmination in massive agrarian reform. "The agrarista struggles left us a trail of blood and dignity," one *matamorense* later recalled.

> The campesinos of our municipality are persecuted, some of them murdered, harassed for participating in political groups, like that famous Socorro Rojo Internacional, affiliated with the Partido Comunista Mexicano, when they circulated the newspaper *El Machete*. A high price was paid by a demonstration of campesinos riddled with bullets in the streets of Matamoros on June 29, 1930. But these agrarista struggles bore fruit because that seed took root among the groups that conspired against the latifundio. . . . In all the agrarian struggles of the lagunera region, matamorenses are always present.[82]

Thus, the PCM's role in mobilizing and unifying the movement gave the party legitimacy in the region for decades to come. In many ways, the dramatic events of the early 1930s indicated the long-delayed arrival of the Mexican Revolution in the Comarca Lagunera, the birthplace of the revolutionary Francisco Madero and the incubator of Villismo. Following the 1936 land collectivization, Communists sought to reclaim and redefine the June 29 spectacle. It became emblematic of the ways that Communist defiance and revolutionary commitment reshaped the postrevolutionary regime from the Maximato to the Popular Front. Over the decades following the incident, the party mythologized it, transforming it, as Antonio Gramsci observed among European Communist parties, into a "concrete fantasy which acts on a dispersed and shattered people to arouse and organize its collective will."[83]

As the PCM continued its struggle for political legitimacy during the dark decades of the cold war, it redeployed the spectacle of the June 29 massacre, transforming it from founding violence into a healing—and overtly gendered—prosthetic that would rebind the "dispersed and shattered" party to reclaim a role in national politics.

Notes

1. *Siglo de Torreón*, June 30, 1930, 1. The story of what *Siglo de Torreón* dubbed the *zafarrancho* dominated the paper's headlines for the five days following the incident.

2. Arno J. Mayer, *The Furies: Violence and Terror in the French and Russian Revolutions* (Princeton: Princeton University Press, 2000), 71.

3. For comparison among different interpretations of revolutionary violence, see Hannah Arendt, *On Revolution* (New York: Penguin Books, 1963). Drawing on Arendt, the historian Arno Mayer distinguishes among force, violence, and terror in revolutionary contexts. Force, an agent of order enjoying the legitimacy of state sanction, stands apart from (and seemingly above) the chaotic, unruly violence of the masses. Terror appears as the "excessive excesses" combining the intentional and disciplinary characteristics of force with the barbaric and arbitrary nature of violence. Mayer, *The Furies*, 93.

4. Mayer, *The Furies*, 30.

5. Lorenzo Mayer, "El primer tramo del camino," in *Historia General de México*, vol. 2, 3rd ed. (Mexico City: El Colegio de México, 1981), 1194.

6. *New York Times*, March 6, 1929, 1.

7. María Vargas-Lobsinger, *La Comarca Lagunera: de la revolución a la expropriación de las haciendas, 1910–1940* (Mexico City: Universidad Nacional Autónoma de México; Instituto Nacional de Estudios Históricos de la Revolución Mexicana, 1999), 121–22.

8. Vargas-Lobsinger, *La Comarca Lagunera*, 122; Barry Carr, *Marxism and Communism in Twentieth-Century Mexico* (Lincoln: University of Nebraska Press, 1992), 353–54, n. 35.

9. Vargas-Lobsinger, *La Comarca Lagunera*, 122–23.

10. Carr, *Marxism and Communism*, 91.

11. Barry Carr, "The Mexican Communist Party and Agrarian Mobilization in the Laguna, 1920–1940: A Worker-Peasant Alliance?," *Hispanic American Historical Review* 67, no. 3 (1987): 385.

12. Vargas-Lobsinger, *La Comarca Lagunera*, 123.

13. For regional history, see Pablo C. Moreno, *Torreón: biografía de la más joven de las ciudades mexicanas* (Saltillo: Talleres Gráficas "Coahuila," 1951); Jorge Tamayo, *Transformación de la Comarca Lagunera, sus perspectivas y problemas* (Mexico City: Academia Nacional de Ciencias "Antonio Alzate," 1941); as well as the novel by Elvira de la Mora, *Tierra de hombres (Comarca Lagunera)* (Mexico City: Información Aduanero de México).

14. Carr, *Marxism and Communism in Twentieth-Century Mexico*, 83–84.

15. For biographical information on *sindicalista-agrarista* collaboration and individual militants moving between industrial and agricultural labor, see Carr, "The Mexican Communist Party and Agrarian Mobilization in the Laguna."

16. Vargas-Lobsinger, *La Comarca Lagunera*, 125–26. Lourdes Romero Navarrete, "Conflicto y negociación por el agua del Nazas, 1888–1936: del dominio público a la propiedad nacional," *Región y Sociedad* 18, no. 36 (2006): 168.

17. *El Universal*, June 23, 1930, 1.

18. Arendt, *On Revolution*, 19.

19. By early 1930, *Siglo de Torreón's* ideological orientation had attracted enough attention that even the averred anticommunist Adalberto Terrones Benítez, the governor of the neighboring state of Durango, wrote a "confidential" note to the Yucatecan governor Bartolomé García Correa calling for limits to freedom of the press to prevent such "reactionary newspapers" from "undermining the revolution" (Archivo General del Estado de Yucatán, February 18, 1930, Fondo Poder Ejécutivo, Sección Gobernación, caja 897).

20. This concept is most recently and fully elaborated in English in Michel Foucault, *Society Must Be Defended: Lectures at the Collège de France, 1975–76*, 1st ed., ed. and trans. David Macey (New York: Picador, 2003).

21. Achille Mbembe, "Necropolitics," *Public Culture* 15, no. 1 (2003): 27.

22. *El Machete*, July 1930, 1.

23. *El Universal* (Mexico City), July 1, 1930, sec. 2, 1; *Excélsior* (Mexico City), July 1, 1930, sec. 2, 1.

24. *El Machete*, July 1930, 1.

25. Ibid.

26. Ibid.

27. *Siglo de Torreón*, June 30, 1930, 1.

28. *El Machete*, September 10, 1931, 2.

29. *Siglo de Torreón*, June 30, 1930, 1.

30. *El Machete*, September 10, 1931, 2; *Siglo de Torreón*, June 30, 1930, 1.

31. *Siglo de Torreón*, June 30, and July 2, 1930, both p. 1.

32. This narrative comes from *El Machete*, July 1930, 1; and September 10, 1931, 2.

33. *El Machete* consistently questioned the authenticity of this group, referring to it as the "so-called defensas ejidales" or putting *defensas ejidales* in quotation marks. The Comarca Lagunera, like other regions of Mexico, had a history of government-sponsored mobilizations of popular antirevolutionary forces in the *defensas sociales* that fought against the revolutionary Villistas. See Friedrich Katz, *The Life and Times of Pancho Villa* (Stanford: Stanford University Press, 1998), 643–49.

34. *Excélsior* (Mexico City), July 1, 1930, sec. 2, 1.

35. *Siglo de Torreón*, July 2, 1930, 1.

36. *Siglo de Torreón*, July 1, 1930, 1.

37. *El Universal*, July 1, 1930, 1; *Excélsior*, July 1, 1930, sec. 2, 1; *New York Times*, June 30, 1930, 1.

38. *El Universal*, June 30, 1930, 1.

39. *Siglo de Torreón*, July 1, 1930, 1.

40. Giorgio Agamben, *Homo Sacer: Sovereign Power and Bare Life* (Stanford: Stanford University Press, 1998), 90.

41. *Siglo de Torreón*, July 1, 1930, 1.

42. *Siglo de Torreón*, June 30, 1930, 1.

43. *Siglo de Torreón*, July 3, 1930, 1.

44. *Siglo de Torreón*, July 2, 1930, 1.

45. *Siglo de Torreón*, July 3, 1930, 1.

46. *El Universal*, July 1, 1930, sec. 2, 1.

47. *Siglo de Torreón*, July 2, 1930, 1.

48. Article 33 of Mexico's 1917 constitution granted the Federal Executive the power to expel immediately and without legal recourse any foreigner whose presence he deems "inappropriate."

49. *Siglo de Torreón*, July 2, 1930, 1.

50. *El Machete*, July 1930, 1.

51. *El Machete*, September 10, 1930, 2; *Siglo de Torreón* July 4, 1930, 1.

52. *El Machete*, December 1930, 1; February 15, 1931, 4; Carr, *Marxism and Communism*, 354, n. 39.

53. On the use of spectacle as prosthetic, see Diane M. Nelson, *A Finger in the Wound: Body Politics in Quincentennial Guatemala* (Berkeley: University of California Press, 1999); Diana Taylor, *Disappearing Acts: Spectacles of Gender and Nationalism in Argentina's "Dirty War"* (Durham: Duke University Press, 1997).

54. *El Machete*, August 1930, 3.

55. *El Machete*, November 1930, 1.

56. Ibid.

57. *El Machete*, December 1930, 1. Although it would not be until the cold war when "disappear" would be used as a transitive verb to refer to the practice of state- or paramilitary-kidnapping, the headline of this 1930 report is "Desaparecidos o Asesinados?"

58. Originally coined by Van Wyck Brooks ("On Creating a Usable Past," *The Dial* 64 [April 11, 1918]: 337–41), the notion of a "usable past" gained credence among scholars of national liberation, most notably Frantz Fanon. Fanon's essay "Concerning Violence" argues for the necessity of violence within anticolonial resistance. In "On National Culture," he explicates the role of intellectuals in excavating the historical roots of this violence. "As for we who have decided to break the back of colonialism, our historic mission is to sanction all revolts, all desperate actions, all those

abortive attempts drowned in rivers of blood." Both essays are in *The Wretched of the Earth* (New York: Grove Press, 1963); quotation on 207.

59. *El Machete*, December 20, 1930, 3.

60. On the 1936 general strike, see Carr, "The Mexican Communist Party and Agrarian Mobilization in the Laguna," 392–404; Jocelyn Olcott, "'Worthy Wives and Mothers: State-Sponsored Women's Organizing in Postrevolutionary Mexico," *Journal of Women's History* 13, no. 4 (2002); Vargas-Lobsinger, *La Comarca Lagunera*.

61. *Siglo de Torreón*, July 2, 1930, 1.

62. *El Machete*, March 15, 1931, 3.

63. *El Machete*, May 30, 1931, 1.

64. For more on this conflict, see Roberto Martínez García, *La visión agrarista del general Pedro V. Rodríguez Triana* (Torreón, Coahuila: Editorial del Norte de México, 1997), 68–72. During the Popular Front, and following the massive general strike and land reform in the region, the PCM would make its peace with Rodríguez Triana, who became governor of Coahuila in 1937.

65. *El Machete*, October 1930, 3; see also July 1930, 1; August 1930, 1; September 1930, 1.

66. *El Machete*, September 29, 1932, 1.

67. On barbaric versus civilized (and civilizing) masculinity, see Ana María Alonso, *Thread of Blood: Colonialism, Revolution, and Gender on Mexico's Northern Frontier*, 1st ed. (Tucson: University of Arizona Press, 1995); R. W. Connell, *Masculinities* (Berkeley: University of California Press, 1995).

68. For a brief mention of Deras's activities prior to the massacre, see Alfonso Porfirio Hernández, *¿La explotación colectiva en la Comarca Lagunera es un fracaso?* (Mexico: B. Costa-Amic Editores, 1975), 72–76. It is difficult to know, however, to what extent this depiction reflects the elevation of Deras's stature subsequent to the 1930 massacre.

69. *El Machete*, July 1930, 1.

70. *Siglo de Torreón*, June 30, 1930, 1.

71. *Siglo de Torreón*, July 1, 1930, 1.

72. *El Machete*, September 10, 1931, 2.

73. "¡A las Obreras, Campesinas y Mujeres Indígenas en General!" Departamento Femenil del Partido Comunista, October 1, 1931, Rodolfo Echeverría Martínez Collection, box 16, folder 7, Hoover Institution Archives, Stanford University. On establishment of the PCM's Departamento Femenil, see *El Machete*, April 15, 1931, 5.

74. Archivo General de la Nación (AGN), Ramo Presidentes (RP), Fondo Lázaro Cárdenas del Río (LCR), exps. 542.1/59, 544/1, 606.3/20, 604.11/171; AGN, RP, Fondo Manuel Avila Camacho, exp. 404.1/984; AGN, Dirección General del Gobierno,

2.331.8(3), vol. 18-A, exp. 31; and Instituto Estatal de Documentación de Coahuila, 1936, caja 3.1.1.8, leg. 25, exp. 2-205.

75. "8 de Marzo: órgano de orientación," AGN, RP, LCR, exp. 437.1/641.

76. "Informe ante la Conferencia Nacional Campesina que se celebrará en la Ciudad de Torreón," May 1, 1957, Mexican Communist Party Collection, Rare Books and Manuscripts Library, Columbia University.

77. Jesús G. Sotomayor Garza, *Anales laguneros* (Torreón: Editorial del Norte Mexicano, 1992).

78. The memorialization of Martina Deras offers a parallel writ small of the phenomenon that Lyman Johnson has examined of popular cults commemorating patriotic figures in Latin America, likening them to martyred Catholic saints. Lyman Johnson, ed., *Body Politics: Death, Dismemberment, and Memory in Latin America* (Albuquerque: University of New Mexico, 2004).

79. Judith Butler, *Bodies That Matter: On the Discursive Limits of "Sex"* (New York: Routledge, 1993).

80. On the PCM's changing stance toward gender and women's organizing, see Jocelyn Olcott, *Revolutionary Women in Postrevolutionary Mexico* (Durham: Duke University Press, 2005).

81. "Informe ante la Conferencia," n.p.

82. Matías Rodríguez Chihuahua, "Matamoros: sudor y sangre," *El Puente: Revista de historia y cultura de La Laguna* 1, no. 6 (1991): 31.

83. Antonio Gramsci, Quintin Hoare, and Geoffrey Nowell-Smith, *Selections from the Prison Notebooks of Antonio Gramsci*, 1st ed. (New York: International Publishers, 1972), 126.

On the Road to "El Porvenir"

Revolutionary and Counterrevolutionary Violence in El Salvador and Nicaragua

JEFFREY L. GOULD

> *Viene la cívica hermano*
> *Con rifles y tartamudas*
> *Vienen los guardias de kaki*
> *Y los soldados azules*
> *Y te buscan campesino*
> *Quieren beberse tu sangre*
> *Y la sangre de tus hijos*
> *Viniendo, vienen, viniendo*
> *Tremenda racha de muerte*
> *El primer soviet de américa*
> *Lo hicieron mierda a balazos*
>
> —PEDRO GEOFFROY RIVAS, "Romance de Enero," 1935

The massacre of ten thousand people, mostly indigenous peasants, in El Salvador in January 1932, was one of the most violent episodes in modern Latin American history. In his introduction to this volume, Greg Grandin, following Arno Mayer, outlines a dynamic of revolutionary and counterrevolutionary violence that aids our understanding of the Salvadoran insurrection and repression that followed. The three coordinates of that dynamic—polarization, contingency, and passion—are all present in the unfolding of events during that fateful January. The process started with state repression against the leftist-controlled labor movement, which directly conditioned intensified forms of militancy. This combination of repression and militancy was the polarizing dynamic that created a critical moment in early January. It was, very clearly, also a moment of "open contingency," not guided by an ideological template. The leadership of the Salvadoran Communist Party (PCS) decided to take "a leap" into the unknown—despite an overwhelming military disadvantage, they launched an insurrection, on the assumption that the alternative was to allow for the slaughter of their leadership and rank and file. This moment of contingency was confronted passionately by both sides. Passion—emotions of loyalty and vengeance—prompted the PCS decision, even if it was anchored in a Marxist-Leninist ideological field. The military easily crushed the insurrection, and then *terratenientes* (landlords) and local politicians aligned with a newly installed military junta intent on establishing authority in the country and legitimacy internationally: together they unleashed the terror of counterrevolution. As in the PCS insurrection, counterrevolutionary moves were also guided by passion. The intensity of the fear provoked by the insurgents' armed occupations provoked a massive, irrational, and lethal response on the part of the military and its civilian allies.

Polarization, contingency, and passion thus played critical roles in January 1932. Also important, in both the insurrection and the repression, were political and ideological factors, as all actors had relatively clear understandings of the goals for which they fought. Ideology—that is, the political calculus of the revolutionaries—restrained "red" violence, just as ideology impelled the violence and coercion of the other side. This essay examines, through an interrogation of the role that symbolic and real coercion played in the insurrection of January 1932, and how survivors inscribed this violence and coercion in their memories. There is a deeply asymmetrical relation between the degree of revolutionary violence or coercion and its weight in collective memory. Indeed, the relatively low level of violence in the insurrection is remarkable, in that insurgents probably killed no more than twenty civilians (some armed) despite controlling a half a dozen towns and villages for over twenty-four hours. The military regime, however, was able to turn the traumatic impact of the repression, combined with the exertion of insurgent authority—including, for example, an order to wear red badges—against, and lump the blame for the indiscriminate killing on, the "Communists."

Following this analysis of the Salvadoran insurrection and its aftermath, I explore a similar relationship between the role of violence and coercion in the Sandinista revolution in Nicaragua, and its effects on the consciousness of its supporters and opponents. Although the duration of the two experiments—a few days in El Salvador versus a decade in Nicaragua—makes comparisons difficult, their juxtaposition does permit a meditation on revolutionary power, the sudden assumption of the "monopoly on violence" by forces acting in the name of the formerly disenfranchised and voiceless. Both revolutionary movements shared certain ideological underpinnings, notably Marxism-Leninism and various forms of Christianity, explicitly "liberationist" in the Nicaraguan case and more "popular" in the Salvadoran one. Both spoke in a populist idiom (though more so in Salvador) that altered the evolving meanings of more formal ideological expressions. Thus, both experiences prompt a reflection on the uses of symbolic and real coercion and their political costs. In Nicaragua and in El Salvador, the counterrevolution effectively magnified such acts and profited immensely as insurgents inserted those acts into their narrative of revolutionary depredations and the need for their particular form of "liberation." The Sandinista response to the Nicaraguan counterrevolution, in particular, merits reflection, as the growing authoritarianism—the sacrifice of social democracy for defense—gathered an aura of objectivity that belied the contingency at play. All of those who experienced the revolution are left to wonder: was an alternative possible? In El Salvador, most of those who might have asked such a question were executed; those who survived were too traumatized to think about such things.

Repression and Radicalization in the Salvadoran Countryside

The transformation of land and labor relations in western Salvador in the early twentieth century occurred rapidly enough to keep the memories of the loss of land and the past prosperity of smallholders quite fresh in the minds of Ladino and indigenous campesinos. Most significantly, the 1920s coffee boom created two new social groups, village-based semiproletarians and *colonos* (resident laborers). Because they shared collective memories of primitive accumulation, neither of these groups viewed the agrarian elite's land ownership as legitimate.[1] In the case of the colonos, when the coffee industry subsequently went into severe decline, harsh and deteriorating contractual terms further eroded any sense of legitimacy, and thus this group, which in some other Latin American countries formed a pillar of the rural social order, in El Salvador became a site of discontent and organized resistance.[2]

During the 1920s, strong currents of social democratic–style reformist nationalism in El Salvador successfully vied with elite forms of political

Workers on El Potosí Coffee Plantation, 1939.
Photo by Carlos Álvarez. Courtesy of Mauricio Álvarez.

discourse to challenge agrarian elite claims to legitimacy. Middle-class reformism, in turn, was tied to a discourse of *mestizaje*, which, unlike in other Central American countries, tended simultaneously to stimulate an indigenous revitalization movement and to open up nonindigenous groups to revolutionary movements. In addition, unlike in most other Latin American countries, the elite could not rely on the church, whose presence was extremely weak in the countryside; in indigenous areas it battled local religious practices. The church could neither integrate nor combat native and popular religious beliefs, and its inability to check millenarian currents among the rural masses became politically significant.[3] The weak church presence in the Salvadoran countryside paralleled the Cuban case during the same period. Although, unlike in Cuba, there were no "imperialist" enclaves in Salvador, the national and regional coffee elite, in the eyes of the rural poor formed a similarly distant and forbidding "other."

Until January 1932, the police and the Salvadoran National Guard held a near monopoly on violence and coercion. Throughout 1930 and 1931, National Guard units repeatedly broke up labor and peasant demonstrations, carting off to jail hundreds of protesters at a time. Organizers usually called the demonstrations to protest repression against the rapidly growing plantation workers' union movement. In 1931, during the reformist administration of Arturo Araujo, the National Guard opened fire on unarmed peasant demonstrators in Sonsonate (three killed in May) and against a union meeting in Zaragosa (fourteen killed in September). These acts of state violence, although not severe by Latin American standards, had the effect of pushing the movement in a more militant direction. The strong push toward militancy was less guided by ideological interpretations of reality than by the cultural repertoires of Indians and peasants—including a sense of embattled dignity tinged with large doses of machismo—which found state repression to be intolerable. In the words of a leftist leader: "Our campesinos will not come to any demonstrations unless they are armed with machetes [*corvos*], and you better believe it."[4] The repression against the rural movement radicalized the forms of struggle and placed the Communist leadership in a position where they had to accept either a retreat of their peasant and Indian militants into passivity or an advance toward some form of armed struggle. PCS leaders in Sonsonate, to cite a key example, informed the Central Committee that the rank and file wanted to storm the city prison to free political prisoners rather than participate in any more unarmed demonstrations. A similar sense of dignity and vengeance can be gleaned from the following statement of an indigenous widow to a PCS militant, in June 1931: "Look, compañero. They killed my compañero, but here are my sons, and they will see the revolution."[5]

On December 2, 1931, a military coup, led by General Maximiliano Hernández Martínez, ousted the ineffectual reformist president, Arturo Araujo, after he had been only nine months in office. The new regime postponed municipal and congressional elections until early January. The Salvadoran Communist Party was poised to win the mayoralties and congressional seats throughout central and western Salvador, but the regime managed to thwart the expected triumphs of the PCS candidates through fraud and intimidation.[6]

Grassroots influence on the PCS became critical on January 4, when party militants and sympathizers in the western department of Ahuachapán (bordering Guatemala) met with the delegate of the Central Committee and "insisted that he demand from the Central Committee that in view of the fact that the party had gained a tremendous majority during the election campaign, they (Ahuachapaneco militants) should be oriented to prepare a movement by which they could secure by force what they had previously failed to secure."[7] At this critical juncture, the Ahuachapanecos, while resisting violent repression, were clamoring for, in effect, a regional insurrection to install their municipal authorities. Acting independently of the Central Committee, on January 7, the local leadership made a direct appeal to soldiers:

> The government, belonging to the rich, has sent forces to crush the workers. Comrade soldiers, you belong to our exploited class and you must not shoot a single cartridge against the workers. The workers and peasants should form workers', peasants' and soldiers' councils in order to establish a workers' and peasants' government. You must disobey the orders of your officers because they are against the workers. Name your delegates so that we can reach an agreement. Let's finish off the officers of the army of the rich and let's organize a red army made up of soldiers and officers who are elected by the soldiers.[8]

Although this dramatic call to mutiny and rebellion probably had little effect on the government troops, it may well have had a powerful effect on the PCS leadership in the capital, San Salvador. At the very least, the Ahuachapanecos placed the entire Left in the line of government fire at the very moment in which the leadership in San Salvador was still looking for ways to forestall an insurrection.

Indeed, at the same moment that PCS militants in Ahuachapán were issuing insurrectionary manifestoes, the national leadership was still considering the viability of the electoral road to power. Legislative elections were scheduled for Sunday, January 10. Notwithstanding the extreme unlikelihood that the regime would allow PCS victories in the legislative elections, the PCS Electoral Commission continued to proceed as if the congressional elections were a real option. The lingering hope for a democratic solution hinged on negotiations with the regime. The same day that the Central Committee laid out its electoral and strike strategy, it named a five-member committee, including a congressional candidate from Ahuachapán, to negotiate with the Martínez regime. Although the minister of defense did meet with the PCS delegation on January 8, the regime exhibited no interest in negotiating a truce with the labor movement.

On January 10, the Central Committee of the PCS convened a plenum in order to discuss the question of insurrection. The leadership by then was convinced—and the day's events would bear them out—that the legislative elections would be a farce and that the regime would not waver in its repressive strategy. Moreover, the fifty delegates to the plenum were under intense pressure from departmental branches in the west to move toward an insurrectionary strategy. In addition to the actions and proclamation of the Ahuachapanecos, strikes and violence were spreading to other western areas: as noted above, on January 7 and 8 government forces crushed strikes and violently broke up meetings in the western departments of La Libertad and Sonsonate. PCS and Socorro Rojo Internacional (SRI) leaders in both departments also began to clamor for armed insurrection.

For the purposes of analysis, it is useful to break down the decision-making process into two components, one driving the grassroots insurrectionary movement and the other, the leadership of the PCS. The Ahuachapanecos' call to the troops to eliminate their officers and fight for a government of workers, peasants, and soldiers indicated that they had already decided to launch an insurrection or to convert a proto-insurrectionary movement into a full-fledged one. As we have seen, the movement had its own dynamic, rooted primarily in class conflict in the fields and political outrage about the municipal elections—and possibly, to a lesser extent, about the overthrow of Araujo. Large groups of rebellious strikers throughout the west were ready for or already engaged in violent conflict with the troops. They had some rudimentary arms and continued to inflict limited casualties on the troops. In short, when the PCS plenum met in San Salvador, they were faced with the choice of either supporting what amounted to the start of a regional insurrectionary movement or pacifying it (only three members publicly supported the latter option).

In addition to the clamor from the west, the decision to mount an armed insurrection was, in another sense, the fruition of ideological struggles of a proinsurrectionary current within the PCS. Throughout the previous eighteen months, this tendency had argued that grassroots support for armed violence as a response to the violent repression provided the rationale and the potential means for revolution. This current gained the support of those present in the plenum who believed that the repression on the election lines and in the fields had already provoked the beginning of a revolutionary movement that would be ruthlessly crushed by the military. Miguel Mármol, a shoemaker union activist and PCS leader who since November had argued in favor of a general strike strategy as opposed to an insurrection, changed his position faced with the brewing civil war in the west. He became a proponent of the insurrectionary option. Ironically, he then had to convince Farabundo Martí (the titular head of the insurrectionary current) that the moment was ripe:

> The discussion was intense and heated. Farabundo Martí [interim PCS secretary] finally agreed with my proposal, accepting that the duty of the party was to take its place as the vanguard of the masses, in order to avoid the greater, imminent danger and disgrace for us of an insurrection that was out of control, spontaneous or provoked by the actions of the government, in the which the masses would go alone and without leadership onto the battlefield.[9]

For Mármol and for his comrades, it was a matter of "honor" that they lead the insurrection.[10] This justifiable and palpable fear of elimination of their comrades in the west combined with more strictly ideological factors. Although the Communist International (Comintern) had nothing directly to do with the January 10 decision, the proinsurrectionary position certainly found ideological support in the fundamental postulates of the Comintern's "Third Phase," notably the "class versus class" strategy. This strategy, based on the assumption of the collapse of the world capitalist system, had some coherence in the European context, however tragically flawed. The policy, however, was never clearly translated to the "colonial" and "semicolonial" world. Rather than present a roadmap to socialism, the Comintern exported to Latin America extreme sectarianism and strong biases against compromise with class antagonists.

Since November 1931, there had been virtually no contact between the PCS or the SRI and the Comintern. That decision-making process was endogenous, as Comintern letters and reports made agonizingly clear. According to a Comintern official, "The Salvadoran comrades made it virtually impossible for us to give them practical, concrete guidance," due to what he referred to as their "self-isolationism."[11] For PCS leaders, their pleas for assistance fell on deaf ears.

Most of the national PCS leadership feared losing the adherence of its political base and, at the same time, believed that with the active support of sympathetic elements in the military the "agrarian, anti-imperialist revolution" could triumph. Although the assessment of military support was mistaken, as noted below, it was not by any means absurd. How can we assess the PCS leadership's reading of the inevitability of a "spontaneous" revolution, with its concomitant probability of extremely violent repression? There is no doubt that by early January some one thousand to two thousand people in Ahuachapán were committed to revolutionary violence against the state. Similarly, in the department of Sonsonate, grassroots militants were pushing for an armed assault on the prison to free their imprisoned comrades. Finally, in La Libertad, the strike movement was beginning to resemble that of Ahuachapán, with machete-armed pickets roaming from farm to farm shutting down operations. Notwithstanding leftist leadership of the movements in the three departments, only an order from the national PCS would have converted these thinly articulated political and social forces into a revolution.[12]

The explosion of strikes and protests also skewed the vision of both the PCS national leadership and of the western rank-and-file leaders. Both leadership groups failed to appreciate that the quality of their support was of uneven depth and quality. An urban artisanal worker, for example, might be ready to vote for the PCS but not to participate in an armed insurrection. The different levels of support would become a significant factor during the insurrection and in its posterior recreation in memory. In addition to failing to differentiate the quality of its support, the PCS leadership did not fully confront the hostility present in virtually all sectors of society. The need for "pressing" tactics during the strike mobilizations indicated that even among their most solid base of support in the coffee sector, a majority or at least a sizeable minority of workers remained on the sidelines out of fear, apathy, or antagonism. The tremendous growth of the labor movement obscured this subaltern sector that, at the very least, would limit the numbers of committed revolutionary troops.

Other groups also opposed the movement. Ladino smallholders in some indigenous areas often bitterly opposed the Left, as did many in the urban middle classes, fearful and resentful of the growing pride and assertiveness of the rural and urban poor. Moreover, although the Left gained massive support from Indians, they remained weak within the "modernizing" factions in indigenous communities split along "modernizing/traditional" lines and had virtually no presence in the highly traditional indigenous town of Santo Domingo de Guzmán. More significant, they had no conceptual tools—nor did any one else for that matter—for dealing with the exceptionally variegated tapestry of ethnic and local identities. Finally, the numerous campesinos who ducked the revolutionary wave also posed objective limits to recruitment and compelled the rebels to use coercive tactics against other subalterns. This serious underestimation of the degree of "antirevolutionary" sentiment would have severe consequences especially during the counterrevolution. In short, the PCS leadership's reading of reality was partially, but fatally, flawed. Of course, they had to read that reality shaped by the violent repression of the military regime. Passion did not sharpen the collective intellect of the PCS.

The insurrection had little chance of success without organized and active support from within the military. The Left did have significant, if relatively inorganic, support in the military establishment. A Secret Police report suggested that 50–60 percent of the regular army and 30 percent of the National Guard were leftist sympathizers.[13] Clandestine groups, including some low-level officers, operated within at least two barracks of the regular army in San Salvador.[14] Yet, through informants, the high command of the military was able to strike before the cells could respond. By January 16, the military had already discovered and eliminated most of the revolutionary conspirators in its ranks.[15] Following leads from the captured soldiers, police arrested the PCS leaders Farabundo Martí, Mario Zapata, and Alfonso Luna and discovered the military plans for the insurrection and other documents. In another arrest, they reportedly found seventy-five bombs. On January 19, according to the British consul, "a large gathering of communists took place in Atlacatl park about a mile and a half north of San Salvador, the object of which was to be an attack on the Cavalry Barracks. National Guardsmen were hurried to the spot and scattered the communists."[16] Through previous accord, the revolutionaries had expected soldiers in the barracks to surrender and join the insurrection. Officers were tipped off, however, and disarmed the company that was prepared to join the revolutionary forces.[17] They then opened fire on the insurgents outside of the barracks. Three days before the planned insurrection, the military had seized the initiative. For the revolutionary Left, there was no Plan B; there was no alternative source of weapons.

Faced with imminent defeat, the remaining members of the Central Committee reconvened on January 20 to debate the postponement of the insurrection. A minority of three argued that the insurrection was doomed to failure but a postponement might avoid the inevitably bloody repression that would follow the crushing of the revolt. The majority of six claimed that the government was already preparing a massacre and that the only option was to fight in order to defend the revolutionaries. In the words of the minority leader, the majority argued against postponing the insurrection "because so many of our comrades were in jail. . . . More arrests were being made and it was clear that all comrades were to be shot, and they thought it would be better that all of us should have the same destiny. None of them showed any logic or clear analysis of the situation and none of them could logically explain why the action was justified."[18]

At this critical juncture, emotional senses of outrage, solidarity, and fatalism influenced the PCS decision. There is no doubt that PCS adherence to Marxist-Leninism created an ideological field in which revolutionary violence was acceptable to both leadership and rank and file. Yet, intense levels of anger against state violence perpetrated on friends and comrades both motivated the resistance in the west and the decision of the Central Committee. The call to arms, issued on January 20, 1932, evoked this sense of outrage and the continued affronts to the dignity of Communists and their supporters. The manifesto underscores the causal relation between the elections and the armed resistance to repression, but most significantly it offers a glimpse of the mentality of the Communist leaders:

> We the workers, they call us thieves . . . and steal our wage, paying us a miserable wage and condemning us to live in filthy tenements or in stinking barracks, or working day and night in the fields under rain and sun. We are labeled thieves for demanding the wages that they owe us, a reduction

in the workday, and a reduction in the rents that we pay to the rich who take almost all our harvest, stealing our work from us. To the insults are added killings, beatings, jailings. . . . We have seen the massacres of workers, men and women and even children and elderly, workers from Santa Tecla, Sonsonate, Zaragoza, and right now in Ahuachapán. According to the wealthy, we do not have a right to anything, and we shouldn't open our mouths. . . . In Ahuachapán, after the National Guard didn't let our comrades vote by order of the rich folks, they beat them. Our compañeros from Ahuachapán are valiantly defending themselves with their weapons in their hands.[19]

The Insurrection

On January 22 and 23, between five and seven thousand insurgents armed mostly with machetes, supplemented by some small arms, assaulted the military barracks in the departmental capitals of Ahuachapán, Santa Tecla, and La Libertad and took over several municipal seats in central and western Salvador.[20] Indians, Ladinos (self-defined as non-Indians), and others with indeterminate and fluid identities participated in the insurrection. The overwhelming majority had experience working on coffee plantations. Cultural details about the rebels have historiographical importance because of the notable imprecision in previous accounts, a deficiency that has had significant political ramifications. With a fair degree of confidence, we can describe various groups of participants. First, those who attacked Ahuachapán and Juayúa were the same people involved in the roving strikes cited by the British official. These people included phenotypically distinct Ladinos from the Atiquizaya/Turín region, as well as many from the Ahuachapán region who did not identify themselves as Indians. Indigenous people from the barrio of Asunción in Izalco and plantation workers (of more indeterminate identities from the outlying cantones of that municipality) participated in the failed attack on the Sonsonate barracks. Similarly, large numbers of indigenous peasants from the Nahuizalco and Juayúa areas joined the forces that occupied their towns. Mostly indigenous and Ladino peasants in the Tacuba area defeated the military garrison there and occupied that town for several days. Finally, coffee workers from the Cumbre de Jayaque—who possessed fluid and indeterminate ethnic identities (they neither wore exclusively indigenous dress nor spoke indigenous languages)—staged the failed attack on Santa Tecla barracks (eight miles west of San Salvador).[21]

Looted store, Izalco.
Photo by Commander Victor Brodeur, National Archives of Canada,
negative no. PA125138. Source: National Archives of Canada.

The insurrectionary forces employed different forms of violence. First, they engaged in military combat, mainly using corvos (long machetes), but also some pistols and shotguns; in Ahuachapán, Tacuba, and Sonsonate the rebels had some rifles (Mausers) that they had appropriated in combat. In addition to the failed assaults on the military barracks, rebels engaged in pitched battles in defense of positions in Sonzacate, Juayúa, Izalco, and Tacuba. In Tacuba, the local rebels joined thousands of retreating rebel troops from throughout the west to make the last stand of the revolution. Machine gun fire decimated the ranks of the revolution in Tacuba, as elsewhere. Government troop losses in all of the battles may have been as low as thirty.

Second, the rebels executed some twenty civilians, some who defended themselves with guns and others who probably were executed in cold blood. The victims fell into two categories: political and class targets. Insurgents killed the mayors-elect in Izalco and Juayúa. In Nahuizalco, the granddaughter of Francisco Brito, the mayor at the time, recalls that he told her how the "Communists marched through the streets shouting, 'We want the head of Chico Brito!'" Brito managed to find refuge during the twenty-four hours of insurgent control.

These political executions were in direct response to the electoral fraud. The insurrectionary leaders placed the Communist candidates who had been denied their victories at the ballot box in positions of power, although rhetorically "soviets" replaced municipal governments. The executions, cold-blooded as they were, seemed to form part of a calculus less guided by vengeance than by political design.

Rebels also executed landowners in unclear circumstances. In some cases, the planters responded with gunfire against overwhelming odds. In others, rebels probably executed them in cold blood. In still others, the planters managed to escape execution. One wealthy Ladino in Izalco recalled: "A group of campesinos, almost all *mozos* from the hacienda showed up led by Lalo's mayordomo, who exclaimed 'Hoy le llega el día al patrón'" (today, the boss's time is up).[22] They ransacked his house, but since they could not find him, they vented their frustrations by killing the boss's horse and mule. Without minimizing the importance of these attempted or successful executions, it is worth noting that insurrectionary forces dominated the cities of Sonsonate and Ahuachapán for at least one night and controlled the towns of Izalco, Juayúa, Nahuizalco, and Tacuba for several days. In the two large cities there were no executions, and in the other four towns there were seven civilian deaths or executions during that period, despite the large numbers of "class enemies" to be found. In Izalco, the rebels imprisoned fourteen "class enemies" during the occupation, without executions. In short, whether or not they were obeying orders from the leadership or their own consciences, the overwhelming majority of the thousands of armed rebels did not set out to execute people.

Other forms of coercion and violence had equally important political consequences. Looting, in particular, has loomed large in the counterrevolutionary reconstruction of events and, most important, in the collective memories of survivors. Dozens of survivors equated "el robo" with "el comunismo" as a way of explaining how "murieron justos por pecadores" (the just died for the sinners). According to documentary and oral sources, in Nahuizalco, Izalco, Juayúa, and Sonzacate, rebels and their supporters looted small stores and some houses. Yet it is difficult to determine the degree of intentionality and spontaneity of those actions. According to the Canadian commander V. G. Brodeur, who, during the latter days of January, received a special military tour of the department of Sonsonate the purpose of which was to demonstrate the Salvadoran army's control:

It was noticed that at each place visited the City Hall had been destroyed, and no other damage caused except in residences of rich plantation owners who had already fled. . . . [T]he residence of a rich planter . . . was left intact though properties on either side were completely destroyed, specially all articles of family value such as priceless old furniture and paintings, this was accounted for by the fact that the above named treated his hands in a far more generous way.[23]

Francisco Sánchez, an indigenous Communist leader in Juayúa, declared upon capture, weeks following the insurrection: "Here, there are only rich people present so I can say nothing. We have robbed nothing, only some clothes to distribute to the poor who were going around naked."[24] Other reports state that Sánchez had all the liquor burned and, like other leaders in other captured towns, tried to centralize the booty and distribute it according to need.

Several survivors insist that the revolutionary leaders broke the locks on the stores in order to provoke the looting by people who would then out of necessity join the rebellion. Although this interpretation is reasonable, it is incomplete. In the cities of Ahuachapán and in Sonsonate there was no looting despite ample opportunity to do so. Rather, rebels and others looted only where the rebels had triumphed completely. At once, the looting represented a chiliastic moment ("the last shall be first") and at the same time formed part of a redistributive or military plan, not only one of gaining provisions but also to commit wavering people to the struggle.

The notion of recruitment through looting is congruent with other forms of what we might call *enforced solidarity*. Thus, for example, the rebels obliged people in the occupied towns to wear red badges or ribbons. An informant in Nahuizalco explained, "They told us we had to put on these red things or they would kill us."[25] The report of the British consul, substantiates the recollection of numerous other informants: "When they occupied the town [Juayúa] they compelled the inhabitants, under pain of death, to put on red badges."[26] There is some evidence that rebels also compelled people to address each other as "camarada," a term that had already become extremely popular among the movement's rank and file during the period of mobilization.

Finally, at least in Juayúa, the revolutionary leaders obliged middle-class women to make tortillas for the troops. This symbolic inversion of roles— a constant in social movements ranging from strikes to insurrections— undoubtedly fueled the widespread hysterical notion among townspeople in San Salvador and the west that the "Indians" were going to rape their women. There were versions of this "noche de bodas" reported in every area that suffered a rebel attack. A written reflection on Sonsonate recreates that particular fear at the core of generalized panic:

> La histeria hizo prezas particularmente de algunas señoras. Cuando se había disipada el ruido de la entrada de los rebeldes, se eschuchaban gritos despavoridos, penetrantes, que revelaban el terror elevado a la enésima potencia. "Mis hijas . . . mis hijas . . . mis hijas!" Las señoras ya veían a sus hijas violadas como se había anunciada. [Hysteria took hold of some women in particular. When the sound of the rebels entering the town dissipated, one could hear petrified, penetrating screams that revealed their incredible degree of terror: "My daughters! My daughters! My daughters!" The women already saw their daughters raped as had been announced.][27]

The Counterrevolutionary Massacres

There is little doubt that the Hernández Martínez regime had provoked grassroots leftists into armed resistance, through the electoral farce and the longstanding recourse to violent repression. The strategy of provocation was due to a variety of factors, ranging from the strategic need for diplomatic recognition from the United States to the need for material support from coffee planters. Yet there is no evidence that the regime, before January 10, was prepared to systematically perpetrate massacres against the grassroots base of the PCS or even to execute political prisoners.

The Hernández Martínez regime's strategy of provocation, however, does suggest that it planned to violently repress the Left into submission. With the discovery of the PCS insurrectionary plans, the regime surely upped the ante, in that they would likely execute their enemies whether legally or extralegally. Yet there would have been no particular logic (and no evidence) underpinning a plan to massacre unarmed Indians, peasants, and workers using the (provoked) insurrection as a pretext.

Rather, the level of violent repression passed through stages, albeit quite compressed ones. First, mainly National Guardsmen relying on machine guns defeated the insurrectionary forces. The regular army, relying on recruits from ethnically distinct and politically marginal eastern Salvador, joined forces with the Guard.[28] In all of the battles, government forces defeated the insurgents in three hours or less of combat. After defeating the revolutionaries, the National Guard pursued the retreating rebels into the countryside. During the hot pursuit, the troops often engaged in indiscriminate killing of males over twelve years old. These killing fields were in the areas surrounding the major sites of rebellion: the countryside around Ahuachapán (mainly nonindigenous), Tacuba (largely indigenous), Juayúa (largely indigenous), Nahuizalco (indigenous), Izalco (largely indigenous), and the Cumbre de Jayaque (some indigenous, mainly self-identified as non-Indian).

The rural areas around Ahuachapán, Juayúa, Tacuba, Izalco, and Nahuizalco suffered the greatest number of deaths, probably several thousand during these critical first days. In the countryside surrounding Nahuizalco and Juayúa, in the words, repeated by dozens of informants, "they killed all males from twelve on up." In Tacuba, apparently, the killing included many women. That the killing had nothing to do with political identification, was driven home by Álvaro Cortez, "My father was a *patrullero* [member of one of the civil patrols organized by the government]; they didn't ask for a declaration, they just shot him."[29]

The question of genocide must be addressed since, with the exception of those in the Ahuachapán/Atiquizaya region, most of the victims were Indians, despite the fact that Ladinos probably composed one-half of the insurrectionary forces. There is no question that the cumulative effect of the massacres amounted to a form of genocide against Indians. However, there is no evidence to suggest the Martínez regime specifically planned to eliminate Indians qua Indians. On one level, the massive killing of Indians immediately following the military defeat of the insurrection had a lot to do with their geographical proximity to the battles and to the order attributed to Martínez, "Take no prisoners!" On another, probably a majority of those who attacked the barracks in the three cities were Ladinos and they were able to retreat without immediate military pursuit.[30]

However, there were two additional factors that conditioned the proportionally high tally of Indian deaths. First, there is no doubt that the ethnic tensions in the above-mentioned municipalities were exacerbated to the point of hysteria, following the occupation by largely indigenous revolutionary forces. Those occupations, despite their relatively small scale of violence, burst the dam holding back the accumulated hostility and hatred toward Indians on the part of the elite but also in distinct degrees shared by middle-class and proletarian townsfolk and villagers. Very quickly Indian, barbarian, and Communist became interchangeable epithets. One survivor recalls townsfolk shouting, "Que se acaben los indios comunistas!" (let's finish off the communist Indians!). Many town residents mobilized into a "Guardia Cívica" as soon as the troops retook the municipal centers. According to a report of a Canadian Christian pastor, "a defense league" in Nahuizalco, composed of Ladinos, "rounded up male believers and had them shot."[31] Although civil guards probably did not play a significant role in the massacres per se, local Ladinos undoubtedly inspired the troops to execute Indians, if they were not already so inclined.

Second, there was at least one case of specific racist actions on the part of the military. One of the National Guard commanders, a Colonel Ortiz, injured while breaking up a peasant demonstration the previous year, reportedly uttered the command: "If a Ladino is suspicious, bring him in for questioning; if it's an Indian, shoot him."[32] In short, the combination of military exigency and brutal excess, local racist hysteria and a desire for vengeance, and at least one racist military commander led to a heavy predominance of Indian fatalities during the latter days of January. Although it is hard to estimate the number of fatalities in these days of battle and the immediate aftermath, General Tomás Calderón's claim that his troops had "liquidated forty-eight hundred Bolsheviks" seems fairly accurate, as it coincides with other partial estimates.[33]

Local racist hysteria undoubtedly played a more distinct role in the next phase of military repression, contributing to at least two large-scale massacres of Indians in Nahuizalco and its environs. On February 13, in Nahuizalco, the mayor called on all the people to obtain identity cards. When a thousand people gathered in the town square, the National Guard corralled them in the market, and then hauled them off to be shot in the cemetery. According to the British consul's report, "388 Indians were killed."[34] The consul maintained that local authorities became nervous because of the threatening attitude of the Indians, but survivors only recall the panic of people trying to escape the machine gun fire.[35]

In El Canelo, a northern canton of Nahuizalco, Gabino Mata, a proto-fascist ideologue, suffered at least a major fright during the insurrection as reportedly a large group of rebels occupied his hacienda.[36] Following their military defeat, Mata decided to seek vengeance. He gathered together his colonos under the pretext of protecting them from the National Guard. As one survivor recalls, "They were going to give out the password but the password was bullets."[37] His father was one of an estimated five hundred to

Corpses in a common
grave, January 1932.
Courtesy of the Museo
de la Palabra y la Imagen.

Salvadoran soldiers.
Photo by Commander
Victor Brodeur, National
Archives of Canada,
negative no. PA125135.
Source: National Archives
of Canada.

eight hundred mostly indigenous peasants who fell under a hail of machine gun fire as they were ordered by the same Colonel Ortiz to make a run for it.

These two massacres, one provoked by municipal authorities and the other by a prominent landlord and political figure, stand alone for both their cunning and unambiguous evil. The principal form of repression engraved in the memory of the survivors, however, were "las listas." National and Civic Guards carried around large lists of voters who had signed petitions to register the PCS. Throughout February and March, Civic Guard patrols and National Guard searched for those PCS supporters and when they found them, they shot them either with or without the benefit of judicial trappings.[38] Executions by lists were carried out in San Salvador and throughout western El Salvador. Again it is impossible to ascertain the numbers killed, but given the large numbers of towns and cities where they were carried out, an estimate of at least fifteen hundred would be conservative.

There are two other pieces of evidence that would necessarily qualify a charge of genocide against Indians. First, as we have seen, there was indiscriminate killing of Ladino peasants in rural areas of Ahuachapán and in

Sonsonate and Sonzacate.[39] Second, there were Indian areas that were untouched by the massacre. Santo Domingo de Guzmán, an almost exclusively indigenous municipality in Sonsonate, suffered no repression, saved—in popular belief—by a miracle. Whereas Santo Domingo residents had not participated in the mobilization or the rebellion, Indians from Panchimalco had participated in both and suffered only light repression.[40] There is no evidence that would help explain why the military authorities acted so differently toward the indigenous rebels and their homes in the Panchimalco region. It is entirely possible that Colonel Emilio Renderos, in charge of the expedition against the retreating rebels, simply had no stomach for massacres and that his superiors, recognizing that their victory was complete, had no interest in further bloodshed. If that explanation were valid, then it would place the onus of guilt for the latter phases of the massacres in the west on local influence on the forces of repression.

Symbolic Coercion, Massacre, and Memory

There are glaring discrepancies between the documentary record of mobilization, repression, insurrection, and massacre and the recreation of those events in the memories of the survivors. Those memories tend to suppress indigenous agency in the insurrection and, at times, categorize the subsequent massacre as the work of "Communists." The trauma induced by witnessing the execution of loved ones and the fear caused by six decades of military rule (the military remained effectively in power until 1992) were the primary causes of the suppression of indigenous agency. Similarly, the trauma erased from memory the events that had precipitated the insurrection, especially the electoral fraud and the violent repression of the prior grassroots mobilizations.

Relatively insignificant in the broad sweep of events, the use of symbolic forms of coercion, "counter-theatre" in the phrase of E. P. Thompson, such as obliging townsfolk to wear a red ribbon, contributed to the creation of the dominant narrative in which the Indians were innocent victims with no agency in an insurrection that amounted to little more than "el robo," induced by the Ladino Communist outsiders.[41] Insurgents practiced other forms of countertheater when the revolutionary leaders compelled middle- and upper-class women to grind corn and make tortillas. Similarly, a lavish funeral for a campesino insurgent in Juayúa contrasted dramatically with the pauper's funeral for an oligarch. These actions were not particularly important in their historical context, but survivors used them as markers to stand for the generic political innocence of Indians.

Most popular rebellions, riots, or social revolutionary triumphs (however brief) unleash similar forms of theater that communicate to a multiclass audience that the world has turned upside down. Such symbolic actions, usually forms of symbolic coercion as in El Salvador, crossed premodern and modern boundaries. For example, William Taylor emphasizes how Indians had often cursed and humiliated officials in colonial-era rebellions in Mexico.[42] The Matagalpan Indians in an 1881 rebellion in Nicaragua, to cite another example, compelled Ladino landowners to perform menial labor for them.[43] The Russian and Spanish Revolutions exhibited numerous similar examples of symbolic inversions of power. For example, the Spanish revolutionaries' exhumations and display of the corpses of nuns revealed their spiritual triumph over the demonized church, a key ally of the counterrevolution.[44] Subversive acts inevitably accompany social revolution, and they are a particularly creative and at times less destructive way of expressing generations of subaltern ressentiment.[45]

Daniel James uncovered actions that he labeled "secular iconoclasm" in the Peronista Mobilization of October 17, 1945. These actions ranged from the chanting of "burlesque slogans" and making vulgar physical gestures against university students and wealthy women to vandalism of selected elite targets. He writes: "In the absence of the direct involvement of the state and its organs—the police and the armed forces—in the October days [along] with the suspension of party activity and with the absence of a direct conflict between capital and labor a situation emerged in which the contest for symbolic domination and cultural power within society was revealed in a peculiarly transparent fashion."[46]

James uncovered these acts of secular iconoclasm largely through an analysis of "silences" in workers' testimonies in the context of written sources. Precisely because of the construction of an official commemorative version of events, memories of these actions remained deeply submerged. This silence stands in stark contrast with the highlighting of analogous actions in the memories of the survivors of 1932.

Some of the Salvadoran insurgent actions not only remained but, indeed, stood out in testimonies, helping to create this memory framework. As mentioned above, compared to the military repression the amount of violence committed by the insurgents was minimal: combat, under twenty executions, some looting, and then numerous acts of more symbolic (and threatened) violence. Yet, in survivor testimonies those acts of violence, co-ercion, and looting are given symbolic weight at times equal to and even confused with the military massacres.

Looting and the destruction of the municipal buildings have loomed large in the counterrevolutionary reconstruction of events and most importantly in the collective memories of survivors. Yet it is difficult to determine the degree of intentionality and spontaneity of those actions. The Comandantes Rojos ordered the destruction of municipal archives (except in Juayúa) and the taking of telegraph offices in every occupied town. A standard target in nineteenth and early twentieth-century agrarian rebellions and revolutions, the municipal archive typically housed land records, the destruction of which laid the groundwork for "free land" or "land without owners." Such an action was fully congruent with the goal of revolutionary agrarian reform and with the de facto transformation of land occupations over the previous month. Notwithstanding, the connection between land distribution and the destruction of the archives is absent in all survivor testimonies. Most likely, the overwhelming power of the trope "el robo" has caused that suppression: dozens of survivors equated "el robo" with "el comunismo" as a way of explaining how "the just died for the sinners." Even among elderly informants on the left, the statement "This was not communism, it was *bandolerismo* [banditry]" is typical, in that it posits no legitimate political or social motive for the looting and destruction.

The most basic explanation for the radically different memory appropriations of these subversive events in Argentina and in El Salvador lies in the immediate political outcomes. In Argentina, the Peronistas triumphed almost immediately after the demonstrations and went on to rule for a decade. During that time, the Peronist leadership was capable of constructing an official history that selectively incorporated aspects of the October 17 protests, creating a strongly peaceful and favorable portrait of the demonstrators. In El Salvador, the triumphant military regime took immediate steps to publicize a version of events that emphasized the "innocence" of the Indians and the barbarity of the Communists.

Although the Salvadoran military's profound impact on the traumatized consciousness of the massacre survivors represents an extreme case, the tension between goals of emancipation and methods of coercion is a constant of twentieth-century social movements in Latin America. In far less violent and dramatic circumstances there was also a tension between the emancipatory and democratic goals of the movements and the forms of coercion, however mild, employed in those struggles. In *To Lead as Equals*, I noted the presence of pickets who physically blocked the entrance to plantations in the first cotton-picker's strike in Nicaraguan history, in 1962: "In the Tonalá strike and in other forms of protest there was a curious relation at once authoritarian and democratic between the leadership and the rank and file. In one sense, their leaders also felt compelled to push the rank and file into action. In this way, workers abdicated full responsibility for action."[47] Throughout the nineteenth and twentieth century most strikes and other forms of social protest have employed some forms of coercion to push wavering supporters into the insurgent camp and, at the same time, to present a united front against their antagonists. Such tactics have often been successful, a key ingredient of many strikes throughout the world.

These revolutionary forms of action and minor acts of enforced solidarity have been problematic in different ways. First, regardless of the degree of violence involved in a given event, the experience did seem terrifying to the enemies of the revolution and to neutral bystanders. To relatively neutral or even sympathetic observers such subaltern acts of subversion were frightening precisely because of their heretical content, expressing an unknown and disturbing alternative to previous social reality. Second, even less intense forms of solidarity enforcement, such as picket lines, have often backfired politically. The Right has rarely had these concerns, relying on the coercion of the market, a reservoir of anticommunist sentiment often connected to religion, and its exercise of state power.

Socially subversive acts of protest and mobilization, however justifiable, form part of a vicious cycle that in part accounts for the Left's political weakness throughout the twentieth century. Invariably outflanked economically, militarily, and ideologically by the Right, such actions by the Left have been often portrayed at the historical moment and in subsequent memory as brutal and terroristic. The Right has been able to use distortion and exaggeration as the basis for mobilization and or a socially constructed memory through several moves. First, the use of any forms of coercion undercuts the Left's claim to be democratic. Second, it allows wavering Left followers to negate voluntary participation in the movement. At the same time, the undemocratic forms and the putative lack of support provide a pretext for repression. Finally, the justifications for the repression intensify the fears of the Right's potential political base. The vicious circle continues as these socially constructed memories continuously debilitate the Left.

A Nicaraguan Counterpoint: Buried Visions

Despite a far more promising situation in Nicaragua following the triumph of the insurrection in 1979, the Frente Sandinista de Liberación Nacional (FSLN) could not break out of such a vicious circle: in the space of a few years the Right successfully magnified moderate forms of coercion into an image of a totalitarian dictatorship, an image that remains active in the present.

No serious analyst can dispute the enormous popularity of the FSLN in 1979. Yet there was a huge difference in the quality of support between, for example, barrio residents of eastern Managua and peasants in the Central Highlands. Like the PCS in 1932, the FSLN leadership had difficulty evaluating the different qualities of its support. In the highlands, to cite a crucial case, the indigenous people did not attribute their dramatic social transformation to the Sandinistas in part because the Frente could neither readily accept a change in consciousness that did not derive from their leadership nor understand indigenous identity among people who no longer had ethnic emblems: "In a dirt-poor indigenous village, people could experience a sense of liberation without any of its national references. The historic antagonists of both the Indians of Matagalpa and the Frente Sandinista have artfully exploited that deep misunderstanding with tragic consequences for all Nicaraguans."[48]

My research during the 1980s suggested a fundamental problem for the Sandinistas or for any other project of national transformation. I observed how local campesinos and nationally oriented actors often share vocabularies but inflect them with different resonance and meaning. These forms of misunderstanding were at times unconscious and at times part of a search for common ground.[49] The shared vocabularies were often quite effective in periods of mobilization. During the Somoza era (1936–79) campesinos in Chinandega and León mobilized and came to understand the world in terms of prevailing notions of private property and necessity.[50] As they struggled through and against the institutions of Somocismo, they developed broader collective understanding of those terms, which allowed them during the 1970s to enter into dialogue with the liberation theology wing of the Sandinista movement.

By the late 1980s, however, the very terms that had solidified the alliance, such as "Land to the Campesinos," led to breakdowns in communication and alliances. The Chinandegan campesino activists who had fought alongside the Sandinistas after ten years broke with them, angered that their goals embodied in their own histories were simply not taken seriously. State cotton farms could not represent the "people's land" for which they had fought so valiantly. The official reconstruction of that local history labeled their pre-1970s struggles as "spontaneous" movements and only granted importance to the battles of the late 1970s, when the campesinos allied themselves with the Frente Sandinista. Yet, on the contrary, the campesinos' political educational process throughout the 1950s and 1960s was largely endogenous, the product of their own reflections on their experiences of alliance and betrayal by forces allied with and opposed to the Somoza dictatorship.

The Nicaraguan Revolution was far more than an accumulation of errors caused by Leninist arrogance compounded by imperial aggression. Indeed, there was an alternative current within the revolution that the counterrevolution helped to bury. Consider an anecdote that outlines that current. On July 21, 1979, two days after the triumph of the Sandinista Revolution, I was working with a Dutch TV crew. We had just descended from "la Cuesta del Plomo," a heavily wooded area on the western outskirts of Managua (a famous battleground in the Liberal Revolution of 1893). During the last days of the regime, it had served as a killing field for Somoza's National Guard. Corpses littered the trails like lethal mushrooms sprouting after a spring rain. Desperate, tearful mothers tried to identify their sons. Some statements I recall: "The Guardia came in and yanked him out of bed!" "He was in jail and they took him away a week ago." "It was a crime to be a young male, they killed anyone they could find!"

After this scene of despair, we descended to a place called OPEN 3—an acronym for Operación Permanente de la Emergencia Nacional—a marginal muddy barrio set up on Somoza-owned land following a flood in 1968; the regime had relocated thousands there following the earthquake in 1972. The impoverished residents were obliged to pay rent to Somoza and had protested against the high cost of water. The barrio became a major base of support for the FSLN. We came upon three teenage kids, armed with automatic rifles, who were standing guard outside of a police station, a small concrete-block building. Inside, four middle-aged men sat dejectedly on the cement floor with another teenager sitting on a stool with a rifle. Outside, a crowd gathered. A woman started shouting, "¡Oreja, oreja, oreja!" (slang for informer). More people suddenly appeared, and the chanting became more ominous, with "oreja" interspersed with "¡Asesino!" "They turned in my kid!" The Sandinista *muchachos* were sweating profusely (as were we). Finally, one of the muchachos, a scrawny kid with the fuzzy outlines of a mustache, stepped toward the crowd and addressed them: "Look, compañeros, we are creating a new Nicaragua and for this we need a new kind of revolution. We are making a humanist revolution that respects human life, even of our enemies. We need to reconstruct the country and not follow along like before with so much killing and destruction. These orejas will be judged by the tribunals and if they are found guilty they will go to prison but we will not kill them!"

Despite a lot of grumbling, people gradually returned home. This was the first of many uneducated youths I would hear who seemed to find a new voice in the revolution. I strongly suspect that the memory of this event is buried along with countless other similar episodes which announced a new type of revolution, one that refused the temptation of *el paredón* (the firing squad wall).

The revolutionary imaginary, the utopian vision announced in 1978 and 1979, did not have a special place on any political agenda. Members of the economic elite were largely content with a political democracy, a free market, and an untouched social structure. The far Left was mired in rank sectarianism, although aspects of that program could have been incorporated into the FSLN's program, entailing, however, a serious challenge to revolutionary orthodoxy. The FSLN would have been obliged to tolerate more or less autonomous labor and peasant movements. Similarly, grassroots militants (allied with the Frente and other leftist groups) expressed a strong desire for the individual appropriation of the fruits of proletarian and peasant labor, with a democratic spirit that resisted all forms of coercion. Campesinos could eagerly participate in the agrarian reform and even cooperatives but did not easily accept being told what to do or have their access to land conditioned by political allegiance. Marxists-Leninists disparaged such revolutionary consciousness as "petit-bourgeois"; the Right recognized it as a dangerous form of popular empowerment.

The revolutionary utopian vision may well have led to all kinds of excesses and expressions of enforced solidarity, and it might have provoked an economic crisis (but of course that occurred anyway). Indeed, the role of a truly democratic revolutionary state would have been to enforce laws that protected citizens and their property against such popular excesses, but not to thwart the movements themselves. Moreover, as the muchachos in front of the Somocista jail announced (as did thousands of unrecognized humanitarian gestures of the Sandinista police), this did not have to be an authoritarian revolution.

If the exigencies of the world market and imperial domination place rigid, objective limits on any revolutionary experiment, they also distorted the guiding ideology of the Frente. The FSLN program of "mixed economy, political pluralism, and nonalignment" recognized those limitations, but the Leninist inflection transformed those terms in decidedly undemocratic and inegalitarian directions. There were some elements within the Frente Sandinista who developed a position that pushed to democratize that agenda, but the military exigencies posed by the growth of the counterrevolutionary forces, the Contra, debilitated this current within the revolution and buried the memory of those scenes and moments that had announced a nonauthoritarian alternative.

The most obvious reason for their burial in memory has to do with the U.S.-sponsored counterrevolution and its devastating consequences of tens of thousands of deaths and billions of dollars of destruction (in an era when Nicaragua earned under $500 million in export earnings annually). The revolution under siege was in no position to pursue this novel course. However that is not the whole story. The institution of the draft, although perhaps a military necessity, was also the culmination of a pernicious coercive trend in the revolution. At their worst (at least among those that I witnessed), those actions included yanking a peasant woman off a bus in order to take a couple of pounds of beans so they wouldn't be sold on the black market (although this policy was stopped rather quickly). There were also arbitrary arrests of suspected counterrevolutionaries and possibly an execution of a civilian leader (in later years in war zones there would be dozens more).

Yet the everyday forms of state coercion never amounted even remotely to the Reaganite description of a totalitarian dictatorship. There were, of course, many people, especially among the politically conscious elites, who believed that they lived in a dictatorship. Yet on countless bus rides, I witnessed people loudly complaining about all sorts of sins of the Sandinistas, including the lack of freedom. And they complained without trepidation in front of soldiers or police officers who happened to be seated near them. Those complaints, however ludicrous as examples of totalitarianism, nonetheless did reflect genuine anger and resentment against the draft and other authoritarian tendencies of the revolution that were only made less digestible by the constant reminders that basic necessities were not available.

The cumulative effect of this coercive strain of the revolution produced ambivalence even among Sandinista supporters. It became difficult to tell if you "had" to go to a demonstration or face some kind of consequence, or if you "should" go because you agreed with its objectives. Only a serious study of the revolutionary process could directly ascertain how debilitating that ambivalence was within the FSLN. Perhaps such ambivalence in wartime prevented militants from questioning the structures of authority that made attendance at a demonstration a source of ambivalence rather than commitment.

Yet the revolution did allow for new voices, new ideas, and new forms of organization. One did not have to believe that you received "revolutionary energy" from every bite of rice and beans in Estelí (as one solidarity worker informed me) in order to recognize that there was something potentially beautiful about this emerging social world. I recall spending a brief period of time on the El Porvenir cooperative, lending a city hand during the *tapisca* (corn harvest). This was a pleasant change: I had spent much time on the Chinandegan plains, bemoaning not only the heat but also the plight of the revolutionary process whose leadership simply could or would not respond to the basic needs and demands of sugar mill and cane workers and poor peasants. Rumors of high-level corruption wafted through the town of Chichigalpa like the fumes emanating from the Flor de Caña plant, a constant reminder that rum was more readily available than milk in this the time of "no hay" (there's none). In El Porvenir, the slight elevation over the plains had a benign effect on the climate, and people actually seemed at peace when they worked. It helped that sweat did not flow from their pores with every movement. Laughter came from all over the fields, kids and adults alike. After work, people cheerfully returned to decently constructed homes, far better than the shacks in which most had lived before the revolution. Like the folks below on the plains, the people of El Porvenir suffered and complained about the hardships of severe food and agricultural supplies shortages and the unmentionable pain of seeing their children drafted to fight the Contra—the Washington-backed, anti-Sandinista mercenaries initially recruited from Somoza's fleeing National guard. Yet the goals of land and liberty were enough of a reality in El Porvenir to soften the harshness. Unlike elsewhere, the complaints did not jab at the heart of the revolutionary project; rather, they begged for a solution that would not jeopardize their forward march out of misery. I left after a few days, wondering why the Sandinista government could not somehow replicate this achievement. In part, the answer, I thought, lay in the historical conjuncture that allowed this local project to flourish: peasant battles against a Somocista *terrateniente* during the late 1970s coincided with massive support for the FSLN. Finally, the land was not particularly important for the agro-export economy. Thus the Frente could stimulate the creation of a production cooperative among a politically predisposed peasantry who, in turn, could use their political capital to push for a reasonable allocation of resources: decent housing, health services, and education.

The ravages of the Contra war and U.S. boycott and the collapse of the cotton economy nonetheless did fatally affect the peasants on the slopes of the Casita Volcano, on whose slopes El Porvenir was located. Although the cash-strapped revolutionary government had made efforts to reforest the hillsides, the lack of cheap, alternative cooking fuels led to growing deforestation. In October 1998—eight years after the Frente was voted out of power—a torrential rain filled the crater of Las Casitas until it burst, pouring thousands of tons of water down its bare slopes. The devastating torrent of water gathered mud, sticks, and stones and came crashing down on El Porvenir and its sister cooperative village, Rolando Rodríguez, burying the houses, the barns, and every living thing. Over a thousand residents who had struggled day and night to make their collective dreams worth living died in the disaster. This was poetic injustice: the burial of a rare revolutionary success under so much muck.

One bitter irony of that horrendous natural disaster is that it could symbolize other human disasters: defeated mobilizations whose profound emancipatory promise has been buried, not with mud but with the toxic sediment of fear, propaganda, and accumulated cynicism. In a world in which the very idea of fundamental social change has become chimerical, where elementary forms of human solidarity seem utopian, those numerous "Porvenirs" that dot the Latin American historical landscape should be excavated and remembered.

Notes

1. Portions of this chapter, originally drafted for the New Haven conference in 2003, appear in chapters five, six, and seven of Jeffrey L. Gould and Aldo Lauria-Santiago, *To Rise in Darkness: Revolution, Repression, and Memory in El Salvador, 1920-1932* (Durham: Duke University Press, 2008). The term "primitive accumulation" suggests that survivors or descendants of people who experienced the loss of land access

and the transformation from independent smallholder or *comunero* remember events related to that process with particular salience. On memories of primitive accumulation, see Jeffrey L. Gould, *To Die in This Way: Nicaraguan Indians and the Myth of Mestizaje, 1880–1965* (Durham: Duke University Press, 1998), 231–38.

2. For a fuller discussion, see Gould and Lauria-Santiago, *To Rise in Darkness*, 16–20.

3. Protestantism was beginning to make some inroads among the indigenous population. The counterrevolution targeted Protestants in the town of Nahuizalco. See Roy McNaught, "Horrors of Communism in Central America," *Central American Bulletin*, March 15, 1932; McNaught, a Canadian, was a minister of religion.

4. Comintern (Communist International) Archive, letter from Ismael Hernández to SRI Secretariado del Caribe, November 29, 1931, 539.3.1060.

5. Comintern Archive, SRI, Comité Ejecutivo, 539.3.1060, June 1931, p. 6.

6. See Gould and Lauria-Santiago, *To Rise in Darkness*, 149–51.

7. Report by Max Cuenca [Comrade Hernández], Comintern Archive, 495.119. 36/46. For an explanation of Hernández as Cuenca, see Gould and Lauria-Santiago, *To Rise in Darkness*, 325.

8. Jorge Schlesinger, *La Revolución Comunista* (Guatemala City: Tipográfica Castañeda, 1946), 157.

9. Roque Dalton, *Miguel Mármol*, trans. Kathleen Ross (Willimantic, Conn.: Curbstone Press, 1987), 240.

10. On gender ideologies and violence in El Salvador, see Jeffrey L. Gould and Aldo Lauria-Santiago, "They Call Us Thieves and Steal Our Wage," *Hispanic American Historical Review* 84, no. 2 (2004), 219–25.

11. Comintern Archive, 495.119.1, 1932, p. 5/30.

12. For a fuller discussion of events preceding the 1932 insurrection, see Gould and Lauria-Santiago, *To Rise in Darkness*, 154–69.

13. "Communist Rising in Salvador, 1932," Report of the British Consul, Foreign Office (FO) 371 15813, p. 10.

14. Schlesinger, *La Revolución Comunista*, 160.

15. British Consul, "Communist Rising in Salvador," 11, describes officers disarming their soldiers in the Sixth Infantry barracks on January 19. Schlesinger depicts a similar event on January 16.

16. British Consul, "Communist Rising in Salvador," 1.

17. Schlesinger, *La Revolución Comunista*, 179.

18. Comintern Archive, report by Comrade "Hernández," Comintern, 495.119.4, p. 52. This leader somewhat feebly also claimed (29) that the PCS had no funds to

publish manifestos explaining its position with respect to the regime. There is no doubt that "Hernández" was, in fact, Max Cuenca. In addition to the argument made in this report, there are numerous points of coincidence between "Hernández's" account of his own positions (for example at the decisive January 20 meeting of the Comité Central) and those attributed to "the intellectual" Cuenca by Mármol. "Hernández"/Cuenca was one of the three-person *comité militar* appointed by the Central Committee of PCS once the insurrection was decided upon. The other two members were Mármol (who escaped and went into hiding) and Martí (who was caught and executed).

19. "Manifiesto del Comité Central del Partido Comunista a las clases trabajadoras de la República," January 20, 1932, appendix, in Mayor Otto Romero Orellano, "Genesis de la Amenaza Comunista en El Salvador" (Centro de Estudios Estratégicos de las Fuerzas Armadas, San Salvador, 1994), 97.

20. See Gould and Lauria-Santiago, *To Rise in Darkness*, chap. 6. The estimate of insurgents based on documentary sources breaks down regionally along the following lines: La Libertad, 900; Sonsonate, 800; Izalco, 600; Juayúa, 600; Nahuizalco, 500–800; Ahuachapán and Tacuba, 1,000–2,000. In addition, hundreds participated in armed actions in the areas south and east of the capital.

21. This ethnographic portrait is based on over 150 interviews with survivors of the massacre. Significantly, most did not identify themselves as Indians.

22. Segundo Montes, *El compadrazgo: una estructura del poder en El Salvador,* 2nd ed. (San Salvador: UCA Editores, 1987), 271.

23. V. G. Brodeur to Naval Secretary, Ottawa, April 7, 1932, FO 371/15814.

24. *Diario Latino*, February 2, 1932.

25. Interview with Gregorio Shul, Nahuizalco, 1998.

26. "Communist Rising in Salvador, 1932," Report of the British Consul, Foreign Office (FO) 371 15813, p. 10.

27. Reynaldo Galindo Pohl, *Recuerdos de Sonsonate* (San Salvador: Comité Pro-Mejoramiento de Sonsonate, 2001), 356. On gender ideologies and violence in El Salvador, see Gould and Lauria-Santiago, "They Call Us Thieves and Steal Our Wage."

28. Only in Sonzacate did the rebels, under the leadership of Julia Mojica, register a victory, a successful defense against a vastly outnumbered unit of the National Guard that attacked them, on the morning of January 23, following the failed assault on the Sonsonate barracks, two miles away.

29. Interview with Álvaro Cortez, El Canelo, Nahuizalco, 1999.

30. The Sonsonate attackers retreated to nearby Sonzacate, where, on the morning of January 23, they defeated a mixed unit of the National Guard and army that

attacked them. Then they dispersed, some going to reinforce the insurrectionary forces in Nahuizalco and Izalco, and others remaining in the countryside. Some of the Sonsonate rebels were Ladino hacienda workers (interview with Margarita Turcios, El Guayabo, 2001). In Ahuachapán it is still somewhat unclear where the rebels went after the attack, but it seems likely that many of them went into hiding. National Guard units did pursue the Cumbre de Jayaque rebels who attacked Santa Tecla, but the results (the number and form of deaths) are not clear (interviews with Doroteo López, San Isidro, 1999 and 2000; Salomé Miranda, Sacacoyo, 2001; Juan Miranda, Sacacoyo, 2001; and Jesús Monterrosa, Jayaque, 2001. For a fuller discussion of the role of genocide in the events of 1932, see Gould and Lauria-Santiago, *To Rise in Darkness*, 217–21.

31. MacNaught, "Horrors of Communism in Central America."

32. Reynaldo Galindo Pohl, *Recuerdos de Sonsonate: Crónica del 32* (Sonsonate: Tecnograff, 2001), 428.

33. *New York Times*, January 30, 1932. Commander Brodeur reported that on January 29 General Calderón had reported the forty-eight hundred Communists "liquidated": "The Commanding Officer [Brodeur] immediately went ashore to verify this statement in a general way, and to pay his respects to General Calderón." He was enthusiastically embraced by the general and invited to lunch the following day in Sonsonate, and to "witness a few executions." "General Resume of Proceedings of H.M.C. Ships whilst at Acajutla," Republic of El Salvador, January 23–31, 1932, FO 371/1584, p. 14.

34. Letter, D. Rodgers to Grant Wilson, February 16, 1932, FO 813/23 no. 24 238/13a.

35. Interviews with Alberto Shul, Nahuizalco 1999 and 2001.

36. José Tomás Calderón, "Anhelos de un ciudadano" (San Salvador, n.d.), 228.

37. Interview with Raimundo Aguilar, Cusamuluco, 1999.

38. Several dozen suspected rebels were imprisoned in Sonsonete and Ahuachapán. Some were still in prison two years later.

39. In all of these cases a certain degree of racism based on phenotype might have played a role. The civilian and military forces might have falsely assumed they were killing Indians, had they bothered to think about it all. Rarely did they bother to talk with their victims and thus potentially discern their accent.

40. Interviews with Alberto Ventura and Ricardo Carillos, Quezalpa, Panchimalco, 2001; *Diario Latino*, February 11, 1932.

41. E. P. Thompson, "Patrician Society, Plebian Culture," *Journal of Social History* 7 (1974), 400.

42. William B. Taylor, *Drinking, Homicide and Rebellion in Colonial Mexican Villages* (Stanford: Stanford University Press, 1979), 117–18.

43. Gould, *To Die in This Way*, 36.

44. Ronald Fraser, *Blood of Spain: An Oral History of the Spanish Civil War* (New York: Pantheon Books, 1979), 150–52.

45. Sheila Fitzpatrick, "Vengeance and Ressentiment in the Russian Revolution," *French Historical Studies* 24, no. 4 (Fall 2001). Fitzpatrick cites a dictionary definition of "ressentiment": "a state of hostility maintained by the memory of an offense which it aspires to avenge." She adds, "Ressentiment (like vengeance) must always be present in the mix of emotions that lead people to support revolutions and commit acts of revolutionary violence" (580).

46. Daniel James, "October 17th and 18th, 1945: Mass Protest, Peronism, and the Argentine Working Class," *Journal of Social History* 21, no. 3 (1989): 68.

47. Jeffrey L. Gould, *To Lead as Equals: Rural Protest and Political Consciousness in Chinandega, Nicaragua, 1912–1979* (Chapel Hill: University of North Carolina Press, 1990), 197.

48. Gould, *To Die in This Way*, 266.

49. This process that I am synthesizing is akin to Bourdieu's notion of misrecognition. Yet in this process campesinos had a more volitional role than that available to people who *misrecognize*. Notwithstanding, one could make the argument that during their struggles in the 1960s for land and then again in the 1980s the campesinos did suffer from *misrecognition*, which Bourdieu defines as "the fact of recognizing a violence which is wielded precisely inasmuch as one does not perceive it as such." Pierre Bourdieu and Loïc Wacquant, *An Invitation to Reflexive Sociology* (Chicago: University of Chicago Press, 1992), 168.

50. Gould, *To Lead as Equals*, 171–77.

Ránquil

Violence and Peasant Politics

on Chile's Southern Frontier

THOMAS MILLER KLUBOCK

In late June 1934, mestizo and indigenous Mapuche peasants on the Rán-quil and Guayalí estates in the southern Chilean province of Lonquimay rose up in rebellion. They invaded large estates, attacked the estates' owners and managers, and, after a week, controlled a large swath of the province, threatening the region's major commercial centers. Pamphlets distributed throughout Lonquimay called on rural laborers to organize soviets of *campesinos* (peasants), *colonos* (settlers), and *indios* (indigenous Mapuches). Workers in the region had organized a union, the Sindicato Agrícola Lonquimay, six years earlier. The union led the uprising with the support of Chile's Communist Party, as well as the Communist-led national labor federation, the FOCH (Federación Obrera de Chile). The rebels were also aided by heavy snowfall in the mountainous region that blocked access to the Chilean military and police. After ten days, however, hundreds of rebels were taken prisoner, while hundreds more fled into the inaccessible mountainous border region with Argentina or to Argentina itself. The prisoners were bound and marched toward the city of Temuco. Many never arrived. Instead, they were executed, their bodies thrown into the Bío Bío river. In effect, they became Chile's first *detenidos-desaparecidos*, disappeared detainees, in one of the worst massacres in Chilean history. In this case, as during other moments of violent repression in Chile, both the massacre committed by the *carabineros* and violent acts committed by rebels were covered by a series of government-declared amnesties.[1]

The 1973 military coup and the seventeen-year dictatorship of Augusto Pinochet are often viewed as aberrations in Chile's twentieth-century history of multiparty democracy and institutional stability unusual in Latin

America. However, viewed from the provinces of the southern frontier, the violence that accompanied the agrarian reform and socialist revolution of the 1960s and early 1970s, and the brutal military dictatorship that put an end to this period of reform and revolution, become more intelligible. In this essay, I argue that the Ránquil rebellion and its repression were not atypical and, indeed, provide an important lens on the long-ignored history of peasant politics in Chile's southern frontier, roughly the huge territory south of the Bío Bío river. The violence unleashed by the state against the Ránquil rebels, while extreme, was part of a broader pattern of violence enacted by local elites and the military against both Mapuche and mestizo peasants during the constitution of the hacienda in Chile's southern provinces.[2]

Viewed from the south, the Chilean state appears far less stable and democratic during the twentieth century. As late as the mid-twentieth century, the state had only the most tenuous administrative and coercive control over its southern frontier, which comprised fully a third of Chile's national territory. Similarly, unlike central Chile—where the power of the hacienda was deeply entrenched, despite episodic challenges from the rural labor movement until the agrarian reform of the 1960s—land and labor relations in southern Chile were contentious, and the legal, spatial, and social boundaries of the landed estate were under constant incursion from both mestizo and Mapuche peasants. In central Chile, *inquilinaje* (resident estate labor) remained a stable system of paternalistically managed resident estate labor until the agrarian reform of the 1960s, and *inquilinos* (estate laborers) composed the most conservative sector of the rural labor force. In southern Chile, however, beginning in the early twentieth century, rural social relations, including *inquilinaje*, were characterized by significant levels of conflict and violence. The uprising of Lonquimay's *ocupantes* (squatters or land occupants without titles), *colonos* (settlers with titles), inquilinos, and members of Mapuche communities had its origin in a decades-long history of confrontations of landowner authority in which rural laborers and smallholders invaded estates and occupied their land, invoking frontier land's "public" status and their rights as putative colonos. In the south, at least, neither the hacienda nor the state enjoyed hegemony; both relied on violence to maintain their rule.

While the Communist Party and the FOCH played a role in organizing campesinos in Lonquimay, their activities cannot be seen as the sole, or even the determining, cause of rural unrest. Read in terms of the broader context of rural social relations, the Ránquil uprising is better understood as one of many violent conflicts that swept southern Chile during the 1920s and 1930s, and that embraced both mestizo and Mapuche transient seasonal and day laborers, squatters, smallholders, members of Mapuche communities, and estate laborers, often acting together in opposition to large landowners.

The Colonization of Chile's Southern Frontier

The southern third of modern Chile, south of the Bío Bío river, did not become part of national territory until the defeat of independent Mapuche groups during the 1880s. While other Latin American states under liberal rule initiated the division and privatization of communally held indigenous land, Chile introduced the colonial policy of *reducción*—literally reducing Mapuche groups to small, circumscribed settlements or communities—and separate legal codes that, at least on paper, made indigenous land inalienable. The state set out to transform the frontier by settling the defeated Mapuche on *reducciones*, auctioning large tracts of land to private individuals and colonization companies, and promoting the settlement of the "vacant" lands once controlled by the Mapuche with European immigrants. The Mapuche, who had controlled territory south of the Bío Bío river until the 1860s, were literally reduced to small settlements organized around male-headed family lines.[3]

During the 1880s, 1890s, and early 1900s, the state relinquished hundreds of thousands of hectares of public land, most covered by rainforest, to private landowners and colonization companies, who established enormous estates. A 1911 congressional commission on colonization noted that as first the military and then the railroad advanced to the provinces furthest south, bringing with them "pacification, industrial progress, and rising land values," interest in acquiring property also grew, and with it the "abusive deforcement of public property; the dispossession of indigenous property, the indeterminacy of boundaries, the fraudulent altering of these boundaries, . . . the preparation of artificial property titles, . . . fictitious contracts, simulated partitions, fraudulent land registrations, etc."[4] The commission found that because of widespread fraud by land speculators, estate owners, and colonization companies, the state had lost large "extensions of land that undeniably belonged to it."[5] While most colonization companies brought only a few European immigrants to Chile, they built large empires of tens of thousands of hectares.[6]

In Lonquimay, the formation of large landed estates followed this pattern of speculation and fraud. The haciendas occupied by peasants during the Ránquil revolt had been formed during the process of colonization and then quickly sold to Francisco Puelma. As minister of war in 1881, Puelma helped to negotiate a key border treaty with Argentina. Perhaps not coincidently, the final border included the land he had purchased in the valley of Lonquimay by making the head of the surrounding rivers (an unusual "natural" border), rather than the peaks of the cordillera, the dividing line between the two countries. Puelma claimed all the land in the valley of Lonquimay that fell to Chile following the treaty. The Chilean government then pressured Puelma to provide lands in his dominion to settle some of the thousands of Chilean peasants who had migrated to Argentina after being expelled from their small plots during colonization. While some of Lonquimay's land was returned to the state for the purposes of colonization, Puelma negotiated a thirty-year lease to five large *fundos*, Rahué (28,000 hectares), Chilpaco (19,739 hectares), Ránquil (37,625 hectares), Lolco (41,791 hectares), and Vilcura (51,607 hectares).

In 1901, Puelma's heirs received titles to the fundos in Lonquimay in an agreement struck by the inspector general of colonization, Agustín Baeza, and the legal representative of the Puelma estate, the then minister of colonization and Baeza's boss, Eliodoro Yáñez. Nobody mentioned any apparent conflict of interest. Nor did anyone seem to notice that, as with so many of the frontier's fundos, the boundaries established in the new titles in 1901 actually differed from the boundaries defined in the original titles by including large extensions of public land that Francisco Puelma had rented from the state, beginning in 1889. By the beginning of the twentieth century, the Puelma family had laid claim to an empire of over 100,000 hectares.[7]

The transfer of frontier land to colonization companies, large landowners, and land speculators led to the expulsion of thousands of Mapuche and mestizo peasants and resulted in their exodus to Argentina or into the stateless valleys of the cordillera along the border. In Lonquimay, Mapuche groups were settled on small reducciones. Many joined mestizo peasants who migrated to Argentina in search of jobs on *estancias* (ranches) or found work on the region's haciendas as inquilinos and *jornaleros* (day laborers). Both mestizo and Mapuche peasants also moved onto marginal public lands high up in the cordillera, where they scraped out an existence as squatter ocupantes, farming, pasturing livestock, and gathering forest products in the native araucaria forests. By the first decade of the twentieth century the population of Chilean peasants across the border in Argentina reached thirty thousand. Nationalists like Nicolás Palacios and social reformers like Malaquías Concha denounced this migration as a threat to Chilean national sovereignty on the southern frontier.[8] In addition, as members of the parliamentary commission warned, two decades before the Ránquil rebellion, the expulsions of Chilean peasants by "land sharks" had led to "the fermentation of class struggle born of the hatred of the poor for the rich. . . . [T]hese people oppressed by the large landowners . . . begin to have . . . those ideas that lead to social convulsion."[9]

From early on, violence directed at indigenous communities and Chilean peasants during the colonization of the frontier was widespread. In 1903, the Inspectorate of Lands and Colonization described the various methods employed by private parties to steal indigenous lands: "In distant places, far from the vigilance of the authorities, individuals who are involved in trafficking alcohol and who have installed themselves on the lands of indios commit murders and abuses. . . . In the rural communes where the Protectorate of Indians only has a weak presence the mayor, the subdelegate, and the judge of the subdelegation conspire together to exploit the indios, stealing their lands."[10] Local tax collectors imposed excessive taxes on reducciones, at times fabricating tax bills and collecting up to ten times the legal tax. Drowning in debt, communities lost their crops, tools, animals, and even their land. As an Inspectorate report observed, local courts were often complicit in the schemes to appropriate indigenous lands: "In these courts they wickedly defraud the natives, often charging them with supposed debts."[11]

Violence was commonly used to acquire land, livestock, and harvests. As one report stated: "There are many people identified in Valdivia as having assassinated indios with the goal of taking their lands . . . and investigations are never carried out to clear up the cases, but, I can confirm, these are wealthy owners of considerable extensions of lands that were once occupied by the indios."[12] Another report observed that "very frequently the country's press reports in its columns on the murders of indigenous people whose authors . . . enjoy the most absolute impunity." Landowners would also kidnap and torture Mapuches, forcing them to sign over their lands or intimidating them into abandoning their lands.[13] In addition, landowners encroached on indigenous lands by pushing their fences into reducciones, clearing forests, often with fire, on the reducciones, and establishing possession of the land. It was common, the protector of Indians for Valdivia and Llanquihue reported, "to find the families of indios living in miserable *rucas* [huts] . . . surrounded entirely by the plantings and crops of some usurper. . . . Fire is so common that there have been cases in which the flames have devoured in one day the extension of forty *cuadras*, six houses, leaving unsheltered thirty-six people, including old people, women, and children."[14] Another report noted that these transgressions of Mapuche reducciones were, for the most part, the work of the "large wheat and timber producers."[15]

Landowner violence and fraud was also directed at poor colonos and ocupantes, both mestizo and Mapuche. According to one 1913 report by the Land Measurement Office, large estate owners, availing themselves of false titles, frequently dislodged and expelled colonos who had cleared and prepared lands for planting: "It is impossible to erase from memory the desolate image of the expulsion of the colono and his family. To burn his house, destroy his crop, and raze everything." The colonos, the report noted, suffered under the burden of constant uncertainty since any day someone with a false title could evict them from the lands they had cleared and cultivated.[16] The report observed that large landowners relied on the fact that state authorities enjoyed only a weak presence and could not oppose the registration of their titles in the Conservador de Bienes Raíces (property title registry) "even when they had no material possession of the land in the title."[17] In 1906, the Inspectorate of Lands and Colonization reported that many large landowners had purchased land from colonos and ocupantes, who chose to sell their rights under the threat of expulsion, and then were left as *arrendatarios* (renters) or inquilinos.[18] Throughout the south, government reports observed, the expansion of the large estate onto land cleared by colonos had led to "disputes that at times degenerate into bloody conflicts. . . . The class struggle in this region has reached its highest point."[19]

As early as 1913, poor mestizo and Mapuche peasants had begun to organize collective movements to claim land they viewed as public from large estates and colonization companies. A typical case was the fundo Pellahuén in Imperial and Cañete, where a bloody battle erupted between colonos and ocupantes on one side and carabineros on the other. The Pellahuén estate had been purchased in 1889 by Jervasio Alarcón from Estéban Freire without any defined boundaries other than rivers and estuaries, which as the Conservative Party deputy Emilio Claro pointed out, allowed Alarcón to expand his recently purchased estate by a number of leagues.

When an administrative change shifted one of the subdelegations the estate was located in from Cañete to Imperial, the reregistration of the property expanded its boundaries to include a number of places occupied by around fifteen hundred peasants or *ocupantes nacionales*, many of them who worked in the region's native forests and saw the wood they cut, as well as their harvests, lost to Alarcón, the nominally new owner of the land. In 1913, Alarcón had rented Pellahuén to Manuel A. Ríos, who threatened to take the land and harvests of the ocupantes and colonos on the estate. When the peasants resisted by occupying the estate land, Alarcón called on his brother, Matías Alarcón, the governor of Imperial, to provide carabineros to evict the peasants, leading to a bloody conflict, described by Claro as "a true battle between an armed force and an enormous group of men, women, and children. Some poor colonos nacionales who had been born and lived in those places that they had made fertile with their sweat, clearing the forest and making the land apt for cultivation, irrigated the land with their blood." The governor's action on behalf of the putative landowner, his brother, was rebuked by the province's intendant as well as the regional and national press, and deputies like Claro, but little was done and the caribineros remained stationed on the estate, in effect a police force in the service of Alarcón and Ríos.[20] This case, like the case of the Puelma estates in Lonquimay, made clear the central role of Chile's small ruling political and landholding class in the formation of enormous haciendas on the frontier, and its use of state power, including regional and local authorities and carabineros, to dispossess mestizo smallholders and Mapuche communities.

Inquilinaje and Rural Labor Relations

For most of Chile's late colonial and modern history, inquilinaje shaped rural labor and property relations. Large estates in central Chile enjoyed a monopoly of arable lands, gradually expelling Mapuche and mestizo peasants over the course of the nineteenth and twentieth centuries. The estates relied on a large population of landless peasants to fill their labor requirements. Inquilinos worked as full-time tenant laborers in exchange for access to small plots of land. Depending on the terms of the contract or agreement established with the inquilinos, *patrones* (landowners) provided seeds, tools, animals, land for crops and pasture, and occasionally even wages to their workers in exchange for their labor. It was not unusual for labor agreements to include inquilinos' entire families, and at times contracts stipulated that inquilionos' children provide labor to the estate. Landowners also established institutions that buttressed their paternalist control of their tenant laborers: chapels, rudimentary health clinics, and *pulperías*, or company stores, at which inquilinos usually built up large debts, thus adding an element of debt-peonage to tenant farming arrangements. Landowners' control of estate labor reinforced their political power. Until electoral reforms in 1958 established the secret ballot and penalties for fraud, adult male laborers provided valuable votes for their patrones' favored candidates. Landowners consecrated the paternalist dimension of their political control by holding fiestas, barbecues, and rodeos for their workers during political campaigns and elections.

In southern Chile, landowners sought to reproduce the paternalist veneer of labor relations. The Puelmas held fiestas and rodeos for their inquilinos during slaughtering season, when the animals were brought in from pasture, and distributed food and aguardiente. During the Ránquil rebellion *El Mercurio*, for example, recalled a visit to the Puelma estates some years earlier, when it had reported on the rodeos and peaceful relations between inquilinos and patrones.[21] In his memoirs, Henry Fahrenkrog Reinhold, an administrator of the Puelma estates, expressed a similar nostalgia for a day of harmonious relations between patrones and inquilinos and a similar confusion about the explosion of violence that accompanied the revolt in his memoirs. Fahrenkrog, like *El Mercurio*, recalled rodeos, fiestas, and a golden era of peace and prosperity. He located the blame for the rebellion on Communist "outside agitators."[22] For many observers, including *El Mercurio* and the region's deputy, Arturo Huenchullán, the rebels were not inquilinos, but colonos and ocupantes from outside Lonquimay who had invaded the region's estates.[23] To recognize the rebels as inquilinos would call into question the claims made by landowners to paternalist beneficence.

Inquilinaje served landowners as a means of establishing claims to large tracts of unoccupied land. They hired inquilinos and *inquilinos-medieros* (estate laborers–sharecroppers) as well as arrendatarios, to clear and cultivate public land, which they then claimed as their property because of their rights of material possession and because they had introduced "improvements."

These laborers tended to be far less permanent than their counterparts in central Chile, where families might work for generations on a single estate. As George McBride observed in 1936, in the frontier region, "There is no such fixed population as that characterizing the agricultural regions of the center. There are few inquilinos proper in the south. Much of the labor is secured only as needed, particularly at wheat harvest. It is supplied largely by migrant harvest hands."[24]

In addition, inquilinaje became a key tactic by which large landowners expanded their estates onto Mapuche reducciones and public land occupied by mestizo and Mapuche peasant smallholders and colonos. Landowners would enter into contracts of inquilinaje with their poor neighbors, whose small plots provided insufficient land for their animals and crops. In these contracts, often signed with thumbprints by illiterate Mapuche and mestizo peasants, the borders of the estate were ingeniously expanded to include the peasants' small plots in the description of the inquilinos' duties. The contract was then proffered as evidence of the estate's legal ownership of land that had once belonged to their laborers, who were then allowed to occupy their old plots as inquilinos. As one government report noted, "They pasture animals on the victim's own lands, they give him a small sum of money as an advance, and charge him with caring for the animals."[25] Contracts of inquilinaje were often used in court to prove that a colono or a Mapuche did not, in fact, have rights to their plots since, rather than colonos or members of reducciones, they were only inquilinos, the dependants of the landowner.[26] Landowners acquired at once both cleared, arable land and an inexpensive labor force to work it.

In 1939, the General Directorate of Lands and Colonization reported on a number of anomalies in the colonization of the frontier. In commenting on the colonization law's provision requiring material possession of land as a prerequisite for a legal title, the memo noted that "it is not enough to pay the taxes on the land . . . because in some cases the lands are full of ocupantes. Nor is it enough to obtain permission to clear the land by fire or to have contracts of inquilinaje with ocupantes who do not know how to sign their names and who by use of their thumbprint authorize a labor contract whose content and consequence they do not know and who are then expelled maliciously." The Directorate noted that peasant ocupantes were frequently enticed to sign contracts of inquilinaje that they did not understand by the promise of a full resolution of their land claims in exchange for small sums of money. The claims were, in fact, resolved, but in favor of the landowners who, contracts of inquilinaje in hand, proceeded to evict their new laborers from their small plots.[27]

Landowners' manipulation of inquilinaje to acquire the land and labor of poor peasants meant that the institution was far less stable on the frontier than in central Chile. Inquilinos were, for the most part, former smallholders (ocupantes or colonos) or members of Mapuche reducciones whose memories of dispossession were quite fresh. In addition, many inquilinos had been installed on public frontier land as a way for land speculators and landowners to demonstrate material possession. Estate owners frequently lived in towns and left their haciendas in the charge of managers (*mayordomos*). Inquilinos had little contact with their patrones. As McBride noted, "Where laborers live on large farms they bear little of the traditional relation to the patron that exists in central Chile."[28] In Lonquimay, the Puelmas left their estates in the charge of mayordomos and visited for only two weeks a year during slaughtering season.[29] Rural laborers nourished an understanding that they had earned rights to public land because they, not the estate owners, had done the work of clearing forest and planting crops and grasses for livestock.

Numerous cases of collusion between landowners and carabineros in disciplining and repressing their estate workers reflect the violence that lay at the core of landowners' precarious and often fraudulent control of their property. Regional newspapers and court cases reflect patterns of landowner violence. In May 1934, for example, *El Diario Austral* led with the headline: "Medieval tortures were revived in order to kill a poor inquilino." The article described the horrible torture and then execution of an inquilino by a landowner. The inquilino had been accused of stealing sheep.[30] That same year military courts heard a number of cases of carabineros accused of detaining inquilinos and jornaleros at the behest of patrones.[31] In one case, a laborer testified that "because of a calumny against me [for stealing a lamb] by my patrón . . . I was detained by carabineros, who locked me in a storehouse [on the hacienda]."[32] Similarly, in 1932, the intendant of Cautín reported that a *mediero* (sharecropper) on the Quilongo estate had reported that the landowners frequently punished their inquilinos by placing irons on their legs, and, "what is even more serious, they do this with the knowledge of the *cabo* (corporal) *de carabineros*."[33]

In Lonquimay, relations between patrones and inquilinos deteriorated rapidly during the 1920s. President Carlos Ibáñez, for example, wrote a telegram to the intendant of Cautín that "the government has concrete information about the true exploitation that inquilinos and smallholders are subjected to by some unscrupulous merchants. The sale of harvests before they are ripe at usurious prices or in exchange for alcoholic beverages or articles of basic necessity and the concession of small credits in exchange for a collateral of the animals belonging to the debtor . . . to then expropriate them under any pretext are the most common and irritating forms in which this exploitation is carried out."[34] In another telegram, Ibáñez noted, "According to the information that I have, in Lonquimay and Alto Bío-Bío there does not exist any respect for the rights of the local population or the inquilinos of the estates and the free transit on public roads has been cut off. The government believes that the increase of the population is important in the regions of the cordillera and does not accept the violation of labor laws and the most elemental rights of men."[35] For Ibáñez, the lack of any state administrative presence in Alto Bío-Bío and Lonquimay had allowed landowners and merchants to operate virtual empires in which both inquilinos and colono smallholders were bound to the estates by debt and coercion.

Political Reform and Peasant Mobilization during the 1920s

The election of Arturo Alessandri to the presidency in 1920 provided a political opening for an explosion of rural unrest in southern Chile. Alessandri's populist campaigns and a military coup by mid-level officers committed to social reform in 1925 created new political spaces for urban and rural workers. Social reforms implemented in 1924–25 provided the framework for Chile's first labor relations system by legalizing unions and the right to strike and institutionalizing state regulation of working conditions and collective bargaining. In 1927, another military coup brought Carlos Ibáñez to the presidency. While Ibáñez, like Alessandri before him, frequently used the military to repress workers' strikes, he also implemented a number of key reforms, including the creation of a labor code (1931), which brought together the 1924 laws and a 1927–28 Southern Property Law that was designed to create a stable property regime out of the infinite lawsuits and violent conflicts in southern Chile by establishing the ownership rights of those in material possession of land as a fundamental legal principle. In addition, the Ibáñez government created the Agricultural Colonization Fund to purchase and subdivide large estates on the frontier and distribute the land to peasants—the first step on what would be a long road to agrarian reform in Chile.

The Southern Property Law required that those who occupied land provide titles and maps in petitions for definitive titles in order to ensure that property claims "did not damage the interests of the state." Beyond resolving decades of struggles over southern land, the law sought to "establish what lands belong to [the state] and what lands belong to private parties, and to form a cadastral map on a solid and certain basis."[36] In addition, the law was designed to regularize the regime of property in the south in response to complaints by landowners who had difficulty in obtaining credit and establishing the legitimacy of their titles "because the courts do not fully recognize the legality of the titles to the immense majority of lands located [in the south]."[37] Ill-defined and illegitimate properties had impeded the economic development of the frontier. The law also permitted the state to redistribute land occupied and cultivated before January 1, 1921, by peasant ocupantes. The goal was to increase production and foment a large population of smallholders, "thus combating pernicious social doctrines." The law, at least in letter, offered thousands of peasant ocupantes on the frontier the possibility of gaining legal title to their small plots.[38]

The Southern Property Law built on earlier laws designed to halt the widespread fraud that had accompanied large land concessions and to "Chileanize" the frontier by repatriating peasants who had fled to Argentina and settling them as *colonos nacionales* (national colonists or settlers). In fact, as early as the late nineteenth century, the Puelma family had negotiated an agreement with the government in which it agreed to allow Chileans repatriated from Argentina to settle as colonos on some of the land it controlled in Lonquimay, while it maintained rental rights to the five estates for which it held a thirty-year lease. In 1908, new colonization legislation had established that public lands would be made available to Chilean colonos who filled certain legal requirements: they had to be "fathers of families," and literate, and they had to clear, fence, and cultivate the land granted them. The 1911 congressional investigation of the constitution of property on the frontier also added fuel to the state's project of reacquiring public land lost to speculators and concessionaires and settling landless Chilean peasants on the frontier. The 1908 colonization law and the 1911 report to congress provided peasants a political and legal language with which to phrase their demands for land. Landless peasants and squatters could assert their rights as Chilean colonos to land on estates that had once been public by invoking the state's interest in recouping land lost during the first wave of colonization, promoting economic development, and Chileanizing the frontier.

More than specific policies or laws, however, the political climate of the 1920s led to an eruption of conflicts over labor and land on the frontier. Members of the Radical, Democratic, and Communist Parties began to call for rural unionization and to critique the vast inequalities in landholding, as well as the fraudulent constitution of haciendas on the frontier that had been highlighted by the 1911 parliamentary commission's report. During the 1920s, critiques of the hacienda became more frequent. In 1927, for example, attacks on southern haciendas were even taken up by the minister of development, who observed that "the economic life of the South was detained" because "the greater part of the land was out of production." The "profound error" of entrusting settlement of the frontier to colonization companies had led to the "formation of the *latifundio* and the stagnation of agricultural production, because only one hand cannot be assigned the exploitation of thousands of hectares."[39]

By the 1920s, then, inquilinos' sense that they had been expelled unjustly from public land, or that they enjoyed rights to public land based on their material occupation, was reinforced by new political movements for social reform, including state policies designed to redress the abuses that had occurred during the process of colonization. Throughout the 1920s and early 1930s, rural workers, organized at times in unions, increasingly thwarted the power of landowners and began to demand their rights to the lands they worked. Inquilinos, medieros, arrendatarios, and colonos occupied land on estates and public land claiming that they had the right to be settled as colonos. They had cleared forests, made the soil productive, and contributed to national progress, while the landowners, who often resided in distant cities, had left their lands idle. Peasants, both Mapuche and mestizo, invoked customary rights to public forests and land, drawing on their rights as citizens to land they defined as public.

In 1925, for example, inquilinos and jornaleros employed by the Cancha Rayada estate in Llanquihue petitioned to establish a colony on Cancha Rayada named for the Democratic Party senator Artemio Gutiérrez. As the minister of lands and colonization noted, "a number of these inquilinos or *contratistas* (contractors), in spite of having signed contracts of inquilinaje, have petitioned the government for the status of colonos nacionales."

The rebellious inquilinos claimed that the land was public and that the nineteenth-century titles were invalid.[40] In another notable case the following year, Mapuche and mestizo peasants, many of whom had been hired as inquilinos or jornaleros, organized a cooperative and occupied two thousand hectares of the infamous forty-thousand-hectare concession made to Luis Silva Rivas in Llaima. In the words of a government forester, the ocupantes were "armed and disposed to resist any effort to evict them."[41] The ocupantes were particularly angered by Silva Rivas's ruthless exploitation of the native forests that they relied on for subsistence and defined as public. In a petition to the Ministry of Lands they wrote: "Three years ago Silva Rivas installed sawmills in Cunco and they are exploiting the forests of *raulí* that are becoming rare in our country." The ocupantes contended, "It is illegal to exploit lands that belong to the government, province, and country."

By 1929 the movement of inquilinos and squatters who claimed the lands of southern estates had reached such large proportions that the intendant of Llanquihue and Chiloé wrote the minister of lands and colonization of "the absolute necessity of authorizing representatives of the government to proceed energetically with all those individuals . . . who have introduced themselves on *fundos* [estates] that belong to others or who, as simple inquilinos, have transformed themselves into the owners of their patrones' lands, becoming *inquilinos alzados*."[42] Throughout Cautín, a report from the Ministry of Development noted, "motivated by the Southern Property Law, a number of people have dedicated themselves today to introducing propaganda among the inquilinos on estates to convince them that said law concedes them property rights to the land they work."[43] Similarly, the government Agricultural Colonization Fund complained of an "uprising of inquilinos ocupantes on estates it had purchased in Cautín."[44] In 1930, the Osorno office of the Ministry of Southern Property similarly reported that on a number of haciendas outside the city inquilinos had revolted against their patrones, claiming that the estates sat on public land. According to the Osorno office, "The inquilinos . . . oppose their patrón, whom they had respected and recognized until yesterday, calling themselves ocupantes of public lands."[45] Inquilinos also increasingly engaged in work stoppages and strikes and their deference to landowner authority diminished noticeably. On the Long-Long estate in Cautín, for example, the landowner, Lamoliatte, reported with alarm that a group of workers were preventing "the normal development of labor in the fields" and "maintaining an active campaign of agitation on the estate." These workers, he reported, "do not show the consideration and respect that they owe to the patrón."[46] The inquilinos, according to police reports, had protested low salaries, as well as an order from the landowner that no worker could leave or enter the estate without authorization and a pass.

Rebellious inquilinos were joined by both Mapuche and mestizo squatters who occupied land on estates that they claimed was public. In 1925, for example, the Sociedad Colonizadora de Llanquihue petitioned the government to send in a surveyor to measure an estate that it had purchased at auction. A large group of "armed persons" had taken possession of the land.[47] In Cautín, the owner of the San Juan de Trovolhue estate wrote the intendant of Cautín: "Lately, with the implementation of the laws on the Constitution of Southern Property . . . my estate, along with a number of other estates in the region have been invaded by a considerable number of audacious ocupantes and *indígenas* who are trying to take possession of my estate without any right."[48] A very similar petition was sent to the intendant by the owners of the Las Ñiochas estate in Imperial, who denounced a land invasion by "numerous groups of indígenas" as well as "some Chilean individuals."[49] And on the Toltén ranching and logging estate, also in Cautín, the minister of the interior reported on the "violent occupations by individuals who claim rights to the land."[50]

In Lonquimay, in 1928, inquilinos and jornaleros who had worked on fundos belonging to the Puelma family for at least two generations and colonos, many repatriated from Argentina at the beginning of the century in the deal struck between the Puelma family and the Chilean government, organized a similar movement to claim land on the region's large estates. They formed the Sindicato Agrícola Lonquimay and petitioned the government for the expropriation of land on the Puelma family's estates. The campesinos were aided by Juan Segundo Leiva Tapia, a schoolteacher and part-time lawyer who had been raised in Lonquimay and in Neuquén on the Argentine side of the border.[51] Leiva had studied the Southern Property Law and understood that the Puelma family did not have legal title to their estates. Because of the material possession enjoyed by both inquilinos and ocupantes the estates could be legally purchased by the Agricultural Colonization Fund and redistributed to those who worked the land. Shortly after the organization of the union, Leiva traveled to Santiago to meet with

President Carlos Ibáñez to request land to colonize and a school. Ibáñez was sympathetic to the union and pledged support for its goals and philosophy, summed up in the slogan "Populate, produce, and civilize."[52]

Despite the union's moderate platform and support from the president, landowners in Lonquimay denounced Leiva and protested that the union was inciting inquilinos in the region to claim estate land as their own. The governor of Victoria noted in a memo that Leiva "has been accused of making subversive or disruptive propaganda among the inquilinos of the Rahue, Villacura, Lolco, Cilpazo, and Ránquil estates, making the inquilinos believe that the lands that they occupy are public and that they have the right to take possession of them, which leads them to disobey their patrones."[53] In 1929, the intendant of Cautín instructed carabineros in Lonquimay to be vigilant, saying, "We have received denunciations of uprisings of inquilinos on the estates of the Puelma Tuppers and others in Lonquimay."[54] By 1931, government reports began to note with alarm that the more than four hundred members of the union, who were once "peaceful and hardworking people," "are today in rebellion [sublevados], they do not obey anyone and they live in an independent Chile under the authority of no one."[55] A year earlier, another major landowner in the region, Martín Bunster Gómez, had requested that carabineros be sent to quell an uprising on his Guayalí estate. According to Bunster, he had received a court order in the city of Los Angeles to have a number of inquilinos, many of them active in the union, expelled from the estate, but they had remained and continued to occupy and cultivate land on the estate independent of his authority.[56]

Yet, although there were accusations of "communist" and "subversive" ideas, no report identified the unions' leaders as from the Communist Party. The influence of political parties in the formation of the union is unclear, but the presence of the Democratic Party, rather than the Communist Party, in the region's politics and in the union's leadership early on was pronounced. One of the union's major supporters, Lonquimay's *El Comercio*, was published by one its original organizers, Froilán Rivera, and was clearly affiliated or aligned with the Democratic Party.[57] Juan Segundo Leiva Tapia wrote frequent columns in the paper. Other members of the Sindicato Agrícola were also members of the Democratic Party. The union's president, until he died in late 1933, was Luis Abelino Astroza Dávila, a member of the Democratic Party.[58] And one of the union's founders and its treasurer was a local merchant and owner of a store on one of the region's estates, Bruno Ackermann, a German immigrant whose political ideas were rooted in German cooperativism, rather than socialism. Indeed, as late as 1931, the union leaders declared that the goal of the union was to colonize public land, the Ránquil estate, and establish "legal cooperatives" of settlers.[59]

In response to protests of the members of the Sindicato Agrícola Lonquimay against a 1929 decree that legalized the Puelma's titles under the Southern Property Law, the director of the Lands Department, Ernesto Maldonado, traveled to Lonquimay to investigate the situation on the ground and was warmly welcomed by the union's leaders and members. He informed the president, Carlos Ibáñez, that, in fact, the titles did not appear to be too "clean" and that it might be a good idea to rectify the situation so as to avoid "the serious consequences the decree . . . would produce for the peace of the ocupantes and their families."[60] On March 27, 1930, Ibáñez issued a decree that named a commission to study the question of the Puelma fundos. Juan Segundo Leiva was named a member of the commission.

After two months the commission presented a report favorable to the Sindicato Agrícola Lonquimay that resulted in another decree (decreto número 1730, July 31, 1930). According to this decree, the 1901 land titles did not correspond to the original 1863 titles and, in fact, "deprived the state of enormous extensions of land." The decree recouped 30,000 hectares of land that had been illicitly incorporated into the Puelma estate in 1901. However, this still left 139,362 hectares on the five fundos in the hands of Puelma's heirs and the new owners to whom they had sold the Lolco property. The decree divided the Ránquil estate into two parts: 7,000 hectares for the Puelma heirs and 30,000 hectares for 130 families of ocupantes, many of them former inquilinos.[61] In addition, the Ibáñez government founded the first town in the region, the pueblo named 23 de Enero, with the requisite political and administrative apparatuses, an assertion of the state's presence in a zone where the Puelma family had reigned since the late nineteenth century. This victory was consolidated when the following year another decree (decreto número 258, May 20, 1931) expropriated 4,000 hectares of the 22,860-hectare Guayalí estate for the purposes of settling the many ocupantes in the region.[62]

The support of Ibáñez was essential and speaks to the populist nature of his government. Despite initiating a wave of repression against organized labor and the Communist Party, Ibáñez intervened to support the legal status of the Sindicato Agrícola Lonquimay, one of the first legal peasant unions in Chile. Over the protestations of the Social Welfare Office in

Temuco, Ibáñez ordered the intendant of Cautín to register the Sindicato and he named its director, Leiva, "a well-intentioned and patriotic man," as *subdelegado*. In addition, Ibáñez demanded from local officials reports on the causes of conflicts between landowners and the union, the release from prison of a union leader, Benjamín Cáceres, and an investigation of those who "maintain in that zone a situation of injustice and abuse the poor."[63]

The success of the Sindicato Agrícola Lonquimay in petitioning for the expropriation of hacienda land in Lonquimay culminated a broader movement of rural laborers and smallholders to claim public frontier land and land appropriated by large estates during colonization. Lonquimay was not unique. Following the Southern Property Law and the creation of the Agricultural Colonization Fund, the state began to purchase land on a small number of large estates in southern Chile and distributed the land to peasant colonos, perhaps the first step on what would be a long and often violent road to agrarian reform and the dismantlement of the hacienda in Chile.[64]

Thermador and Political Retrenchment during the 1930s

When Arturo Alessandri returned to the presidency in 1932, following the fall of the Ibáñez regime and a series of short-lived governments, he began a concerted campaign to shore up the old social and economic order. Alessandri backed conservative economic policies with rigorous repression of workers' movements in cities and mining districts, as well as peasant movements in the countryside. The reform of the system of colonization and land ownership in the south introduced under Ibáñez was quickly halted. The new administration sought to push back the challenge to the rule of the hacienda and put a lid on the militant movements for land redistribution. In the case of Lonquimay, a 1932 report by the Alessandri-appointed governor of Victoria noted with alarm that the leaders of the Sindicato Agrícola Lonquimay "have incited the inquilinaje on the cordillera's estates to disobey their patrones under the pretext that they have usurped public land; they have made the inquilinos believe that . . . they, as the people who actually live on the land, will be legally recognized as in material possession of public land and will have the right to titles."[65]

Southern landowners seized the opportunity presented by Alessandri's political about-face to initiate a counteroffensive against the region's rural laborers. In March 1933, for example, landowners held a large meeting in

Angol to hear the report of a commission that had traveled to Santiago to discuss the situation of southern agriculture. The meeting was motivated by a deep sense of concern about the state of labor relations on the region's estates. The landowners present at the meeting denounced "the usurpation of private properties by inquilinos and medieros on the region's estates, who, instigated by a few professional agitators, refuse to recognize the authority and rights of the patrón with the false pretext that they are occupying public lands. And they violently resist accepting the conditions that they agreed to with their patrones."[66]

The Angol meeting was part of a broader campaign by landowners to reassert the authority of the patrón over land and labor relations in the south. In January 1933, for example, the recently founded Socialist Party's Socialist Colonization Central sent a letter to southern newspapers denouncing a wave of expulsions of ocupantes or *aspirantes de colonos* (settlers) and colonos. According to the Central, large concessions and estates had burned the houses and taken the lands of thousands of colonos throughout southern Chile. That same month a surveyor from the office of the Ministry of Lands and Colonization traveled to Temuco to look into a wave of expulsions of rural laborers instigated by colonization companies and estates, especially the Budi and Toltén logging and livestock companies.[67] In April 1934, the Socialist Party paper, *La Opinión*, published a letter from the Socialist Colonization Central about "the problem of southern land." The Central had spent three years "tirelessly demonstrating to the authorities . . . the problems of colonization and the ocupantes of land . . . who from time immemorial have been cultivating the soil."[68] According to the Central, colonos and ocupantes who had worked for years clearing and cultivating lands "in the middle of the jungle, in inclement weather," were being evicted by the owners of large concessions who enjoyed the support of regional authorities.[69]

The Alessandri government's effort to restore social order in the southern countryside was expressed in a report by the minister of the interior to the intendant of Cautín. The minister noted the "serious problems produced by the acts of [land] invasion. . . . In the region of the South agricultural labor is suffering disturbances, and in some parts, the harvests, already begun, will be very difficult for this reason. These individuals violate the right to private property and disrupt the public order." The minister instructed the intendant to send carabineros to expel rebellious workers and squatters from southern estate lands and to work with the Servicio de

Investigaciones (the Chilean equivalent of the FBI) to investigate the "instigators" and "professional agitators" who provoked land "usurpations."[70] That same year, Juan Segundo Leiva Tapia was arrested and sent into internal exile for six months to the islands of Guaytecas and Chiloé because of his membership in the FOCH and his attendance, as a FOCH delegate, at the international conference of the Communist Confederación Sindical Latino Americana in Montevideo.[71] Leiva had moved back and forth across the cordillera clandestinely in the company of the Communist Party leader, Elías Lafertte. Between 1930, when he was aligned with the Democratic Party and appointed subdelegate by Ibáñez, and 1933, when he traveled to the Montevideo conference with Lafertte, Leiva had moved to the left to an alliance with the Communist Party. Perhaps the growing presence of the FOCH in the region as a major ally of the Sindicato Agrícola Lonquimay, and perhaps the repression unleashed by landowners with the support of the Alessandri government against the rural labor movement, perhaps both, contributed to the radicalization of Leiva and the union leadership, which changed in 1933 to reflect a more leftist identity.[72] In early 1933, after his return from internal exile, Leiva began to employ radical and revolutionary language in interviews and articles published in *El Comercio*, though his rhetoric did not stay strictly in line with the positions and ideology of the Communist Party.[73]

Indeed, the radicalization of rural politics in the south was not exclusively channeled through the Communist Party. The presence of the Socialist Party, organized in 1933, also played a role in the, at times, violent conflicts between rural laborers and large landowners on the frontier. In March 1934, only a few months before the Ránquil rebellion, an armed conflict erupted southwest of the city of Temuco, where the Socialist Colonization Committee had worked for a number of years to resettle two hundred colonos and ocupantes on public land claimed by the Compañía Ganadera y Agrícola Toltén. The company had used force to expel Mapuche and mestizo peasants from their land and burned their *rucas* (huts) and harvests. The ocupantes had demanded that they be settled as colonos on the company's land, invoking the Southern Property Law.[74] They held secret meetings in hidden valleys covered by the company's forests, on the run from the private forest guards. As *La Opinión* reported, the ocupantes "had the goal of confronting the company's police force, which would have provoked a bloody struggle since these are strategic forest and mountain lands." The conflagration was averted at the last minute, however, when the president of the Socialist Central, Juan de Dios Moraga, intervened and mediated an arrangement between the Ministry of Lands and Colonization and the ocupantes. Moraga spoke to a meeting of 350 peasants about the agreement. The entire speech was translated by "the indígena Segundo Colil Jiménez in the aboriginal language." The presence of both mestizo and Mapuche ocupantes meant that the protector of Indians was also brought in to help broker the deal.[75]

In Lonquimay, the agreement engineered by the Ibáñez government failed to hold. As early as 1929, the Sindicato Agrícola Lonquimay had denounced "the abuses and violations of rights that they are committing on the Puelma estates against the residents there because they belong to our Institution, evicting them and thus appropriating their *adelantos* [crops] and harvests or preventing them from cultivating."[76] Following Alessandri's return to office, the distribution of lands to the ocupantes was stalled. The owners of the estates began a slow war of attrition against the region's peasants. The first blow was the mysterious theft of 23 de Enero's town charter, a symbolic slap in the face to both the state's assertion of power in the region and the political autonomy of the peasant population. Then the Puelmas, with the support of the local police, began to use force to expel the ocupantes-colonos from Ránquil.[77] Union members complained that Gonzalo Bunster had begun to terrorize those settled on the Guayalí estate. Accompanied by a group of friends he "entertained himself by shooting the colonos' pigs and threatening to dispossess them. As he left, like a great magnate, he brutally beat the old man Albino Acuña because he has initiated a court case against him in Victoria for violating the domicile of his daughter Delfina last autumn."[78] Despite numerous petitions for assistance, trips to Santiago, and meetings with congressmen by delegations from the Sindicato Agrícola Lonquimay, the evictions of small groups of peasants proceeded apace during the first years of Alessandri's government.

On February 11, 1932, Democratic Party senators Gutiérrez and Concha described in congress "the persecution of the *ocupantes de tierras* in Alto Bío-Bío" and read a petition from the Sindicato Agrícola Lonquimay denouncing the theft of lands in the Nitrito Valley that had been allotted to its members on the fundos Ránquil and Guayalí. Carabineros sent to enforce evictions reported that they had killed a number of peasants during conflicts with members of the Sindicato.[79] Rather than provide support for the Lonquimay peasants, however, Alessandri's minister of lands and colonization issued a report stating that the Ibáñez regime's decrees were illegal.[80]

At issue were eight thousand hectares of winter pasture land in low alti-
tude valleys, *invernadas*, which the 1930 commission charged with dividing
Ránquil had allotted to the members of the Sindicato Agrícola Lonquimay.
In addition, while the director of lands and colonization had promised four
thousand hectares of lowland *invernada* belonging to the Bunsters' Guayalí
to the ocupantes during the division of the estate, the Bunsters had "ordered" the surveyors who had made the final measurements to designate
a high-altitude craggy land known as Llanquén for settlement by the pro-
spective colonos.[81] The inquilinos-ocupantes protested their settlement on
the rocky Llanquén plots, refused to recognize the maps drawn by surveyors, and threatened to take up arms.[82]

During the conflict with the Puelma and Bunster families, the Sindicato
Agrícola Lonquimay received support from left-wing political parties in
congress, the FOCH, and an active, if embryonic, regional labor movement.
In 1933, the FOCH declared that it had organized in Cura-Cautín a "Consejo
de Oficios Varios" (workers' council) with more than one hundred workers
and campesinos.[83] The Consejo maintained "close contact with the Sindicato Agrario de Lonquimay that has numerous consejos of Colonos and
Ocupantes de Tierras." These consejos (councils) had "formed campesino
guards to defend themselves from the usurpers of land . . . the evil concessionaires Bunster and Puelma."[84]

In the summer of 1934, a commission of surveyors traveled to Lonquimay
to redraw the boundaries of the lands granted to the ocupantes, inquilinos,
and colonos. Their goal was to move the peasants further up the cordillera
to join workers, many of them repatriated from the northern nitrate mines,
who labored in the mountains' gold placer mines. The pretext was that the
land on Ránquil would yield only meager harvests. According to government officials, the peasants were not being expelled from Ránquil, only
resettled, albeit with the assistance of carabineros.[85] While many members
of the Sindicato Agrícola de Lonquimay accepted the resettlement, a significant number continued to assert their rights based on the decrees issued
by the Ibáñez government. Even those who accepted the move and began
to work in the placer mines soon encountered trouble. When winter arrived, it became impossible to work in the mines washing gold because of a
thick snow cover. The workers had exchanged their gold at pulperías run by
the mining concession, but now with no gold to sell, the doors of the pulperías were closed to them. Workers employed in building the Túnel de Las
Raíces in the cordillera, many of them also former nitrate miners, suffered

a similar fate. *La Opinión* reported that hundreds of workers continued to work in freezing water and snow with little clothing and no medical attention. The workers' only recourse was to seek help from the *machis* (healers) on neighboring Mapuche reducciones.[86] Shortly before the rebellion, these workers declared a strike.

The final straw, however, was the eviction of sixty peasant families from Ránquil in April 1934. A month before, a force of twenty carabineros had expelled the ocupantes on the Guayalí fundo from the invernadas in the Nitrito Valley. Many accepted small plots in Llanquén, while others found refuge with relatives who had been settled on Ránquil.[87] As newspapers in the region noted, the peasants' situation was exacerbated by an unusually harsh winter that had killed many of their cattle. At the end of June, starving and ill-clothed, hundreds of laborers sacked the pulperías belonging to the estates and concessionaires. Armed with revolvers, carbines, and rifles, they built trenches and attacked pickets of carabineros and the big houses of the local landowners. On the Guayalí estate they assaulted the manager and carabineros. They also invaded the Lolco estate. The movement of over six hundred men began to sweep through neighboring fundos, attacking the Mulchén Forest Reserves and gaining adherents among the inquilinos of the Mariposa, El Morro and El Aguila estates.[88] On the Amargos estate, workers in the sawmills joined the rebellion, "incited by Communist emissaries."[89]

For over a week the rebellion controlled a significant area of Lonquimay and threatened to sweep through the region's commercial centers, Mulchén and Cura Cautín. Reports of Communist Party pamphlets distributed throughout the zone and a planned Communist-led revolt circulated in the press. Concepción's *El Sur* reported that the rebellious peasants and laborers had issued proclamations declaring the establishment of "soviets of workers and peasants and indios."[90] This claim was repeated in the pages of Santiago's *El Mercurio*, which described Communist Party pamphlets that read: "Let's struggle for the constitution of soviets of workers, peasants, and indios, the only way to obtain the free enjoyment of the land, liberty and bread."[91] On the El Rosario estate, outside the city of Victoria, members of the movement had incited the inquilinos to rebel against "those who own the land."[92] According to *El Sur*, the towns of Victoria and Cura-Cautín were "inundated" with "subversive proclamations inciting rebellion."

The rebellion received support from the national labor federation, the FOCH. *El Sur* reported, for example, that delegates from the FOCH had traveled to Lonquimay to incite workers to cut off carabineros' access to the cordillera.[93] Both the FOCH and the Communist Party called on "obreros, campesinos e indios" to form "Comites de Campesinos e Indios" and to constitute "soviets of *obreros, campesinos e indios*" in order "to obtain the free dominion of the land."[94] The Chilean Communist Party and the FOCH had begun organizing rural laborers since the early 1920s with some success, including by 1924 the formation of a number of FOCH consejos in diverse regions of central Chile, though reports from the party's central committee noted that as late as 1927 it had almost no influence in the southern provinces of Cautin and Malleco, a situation that was basically unchanged by the early 1930s.[95]

Nonetheless, reports by the party's general secretary, Carlos Contreras Labarca, after the Ránquil rebellion claimed that the party had focused its organizing activity in Lonquimay "to prevent the eviction of the campesinos from their land, calling for a shared struggle and solidarity between indigenas and campesinos in this region." Indeed, the presence of the FOCH consejo in Lonquimay and its role in organizing campesino guards to defend against evictions by landowners and carabineros, as well as the presence of delegates from Lonquimay's union at the FOCH conference that same June, 1934, indicate the influence of the FOCH and the Communist Party in the region by 1933 and 1934.[96] And it seems clear that the rebellion was initiated at a union meeting in which the union's new, leftist leadership organized and directed its members to assault the estates and their pulperías.[97] Yet, the presence of the Communist Party and the FOCH in the region was recent and there is no evidence that the rebellion was initiated according to plans elaborated by the party or conformed to its general program. The rebellion appears to have been a local initiative, shaped by events on the ground, rather than a result of an insurrection planned by the party's national leadership or by the Communist International (Comintern), even if it did coincide in some ways with the party's general ideology of "agrarian and anti-imperialist revolution" throughout Latin America.[98]

Concepcion's *El Sur* concluded that, despite the role of Communist Party and FOCH militants, "the cause of this uprising does not exactly obey in a precise form a Communist movement. . . . The Communist agitators have played a secondary role . . . exploiting the difficult situation of a numerous group of colonos who were expelled violently from their lands."[99] As even *El Sur* seemed to understand, while the Communist Party and the FOCH had supported the region's rural laborers organized in the Sindicato

Agrícola Lonquimay and had helped to form campesino guards to defend the lands granted by the Ibáñez regime, the revolt was part of larger pattern of rural violence and unrest that shook southern Chile throughout the late 1920s and early 1930s.[100] In a lengthy article on the revolt, *Hoy* reproduced this analysis, concluding that "the Ránquil uprising has undoubtedly been led by extremist agitators, but the actual uprising is not their work, but the work of the difficult and miserable [social] circumstances that exist in that region, without any state assistance, abandoned to their own fate." As the commentary in *El Sur* and *Hoy* underlines, while Communist Party activists had played a role in the politics of the region since 1933, and then supported the revolt, perhaps even taken over leadership of the movement, it would be difficult to describe the revolt as having been planned by the party.[101] Indeed, as the historians Sebastián Leiva and Olga Ulianova have shown, Comintern documents and documents authored by Communist Party leaders in Chile demonstrate no international or national plan for promoting an insurrection in Lonquimay.[102] Even if the Communist Party and the FOCH had begun organizing in Lonquimay, it seems clear that their efforts had been directed at organizing unions and peasant guards to defend the land conceded to Lonquimay's rural laborers during the Ibanez regime. The constant low-level violence that accompanied conflicts between peasants and landowners in Lonquimay was repeated throughout southern Chile and had a history decades long. What distinguished the Ránquil revolt was the organization of a strong union with the prominent support of first the Democratic Party and then the Communist Party in the region, and the role of this union and its leadership in organizing and directing what was one of many movements by rural laborers to claim estate land for colonization.

Mapuches, Ethnic Nationalism, and Peasant Mobilization

It quickly became apparent that the estates' laborers had been joined in the revolt by some members of the region's indigenous Mapuche reducciones. The Ránquil uprising fits a broader pattern of Chilean and Mapuche colonos, inquilinos, and ocupantes joining together in shared conflict with large estates throughout the frontier region. *El Sur* reported, for example, that "one hundred indios have joined the revolt."[103] The local indigenous reducciones Minas Queco and Cauñicú, as well as "indígenas" who lived and worked on the Guayalí estate, were reported to have also joined the uprising.[104] And in Queco, one report declared, perhaps with a dose of hyperbole and racist hysteria, that the "indiada" (mob of Indians) in the region had risen up and formed a band of hundreds that sacked the fundos in the region.[105] *El Sur* reported, and this report was backed by other sources as well, that the cacique Ignacio Maripe and other members of the Ralco reducción had also participated and suffered violent retribution from carabineros when the rebellion was crushed.[106]

Immediately following the outbreak of the rebellion, the Communist Party's *Bandera Roja* declared that the rebels of Lonquimay had announced their support for a "government of soviets and a República Araucana"[107] and that "the Communist Party and the FOCH have demanded the return of stolen lands to the Mapuche and support their right to full political and cultural independence and the formation of their own República Araucana."[108] For the Communist Party, the participation of the *reducción indígena* of Ralco in the revolt reflected "the problem of national liberation, which is a problem that is of the first order today and that the bourgeois-democratic revolution will have to establish a plan to concede the right of self-determination and the formation of their own republic to the Araucanian race."[109] The Mapuche "suffer today a double oppression of the feudal-bourgeois state that starves and exploits the working masses in general and the national oppression that steals their land and denies their right to maintain their customs, schools, language, etc." The Communist Party lauded the active Mapuche participation in the insurrection as a sign of their revolutionary will and imminent "national liberation." The party also supported the right of the Mapuche "to form their own republic and separate themselves from Chile if they wish."[110] A year earlier, the FOCH had also supported the right of Mapuches to establish a "República Araucana with freedom for their languages and customs."[111]

Both the call for an independent indigenous republic and the Communist Party's support for Mapuche national political and cultural self-determination reflected the Comintern's ideological platform that called for national liberation for ethnic minorities. Yet the ideology of national self-determination evoked in the call for an Araucanian Republic did not remain restricted to the Comintern. This Communist Party platform was taken up by a Mapuche political organization, the Federación Araucana, founded by Manuel Aburto Panguilef. The Federación had begun as a mutual aid society for "araucanos" in 1916 in the southern city of Pitrufquén, but by the 1920s, Aburto organized the Federación Araucana in alliance with the Communist Party and the FOCH. The structure of the Federación mimicked the structure of the FOCH, and FOCH militants attended the Federación's meetings and congresses. In 1927, for example, the intendant of Cautín noted a new political effervescence among the Mapuche, inspired, he argued, by the Communist Party. "Within the tendencies that have been awoken among the indígenas," he contended, were "currents or influences of a Communist cast and model; the Federación Araucana has constituted Juntas Provinciales and Consejos Federales headed by Secretary Generals that have tirelessly sown among the mass of ignorant indios demands for the right to land and that have provoked dissatisfaction among them."[112]

The Federación Araucana also, however, advocated a return to traditional Mapuche religious and cultural practices, defense of the indigenous reducción from division and privatization, and the establishment of an "independent indigenous republic."[113] Aburto sought to reaffirm and draw on Mapuche traditions to articulate a radical ethnic nationalism. He resorted to congresses and organized federations, but within the framework of these institutions he also promoted indigenous practices of social organization. As the historian José Bengoa has noted, the congresses and meetings held by Aburto and the Federación were organized in traditional style. Mapuche caciques and *mocetones* (commoners) from reducciones all over the south would come together for days of meetings organized around religious ceremonies. At times, thousands of Mapuches would meet to plan strategies to defend the lands of reducciones.[114]

There is little evidence, however, that the call for an Araucanian Republic shaped the land claims and political culture of Mapuche reducciones during this period. Instead, for the most part reducciones continued to defend their land by invoking land grant titles made by the state during the process of reduccion, as well as their years of land occupation, rather than by demanding national sovereignty or asserting their rights as members of a separate republic or nation. Yet, even as Mapuche communities tailored their demands to legalistic claims within the Indian courts and protectorates set up during the process of reduccion, they also aggressively confronted the violence of local state authorities, carabineros, and landowners. During the late 1920s and 1930s low-level violence between Mapuche reducciones and carabineros was a constant feature of rural social relations in southern Chile. Police, enlisted to expel Mapuche from land they claimed, either public or on estates or reducciones, met frequent resistance and, in turn, employed force. In 1933, for example, Mapuche "squatters" on land claimed by the Budi concession were forcibly evicted by carabineros.[115] That same year, three hundred Mapuches from Temulemu went to Temuco to protest to the regional government abuses by carabineros in Lumaco and Capitan Pastene who "commit all kinds of abuses against them, becoming so extreme, that they cannot live in peace since they fear being assaulted and assassinated by them as has occurred recently when they had to mourn the assassination of the youth Segundo Paine by Lumaco's carabineros under the pretext that he was a thief. . . . [T]his is something that enrages, what occurs with the abuses committed by carabineros, . . . who should be protectors, who have become persecutors."[116] In November of that same year, seventy Mapuches in Temulemu assaulted carabineros who had detained a group from the reducción for allegedly stealing cattle.[117] Similarly, in April 1934, a large group of Mapuches assaulted carabineros who had attempted to detain three members of a reducción in Curihuin.[118] In another typical case, carabineros shot the two brothers Ancamilla from the Huequén reducción. They had been accused of stealing six pigs and, according to the police, had resisted arrest with sticks and a whip.[119]

In Lonquimay, Mapuche reducciones had engaged in a longstanding conflict with local landowners. Among the different indigenous communities, the Ralco reducción's participation in the revolt was most prominent and members of the reducción suffered the most from the repression. Land on the fundo Ralco, just north of the Bío Bío river, had been sold originally with the provision that the owner respect the rights of material occupation of the indigenous Pehuenche Mapuche and nonindigenous peasant ocupantes. However, the owners marshaled titles based on fraudulent sales to twenty-three of the 250 members of the reducción in 1881 and had the police forcibly expel all of the Mapuches on the Ralco estate, at least on two occasions. The Ralco Mapuches, however, continued to return and occupy roughly thirty-nine thousand hectares they claimed in a permanent state of "rebellion," as one Indian court put it, during the first two decades of the twentieth century.[120]

During the mid-1920s, as conflicts over land spread throughout southern Chile, the community engaged in bitter confrontations with the owners of the Ralco estate, the Bunster family, the same family that owned the Guayalí estate. The community continuously petitioned to be settled on land claimed by the Bunsters and protested incursions onto the lands of the reducción. By the early 1930s, Mapuches from the reducción, along with Chilean ocupantes numbering roughly 550, had occupied an invernada of 11,493 hectares on the Ralco estate, which they claimed was public land.[121] A year before the rebellion, the Bunster Gómez family, with support from the courts and carabineros, had evicted members of the Ralco reducción from land claimed by the estate and the reducción.

Like many of the conflicts between large landowners and peasants on the frontier during the 1920s and 1930s, the Ralco reduccción's confrontation with the Bunsters included mestizo or "Chilean" ocupantes. While they defended their rights to land in terms of their indigenous status and the legislation that governed indigenous affairs, invoking the Títulos de Merced (land titles) granted their *reducciones*, they also defended the rights of poor nonindigenous peasants to occupy public land. In fact, as government censuses reflected, nonindigenous and Mapuche ocupantes occupied the same space on the Ralco estate living and working, if not together, then as neighbors. Thus, members of the Ralco reducción petitioned that the state settle them on the Ralco estate land together with the "poor Chileans" who were also squatting and who claimed the status of colonos. A few years after the Ránquil revolt, the Ralco reducción petitioned the Ministry of Lands and Colonization for support in their continued conflict with the Bunster Gómez family:

> We declare that we occupy the lands in Ralco since time immemorial, since our ancestors were the first to populate [the region]. . . . And now we ask that the supreme government take interest in us, send us a surveyor to determine the borders of our reducción respecting the rights that the poor Chileans may have who occupy the place on public lands that neighbors our possession, excepting the representatives of the Bunster Gómez family who have always abused us and now are trying to take our land from us.[122]

That Mapuches from the Ralco community participated in the Ránquil rebellion is hardly unusual. As this petition makes clear, as in many of the land conflicts cited above, poor mestizo inquilinos, ocupantes, and colonos, often worked side by side or lived as neighbors with members of Mapuche communities, and they often shared common enemies in large landowners like the Bunsters and Puelmas.

There is no evidence that the Federación Araucana and Communist Party's ideology of an Araucanian republic played any role in either the enduring conflict between the Ralco reducción and the Bunsters, or in the participation of members of the reducción in the revolt. Some of Lonquimay's Mapuche reducciones had participated in congresses held by the Federación

Araucana, but there is no evidence that the call for an indigenous republic shaped either the longstanding land conflicts between the Bunsters and the reducciones or the politics of the region. In addition, it is important to note that there is no evidence that any reducción participated as a reducción. While around 15 percent of those detained after the revolt and listed in court records had indigenous names, and there is ample testimony to the participation of Ignacio Maripe and members of the Ralco community, what seems clear is that those who participated were members of the reducción who labored on the region's estates as either seasonal laborers or inquilinos, some of whom may have joined the Sindicato Agrícola Lonquimay.[123]

The calls for soviets and the indigenous republic in pamphlets that were circulated in towns did, however, allow the press to inflame fears about an uprising of the indiada, much as the calls for soviets more generally allowed the local press to articulate a hyperbolic anticommunist hysteria, and to paint the Ránquil rebels with the brush of barbarism, placing them outside the civilized nation. In some ways, this rhetoric also eclipsed the realities on the ground of longstanding conflicts between rural laborers and large estates that often included both Mapuches and "Chileans" and to define the rebellion as something unusual, outside of the common, and not intrinsic to rural social relations. It is notable that following the revolt, there was relatively little mention of the participation of Mapuches or reducciones in the uprising in either the press or in congress. Rather, almost all accounts described the rebels as colonos, ocupantes, or inquilinos. And, despite the fears of a Communist insurrection and the application of Chile's National Security Law to the rebels, the 1935 amnesty based in the investigation of a Santiago appellate court judge efficiently minimized the role of the Communist Party in the rebellion.

Conclusion

The *sucesos* (events), as they were often referred to, in Ránquil reflect several important points about modern Chile. First, the revolt indicates the limits of the Chilean state's administrative, military, and hegemonic presence in the southern frontier region, especially in the cordillera along the frontier with Argentina. Landowners' capacity to defraud the state of literally hundreds of thousands of hectares of public land and the state's inability to establish a cadastral survey of Lonquimay's properties or to define the boundaries enshrined in fictive titles, lay at the root of rural unrest in the south. In addition, the state's ability to maintain a stable social order on the frontier was quite limited. Lonquimay's rural laborers did not inhabit longstanding villages or municipalities. Rather, they were a transient and migrant population that had moved into the region from Chile's central valley and from other zones of the frontier. Many had fled across the border to Argentina when the state began to auction and grant land on the frontier and landowners had initiated the massive expulsion of ocupantes during the process of colonization. In the mountainous border region they had little contact with the state at any level—local, regional, or national. This was the situation that the Sindicato Agrícola Lonquimay's original program of "populating" and "civilizing," and Ibáñez's support for the settlement of the region, and the establishment of a municipality and schools, sought to redress. With limited administrative presence on the frontier, the state's authority over society and territory was exercised through the coercive powers of local carabineros.

Second, the peasant movement in Lonquimay, placed in the context of broader patterns of peasant opposition to the authority of landowners and the state, reveals the deeply conflictive and unstable nature of land and labor relations in southern Chile. Unlike central Chile, where the hacienda and the state enjoyed a powerful hegemony that effectively postponed any subaltern challenge to the rural order until the agrarian reform of the 1960s and 1970s, in the south peasants and laborers of all sorts, inquilinos, medieros, arrendatarios, jornaleros, ocupantes, and colonos, both Mapuche and nonindigenous or mestizo, responded to the dubious and often fraudulent legal status of many estates by invading, squatting, and claiming land they defined as belonging to the public domain. Memories of landlord violence, expulsions, and land appropriations were fresh in the minds of the frontier's rural laborers. A petition from the Sindicato Agrícola Lonquimay for government protection from the abuses of the Bunsters and Puelmas made this clear: "We don't want to repeat here the massacres that are registered in our legendary history. We do not want to once again experience the horrible acts that were carried out on this land against our ancestors—fires, violent expulsions, and long caravans of refugees crossing the Chilean-Argentine Andes. These memories live in the memories of today's children of this land."[124]

Finally, unlike the relatively quiescent rural land and labor relations of central Chile, in the south rural laborers, smallholders, and Mapuche reducciones frequently confronted the violence wielded by large landowners and the state with their own violence, even as they continued to make claims to land shaped by the legal codes that governed colonization. They demanded land either in terms of their rights as colonos or members of reducciones. Yet, confronted with violence exercised by landowners in collusion with local authorities and the police, they also resorted to violent confrontations. While Ránquil was the most extreme occasion of peasant violence, smaller-scale forms of opposition, including squatting, land invasions, or confrontations with police, or, as many of the cases above noted, simple refusal to recognize the authority of patrones, were frequent on the frontier. The Ránquil revolt belonged to a broader moment of rural unrest with roots in the violent colonization of Chile's southern frontier.

Notes

1. For a discussion of the role of amnesties in forging political reconciliation in Chile, see the pioneering work of Elizabeth Lira and Brian Loveman, *Las suaves cenizas del olvido: via chilena de reconciliación política, 1814–1932* (Santiago: LOM Ediciones, 1999), and *Las ardientes cenizas del olvido: via chilena de reconciliación política, 1932–1994* (Santiago: LOM Ediciones, 2000). Lira and Loveman refer to the victims of the Ránquil massacre as Chile's first *detenidos-desaparecidos* even though, as they point out, the term was not used in 1934. See Lira and Loveman, *Las ardientes cenizas del olvido*, 40. Some details of the repression can be found in the military judicial processes of the Juzgado Militar de Concepción, Archivo Nacional de la Administración, Santiago henceforth referred to as AAN. Using language and arguments that would be repeated by the Pinochet regime decades later, carabineros testified that the disappeared detainees had escaped, thrown themselves in the Bío Bío, and were probably in Argentina. See especially the testimony in the case against carabineros initiated by the FOCH on July 18, 1934, Causa 195–34. According to *El Diario Austral* (June 29, 1934), carabineros were aided by two paramiliary organizations: the Milicia Republicana (Republican Militia) and the Guardia Blanca (White Guard). The numbers of those killed, executed, or disappeared are difficult to fix, and range from around twenty to sixty to over four hundred, depending on the source. In congress, deputies and senators cited all these figures.

2. While the Ránquil rebellion, as it is known in Chile, acquired iconic status in the popular culture of Chile's Left, very little has been written about the uprising itself or about the rural social relations that gave rise to it. Sebastián Leiva, "El partido comunista de Chile y el levantamiento de Ranquil." *Cyber Humanitatis* 28 (Spring 2003); Eduardo Téllez Lugaro et al., "El levantamiento del Alto Biobio y el Soviet y la Republica Araucana de 1934," *Annales de la Universidad de Chile*, 6th ser., no. 13

(August 2001). There are also a number of memoirs written by observers or tangential participants. See Harry Fahrenkrog Reinhold, *La verdad sobre la revuelta de Ránquil: memorias de Harry Fahrenkrog Reinhold* (Santiago: Editorial Universitaria, 1985), and *Los sucesos del Alto Bío-Bío y el Diputado Huenchullán* (Santiago: Selectam, 1934). A couple of important works on peasants in twentieth-century Chile deal briefly with the Ránquil uprising. See Brian Loveman, *Struggle in the Countryside: Politics and Rural Labor in Chile, 1919–1973* (Bloomington: Indiana University Press, 1976); José Bengoa, *Historia social de la agricultura chilena II: haciendas y campesinos* (Santiago: Ediciones SUR, 1990); and Almino Affonso et al., *Movimiento campesino chileno*, vol. 1 (Santiago: ICIRA, 1970).

3. For excellent overviews of this history see José Bengoa, *Historia del pueblo Mapuche siglo XIX y XX* (Santiago: Ediciones SUR, 1985), and *Historia de un conflicto: el estado y los Mapuches en el siglo XX* (Santiago: Planeta, 1999).

4. Congreso Nacional, *Comisión Parlamentaria de Colonización: informe, proyectos de ley, actas de las sesiones y otros antecedentes* (Santiago: Sociedad Imprenta y Litografía Universo, 1912), lvii.

5. Ibid.

6. The state Colonization Agency was deeply disappointed by Chile's comparatively low levels of immigration. Santiago's *La Nueva República* cited a pessimistic report by the Colonization Agency that demonstrated that between 1857 and 1897 Argentina had received, 2,275,521 immigrants, while during roughly the same period (1850–97) only 38,528 immigrants had traveled to Chile. In 1897 alone 105,143 immigrants had gone to Argentina and only 885 to Chile (*La Nueva República*, October 3, 1898). See also *Memoria de la Inspección Jeneral de Tierras y Colonización* (Santiago, 1904), 9.

7. For a brief discussion of this history, see Fahrenkrog Reinhold, *La verdad sobre la revuelta de Ránquil*. Also see a detailed description of the property titles in *Boletín de Tierras y Colonización*, decreto número 265, March 27, 1930, published in its entirety in Chile, Cámara de Diputados, Sesión Ordinaria, July 9, 1934, Biblioteca del Congreso, Santiago, henceforth referred to as BC. An excellent account of all the events leading up to the uprising and massacre can also be found in *El Sur*, July 22, 1934.

8. See Nicolás Palacios, "Algunos efectos de la colonización extranjera," in Congreso Nacional, *Comisión Parlamentaria de Colonización*, and speeches by Malaquías Concha included in the same volume.

9. Speech by the Democratic Party deputy Gutiérrez, Camara de Diputados, Sesión Ordinaria, January 7, 1911, BC.

10. *Memoria de la Inspección Jeneral de Tierras i Colonización* (Santiago, 1902), 33.

11. Ibid., 182.

12. Ibid., 190.

13. *Memoria de la Inspección Jeneral de Colonización e Inmigración* (1908), 224.

14. Ibid.

15. *Memoria de la Inspección Jeneral de Tierras y Colonización* (1902), 164.

16. *Sesta Memoria del Director de la Oficina de la Mensura de Tierras para el Señor Ministro de Colonización* (Santiago, 1913), 157.

17. *Memoria del Interventor de Colonias Correspondiente al año 1911*, 59.

18. *Memoria de la Inspección Jeneral de Tierras i Colonización* (Santiago, 1905), 25.

19. *Sesta Memoria del Director de la Oficina dela Mensura de Tierras para el Señor Ministro de Colonización* (Santiago, 1913), 158.

20. See the account by the Conservative Party deputy Emilio Claro in *Diario de Sesiones*, Sesión Extraordinaria, January 16, 1914, BC, as well as accounts in the press, especially *El Sur*, October 15–27, 1913.

21. *El Mercurio*, July 1, 1934.

22. Fahrenkrog Reinhold, *La verdad sobre la revuelta de Ránquil*, 26–32.

23. *Los sucesos del Alto Bío-Bío y el Diputado Huenchullán*. Huenchullán quickly recognized that many of the rebels were, in fact, former inquilinos, as did Fahrenkrog Reinhold and the regional press.

24. George McCutchen McBride, *Chile: Land and Society* (New York: American Geographical Society, 1936), 294.

25. *Memoria de la Inspección Jeneral de Colonización e Inmigración* (Santiago, 1908), 227.

26. For the many cases of smallholders who lost their land after signing inquilinaje contracts, see Ministerio de Agricultura, Industria, y Obras Públicas, Sección Colonización, decretos números 133–96, May 1926, AAN.

27. Ministerio de Tierras y Colonización, Providencias, vol. 1814 (1939), AAN.

28. McBride, *Chile*, 294.

29. Fahrenkrog Reinhold, *La verdad sobre la revuelta de Ránquil*.

30. *El Diario Austral*, May 26, 1934.

31. See, for example Juzgado Militar de Concepción, Causa 187–34, Evasión de Detenidos; Causa 189–34, Desaparecimiento de Juan Jara; Causa 252–34, Flagelaciones a Alfonso Wencesla—jornalero, AAN.

32. Ibid., Causa 189–34.

33. Communication from the Intendente to the Prefecto de Carabineros, December 9, 1932, Intendencia de Cautín, vol. 387 (1932), Archivo Nacional, Santiago, henceforth referred to as AN.

34. Telegram from Carlos Ibáñez to the Intendente, January 23, 1930, Intendencia de Cautín, vol. 298 (1930), AN.

35. Telegram from Carlos Ibáñez del Campo, November 11, 1929, Intendencia de Cautín, vol. 279 (1929), AN.

36. See Ministerio de Fomento, *Memoria de Fomento, 1927*, 112–13.

37. Ministerio de Fomento, *Memoria de Fomento, 1928*, 194.

38. Ibid., 11–13.

39. Ministerio de Fomento, *Memoria de Fomento, 1927*, 112, 123.

40. Ministerio de Tierras y Colonización, Oficios 1–341 (1925), AAN.

41. Ministerio de Agricultura, Industria, y Obras Públicas, decretos números 197–226 (April 1926); Ministerio de Tierras y Colonización, Oficios 1–341 (1925); Ministerio de Tierras y Colonización, Oficios Dirigidos y Antecedentes, 301–484 (1925–26); Ministerio de Agricultura, Industria, y Colonización, Sección Colonización, Providencias (July–September 1927), AAN.

42. Ministerio de Tierras y Colonización, Providencias, vol. 165 (1930), AAN.

43. Circular from the Ministerio de Fomento to the Intendente, April 29, 1929. Intendencia de Cautín, vol. 281 (1929), AN.

44. Telegram from the Director, Caja de Colonización, to the Intendente, December 22, 1930, Intendencia de Cautín, vol. 307 (1930), AN.

45. Ministerio de Tierras y Colonización, Providencias, 1930, vol. 167, AAN.

46. Communication from the Secretario de Bienestar to the Intendencia, April 7, 1930, Intendencia de Cautín, vol. 305 (1930), AN. Memorandum from Carabineros to the Prefectura de Cautín, April 20, 1930, AN.

47. Ministerio de Tierras y Colonización, Oficios 1–341 (1925), AAN.

48. Petition to the Intendente from Pedro Ugalde Barrios, *arigcultor*, October 13, 1926, Intendencia de Cautín, vol. 261 (1928), AN.

49. Petition to the Intendente from Eduardo Slano Illanes and Santiago Viñuela, *agricultores*, October 13, 1928, Intendencia de Cautín, vol. 261 (1928), AN.

50. Communication from the Ministerio del Interior to the Intendente, July 23, 1930, AN.

51. Fahrenkrog Reinhold, *La verdad sobre la revuelta de Ránquil*; *El Sur*, July 22, 1934.

52. *El Comercio*, December 9, 1928.

53. Communication from the Gobernador of Victoria, October 14, 1929, Intendencia de Cautín, vol. 279 (1929), AN.

54. Communication from the Intendente to the Prefecto de Carabineros, October 14, 1929, Intendencia de Cautín, 279 (1929), AN.

55. Memorandum from the Subdelegado of Lonquimay, December 30, 1931, Intendencia de Cautín, VOL. 378 (1932), AN.

56. Communication from the Prefectura de Carabineros to the Intendente, April 22, 1930, Intendencia de Cautín, VOL. 299 (1930), AN.

57. *El Comercio*, August 30, 1931.

58. *El Comercio*, October 8, 1933.

59. *El Comercio*, January 11, 1931.

60. The language is that of the deputy Carlos Alberto Martínez in Chile, Cámara de Diputados, Sesión Ordinaria, July 9, 1934, BC.

61. This decree was published in its entirety in ibid.

62. Telegram from Carlos Ibáñez del Campo to the Intendente, September 20, 1929, and telegram from Carlos Ibáñez del Campo, November 11, 1929, Intendencia de Cautín, VOL. 279 (1929), AN.

63. Telegram from Carlos Ibáñez to the Intendente, January 18, 1930, Intendencia de Cautín, VOL. 306 (1930), AN.

64. On May 12, 1934, *El Diario Austral* reported, for example, that three large estates, Toltén, Nueva Italia, and Ránquil would be divided and their lands distributed.

65. Memorandum on colonization in Alto Bio-Bio, from the Gobernador of Victoria to the Ministro de Tierras y Colonización, January 5, 1932, Intendencia de Cautín, VOL. 378 (1932), AN.

66. *El Sur*, March 10, 1933.

67. *El Sur*, January 22 and 27, 1933.

68. *La Opinión*, April 12, 1934.

69. For other examples see *El Diario Austral*, "Colonos habrían sido violentamente expulsados en Traiguén," October 29, 1933; "Segunda Asamblea Plenaria de la Gran Convencíon de Aspirantes a Colonos," November 8, 1933.

70. Communication from the Ministerio del Interior to the Intendente, April 6, 1933, Intendencia de Cautín, VOL. 342 (1931–33), AN.

71. *El Comercio*, November 5, 1933. Also see Elías Lafertte, *Vida de un comunista* (Santiago: Editoral Austral, 1971).

72. *El Comercio*, November 5, 1933. See also Olga Ulianova, "Levantamiento campesino de Lonquimay y la Internacional Comunista," *Estudios Públicos* 89 (2003), 190.

73. Ulianova, "Levantamiento campesino de Lonquimay," 190.

74. *La Opinión*, May 19, 1934.

75. *La Opinión*, March 26, 1934.

76. Communication from the Sindicato Agrícola de Lonquimay to the Intendente, September 29, 1929, Intendencia de Cautín, vol. 278 (1929), AN.

77. *La Opinión*, July 1, 1934.

78. *El Comercio*, January 8, 1933.

79. *La Opinión*, June 30, 1934. Copies of petitions to congress from the Sindicato Agrícola Lonquimay are also located in Chile, Cámara de Diputados, Sesión Extraordinaria, February 4, 1932, BC.

80. *El Sur*, July 22, 1934.

81. Fahrenkrog Reinhold, *La verdad sobre la revuelta de Ránquil*, 43–44.

82. Ibid., 44–45.

83. *Justicia*, February 10, 1933.

84. Ibid.

85. Chile, Cámara de Diputados, Sesión Ordinaria, July 9, 1934, BC.

86. *La Opinión*, June 26, 1934.

87. Fahrenkrog Reinhold, *La verdad sobre la revuelta de Ránquil*, 46–47. See also *El Comercio*, April 2, 1934.

88. For accounts of the events, see *El Sur*, July 1–22, 1934; *El Malleco*, June 30–July 10, 1934; *El Diario Austral*, June 29 and 30, 1934; *El Mercurio*, July 1–4, 1934; *La Opinión*, March 26, April 2, May 9 and 19, June 13, and June 30–July 4, 1934.

89. *El Mercurio*, July 4, 1934.

90. *El Sur*, July 22, 1934.

91. *El Mercurio*, July 4, 1934.

92. *El Malleco*, July 5, 1934.

93. *El Sur*, July 1, 1934.

94. *Bandera Roja*, July 28, 1934. I would like to thank Florencia Mallon for providing me copies of *Bandera Roja* issues.

95. Leiva, "El partido comunista de Chile y levantamiento de Ránquil," 10–11.

96. Quoted in ibid., 14.

97. This is the testimony of many rebels taken prisoner, as well as the account of Harry Fahrenkrog Reinhold, and coincides too with the account by the head of the Chilean Communist Party, Carlos Contreras Labarca. See testimony in Corte de Apelaciones de Temuco, in the Conservador de Bienes y Raices, Temuco; and Jaime Flores, "Un episodio en la historia social de Chile: Ránquil, una revuelta campesina,"

M.A. thesis, Universidad de Santiago de Chile, 1993. Also see Uliavanova, "Levantamiento campesino."

98. Quoted in Ulianova, "Levantamiento campesino," 204.

99. *El Sur*, July 1, 1934.

100. *Hoy*, July 6, 1934.

101. This is the argument made by Leiva in "El partido comunista y levantamiento de Ránquil," 18.

102. Based on an analysis of Comintern documents, Sebastián Leiva arrives at the conclusion that the uprising was the result of the miserable conditions in Ránquil, not a planned conspiracy of the Communist Party, despite the presence of the party in the region. Leiva, "El partido comunista de Chile y levantamiento de Ránquil." Also see Ulianova, "Levantamiento campesino." Elías Lafertte, secretary general of the FOCH and president of the Communist Party, also affirms this position in his memoirs: "The Ránquil uprising was in reality a spontaneous rebellion, unprepared, an explosion of anger of impoverished campesinos cheated of their lands for centuries when they had finished stealing their meager and poor lands" (Lafertte, *Vida de un comunista*, 274.

103. *El Sur*, July 2, 1934.

104. *El Mercurio*, July 4, 1934; *El Sur*, July 6, 1934.

105. *El Sur*, July 6, 1934.

106. *El Sur*, July 21, 1934.

107. *Bandera Roja*, July 28, 1934.

108. Ibid.

109. Ibid.

110. Ibid.

111. *Justicia*, February 10, 1933.

112. Memorandum of the Intendencia de Cautín, Temuco, August 1, 1927, Ministerio del Interior, Providencias , vol. 7062 (1928), AAN. By 1933, however, Aburto and the Federación seem to have split with the Communist Party. According to *El Diario Austral* (November 6, 1933) at the second convention of the Central Socialista de Colonización, Aburto protested against the "attitude" of the Communists and made it clear that "the indígenas were respectful of the law."

113. See the very interesting discussions of Manuel Aburto Panguilef in José Bengoa, *Historia de un conflicto: el estado y los Mapuches en el siglo XX* (Santiago: Editorial Planeta, 1999), 127–33; and in Rolf Foerster and Sonia Montecino, *Organizaciones, lideres y contiendas mapuches (1900–1970)* (Santiago: Centro de Estudios de la Mujer, 1988).

114. Bengoa, *Historia de un conflicto*, 131.

115. *El Diario Austral*, January 7, 1933.

116. Protest by the Mapuche of Temulemu ("reclamo de los indigenas del lugar denominado 'Temulemu'") November 28, 1933, Intendencia de Cautín, vol. 418 (1933), AN.

117. *El Diario Austral*, November 14, 1933.

118. *El Diario Austral*, April 13, 1934.

119. Juzgado Militar de Concepción, Detenidos por Lesiones Graves, Causa 191–34, AAN. See also Causa 152–3 in which a group of indígenas was arrested for beating carabineros sent to arrest them for theft of crops and cattle from a neighboring estate.

120. November 1942, Sentencia, Juez Titular de Indios de Victoria, don Gustavo Risquertz Susarte, Archivo General de Asuntos Indigenas, Archivo Regional de la Araucanía.

121. Juzgado de Indios de Victoria, Radicación, no. 2099, January 19, 1939, Archivo Regional de la Araucanía.

122. Ibid.

123. See Flores, "Un episodio en la historia social de Chile," and Ulianova, "Levantamiento campesino," 200.

124. *El Comercio*, October 23, 1929.

PART TWO   *The Cuban Conjuncture*

The Trials

Violence and Justice in the Aftermath

of the Cuban Revolution

MICHELLE CHASE

On January 1, 1959, Cubans stood on the threshold of a new era. The insurrection against the increasingly unpopular dictator Fulgencio Batista had triumphed. As Batista boarded a plane for the Dominican Republic, bearded rebels swept into cities filled with cheering crowds. The final months of the uprising had been particularly violent, especially in urban centers, and the rebels' first order of business was to arrest men suspected of torturing and killing. It was in this context, amidst popular euphoria and widespread expectations of change, that the first trials and executions of members of Batista's security forces began.

Most concede that the men executed were probably guilty as accused, but have criticized the trials for not following due process.[1] Thus the major questions with respect to the revolutionary tribunals have to do with their legality or lack thereof, not what political and ideological role the trials might have played in helping the movement headed by Fidel Castro establish authority during a moment of fractured sovereignty, as well as how the trials themselves enacted popular, historically conditioned notions of morality and justice. Quick consolidation of power was imperative in the vacuum of power left by Batista's flight. For despite the popular focus on the guerrilla forces led by Castro, known as the 26th of July movement (M-26), a wide range of opposition groups contributed to the gradual disintegration of Batista's regime.[2] Throughout its six-year insurgency, the M-26 had struggled to build alliances with other opposition groups while simultaneously claiming the role of revolutionary vanguard. These efforts took on new urgency with Batista's flight. While the M-26 was the best-organized and most visible group, other revolutionary and political groups still enjoyed varying degrees of prestige and power.

Thus in the first days of the revolution, the M-26 moved quickly to prevent General Eulogio Cantillo, Batista's chief of staff, from occupying Camp Columbia, the headquarters of the Cuban military, to disarm the most important rival revolutionary group, the university-based Revolutionary Directorate, which had briefly occupied the Presidential Palace and the capital building.[3] As Castro warned in a televised speech on January 8, there was only one revolutionary force in Cuba; there would be no "private armies."[4] M-26 members in Havana also moved swiftly to contain spontaneous rioting in the capital, where crowds had taken to attacking the symbols of Batista's regime.[5] Thus the M-26 was able to position itself as the new revolutionary leadership and the sole guarantor of order in the power vacuum left by Batista's flight.[6]

Still, while many accounts of the Cuban Revolution explain how the M-26 established a literal monopoly of force, they do not entirely explain how this was transformed into a *legitimate* monopoly of force. To a large degree, that early legitimacy was consolidated through the trials and executions of former *batistianos*. These tribunals, presided over by members of the rebel army and some civic leaders, contributed to the M-26's consolidation of victory in several ways. First, they eliminated those who might have been the staunchest opponents of the new regime. More broadly, they publicly exposed and dramatized the horrors of Batista's counterinsurgency campaign, horrors that served to demarcate legitimate from illegitimate violence, and thus graphically juxtaposed revolutionary justice and dictatorial terror. These distinctions, in turn, resonated with a broader political discourse of morality, which cast the conflict of 1952–58 in terms of honor versus corruption. Finally, the tribunals channeled popular demands for retribution through procedures led by the new authorities, in a move that fulfilled a widespread desire for vengeance as it simultaneously cast itself as the antithesis of uncontrolled mob justice. But while the trials allowed the new regime to consolidate domestic authority, they also exposed ideological and political fractures in the field of interstate relations, as the summary executions became a flashpoint for early friction between Havana and Washington, revealing divergent opinions about sovereignty, the right of self-rule, and the historical role of the United States in the region.

Justice and Outrage

Long before the revolution's triumph, Castro and other M-26 leaders had made reference to the importance of quick trials for the perpetrators of the worst abuses during the insurrection, and immediately after Batista's departure, the rebel leadership made the first overtures toward delivering the promised retribution. Speaking on the radio while still in Santiago, Fidel assured listeners that there would be no need to take justice into their own hands.[7] On January 6, the interim president, Manuel Urrutia, echoed the promise, speaking at a rally on the steps of the University of Havana.[8] Soldiers captured in the final battles—in Cienfuegos, Santa Clara, and Santiago—awaited trial. In Havana and other cities, M-26 fighters exhorted the general public to help them round up policemen, politicians, and informers of the Batista regime before they could reach foreign embassies to ask for safe haven.[9] In early January, news of the first executions in Santiago began to circulate.[10]

During the next few days, several particularly notorious figures were executed in Las Villas, including Colonel Cornelio Rojas, police chief of Santa Clara, and General Joaquín Casillas Lumpuy, suspected of murdering the labor leader Jesús Menéndez in 1947 and for terrorizing campesinos in the Sierra Maestra.[11] These executions were quickly followed by more in Oriente, and other provinces began setting up tribunals as well. Reportedly some three thousand prisoners were being held across the island, six hundred of these in La Cabaña in Havana.[12] On January 12, in Santiago, several army officers accused of multiple acts of torture and murder stood before a massive public trial. The defendants included Enrique Despaigne Nordet and other policemen, some of whom confessed to murder and testified against each other. One even volunteered to demonstrate torture tactics used by the police during interrogations. At least four men were shot after the trial, including Despaigne Nordet, who chose to direct his own firing squad. Perhaps for this reason, his execution was postponed from four o'clock in the morning to six o'clock, so that it could be filmed in the morning light and televised.[13]

It may have been details such as these that first caught the eye of U.S. observers, for the trials had hardly begun when they were met by an outpouring of fierce denunciations. Several senators, notably Wayne Morse, and several publications, particularly *Time*, denounced the executions as a "bloodbath," called the tribunals "kangaroo courts," and so on. *Time* described how rebels quickly condemned defendants in a makeshift court, then dragged them out back for a few puffs of a cigarette and a word with the local priest before shooting them over a hastily dug ditch. "Capable of high idealism and warm generosity, Cubans are also endowed to the full with the Latin capacity for brooding revenge and blood purges," the magazine explained breezily.[14] By mid-month, events had reached a crescendo of podium-thumping congressional speeches and sensationalist magazine features, which provoked a swelling indignation in Cuba in response.

Stung by international criticism, Cuban civic groups planned demonstrations to show their support of the trials and—very pointedly—the firing squads. Crowds gathered outside the presidential palace and in parks, passing out flyers and holding banners in support of the executions.[15] Women—likely those already organized into support groups for political prisoners during the insurrection—staged a meeting in Havana's central park to show support for the trials.[16] Student groups, professional associations, and even some members of the clergy released statements of support to the press and personally wrote to President Eisenhower to plead that he put a stop to criticism of the executions.[17]

On January 13, Castro decided to meet the criticisms head-on in spectacular fashion. He announced the public trial of Captain Jesús Sosa Blanco, commander of the military garrison in Holguín. The trial would take place in Havana's central stadium under the watchful eyes of the international media. It would be preceded by a major rally held to demonstrate the public's enthusiasm, a massive demonstration that the revolutionary leadership hoped would serve as a sort of plebiscite. The world would see, he insisted, that the men on trial were guilty of the most unimaginable crimes, and that the people of Cuba soundly supported the executions.

On the day of the rally, between 500,000 and one million people flooded the streets of Havana, seeming to demonstrate unquestionable mass support for the revolutionary tribunals.[18] Crowds overflowed the plaza and filled the streets surrounding the Palacio Nacional. People marched organized by unions, commercial associations, student groups, and other civil groups. They held banners in Spanish, English, French, and Italian reading "Cuban mothers want the execution of murderers" and "Cubans are Beside Castro's Justice." Women marched in red blouses and black skirts, the colors of the M-26. Students marched shouting for the heads of Batista and Ventura Novo as people watching from windows above applauded. The following night Sosa Blanco stood handcuffed on a stage in the center of Havana Stadium, surrounded by international press crews and bleachers packed to the rims with some eighteen thousand spectators. Audiences the world over might dispute the legality of the proceedings, but there was no denying that the trials and executions drew on massive public support.

Insurrection and Popular Violence

How can we explain this dramatic outpouring in favor of the trials and executions? First, we must recall the period of intense political conflict and deepening violence that preceded the rebel victory, and sketch out at least briefly when, where, and how violence escalated. Scholars of the insurrection concur that the total number of casualties of the insurrectionary period of 1952–58 was far lower than the official figure of twenty thousand proclaimed by the revolutionary government. Around two to three thousand deaths is a more reasonable estimate.[19] However, those deaths were concentrated geographically and temporally and were predominantly visited on young men with links to certain political groups. This concentration explains how a relatively low number of casualties coincided with the perception, at least among certain sectors, that the insurrection was a virtual holocaust.

In terms of periodization, we can outline an early period (1953–55) of more contained violence that coincided with conspiracies of planned coups and armed uprisings, of which the Moncada attackers led by Fidel Castro were the most sensational.[20] This period also saw concerted attempts to convince Batista to step down or at least call early elections, directed by fractions of the existing political parties such as the Auténticos and Ortodoxos, or by established political and intellectual figures. These initiatives failed due to a combination of government intransigence, growing state repression of political dissent, and self-interested squabbling among various political contenders of the opposition.

The year 1955 witnessed various attempts at civic organization, some more successful than others. For example, the broad campaign for amnesty did result in the release of political prisoners, including the *moncadistas* led by Fidel Castro.[21] Yet successive attempts to negotiate with Batista to call for early elections had failed utterly by late 1955, and by 1956 it had become evident to many in the opposition that Batista would not be removed by civic forms of protest. As a result, the political initiative passed from the established political parties to the new insurgent groups, especially the 26th of July Movement and the Revolutionary Directorate, both formally organized in 1955. The period 1956–58 witnessed broader mobilization in cities, particularly visible in a city-wide uprising in Santiago to coincide with the landing of M-26 expeditionaries in the Granma in late 1956, and in a failed general strike in April 1958. During this period we see a transition to a more generalized violence, as state repression became less discriminate. Violent conflict in urban settings now spread spatially beyond organized university protest to a more ambient street violence affecting residential and commercial areas, and the army was deployed to rout rebels now deeply ensconced in the mountains of Oriente Province.[22]

Additionally, this period (1956–58) also saw various transformations within the state security apparatus. They included the formation of the Buró de Represión de Actividades Comunistas in 1955, the combination of various security forces under unified command (*mando único*), and the recruitment and training of thousands of new soldiers in spring 1958. Government counterinsurgency was facilitated by the suspension of constitutional guarantees, which occurred at regular intervals beginning in January 1957, as well as presidential decrees that, among other things, virtually depenalized the killing of oppositionists. This period witnessed the increasing infiltration of opposition groups and the engagement of paramilitary forces in urban and rural settings.[23] Urban police forces in this period also increasingly used irregular tactics such as unreported detentions, and torture or killings during detention. Finally, the police increasingly undertook the direct, public assassination of insurgents.[24]

Geographically, we can identify two overlapping theaters of violence: first, the cities, especially Havana and Santiago, where political opposition was most organized, and second, the Sierra Maestra mountains and surrounding plains of Oriente Province, which was the site of the rebel stronghold. In these two settings we can identify various patterns of violence. In the Sierras there were clashes between the rebel army, the regular army, and to some extent paramilitary forces.[25] In the cities, we see cyclical violence—reprisal killings—between police and urban militants. This cyclical violence also frequently spiraled out to include opposition sympathizers or people completely uninvolved in the opposition, a process that was crucial in turning urban public opinion against Batista's regime. In the rural areas surrounding the Sierra Maestra in Oriente Province, we also see army violence directed at civilians, including aerial bombings, arson (to forcibly

This August 1958 edition of the clandestine periodical *Resistencia* denounces the aerial bombing of peasants in the Sierra Maestra. Source: Instituto de Historia de Cuba.

displace peasants thought to be supporting rebels), and direct assassinations of peasants or squatters. There were also incidents of army violence against sugar workers on plantations and against employees of nonsugar industries, such as mining.

Indeed, while Havana was undoubtedly the site of major waves of police repression and killings, usually following some concerted action by the opposition, it seems that Oriente Province was the site of more consistent violence, including rashes of police and army killings of civilians that might properly be called massacres; more frequent M-26 executions of *chivatos* (informers) and security officials, especially after the M-26 declared a major campaign to eradicate them; and—although this may be the result of a bias in the documents—more frequent killings of people uninvolved in the opposition. Finally, the more spectacular forms of killing that have been recorded seemed to take place in Oriente Province. For example, while police in both Havana and Santiago occasionally killed detainees in public and frequently left the mutilated bodies of insurrectionists in outlying areas, it is in Oriente Province that one more often reads of the killing of young teenagers, men found hanged from trees and lampposts, and, in one case,

Relatives of men killed during the insurrection display portraits and newspaper photos of loved ones at the trial of Jesús Sosa Blanco. Credit: Cuban Revolution Collection, 1955–70 (inclusive). Manuscripts and Archives, Yale University.

the gruesome promenade of the body of a dead rebel through the streets of Santiago on the hood of an army jeep.[26]

This exploration of the patterns of violence during the insurrection helps explain why Fidel Castro chose Jesús Sosa Blanco as the old regime figure most appropriate for a show trial. The man who stood before hundreds of cameras and thousands of spectators in a sports arena that night in January 1959 was not among the most notorious security agents of the period, at least not for the urban underground. But Sosa Blanco, captain of the army garrison at Holguín, was accused of perpetrating the last type of violence outlined above — attacks on unarmed campesinos in rural Oriente — in a series of local incidents that the leadership must have concluded would seem reprehensible to anyone, including foreign observers, and which would most clearly fit the definition of "war crimes."[27] For many national observers, Sosa Blanco was associated with the vortex of violence that had engulfed Oriente Province and the extreme measures taken by the army against locals during the last two years of the insurrection. In fact, clandestine and exile publications sometimes referred to these attacks on local campesinos as "genocide."[28]

Sosa Blanco's trial, which was televised, dramatized these army abuses of local peasants. Throughout the twelve-hour long trial, Sosa Blanco stood handcuffed, visually suggesting his culpability, while he defiantly proclaimed that this had been war, that he had done his duty, and that he had acted as a man of honor. In contrast with his obdurate denial, some forty witnesses took the stand to describe in emotional detail the havoc Sosa Blanco and his troops had wrought on their towns. Many of these victims' relatives were likely included for the cumulative effect of dozens of emotional denunciations, for not all had been eyewitnesses, as the defense lawyer pointed out. Women whose relatives had been killed by Sosa Blanco wept and flew at the accused in rage. A former soldier under Sosa Blanco's command expressed horror at the atrocities he had seen and concluded, "I couldn't stand the situation any more, seeing the crimes he committed, and I joined the rebels [*me alcé*]."[29]

The tribunal tried to establish that the violence perpetrated against locals had occurred in an area where rebels had not been present, and that the victims had not been involved with the rebels. Witness after witness swore they had never been *alzados*, and that the army had attacked locals although there had been no skirmish with rebels in the area. Whether or not locals in these areas had in fact been involved in provisioning or otherwise aiding the rebel forces is unclear. The territory under Sosa Blanco's command was heavily contested by Raul Castro's column, and was also the site of smaller, independent groups of belligerents and displaced peasants.[30] But the emotional impact of "innocent" campesinos besieged by a bloodthirsty army was not lost on an urban audience; the imagery in fact resonated with opposition propaganda printed during the insurrection, which often cast campesinos as victims rather than protagonists of the struggle. The drama was summed up neatly when the president of the tribunal asked a twelve-year-old boy if his deceased father had been a *fidelista*. "No," the boy replied, "He was a carpenter."

The Legitimacy of Violence

Much of the emotional outpouring and debate generated by the trials and executions and subsequent U.S. opposition to them could be described as a process of articulating the difference between legitimate and illegitimate violence. In this case, legitimate violence encompassed both the guerrilla actions and the rebel-led executions, while illegitimate violence encompassed both that of Batista's security forces and the specter of uncontrolled popular retribution.

These distinctions had to some extent been established during the course of the insurrection, and this helps explain why the opposition increasingly embraced, or at least accepted, armed struggle. Although opposition to Batista had mounted gradually following his coup on March 10, 1952, violence was not widely accepted as a legitimate strategy of opposition until 1957 or even 1958. As noted above, it was only after the definitive derailing of civic negotiations led by moderate opposition groups such as the Sociedad de Amigos de la República in 1955, the killing of the high-profile student leader José Antonio Echeverría and respected urban underground organizer Frank País in 1957, and the failure of the general revolutionary strike of April 1958, that increasingly large numbers of Cubans despaired of any civic solution and began to accept a violent overthrow of Batista. This shift responded to both pure tactical necessity (that is, the weakening of opposition groups other than the M-26) and the engulfing of ever-larger numbers of people in the repressive actions that the state undertook, enflaming the country and bolstering the opposition.[31] Each surge forward by the opposition brought a corresponding crackdown; the violence of each crackdown pushed more people into the arms of the opposition. By December 1957 the U.S. Embassy noted that a "considerable proportion of the opposition now advocates and practices violence" and that the Cuban government was taking increasingly harsh countermeasures.[32] By spring 1958, a state department research report commented that any chances for a peaceful solution to the conflict were gone: "Moderate middle elements have either withdrawn from political activity or aligned themselves with the opposition, and a showdown involving violence and blood shed appears inevitable. Batista is dependent on the armed forces and organized labor, whose leaders remain loyal, to maintain his position. His support among the rank and file of these organizations is much less certain."[33]

As much of the opposition gravitated toward supporting some type of violent opposition to the dictatorship, it may be useful to ask how the opposition understood its own recourse to violence. Some members of the M-26 proclaimed the universal necessity of violence in revolutionary upheavals, referring to historical precedent.[34] However, this was a minority view, even within the M-26. Insurrectionists much more frequently portrayed revolutionary violence as defensive, a tragic but necessary response to Batista's "crimes." The clandestine press frequently narrated the insurrectionary period as a long descent into state terror. The need for the opposition to take up arms in defense was often merely implicit. A 1958 handbill circulated by the M-26 is representative in this regard:

Since March 10 [1952] . . . hundreds of youths—students and workers—have been assassinated in the streets of Cuba's cities for opposing Cuba's transformation into a military barracks directed by delinquents. Thousands of these youths have been tortured . . . in barracks and police stations. . . . [T]he jails are full of political prisoners, among which are found dignified and honest men, both civilian and military; a city was recently air-bombed, resulting in hundreds of deaths and injuries; in the city of Holguín Cubans of all classes and [political] militancies have been shot to death and hanged; various Cuban doctors have been assassinated by security forces for attempting to comply with their sworn duty to lend assistance to any injured or sick person without inquiring their [political] affiliation. Apart from all this . . . in the Sierra Maestra a civil war rages.[35]

The insurgent opposition also often described the anti-Batista struggle as an anticolonial struggle, drawing parallels between the insurrection of the 1950s and the War of Independence of 1895–98. This analogy was partly a strategic rebuttal to the Batista regime's claim that the opposition had provoked violence within the "Cuban family" or "violence between brothers." The clandestine press eschewed this comparison with a civil war, suggesting instead an anticolonial struggle. References abound to Batista as the "antipatriot," as "anti-Cuban," or as Fulgencio "Weyler" Batista—a reference to the notorious Spanish general Valeriano Weyler, sent to pacify the island during the War of Independence. One article openly compared the two struggles by arguing that the War of Independence was not essentially a war between nations; instead, it was a war against despotism in which Cubans and Spaniards participated on both sides. In fact, both struggles were primarily against "dishonor and tyranny." The article used this analysis to goad "indifferents" into action, arguing provocatively that those indifferent toward the anti-Batista struggle were tantamount to the antinationalists of the late nineteenth century: "Those apathetic today would have been apathetic yesterday; they would have seen Martí die without a tremor, Maceo without a protest."[36] Demonstrations held on the anniversaries of important dates in the anticolonial struggle also suggested parallels between the two insurrections, and protesters often sang the national anthem as they clashed with police.[37]

The growing acceptance of armed insurrection was also facilitated by the emergence of certain distinctions—what we might describe as moral distinctions—between state violence and the violence of the opposition. While the violence of the Batista regime was almost universally considered abhorrent, guerrilla violence was increasingly seen as legitimate, both because it could be read as defensive in nature and because the M-26 was considered to have eschewed the crueler aspects of punishment, even in battle. In contrast to the sadistic excesses employed by Batista's men, the guerrilla fighters' violence was considered instrumental only, hence the occasional reference to the revolution as "clean."[38]

While the groundwork for these differences had been established during the insurgency, the days and weeks following Batista's flight served to shore up these distinctions. As mass graves were exhumed and horrific stories of Batistiano terror circulated in conversation and in the media,[39] the trials served to publicly dramatize and clarify the perceived difference between rebel violence and the violence of Batista's forces.

In delineating the illegitimacy of Batistiano violence, popular outrage seemed to coalesce around two central concepts. The first was the linking of violence with enrichment. This connection took various forms. Anecdotes abounded of police who robbed as well as killed their victims: it was said that police stole all money and jewels found in one victim's home, and then even returned the following day to remove and sell the furniture![40] Stories ranged from petty theft to embezzlement, extortion, and the amassing of extensive property by Batista's men. *Bohemia* reported that one policeman had "lands, houses, cattle. But . . . he continued being a despot who wouldn't let go of the whip, who opresed and humilliated the campesinos." Brothers Rafael and José Salas Cañizares, both police chiefs, continued perpetrating violence "despite already being rich," the magazine noted. As *Revolución* angrily fired off lists of former Batista officers' riches, allegations of outrageous wealth seemed nearly tantamount to having committed murder.[41] In the highly emotional atmosphere of January 1959, denunciations ranged from an anecdotal focus on particularly demonized figures to more systemic critiques of government corruption.

The second factor marking state repression as illegitimate was the dishonorable nature of the violence employed. That is to say, it was not simply the use of force that was objected to in the case of Batista's security forces. Rather, certain aspects of the repression were particularly demonized: the killing of civilians (as opposed to those actually involved in the revolutionary underground), the rape of women prisoners, the killing of children as young as twelve, or the killing of various members of one family. Torture was singled out as particularly abhorrent.[42] Rumors alleged that Batista's men had actually enjoyed the tortures and that some policemen had even carried photos of mutilated bodies to brag about their exploits.[43] Testimonial descriptions of the insurgency also reserve particular fury for the way certain respected opposition leaders were killed, their corpses left alongside highways or in other strategic places for display and often bearing marks of torture. Images such as these—the dishonorable killings of honorable men—were at the core of the widespread abhorrence of Batistiano violence.

In this context Batista's overthrow could be perceived as a restoration of national honor. The discourse of the political opposition had long stressed the rotten, corrupt nature of the island's politics. Since its formation in 1947, the Ortodoxo Party in particular had promised the restoration of honor and cleanliness to the diseased body politic after high hopes for the Auténtico governments of 1944–52 were dashed in scandals of embezzlement and graft.[44] The 1951 suicide of the Ortodoxo presidential candidate and figurehead, Eduardo Chibás, lent the drama of martyrdom to calls for honor in government. Thus even before Batista's March 1952 coup, opposition groups had expressed their frustration with a strikingly passionate discourse of moral decay.[45] Over the course of the anti-Batista insurgency, these juxtapositions—contrasting corruption and dignity, immorality and honor, degradation and restoration—were grafted onto two contrasting types of violence, rather than violence versus nonviolence. Upon sweeping to power, the M-26 successfully appropriated this discourse of political redemption, and the trials and executions could thus be seen as transcending simple juridical punishment to restore the republic's lost moral order.

In her study of the persecution of Nazi collaborators in the aftermath of the Second World War in France, Megan Koreman identifies several types of justice operating simultaneously: legal justice, which she describes as the punishments prescribed by the rules of the state; social justice, understood as the just distribution of goods within a community; and honorary justice, which "apportions honor among the living and the dead."[46] Koreman argues that part of the problem of political consolidation in postwar France lay in the fact that the government meted out only legal justice; honorary justice was either carried out by local communities themselves, or simply left unfulfilled. In the case of Cuba in 1959, in contrast, one could argue that the trials led by the new revolutionary authorities wove together legal and

honorary justice in a way that garnered mass support and laid the foundations for the consolidation of the new regime.

The revolutionary tribunals thus served an important political function;
rather than merely mete out formal punishments, they dramatized Batistiano excess and rebel restraint. For example, the contrast of the Batistiano
security forces' "sadism" toward their victims with the benign and even
dignified treatment awarded the war criminals by the M-26 was something
much commented upon during the days of the trials. While the soldier José
Rodríguez openly demonstrated during his trial the torture tactics he had
used against captured revolutionaries, "with him, in contrast, these procedures were not used and [in fact] he was given every kind of [constitutional]
guarantee," *Bohemia* noted.[47] Questioning the Batista spokesman Otto
Meruelo, who turned himself in, reporters asked if he had been treated well
by his captors. When Meruelo replied that he had not even been spoken
to harshly, one reporter shouted, "So they've treated you like [the police
chief] Ventura used to treat us," provoking roars of laughter.[48] And *Revolución* ran a photo that seemed to capture the very essence of the distinction
between the conduct of the rebels and Batista's strongmen: an M-26 soldier
graciously served coffee to four seated detainees accused of war crimes; the
caption declared that the photo spoke "eloquently."[49]

The exemplary treatment of the detained Batistianos at the hands of the
M-26 was also important in that it reinforced another central claim of the
trials' proponents: that execution in these circumstances was not motivated
by revenge. Indeed, much of the debate around the executions centered
more on the tone of the trials than on the fact of the killing. Perhaps sol-
emn, "rational," privately conducted executions might have been acceptable to U.S. critics, but the Cuban newspapers' daily gloating over the
Batistianos' comeuppance and the circus-like atmosphere of the trials (the
"popcorn-munching atmosphere," as described by *Time* magazine) seemed
suffused with a vengeful relish. As two journalists wrote, "To those accustomed to Anglo-Saxon justice, it was repulsive to see a defendant tried in a
sports arena."[50] Yet many Cubans insisted it was not revenge, it was simply
justice. If Batista's men fell before firing squads, they had been condemned
"without the spirit of revenge."[51]

In his book *The Furies*, Arno Mayer notes that vengeance has long been
repudiated as antithetical to the rational legality of the modern state. Vengeance is seen as "irrational, uncontrolled, without end, and beyond appeal"; the channeling of justice through the state apparatus transforms this

personal, private revenge into public, dispassionate punishment.[52] Vengeance may resurface, however, during periods of political upheaval such as revolution, and is again constrained by the rise of the new state, which uses "violence to end violence."[53] So the denial of revenge as an animating factor in the trials served to confer legitimacy on the new authorities partly by constructing revolutionary justice as "modern," exactly the opposite of the archaic, "Banana Republic"–style justice foreign critics imagined (recall the *Time* comment about "blood purges").

Vigilante Justice and Popular Memory

As they justified the revolutionary tribunals to foreign critics, the rebel leaders frequently repeated the need to preempt mob violence; this was one of the earliest and most often repeated justifications given for the executions. This fear of vigilante justice was not, in fact, unjustified. There were some reports that angry crowds were held at bay only by the M-26 militias, narrowly preventing the lynching of a known torturer or informer.[54] Yet, in general, popular fury in the immediate aftermath of Batista's flight either expressed itself in symbolic censure, such as hanging effigies of Batista or painting new names over streets bearing his name, or targeted property rather than people. Thus crowds sacked the houses or other properties of such well-known Batistianos as the paramilitary leader Rolando Masferrer, the police chief Esteban Ventura Novo, Colonel Pilar García, and Sosa Blanco.[55] M-26 militants and prisoners' relatives stormed the Castillo de Principe prison to release political prisoners. Casinos, public telephones, and parking meters—all symbols of the extensive extortion practiced under Batista—were destroyed. The Shell Petroleum headquarters were also targeted, in reprisal for the British government's having sold Batista military supplies.[56] There were other scattered acts of vandalism. But, on the whole, restraint predominated and the M-26 managed to establish authority quickly, stationing militia patrols on the streets of Havana before noon; gleeful crowds turned suspects over to the revolutionary army and boy scouts aided rebels in directing traffic.[57]

More important, vigilante justice had a historical precedent firmly etched into popular memory. The bloodshed that followed Gerardo Machado's removal from office in August 1933 was remembered with horror, and the parallels between Machado's regime of the early 1930s and Batista's rule in the late 1950s were not lost on contemporary observers. Like Batista,

Machado had increasingly relied on violence as internal opposition grew. He set up a huge police apparatus, including the Sección de Expertos, a group reported to specialize in torture, and the Partida de la Porra or *porristas*, a government-sponsored death squad. Particularly after an attempted uprising in August 1931, the struggle between Machado's regime and more radical opposition groups approached open warfare.[58] When Machado finally fell, riots and looting rocked Havana for days. Crowds immediately sacked the presidential palace and lynched the chief of the Porra, Colonel José Antonio Jiménez.[59] Members of an anti-Machado group and victims' relatives systematically hunted down Machado's policemen, then improvised public executions, which were announced daily by drum rolls at dawn.[60] The dead bodies of the most infamous Porristas were dragged triumphantly through the streets. It was estimated that, all told, a thousand people were killed and three hundred houses sacked.[61] When Carlos Céspedes was installed as provisional head of state, he announced that those guilty of atrocities would be tried, yet prosecutions lagged and sanctions were light.[62] It was not until more than a month after Machado's removal that the provisional government decreed the formation of *tribunales de sanciones*, which adhered to ordinary legal procedure, thus disappointing the many Cubans who hoped for more abrupt and exemplary punishments.[63] In the meantime, many of those guilty of the most heinous crimes had fled the island.

These events were present in the minds of many observers as the trials and executions began.[64] As one columnist wrote angrily, the island's collection of corrupt politicians and abusive policemen were "not the product of March 10, 1952. They are the product of 1895, successively ratified in '33 and '44."[65] Another warned that in the debate over the trials, "[they] should keep very clearly in mind the experiences with criminals of prior regimes, who, after killing and robbing, were able to go around Havana with impunity, and, what's more, were rehired."[66] Among the rebel leadership, some also feared a repeat of the 1954 overthrow of Jacobo Arbenz in Guatemala, which had been orchestrated by the U.S. Central Intelligence Agency and carried out by right-wing elements of the Guatemalan army. They were thus anxious to purge the military of those most loyal to Batista.[67] So the revolution of 1959 learned from its predecessors: this time justice would be swift and thorough, and the tribunals would be organized by the revolutionary leadership rather than through the legal infrastructure inherited from the previous regime.[68] The rebel authorities would usurp popular justice by implementing it themselves.

From Anti-Batista to Anti-Imperialist

The angry outpouring over the U.S. media's characterizations of the trials also seemed to push public opinion to more closely scrutinize U.S. foreign policy. It was pointed out repeatedly in editorials and on placards that the U.S. government had never bothered to criticize the violence Batista had unleashed across the island. Many journalists, protesters, and Castro himself noted that the United States had supported the Nuremberg trials, and argued, "Our Himmler is Ventura, our Goering the Tabernillas, the Pilar Garcías. . . . Our Hitler is Batista." Some denounced U.S. hypocrisy in expressing shock over the Cuban executions while engaging in violence abroad and at home. As an editorial in *Bohemia* noted, the trials were judging hardened killers, not "massacring Colombian banana workers or Nicaraguan patriots."[69] An editorialist in *Revolución* compared the tortures practiced under Batista to the atrocities committed by U.S. marines in the Dominican Republic and Nicaragua "in the name of dollar diplomacy." The writer argued, "You cannot compare . . . the shooting of a monster with the lynching of a black man for having whistled at a white woman. It is not the same to punish a man who drove nails into the head of another human being, as to condemn a black man to the electric chair for having stolen 95 cents."[70] Another accused the United States of using the trials as a pretext for reprisals, while the real motivation was the ousting of a business-friendly dictator: "It's not the executions they're trying to stop," he wrote, "but the firm and sure progress of the revolution."[71] And, as the Mexican journalist Armando Rodríguez Suárez warned Cuban readers, "It's clear that . . . along with these intentions against Cuba go the attempts to discredit any popular movement in Latin America . . . [I]f today they make the people yield in their drive toward justice, tomorrow it will be that much easier to detain . . . agrarian reform or . . . the redistribution of wealth . . . or nationalizations" of foreign-owned firms.[72] Similarly, around mid-month Castro began to cast criticism of the trials as a kind of extension of U.S. imperialism, implying that to hold back the executions would be to adopt a "submissive" attitude toward the United States.[73]

Thus, as the controversy over the trials spread, some observers expanded their denunciations of political violence to a more systemic critique of the violence of Batista's regime, one that saw Batista as a frontman for U.S. corporations and expressed expectations that the revolution would alter these power relations. It also contrasted the judicious violence practiced by the new Cuban authorities with the United States' infamous legacy of imperialist violence throughout the hemisphere and against its own "colonized" populations at home. The struggle over the meaning of the trials thus began to stand in more broadly for the fraught relations between Cuba and the United States, and between the United States and Latin America.

These connections were of course most sharply articulated by longstanding members of the anti-imperialist Left and the left wing of the M-26; as many scholars have noted, since the Ten Years' War of 1868–78, radical Cuban nationalism had been infused with an anti-imperialist critique.[74] And it is clear that many Cubans—particularly elites—continued to identify strongly with the United States in this period.[75] But the controversy surrounding the trials briefly provided a highly charged public venue for these critiques, allowing them to spread to some extent across the political spectrum and throughout the class structure. As the journalist Carlton Beals noted,

> Nothing has done more to solidify the Cuban people behind the revolutionary Government than the "bath of blood" statements by our Congressmen, the veiled threats of intervention, the possible cutting off of trade, the imposition of sanctions, the proposal that American tourists be prevented from going to Cuba. From end to end of this island, the cry goes up, "*Unidad! Unidad!*" and it sounds forth from the Communists to the extreme Catholic Right. On every corner, in every bar and restaurant, on every autobus, comes a bitter anti-American reproach.[76]

It could be argued that the potential spread of these more radical sentiments—those denouncing U.S. intervention in the hemisphere or directly linking violence with the maintenance of a certain economic or racial order—were what most concerned State Department officials. While some senators in Washington publicly expressed their outrage over the executions, U.S. government representatives on the island privately took a more conciliatory tone, attempting to downplay U.S. senators' denunciations and elicit promises of more restrained rhetoric from Cuban officials in exchange. In a meeting with the minister of state Roberto Agramonte, the embassy chargé d'affaires Daniel Braddock expressed dismay over the "misunderstanding that had occurred over [the] trials and executions," and asked Agramonte to "carefully distinguish between unofficial statements in [the] U.S. and those of [the] government."[77] Shortly after the execution of some seventy people in Santiago, the consul there recommended easing bilateral relations rather than adopting punitive measures. Perhaps the U.S. government could publicize the "positive aspects" of its policy toward Cuba, he suggested—for example, by publishing a document related to the banning of arms sales to Batista in 1957 or producing evidence that the napalm used against Oriente campesinos had not originated in the United States. He also recommended the extradition of the paramilitary leader Senator Rolando Masferrer, who, under the circumstances, would certainly have received the death penalty.[78]

Maintaining a more or less restrained posture toward the executions, U.S. officials did, however, express serious concern with the public questioning of Cuba's relationship with the United States and of the U.S. role in global politics generally. Worried that speakers might voice "anti-American" sentiments at the major rally of January 21, Braddock broached the subject with Agramonte the night before the rally to seek assurances of moderation. But the speeches made at the rally struck U.S. officers as relatively measured, and that evening Castro further assuaged concern when he met with the diplomatic corps and explained that "on a public occasion like the rally he had to express 'certain points of view,' and added something to the effect that of course the two countries would get along together." Braddock concluded with relief that the "dominant note of the day was not anti-Americanism but national pride."[79]

These glimpses of diplomatic meetings reveal a mixture of public denunciation and private cajoling on both sides of the fence. While this could be seen as simple everyday realpolitik, it also seems to capture a genuine ambiguity on the part of Cuban officials. Denunciations of U.S. criticism went hand in hand with attempts to sway those same U.S. critics through invitations to journalists and senators. Jumbled references to Nuremberg and Nagasaki sought to establish precedent and legitimacy by appealing to a political process sanctioned by the United States, on the one hand, and to denounce the United States as a perpetrator of war crimes of its own, on the other.

Similarly, while Castro and other leaders exclaimed loudly that they would prove to U.S. observers that revolutionary justice was morally impeccable, there is evidence that the leadership may have tried to accommodate U.S. pressure. Following the initial media frenzy, for example, attempts were made to formalize the trial proceedings. A *New York Times* reporter, Herbert Matthews, wrote: "Often the [earliest] trials consisted of an accused man appearing before a small group of rebel officers and being identified by a number of citizens of the locality as a man who had tortured and killed. That would be enough. In most places, especially after the first few days, a more elaborate procedure was used with a panel of military judges, a prosecutor, and with the accused having the right to counsel."[80]

Despite the impression the U.S. media gave of the executions, there were some efforts to formalize, and even slow down, the trials. For example, on January 16, Raúl Castro announced that trials would be temporarily suspended in order to put together more convincing evidence against the defendants. The pace of executions may also have slowed as invitations were extended to several U.S. congressmen to attend the massive January 21 rally.[81]

Yet the executions were popular, and lags in the pace of the trials provoked public outrage. Presiding over the trials, the revolutionary leadership also felt itself pushed from below regarding the terms of punishment, about which M-26 leaders and the general public frequently differed. Was a long prison term sufficient punishment for killing? Should defendants have a right to appeal? Did informers (*chivatos*) also deserve capital punishment? As Castro warned, "Be assured that we are going to be much more benign than what the people want. . . . [I]f we follow what the people want, we would have to shoot all the informers, which is a considerable quantity, but you can't. One has to punish the exemplary cases, the minimum. For the rest, there are other punishments. Not everyone has to be shot."[82] But the public often felt the sentences were not harsh enough. As a tribunal member, Orlando Borrego, later recalled, people "thought the sentencing was too benign. . . . Sometimes one asked for [a sentence of] ten years and the people wanted it to be twenty."[83] Toward the end of the month trials were again delayed, and now appeals were permitted in all cases.[84] Again the delays caused consternation, and soon new legal steps were taken to hasten the trials: the constitution was altered for ninety days in order to hasten detentions; prisoners were now allowed to be tried in any part of the island, not simply where the alleged crime had taken place; and six new courts were created in Havana to try war criminals.[85]

Meanwhile, local protests continued. In Manzanillo, when two soldiers received prison terms instead of death, and one corporal was acquitted, the decision sparked a two-day riot.[86] In Santiago the acquittal of a notorious man provoked tumultuous protests;[87] and when the Tribunal Superior de

Guerra overturned the death sentence given by a local tribunal in Pinar del Rio, sentencing the three defendants to prison sentences instead, public outrage took on ominous overtones, including veiled references to the potential such decisions had to breed counterrevolution.[88]

The new revolutionary authorities sought to curb these expressions of discontent. In February 1959, in several towns in Oriente Province, local anger over what were considered insufficiently harsh sentences developed into organized protests, including a brief transportation strike and declarations to a local newspaper.[89] Two rebel army commanders were sent to stop the disturbances and release a statement of warning:

> The problem posited by the people of Palma Soriano, protesting because Revolutionary Justice is being applied slowly and benignly [con mucha demora y benigdad] has served to allow Contramaestre to use the same incorrect procedure [protests]. . . . We say it is incorrect because they are using the same demagogic methods from 20 years ago, using public agitation to get attention. [But] a popular government, a government whose leaders cannot be called politiqueros or demagogues, a government that is resolving as quickly as possible all the problems brought on by the disintegration of a corrupt state, a government that loves liberty, respects individual rights, and is incapable of using public force against the people, because it emerged from the people . . . a government like this cannot be blackmailed with demagogic protests, disturbances of public peace. . . . We responsibly demand . . . that there be no more acts such as those in Palma and Contramaestre. [We ask that] when some injustice is committed, you go to the corresponding organisms, and you will see that justice will be done quickly.[90]

So throughout the trials and subsequent international controversy the revolutionary leadership navigated pressure from abroad and from below, responding to popular anger as well as channeling and containing it.

Popular Support and Political Maneuver

Is it justified to describe the vast majority of Cubans as supporting the revolutionary tribunals? Many contemporary observers described nearly complete consensus in favor of the trials and executions. As Herbert Matthews reported for the *New York Times*, there was "hardly a family in Cuba that did not have a member at least arrested and at worst tortured and killed. . . . Moreover, in every city, town and village, the killers and torturers were known." There were, therefore, "very few Cubans indeed who would disapprove of the executions."[91] The U.S. consul in Santiago concurred, noting widespread support in the capital and villages of Oriente Province. Upon visiting a nearby town whose inhabitants were outraged by the discovery of secret mass graves, he remarked that "While U.S.-style evidence might be lacking without a thorough investigation by trained personnel . . . there appears no doubt but that the inhabitants were terrorized. . . . Needless to say, these people were fully in favor of revolutionary justice."[92]

At this early stage it would be incorrect to ascribe a class character to the support of the tribunals.[93] Although some segments of Cuba's elite (such as sugar magnates) harbored suspicions about reforms the revolution might usher in, by 1958 even the elites who had initially supported Batista had abandoned him, reducing his base of support almost entirely to the armed forces and those on the government payroll. Thus, with the exception of Batista's closest supporters, now scurrying to seek safe haven in foreign embassies, approval of the trials and executions seems to have been nearly universal.[94]

Still, there are a few scattered suggestions that the rebel leadership may have been concerned to portray support for the tribunals as overwhelming, perhaps revealing some anxiety that domestic criticism might emerge.[95] While televising the trials and executions can be seen as contributing to the national catharsis that followed years of state repression and censorship, perhaps it was also partly meant to convey a sense of irrevocable political rupture to those not yet fully convinced of the M-26's claims to power. Similarly, the mammoth rally of January 21, while primarily directed toward foreign critics, may have also been a calculated display of support for domestic as well as foreign observers.

This is not to say that the phenomenal attendance at the rally—which neared the total population of Havana, if the figure of one million can be believed—was not motivated by genuine support for the trials. Though the rally was called for by Castro, the new authorities did not yet have the mechanisms, developed in subsequent years, to mobilize those who fell outside the original organizational structure of the M-26. In fact, in its published instructions the rally's organizing committee envisioned the march as being organized into sections of schools, labor unions, professional and civic associations, and so on. That is to say, those people who

Mass rallies against U.S. criticism of the trials, called by the revolutionary
leadership, drew hundreds of thousands of people in Havana.
Credit: Cuban Revolution Collection, 1955–70 (inclusive).
Manuscripts and Archives, Yale University.

did not attend the rally as individuals were to be organized into groups
that reflected existing loyalties, and press accounts and photos suggest this
was the case. For example, the Confederación de Trabajadores de Cuba led
a large feeder march from its headquarters to the Palacio Nacional, seg-
mented into unions of sugar workers, office employees, service workers,
and so on. Multiple student groups, professional and civic organizations,
and neighborhood groups were visible in the crowd. A group of elderly
mambises (veterans of the War of Independence), their *guayaberas* adorned
with faded medals, were met with particularly loud clapping.[96]

Notable for their absence were groups organized under the banners of
political parties. This was no accident. A U.S. embassy officer was informed
that "political slogans, or the mentioning of any political party, had been
banned, and the PSP [Communist Party] banners which had been unfurled
near the Palace were at some period during the proceedings quietly put
away."[97] Much as they had when excluding rival revolutionary groups and
political parties from the triumphant march into Havana in early January,
the leaders of the M-26 attempted to shape the appearance of the large rally
in order to emphasize their own political strength.

Other groups engaged in similar maneuvers. Although it would be several months before the revolutionary leadership proclaimed the working class and peasantry their base of support, putting Cuban elites on the defensive, the social tensions that would eventually polarize and radicalize the revolution were already visible in subtle disagreements over how to carry out rallies. For example, on the same day of the massive rally of January 21, Oriente Province was "strikebound for eighteen hours . . . when local labor unions decided to demonstrate their support of revolutionary justice."[98] Timed to coincide with the massive rally in Havana, the labor-led demonstrations in Oriente shut down businesses throughout the day, irritating some merchants and businessmen who felt that "there could have been a token strike or an evening 'manifestation' without interrupting commerce and industry." Several days later, a Catholic rally was held in Santiago's central plaza, in tribute to both the new government and Archbishop Enrique Pérez Serante, who had systematically denounced the Batista government's repression. While similarly supportive of the trials and executions, the Catholic rally was meant to offset the left-leaning tone of the prior labor-led demonstration: while criticizing monopolies and calling for social justice, the Catholic speakers took care to express their resolute anticommunism.[99] So beneath the broad consensus over the tribunals, various groups tried to shape displays of support in ways that would showcase their own strengths and further their own interests.

Conclusions

After the show trial of Sosa Blanco, the trials were moved to less spectacular venues and were no longer televised. By July 1959, the work of the revolutionary tribunals had been shifted to tribunales ordinarios,[100] which now turned to the different task of prosecuting internal opposition. It was the end of the era of revolutionary justice, and the beginning of the institutionalization of the revolution. All told, perhaps between three hundred and seven hundred people were executed, a figure which, in retrospect, marks the aftermath of the Cuban Revolution as distinctly less bloody than the other tumultuous regime changes that have punctuated the twentieth century.[101]

It is clear that the trials helped consolidate popular support for the revolution. The quick organization of the trials and the firm response to foreign disapproval lent the revolutionary leadership credibility in the eyes of the

Cuban public and channeled popular anger into state-sanctioned justice. The outpouring of denunciations of violence suffered under Batista generated by the trials extended public knowledge of the abuses of the prior regime, occurring within and contributing to a framework that contrasted legitimate and illegitimate violence. The public repudiation of Batistiano violence, viewed in contrast to the purported civility and humanity of the M-26, helped cast the trials and executions as a restoration of the country's lost moral compass.

This essay has attempted to go beyond existing interpretations of violence during and in the aftermath of the insurrection. Critics of the Cuban Revolution have tended to explain the outbreak of armed insurrection and the executions of 1959 as a reflection of some ahistorical Marxist propensity toward violence and hatred, imposed downward from the leadership onto the impressionable hordes in a kind of mass hysteria.[102] This view does not explain the context in which many Cubans eventually came to support or at least tolerate armed insurgency; overlooks clear expressions of middle-class approval of the trials and executions;[103] provides no model for understanding the violence of the anticommunist counterrevolution; and fails to ask even such simple questions as whether, for example, the thousands of participants in the anti-Batista insurrection—the revolutionary rank and file, so to speak—saw civic and armed opposition as incompatible strategies.

Cuba's official history, on the other hand, has created its own set of myths. Since 1961, the Cuban leadership has sought to place the insurrection within the postwar revolutionary wave of the decolonizing world, along with Algeria and Vietnam; by implication, it is assumed that revolutionaries saw themselves as enacting an anti-imperialist, "third world-ist" revolution. But contemporary actors rarely saw this parallel themselves; not even the farthest left wing of the M-26 theorized violence as an act of national liberation and personal affirmation, as would Frantz Fanon a few years later.[104] Although some members of the M-26 and other opposition groups did express a burgeoning anti-imperialist sentiment, the anti-Batista insurrection was predominantly understood by its participants as a nationalist, democratic struggle. The most consistent parallels drawn by contemporaries were either to Hungary, which a few years earlier had been involved in a bloody uprising against the Soviets, or to the Cuban independence struggle of 1895–98. The move from "Cuba: Hungary of the Americas" to "Two, Three, Many Vietnams" was largely provoked by post-1959 developments.

For this reason it is significant that the debate surrounding the trials provided an early platform for the public articulation of certain concepts—the fundamental incompatibility of radical Cuban nationalism with U.S. interests, for example, or the need for deeper structural change than that implemented after the revolution of 1933—concepts that became increasingly central to the revolution during the next two years. Similarly, the widespread outrage over Batistiano violence, often linked in the popular imagination with illicit enrichment, helped garner mass support for radical early measures that paved the way, one could argue, for the more sweeping economic restructuring of 1960 and 1961. For example, the fact that even *El Diario de la Marina*, the conservative mouthpiece of Cuba's *clases económicas*, applauded the formation of a ministry to oversee the confiscation of property belonging to Batistianos—what were, in effect, the revolution's first nationalizations—is a sign of how far bitterness and frustration with the previous regime had spread.[105] Thus at a time when the ideology of the revolution was still vaguely described as "nationalist," and the period of class struggle ultimately resulting in socialism had yet to be ignited, the debate concerning the trials stood as an early testament to the more radical undertones of the revolution, permitting the articulation of a vision of deep social transformation and profound rupture with the previous regime.

Notes

1. The most complete sources on the trials are John Lee Anderson, *Che Guevara: A Revolutionary Life* (New York: Grove Press, 1997), and Hugh Thomas, *Cuba: The Pursuit of Freedom* (New York: Harper and Row, 1971). For a description of the trials from the perspective of the legal innovations involved, see José García Álvarez, "Los tribunales revolucionarios," in *Legalidad y poder popular en Cuba* (Buenos Aires: Editorial Convergencia, 1976). On the historical Iberian conception of "justice" as opposed to "law" in the March 1959 retrial ordered by Fidel Castro of air force pilots accused of genocide, see Francisco José Moreno, "Justice and Law in Latin America: A Cuban Example," *Journal of Interamerican Studies and World Affairs* 12, no 3 (July 1970): 367–78. For an emphasis on criticism of the executions within the United States, see Reinaldo Suárez Suárez, "Oriente: Criminales de guerra y justicia revolucionaria," trabajo de diploma, Universidad de Oriente, Facultad de Derecho, 1989.

2. The classic account of the insurrection is Nelson Bonachea and Marta San Martín, *The Cuban Insurrection, 1952–1959* (New Brunswick, N.J.: Transaction Books, 1974). On the emergence of the M-26 as the strongest among the various opposition groups,

see Marifeli Pérez-Stable, *The Cuban Revolution: Origins, Course, and Legacy* (Oxford: Oxford University Press, 1993); Samuel Farber, *Revolution and Reaction in Cuba: A Political Sociology from Machado to Castro* (Middletown, Conn.: Wesleyan University Press, 1976); Louis Pérez, *Cuba: Between Reform and Revolution* (New York: Oxford University Press, 1988); and Gladys Marcel García-Pérez, *Insurrection and Revolution: Armed Struggle in Cuba, 1952–1959* (Boulder, Colo.: Lynne Rienner Publishers, 1998). On the urban civic resistance groups led by the M-26, see Lucas Morán Arce, *La revolución cubana (1953–59): una versión rebelde* (Ponce, Puerto Rico: Imprenta Universitaria Universidad Catolica, 1980), and José María Cuesta Braniella, *La resistencia cívica en la batalla de liberación de Cuba* (Havana: Ciencias Sociales, 1997). For a focus on the failure of moderate civic opposition groups led by the old political elites, see Jorge Ibarra Guitart, *Sociedad de Amigos de la República* (Havana: Ciencias Sociales, 2003) and *El fracaso de los moderados en Cuba* (Havana: Editora Política, 2000). On the internal developments of the M-26 and its growing strength relative to other opposition groups, see Julia Sweig, *Inside the Cuban Revolution: Fidel Castro and the Urban Underground* (Cambridge, Mass.: Harvard University Press, 2002).

3. Carlos Franqui, *Diary of the Cuban Revolution* (New York: Viking Press, 1980), 483, 513–14. On the rise and eclipse of the Revolutionary Directorate, see Jaime Suchlicki, *University Students and Revolution in Cuba, 1920–1968* (Coral Gables: University of Miami Press, 1969), 70–86; and also Bonachea and San Martín, *The Cuban Insurrection*.

4. Anderson, *Che Guevara*, 381.

5. *New York Times*, January 2, 1959.

6. On the immediate postrevolutionary period, Richard Welch writes that rather than any specific political platform, Castro's strength as a leader lay in immediately "capitalizing on the confusion and weakness of other anti-Batista organizations" (*Response to Revolution: The United States and the Cuban Revolution, 1959–1961* [Chapel Hill: University of North Carolina Press, 1985], 9).

7. *Revolución,* January 5–6, 1959; *New York Times*, January 5–6, 1959.

8. *Revolución*, January 7, 1959.

9. Roughly three hundred of them left in the first days of January, including the senator and paramilitary leader Rolando Masferrer, who escaped to Miami on a yacht, and the Havana police chief Esteban Ventura Novo, who also escaped to the United States. See Paco Ignacio Taibo II, *Guevara, Also Known as Che* (New York: St. Martin's Press, 1997), 266, and Thomas, *Cuba*, 1075. The U.S. ambassador, Earl Smith, personally intervened by helping to assure the safe passage of the several hundred Batistianos who had made it to foreign embassies, including General Cantillo. See Karl E. Meyer and Tad Szulc, *The Cuban Invasion: Chronicle of a Disaster* (New York: Praeger, 1962), 31.

10. Associated Press (printed in *New York Times*), January 8, 1959.

11. *New York Times*, January 11, 1959.

12. *Revolución*, January 14, 1959.

13. *Revolución*, January 13, 1959; Associated Press (printed in *New York Times*), January 13, 1959; *Time*, January 26, 1959.

14. *Time*, January 26, 1959.

15. *New York Times*, January 15, 1959; *Revolución*, January 17, 19, 20, 1959.

16. Carlos Todd, "Let's Look at Today," *Times of Havana*, January 17, 1959.

17. Colegio Nacional de Profesionales Publicitarios to Eisenhower, February 5, 1959. Confidential Records of the Department of State, Record Group (hereafter referred to as RG) 59, consulted on microfilm.

18. Revolutionary leaders put the number at one million; U.S. embassy officials estimated some 500,000.

19. See Rafael Fermoselle, *The Evolution of the Cuban Military: 1492–1986* (Miami: Ediciones Universal, 1987), 15, 224.

20. For a useful contextualization of Fidel Castro's 26th of July movement among the various small armed groups that emerged in the immediate aftermath of Batista's 1952 coup, see Rolando E. Bonachea and Nelson P. Valdes, "Introduction," *Revolutionary Struggle, 1947–58*, vol. 1 of *Selected Works of Fidel Castro* (Cambridge, Mass.: MIT Press, 1972).

21. The amnesty campaign was led by various civic committees formed for the purpose, including the Comité Nacional Pro-Amnistía and the Comité de Madres de Detenidos. The Communist Party (PSP, or Partido Socialista Popular) also lent its support. See Angelina Rojas Blaquier, *1955: cronica de una marcha ascendiente*, Avance de Investigacion no. 7 (Havana: Instituto de Historia, 1998).

22. The best sources on the transformations in violence during this period are the correspondence of the U.S. Embassy in Havana and the Department of State. Also see Linda Ann Klouzal, "Rebellious Affinities: Narratives of Community, Resistance, and Women's participation in the Cuban Revolution (1952–1959)," Ph.D. diss., University of California at Santa Barbara, 2006.

23. Cuba's main paramilitary group was the "Tigres de Masferrer," led by Senator Rolando Masferrer. The Tigres were estimated to have between five hundred and fifteen hundred men and were thought to be responsible for some of the worst atrocities committed by security forces during the insurrection. The group had its origin in the "action groups" of the 1940s, which struggled with one another for control of Havana University and were sometimes used by the Auténtico administrations (1944–52) as bodyguards and to assassinate Communist labor leaders. The coup of 1952 disrupted the action groups' activities, as former members of some groups (for

example, Fidel Castro) became involved in conspiratorial activities to overthrow the new regime, while others (Rolando Masferrer and his followers) aligned themselves with Batista and grew into much larger, better-armed paramilitary forces. On the formation of the action groups, see Samuel Farber, *Revolution and Reaction in Cuba*, 119–22. Also see Bonachea and Valdés, "Introduction," *Revolutionary Struggle*, 16–27.

24. The most notorious examples of such assassinations were the killing of the Oriente leader of the M-26, Frank País, in summer of 1957 in broad daylight on a residential street of Santiago, and the infamous "Humbolt 7" incident, in which police killed several Revolutionary Directorate leaders found in a safe house in Centro Habana. This tactic was also used in the repression of the failed April 9, 1958, general strike. As one journalist reported, victims in Havana were "taken from residences and then killed and were not shot down in the streets as they attacked police as reported by the government" ("Notes on phone conversation with Ruby Hart Phillips," April 11, 1958, Herbert Matthews Papers, Columbia University, box 1, folder "Correspondence 1951–1954").

25. With the August 1957 reorganization of security forces in the eastern region, Masferrer's forces were apparently deployed in open combat in the Sierra. (See despatch from American Consulate, Santiago, to Department of State, August 28, 1957, RG 59.)

26. On this last incident, see American Consulate, Santiago, despatch to Department of State, October 6, 1958. On incidents of violence in Oriente more broadly, see, for example, "Alleged atrocities committed by Cuban Government, December 2, 1956–November 13, 1957," enclosed in memo from Leonhardy to Weiland, November 25, 1957, RG 59, lot 59 D2, General Records of the Department of State, Subject Files Relating to Cuba, 1951–57, box 1, file "Consulate Santiago Reports 1957," Nation Archives and Records Administration; and DRA Special Paper no. A-8-2, "Increased Incidents of Violence in Cuba," February 20, 1958, RG 59, lot 75 D 242, INR records 1947–63, box 15, Nation Archives and Records Administration.

27. Sosa Blanco was accused of killing twelve mine workers near Nicaro, killing close to forty campesinos in Oro de Guisa, and of burning one local alive by leaving him restrained in a house that soldiers set on fire. He was also accused of using locals as a human shield during subsequent battles with rebel forces. Two other army commanders from the zone, Ricardo Luis Grao and Pedro Morejón Valdés, were also brought from Oriente to Havana, accused of similarly horrific crimes, but their trials were not televised. See Suárez Suárez, "Oriente," 98–110.

28. See, for example, "Manifiesto al pueblo de Cuba," in *Sierra Maestra* (Miami), June 1958, and Dysis Guira, "Cuba partida en dos," *La Vanguardia* (Buenos Aires), December 8, 1958.

29. "Batista es un canalla que me embarcó—Sosa," *Prensa Libre*, January 24, 1959, 1.

30. On Raul Castro's Segundo Frente, see Bonachea and San Martín, *The Cuban Insurrection*, 187–97. On the presence in the area of small groups of rebels, sometimes forced into taking up arms after a failed local attack, see Morán Arce, *La revolución cubana*, 250–51. Morán Arce suggests that some of these small independent groups were later incorporated under Raul Castro's command.

31. On the acceptance of armed insurgency by segments of the opposition who had previously put their faith in public dialogue or civic resistance, see Pérez-Stable, *The Cuban Revolution*, 56–58, and Suchlicki, *University Students and Revolution in Cuba*, 81–86.

32. Despatch, American Embassy, Havana, to Department of State, December 7, 1957.

33. Memo from deputy director of intelligence and research to secretary of state, April 1, 1958, reprinted in *Foreign Relations of the United States, 1958–1960*, vol. 6, *Cuba* (Washington, D.C.: Department of State, 1991), 77–78.

34. See, for example, the editorial "Paz, pero sin Batista," which claims, "Violence is necessary. To not use violence when the conquest of liberty or recovery of the state of law depends on it, is an unpardonable crime. . . . The revolution raises its historical right [*razón*] and proclaims the urgent necessity of violence!" In *Revolución*, February 15, 1957 (Herbert Matthews Papers, box 8).

35. "La feria ganadera y el pueblo de Camagüey," July 26, undated handbill circa 1958, RG 84, box 5, file 350, "Island Reports 1956–58," Nation Archives and Records Administration. This view was by no means limited to the M-26; in fact it was dominant. Another example is the manifesto of the armed group related to the Auténtico party, the Organización Auténtica. The manifesto makes scant mention of the systemic political and economic problems that plagued Cuba, instead describing the rise of state violence as the reason for insurrection. See Organización Auténtica, "Manifiesto," pamphlet, May 1957 (Herbert Matthews Papers, box 8).

36. "Las cosas como son: ayer y hoy," *Resistencia*, August 5, 1958 (Prensa Clandestina collection, Instituto de Historia). The references are to the independence leaders José Martí and Antonio Maceo. On the centrality of the figure of Martí to Cuban nationalism, see Lillian Guerra, *The Myth of José Martí: Conflicting Nationalisms in Early Twentieth-Century Cuba* (Chapel Hill: University of North Carolina Press, 2005).

37. Handbill, "24 de Febrero de 1958," Movimiento de Resistencia Cívica (Camagüey), RG 84, box 6, file "Propaganda," Nation Archives and Records Administration.

38. As Timothy Wickham-Crowley argues, left-wing guerrillas in Latin America prior to the 1970s did not typically resort to excessive violence, torture, or rape; when killings of prisoners occurred, for example, they generally took the form of straightforward executions. "Guerrilla terror is generally far more selective than government

terror," he writes, partly because "socialist guerrillas are often fundamentally motivated by a moral vision of a better world, which precludes terrorist actions as inconsistent with such a vision" ("Terror and Guerrilla Warfare," *Comparative Studies in Society and History* 32, no. 2 [April 1990]: 216). The few Sierra Maestra executions described in Franqui uphold this generalization, although the majority of the guerrillas would not at that time have defined themselves as "socialist." However, the men executed were never captured soldiers (who seem to have been used for prisoner exchange), but were M-26 turncoats and rebels guilty of perpetrating crimes among the locals, such as rape. Of course, the M-26 leaders also consciously promoted an image of principled violence during the insurgency and afterwards, both to ensure broad public support and, more pragmatically, to encourage army members to defect to the rebel side without fear of undue reprisal. See the transcripts of *radio rebelde* broadcasts, held in the Carlos Franqui Collection at Princeton University Library, which assure soldiers they will be treated well by their new comrades.

39. Some of these stories may have been more fiction than fact, for example, reports that the Escuadrón 66 commander, Jacinto García Menocal, based in Pinar del Rio, asked his men to bring him the ears of victims to ensure they had been killed. See Rolando Pérez, "Menocal, el Chacal de Occidente," *Carteles*, January 21, 1959, 30–32.

40. Rine Leal, "Cerca de 300 las ejecuciones," *Carteles*, February 22, 1959, 30–31, 79–80.

41. The following is a typical denunciation that seamlessly merges allegations of violence and enrichment: "Under what moral or juridical precept can individuals be protected who kidnapped our youth . . . tore out their eyes, ripped out their fingernails, applied electric current to their genitals . . . ? How many private cemeteries did [those security officers] have? How many torture chambers were maintained to impose political terror, drag out confessions, and continue the scandalous usufruct of productive businesses? How many *fincas* were stolen from the state . . . ? How many payrolls were swollen?" Lolo de la Torriente, "Un tratamiento de cauterio . . ." *Carteles*, February 1, 1959, 55.

42. As Batista increasingly relied on force to stay in power, security forces intensified the use of torture to persecute dissidents. See Franqui, *Diary of the Cuban Revolution*, 443–44. On Batista's early rise to power as a populist reformer, using repression but also attempting to establish alliances that would broaden his bases of support, see Luis E. Aguilar, *Cuba 1933: Prologue to Revolution* (Ithaca: Cornell University Press, 1972), and Robert Whitney, *State and Revolution in Cuba: Mass Mobilization and Political Change* (Chapel Hill: University of North Carolina Press, 2001).

43. *New York Times*, January 24, 1959. The role of the mass media in contributing to people's knowledge about the extent of violence is notable. By the time of the rebels' triumph, the brutality of the Batistiano police force had already become legendary.

But in the following days the lifting of press censorship, the exhumation of mass graves, the discovery of secret torture chambers in police stations, and the disturbing testimony given at the trials formalized people's knowledge of the extent of violence. As one columnist wrote, "Every indictment, every confession, every testimony made manifest the horrors imposed by these criminals. Despite the prevalent rumors and deep suspicions, the citizenry could never imagine what was [really] happening in Cuba" (*Bohemia*, February 8, 1959).

44. On the disappointments of Auténtico rule, see Pérez, *Cuba*, 284–88. On opposition to the Auténtico government, see E. Vignier G. Alonso, *La corrupción política y administrativa en Cuba, 1944–1952* (Havana: Ciencias Sociales, 1973). For a more positive assessment of the Auténtico period, stressing democratic procedure over corruption, see Charles Ameringer, *The Cuban Democratic Experience: The Auténtico Years, 1944–1952* (Gainesville: University of Florida Press, 2000).

45. See Samuel Farber, *The Origins of the Cuban Revolution Reconsidered* (Chapel Hill: University of North Carolina Press, 2006), on the importance of honor and morality in the Cuban populism of the late 1940s and 1950s. On the articulation of a discourse of moral crisis by liberal intellectuals from the 1920s through the 1940s, see Velia Cecilia Bobes, *Los laberintos de la imaginación: repertorio simbólico, identidades y actores del cambio social en Cuba* (Mexico City: Colegio de Mexico, 2000), 58–70.

46. Megan Koreman, *The Expectation of Justice: France, 1944–46* (Durham: Duke University Press, 1999), 6.

47. *Bohemia*, February 1, 1959.

48. *Revolución*, February 3, 1959.

49. *Revolución*, February 7, 1959.

50. Meyer and Szulc, *The Cuban Invasion*, 32.

51. As one *Revolución* columnist wrote: "It's not about vengeance. Because revenge won't return life to the dead, nor health to the wounded. It's not even about punishment, because taking one life one can never punish the taking of fifty lives. It's about something much more important" (January 13, 1959).

52. Arno J. Mayer, *The Furies: Violence and Terror in the French and Russian Revolutions* (Princeton: Princeton University Press, 2000), 127.

53. Ibid., 137.

54. See, for example, Angel Abascal Ledesma, "Salvó mi vida la justicia revolucionaria," *Carteles*, February 1, 1959, 62; Antonio Llano Montes, "Los criminales murieron al amanecer," *Carteles*, February 1, 34–36; and "Quisieron linchar a los acusados de criminals de guerra Grao y Morejón," *Prensa Libre*, January 25, 1959, 3.

55. The building of Masferrer's newspaper, *Tiempo en Cuba*, was targeted. For a detailed description of the looting and vandalism that occurred in the first days of

January, see Enrique Gutiérrez, "La justicia del pueblo," *Carteles*, January 21, 1959, 90–92, 110–12.

56. Thomas, *Cuba*, 1029.

57. Braddock to Department of State, February 25, 1959, RG 59.

58. Louis A. Pérez, *Cuba under the Platt Amendment, 1902–1934* (Pittsburgh: University of Pittsburgh Press, 1986), 284–93.

59. Thomas, *Cuba*, 625.

60. Ibid., 628.

61. Ibid.

62. Pérez, *Cuba under the Platt Amendment*, 319; Thomas, *Cuba*, 630; Aguilar, *Cuba 1933*, 157–58.

63. García Álvarez, "Los tribunales revolucionarios," 127.

64. Gervasio Ruiz, "300 milicianos evitaron a la Habana otro 12 de Agosto," *Carteles*, February 15, 1959, 30–31, 83.

65. *Revolución*, January 15, 1959.

66. Bernardo Diaz, "Justicia Americana," *Revolución*, January 16, 1959. In the late 1930s, Batista reappointed many of the officials of the *machadato* (Pérez-Stable, *The Cuban Revolution*, 43).

67. As Anderson notes, "The lessons of 'Guatemala 1954' had been a watershed experience for both victors and losers." Guevara and others tried to apply "preventive medicine" to prevent a US-backed coup, while US officials measured the Cuban Revolution's strengths relative to the rise of Arbenz (*Che Guevara*, 421).

68. See García Álvarez, "Los tribunales revolucionarios," 127–28. As Sweig points out, many of the Cuban Revolution's participants were highly conscious of the historical antecedents to the 1959 revolution. Armando Hart, for instance, warned fellow M-26 members that neither in the 1890s nor 1930s had the revolutionary forces developed sufficient resources for "confronting and surviving the confusion and counterrevolution" that ensued (*Inside the Cuban Revolution*, 57, 88).

69. *Bohemia*, February 1.

70. *Revolución*, January 21, 1959.

71. *Revolución*, January 16, 1959.

72. Armando Rodríguez Suárez, "Lágrimas de cocodrilo," *Revolución*, February 2, 1959.

73. *Revolución*, January 16, 1959.

74. On the forging of a radical nationalism during the Ten Years' War and War of Independence, see Ada Ferrer, *Insurgent Cuba: Race, Nation, and Revolution, 1868–1898*

(Chapel Hill: University of North Carolina Press, 1999). On the continued legacy of radical nationalism and its importance in the 1959 revolution, see C. A. M. Hennessy, "The Roots of Cuban Nationalism," *International Affairs* (Royal Institute of International Affairs) 39, no. 3 (July 1963): 345–59, and Antonio Kapcia, *Cuba: Island of Dreams* (New York: Berg Press, 2000). Also see Sheldon Liss, *Roots of Revolution: Radical Thought in Cuba* (Lincoln: University of Nebraska Press, 1987). On the continued legacy of Communist Party organizing in Cuba throughout the 1950s, despite the isolation of the party during the cold war, see Maurice Zeitlin, *Revolutionary Politics and the Cuban Working Class* (Princeton, N.J.: Princeton University Press, 1967).

75. On the depth of Cuban identification with the United States, particularly among the urban middle class, and the potential of such identification to turn into resentment, see Louis Pérez, *On Becoming Cuban: Identity, Nationality, and Culture* (Chapel Hill: University of North Carolina Press, 1999).

76. Carlton Beals, "As Cuba Sees It . . .," *Nation*, January 31, 1959, 83. U.S. Embassy officials tended to portray organized labor and revolutionary leaders as the most "anti-American" groups. See Wollom to Department of State, January 26, 1959, Wollom to Department of State, January 30, 1959, and Braddock to Department of State, February 16, 1959, RG 59.

77. Braddock held the fort after the resignation of Ambassador Earl Smith, and before the arrival of the newly appointed Ambassador Philip Bronsal. When pressed, Braddock asserted that even congressmen "did not speak for [the] government" (Braddock to Department of State, January 20, 1959, RG 59).

78. Wollom to Office of Caribbean and Mexican Affairs, January 19, 1959, RG 59.

79. Braddock to Department of State, January 23, 1959, RG 59.

80. *New York Times*, January 18.

81. As Wollom noted on January 26, 1959, no executions had taken place in Santiago since January 12, but they were now expected to resume (Wollom to Department of State, January 26, 1959, RG 59).

82. *Revolución*, January 14, 1959. It should be noted that the tribunals did occasionally hand down acquittals, and some imposed imprisonment rather than capital punishment. Indeed, when all was said and done, those policemen and some officers against whom nothing could be proven were often left in position (Thomas, *Cuba*, 1071–73). Furthermore, capital punishment was only applicable to members of the police and armed forces. Civil government officials were to be tried in civil courts and would receive only prison sentences. Also, the constitution was amended to include new punishments, such as the confiscation of all goods, for those accused of committing crimes against the national economy or the public good (Adele Van der

Plas, *Revolution and Criminal Justice: The Cuban Experiment, 1958–1983*, [Amsterdam: CEDLA, 1987], 11).

83. Quoted in Anderson, *Che Guevara*, 389.

84. However, in Havana appeals were apparently reviewed by the same judge and prosecutor assigned to the original hearing (Braddock to Department of State, February 25, 1959, RG 59).

85. *New York Times*, January 31, 1959.

86. *New York Times*, January 29, 1959.

87. *Bohemia*, February 8, 1959, 87.

88. *Revolución*, February 12, 1959.

89. Suárez Suárez, "Oriente," 39–41.

90. *Sierra Maestra*, February 28, 1959, quoted in Suárez Suárez, "Oriente," 40–41.

91. *New York Times*, January 18, 1959. Also see Wollom to Department of State, January 28, 1959, RG 59.

92. See Wollom to Department of State, January 26 and 28, 1959, RG 59.

93. Pérez-Stable, *The Cuban Revolution*, 63–64. According to James O'Connor, Batista's regime had integrated one segment of every major social class, such that the revolution began not as a social revolution, but as a multiclass alliance against a political in-group. See *The Origins of Socialism in Cuba* (Ithaca: Cornell University Press, 1970), 41–46.

94. It is notable that even the most prominent associations of Havana's *clases económicas* exhorted their members to attend. See the list of associations that supported the rally in *Diario de la Marina*, January 21, 1959. Although the church seems to have been divided on the executions in January, the first major call for "moderation" in punishment was issued by the archbishop of Oriente in early February. While soundly denouncing Batista and conceding the need for justice, the public letter called for "compassion" and "careful justice" (Wollom to Department of State, February 5, 1959, RG 59).

95. For example, Wollom reports rumors that the archbishop had been prevented from publishing the letter mentioned above (Wollom to Department of State, February 5, 1959, RG 59); he also notes that a delegation of civic and religious groups from Oriente province met with Raul Castro to present complaints specific to Oriente, but that an M-26 radio reporter later described the meeting as "one of support for revolutionary justice" (Wollom to Department of State, January 26, 1959, RG 59).

96. *Revolución*, January 22, 1959.

97. Braddock to Department of State, January 23, 1959, RG 59.

98. Wollom to Department of State, January 26, 1959, RG 59.

99. Ibid.

100. García Alvarez, "Los tribunales revolucionarios," 130.

101. For a list of those executed up to January 16, see Braddock to Department of State, January 20, 1959, RG 59. Braddock records at least 156 executions in total. A month later, Braddock reported that over 300 people had been executed, with more sentenced to imprisonment (Braddock to Department of State, February 25, 1959, RG 59).

102. Efrén Córdova, "Represión y violencia," in Córdova, ed., *40 años de revolución: el legado de Castro* (Miami: Ediciones Universal, 1999), and Álvaro Vargas Llosa, "The Killing Machine: Che Guevara, from Communist Firebrand to Capitalist Brand," *New Republic,* July 11, 2005.

103. See, for example, "Declaración de la Confederación de Profesionales Universitarios," published in *Prensa Libre*, January 24, 1959, 2; "Presenciarán los juicios periodistas de toda America, declaró Fidel en el Hilton," *Prensa Libre*, January 20, 1959, 19.

104. Frantz Fanon, "Concerning Violence," in *The Wretched of the Earth* (New York: Grove Press, 1963).

105. See the editorial by Miguel Penabad Fraga, "Conciencia agrícola," January 6, 1959, 4-B, which supports the formation of the Ministerio de Recuperación de Bienes Malversados and calls for the confiscation of Batistianos' houses, *fincas*, bank accounts, and cars. Also see O'Connor, who argues that the rapid transition to socialism is partly explained by the fact that many members of Cuba's elites and middle classes supported early revolutionary measures, contributing to rather than braking momentum: "In the heat of the social revolution it was difficult for many Cubans to distinguish between reform measures and policies that went to the heart of the prevailing property relationships. For these reasons the Revolutionary Government had near unanimous support until the political initiative shifted altogether to the revolutionaries, that is, until it was too late to even attempt to salvage Cuban capitalism" (*The Origins of Socialism in Cuba*, 280).

Beyond Paradox

Counterrevolution and the Origins of Political Culture in the Cuban Revolution, 1959–2009

LILLIAN GUERRA

"A paradox considers the possibility that what appears real inside a certain reality only makes sense and only becomes real when viewed from *out-side* that reality; one must stand *within* and look out," remarked Manuel López Oliva, a Cuban artist and cultural critic, to a group of young Boston-area art students gathered in his studio in the summer of 2003. Everyone laughed, collectively trying to decipher López's deliberately paradoxical effort to define the role of paradox in his paintings. "They are all—and they are none—an allegory for the experience of Cubans," he said, his eyes twinkling. These words directed the students' gaze toward a large, painted close-up of Antigone. As López responded to their interest, I remember thinking that their time in Cuba (less than a week) had already taught them well. *Antigone* spoke volumes about the dichotomous internal world that the Cuban Revolution had forged.

Flowing from the folds of a toga stamped with tiny, silhouetted images of Havana's Cathedral, López Oliva's *Antigone*, like the figure in Sophocles' ancient play, embodies the despair of a woman whose violation of the rules of society and loyalty to her father, Oedipus, earns her the status of a pariah and the death sentence of imposed isolation. Antigone, like Cuban society under the much-mythologized rule of Fidel Castro, reminds us that often the most censurable sins a father can commit are often not so much literal sins as symbolic ones. Well-intended and valiant in his day, Antigone's father had become, in Sophocles' plays, a misguided, self-deceiving, and blind ruler, whose actions ultimately resulted in fratricide and worse. His daughter is caught in a deadlocked war between uncompromising sides, each of which claims moral authority over the other; she plays the role of

Antígona by Manuel
López Oliva (1998), oil
on canvas, 180 × 130 cm.
Courtesy: Manuel
López Oliva.

spectator in her own life, while her younger brother leads their national
forces against an older brother whose army comprised exiles and foreign
allies coming from abroad.

Living in Cuba, it is easy to see Antigone's admirably stoic and tragic
condition as a metaphor for the experience and perspective of the Cuban
people. Few educated observers have been able to dismiss the vortex of
external hostility and the imperial alliance of wealthy exiles with the United
States that has confined revolutionary Cuba since 1959. Much as Cuba's
own state leaders have done since the early 1960s, analysts often dismiss
the ideological contradiction to national liberation that extreme limitations
on collective and individual political freedoms have represented for the
Cuban people. In general, such accounts depict these limitations as mere side-
effects of a U.S.-supported counterrevolution rather than as foundational
building blocks to Fidel Castro's five-decade-long rule. Insulated from the
myriad ways in which the state's reliance on the counterrevolution to maintain "the Revolution" in power has affected everyday life, observers who

analyze Cuba from afar find the reasoning for their convictions clear and convincing.

Perhaps no other revolution since the eighteenth-century revolution led by slaves in the French colony of Saint Domingue has so directly threatened the existing social and political world order. Symbolically and practically, the Cuban Revolution attacked the validity of the ideology of U.S. exceptionalism, the structures of U.S. capital, and the myth of the United States' "democratic" intentions toward Latin American nations whose internal political processes it strove to manipulate for over two hundred years (despite official proclamations of respect for national sovereignty). As a result, Cuba became the first country in the hemisphere to divest itself of U.S. political and economic controls, despite over fifty years of repeated U.S. military and diplomatic interventions. Before and after its fusion with Soviet-style communism in 1961, the Cuban Revolution's own enduring ideology of anti-imperialist nationalism aggressively promoted the idea that surviving colonial legacies of inequality and disenfranchisement could be swiftly overturned through popular action and sheer force of will. Like Haiti, Cuba's historic precedent forced a global reconsideration and questioning of everything that the world's elites once took for granted. And like Haiti in the nineteenth century, Cuba became, for the last half of the twentieth century, a hemispheric pariah. Judging from continuities in U.S. foreign policy across eight administrations, it still is.

Arguably meant to serve U.S. corporate interests and imperial power rather than combat any presumed threat of a Sovietization of America under the cold war, U.S. policy toward Cuba remains locked in a dead-end struggle to discredit, isolate, and deliberately impoverish the island society as a means for dislodging its government. This policy retains all the same features that it acquired during the early cold war, despite the fact that Cuba's government has, for nearly seventeen years, like that of China and Vietnam, exchanged its communist economic system for one based on state monopoly capitalism. Moreover, the state's reliance on foreign investment and military control over government enterprises has also deepened comparisons with the oligarchic regimes and Latin American dictatorships that the United States traditionally supported, raising more questions about the logic behind U.S. policy toward Cuba than ever before. Meanwhile, much of the Cuban exile elite based in Miami continues to sustain itself economically and politically through lobbying, government subsidies meant to "democratize" Cuba, and propaganda meant to obstruct the reestablishment of diplomatic ties.[1] Thus, paradoxically, by dint of their very *absence*, the interests of a U.S.-supported counterrevolution remain ominously *present* in Cuban leaders' decision-making and in the enduring international image of Cuba as an innocent, morally righteous David fighting an imperial Goliath.

Over time and especially since the demise of the Soviet Union, the words "paradox" and "contradiction" have begun to serve as a kind of universal shorthand for describing the complex internal dynamics of popular complicity with a top-down, authoritarian state that the counterrevolution is credited with creating in revolutionary Cuba. Today, mainstream sources as diverse as the entertaining PBS documentary *Cuba: Paradox Found*, by the production group Adventure Divas, and the engrossing travel memoirs of the sardonic food critic Alan Richman, written for *GQ* magazine, recognize what has become a routine form of discourse to most Cubans.[2] "Whenever I asked for an explanation of the appalling inequities in their so-called workers' paradise," writes Richman, "Cubans would offer a one-word explanation: 'contradictions.' It is the standard explanation for everything incomprehensible about Cuba. . . . Why does a country with more doctors per capita than anywhere else on earth have no aspirin? 'Contradictions.'"[3] For related reasons, Cuban exile leaders' obsessive struggle to reassert control over a home society that most have not known for over forty years has inspired increasing degrees of ridicule among diverse sectors of the U.S. public in recent years. Reflecting this, a 2001 edition of the parodic tabloid *Weekly World News* featured a report that Castro planned to launch weapons of mass destruction in the unlikely form of scientifically modified sharks. The report cited a spy network of Miami Cubans as the source for the story. Alongside headlines announcing that the "Shroud of Turin" had "open[ed] its eyes" and that a three-breasted woman and three-armed man had produced a three-legged baby, the tabloid's front page declared: "Castro's Evil Plot to Terrorize our Beaches! Cuba Launches Shark Attack on US!"[4] But acknowledging the depth of paradox and contradiction that govern daily life in Cuba achieves little more than a fatalistic assessment of the origins of these problems and their relevance to explaining the attitude of the Cuban people toward revolutionary rule, an attitude Cubans often describe as *conformismo*.

For the first generation of Cubans to witness and participate in Cuba's communist transformation and Fidel's paternalistic system of totalitarian

Exaggerating official U.S. characterizations of Castro's Cuba as a threat to national security, *Weekly World News* framed a 2001 report on Fidel using, among other equally ludicrous stories, sharks as weapons of mass destruction against exiles in Florida. Source: *Weekly World News*, September 4, 2001.

tutelage, believing in and fighting the counterrevolution became a way of life and *fidelismo* a new religion. For those who trusted the often ubiquitous voice of Fidel, defending the revolution took on millenarian significance as Cuba became the center of U.S.-Soviet concerns and Fidel's international relevance grew by leaps and bounds.[5] As Fidel Castro himself declared, months before the catastrophic failure of the CIA-organized invasion at the Bay of Pigs in April 1961, overt and covert efforts to topple Cuba's revolutionary government only succeeded in strengthening it.[6] "The revolution needs to do battle [*combatir*]," he stated. "Battle is what makes revolutions strong. . . . A revolution that is not attacked might not be a true revolution in the first place. Moreover, a revolution that did not have an enemy would run the risk of falling asleep, of weakening itself. Revolutions need to fight, revolutions need to do battle, revolutions, like armies, need to have an enemy in front of them in order to become more courageous and self-sacrificing!"[7] Ironically, Fidel gave this speech at a school that, like many after 1959, had been refashioned from the rubble of a former military barracks that had once served Batista's army. Rather than reject the centrality of the military to Cuba's post-1959 political system as he regularly promised in 1959, Fidel Castro embraced, deepened, and expanded it.

In a society defined by a constant state of alert against U.S. military assaults (which, after 1961, never materialized), the militarization of workplaces, education, and public culture that consumed so much of the nation's energy and resources until the mid-1980s now seems as worthy of critique to many Cubans as the alliance between the U.S. government and Cuban exiles living in the United States appears to the U.S. public. Because the effects of U.S. policies of supporting dictatorships and sponsoring state terror in the name of "democracy" were so evident in the first two decades of the revolution, most Cubans probably agreed that Castro's demonizing of the United States was justified. However, they also recognized that invoking the phantom of the counterrevolution and warning of its forces' desire to turn back the clock to the pre-1959 age became the primary material with which government leaders crafted the incontestability of the revolution and thereby ensured the impenetrability of their own rule.

Understood in the broadest of terms from the beginning of the revolution, the forces arrayed *against* Fidel Castro's rule, rather than for it, have proved critical to the definition and stagnation of its political culture since 1959. Indeed, I suggest in this essay that the counterrevolution, both real and imagined, proved critical to the cyclical nature of state repression as well as the role of popular complicity and conformity in ensuring that such state repression would take a less overtly violent and more disciplinary form. Put simply, revolutionary leaders used U.S. hostility as a means for justifying a permanent state of war that entailed strict policing of the actions and attitudes of citizens and fellow revolutionary activists alike. However, control was generally asserted not through terror and disappearances but through selective repression of key individuals and the popular intimidation that could result from making their example public. Most important of all perhaps, revolutionary leaders' constant referencing of the threat posed by the counterrevolution and the series of national crises provoked by early confrontations with the United States helped facilitate both a political culture of support—ranging from genuine activism to tacit complicity—and a set of semicoercive structures that ensured a collective expression of support over time.

Exploring how counterrevolution came to define the political culture of Cuba after 1959 on both micro and macro levels reveals the frequency with which expansive, ideologically arbitrary definitions of the term were applied to many revolutionaries who had themselves formerly endorsed or implemented policies that policed, curtailed, or repressed overt opposition to the state at different points in time. The Cuban state could not have sustained its most foundational and enduring myths nor justified policies of selective repression without reference to the external threat posed by an openly counterrevolutionary U.S.-exile alliance. More often than not, Cuban leaders relied on the existence of a genuine, foreign-based counterrevolution in order to discredit the legitimate dissent of prorevolutionary critics whose involvement in any active (armed or unarmed) counterrevolution was more imaginary than real. The fact that some key officials in charge of justifying or carrying out the persecution of phantom counterrevolutionaries eventually fell victim to the same charge themselves established a certain insecurity and unpredictability in the political process. This insecurity ironically prompted greater popular conformity to state control and tacit acceptance of the unpredictability of its self-serving rules.

At the same time, the Cuban state sought to cover up the relevance and nature of explicitly subversive movements like the one that consumed the peasant-based coffee region of El Escambray from 1961 to 1965. Called simply El Movimiento Contra Bandidos (the Movement against the Bandits), this bloody armed conflict between pro-government peasant militias and anticommunist peasant insurgents dramatizes the degree to which leaders' enforcement of the myth of unconditional support and popular unanimity behind the state led them to silence the events and importance of what might have amounted to Cuba's most significant counterrevolution.

Coopting Memory and Countermemory: Culture as Politics and the Counterrevolution that Everyone Forgot

Besides the allegations offered in counterrevolutionary rhetoric, there is little known evidence that the Cuban government has continually used violence and wide scale terror as a means for maintaining rule or drowning dissent. U.S.-backed military dictatorships in Chile, Argentina, Guatemala, El Salvador, Brazil, Paraguay, Uruguay, and surrogate armies like the Contras annihilated hundreds of thousands of people seeking economic equity and political rights from the 1960s through the 1980s, and into the mid-1990s, in some cases. During this time, Cuba apparently remained a haven from both right-wing and left-wing violence. As the Cuban minister of foreign relations Felipe Pérez Roque pointed out in an address to the United Nations in 2001, "Is there somebody in this room who could mention one sole case of torture, murder or a disappeared person in Cuba? Does anyone in this room know of one single case of a journalist murdered in Cuba, or of kidnapped children . . . or of the sale of children or of slavery? Has anyone heard talk of a death squad in Cuba?"[8] Although dozens of cases of harassment and appalling abuses of homosexuals and other ideological "undesirables" had occurred in Cuba, especially in the late 1960s, the country's record on human rights abuses then and today pales by comparison with the excesses of capitalist military regimes operating with full U.S. support in the same decades.[9] Whatever their view on the Cuban state's attitude to freedom of expression, assembly, and protest, most knowledgeable analysts can only conclude that there is no comparison.

Still, the Cuban Revolution's search for unanimity as an antidote to counterrevolutionary attitudes and actions has come at tremendous political cost and collective as well as individual sacrifice. Arguably, the greatest challenges the revolution has faced lie in the state's ability to control the ideological realm. The inscription of mandates against individual rights in Cuban law and official discourse over the last twenty years represent the culmination of an experimental process begun much earlier, from the late 1960s through the mid-1970s. In these years, fighting the credibility of a U.S.-supported counterrevolution for the sake of radical change and national sovereignty entailed defining exactly what "counterrevolution" meant in ways that transcended the use of armed violence and entered the field of individual expression and identity. Importantly, as Greg Grandin argues in the introduction to this work, contradictions in this definition derived from the origins of the post-1959 state in an anti-imperialist movement that abhorred state violence and saw itself as part of a moral crusade for equality, liberty, and freedom of expression in a neocolonial context. However, whenever state officials perceived the revolution in an acute state of war, they often defined that war in ideological and cultural terms, not just military ones. These moral crusaders not only turned outward to fight their opponents to the death, but inward as well.

Thus, from the late 1960s to early 1970s, the Revolutionary Armed Forces and Raúl Castro's campaign against political "microfactions" and "ideological diversionism" launched weapons of intimidation that struck at the heart of Cubans' faith in the ability of the revolution to encourage creative thought and free expression.[10] Amazingly though, much of the artistic community, arguably the community most vulnerable to such charges, responded to official mandates armed only with a good sense of humor and the courage to criticize *within* the discursive confines of Cuba's unique experience. Artists have also gone as far as to criticize those discursive confines themselves, a powerful indictment of the paradoxical policy of promoting creative expression by policing its boundaries and paradigms. Irony, then as now, seems the most popular building material in the structures and discourses of Cuba's political life. Irony, then as now, also became the sweet nectar of freedom for creative thinkers. While broad discussion of this phenomenon lies beyond the scope of this essay, the film career of the internationally renowned director Tomás Gutiérrez Alea provides a case in point.

Gutiérrez Alea launched his career with the hilariously comic film *Death of a Bureaucrat*, made in 1966, and ended it with *Guantanamera*, released in 1996. The movies are based on the same plotline: a Cuban protagonist struggles to bury the past symbolically and literally in the form of a beloved dead relative while navigating a state-constructed ideological obstacle course filled with near-sighted hypocrisy and historical denial. His films provide appropriate bookends for a political process characterized by paradoxical tensions that pulled in two opposing directions: *against* dissent, criticism, or even debate; and *for* cultural and artistic ingenuity. Together, the films demonstrate one of the most striking and perhaps unique features of the Cuban Revolution: its capacity to tolerate and even encourage strident expressions of nonconformity to state political control as a form of cultural contemplation and creative analysis. Yet, the apparent "openness" of Cuban officials in revealing that the revolution's closets were filled with dirty laundry has potentially obscured painful, violent conflicts that proved much harder to explain than the counterrevolutionary terror generated by the exile-imperialist alliance.

Neither the revolution nor the forces of external counterrevolution have engaged in any serious, open analysis of the most damaging and threatening of internal conflicts that rocked the first two decades of the revolution: the clandestine, peasant-led guerrilla war against the Cuban state in El Escambray and its drawn-out aftermath of forcible peasant relocation. Arising in the Escambray Mountains of Santa Clara province and lasting five years or more, the armed insurgency of 1961–65 represents both a forgotten peasant-led rebellion against the practical implications of communism for their daily lives and a historically ignored, incipient civil war.

Born of CIA recruitment programs and the fears generated by counterrevolutionary propaganda predicting a Soviet-style seizure of all agricultural properties, peasant coffee farmers in the Escambray Mountains organized an armed revolt meant to topple the revolution in the province of Santa Clara shortly before and after the Bay of Pigs invasion. Unbeknownst to most students of Cuban history, the "Movement against the Bandits," as Cuban officials dubbed it, lasted nearly five years and encompassed three, hard-fought phases of violent military action to suppress the insurrection between January 1961 and January 1965. With the exception of a still un-published but excellent comparative analysis of the resistance of Escam-bray peasants to the revolution and the Oriente peasants' embrace of it, no in-depth history of the movement, its repression, or implications ex-ists.[11] Although the state has never released any official totals on the number killed or wounded, Norberto Fuentes, a former personal friend of Cuba's heads of state and semiofficial chronicler of the experience until his defec-tion in the early 1990s, offers these casualty figures: 3,478 killed and 2,099 wounded on the revolutionary side, and approximately 3,000 killed on the insurgent side. Fuentes gives a precise figure of 3,995 as the total number of insurgent fighters encountered by the Cuban armed forces during the war, that is, between 1961 and 1965.[12]

Few, if any official histories of the Movement against the Bandits exist besides those written by Fuentes himself. The first of these, *Nos impusieron la violencia* (They Imposed the Violence on Us), recounted the repression of peasants that followed the 1961 Bay of Pigs Invasion. Its title reveals the ambivalence with which the repression was remembered and the dis-course of reluctance that the Cuban state has gradually constructed to make sense of violence or evidence of mass popular dissent within its borders. *Nos impusieron la violencia* made heroes of the young men who comprised the revolutionary militias, describing the "bandits" as "peons" that "Yankee im-perialism launches onto our soil in its struggle to destroy the Revolution." Fuentes described the "functions of the bandit" to produce "terror, the de-struction of resources, the distraction of our [armed] forces so that they may remain occupied in case of a [U.S.] invasion."[13] Years later, military officers who directed the counterinsurgency campaign described the ante-cedents of the rebels in similar terms: "These gangs of bandits were always fed, paid, supplied, and inspired by the United States, by its agencies of espionage and subversion. They focused on the Escambray, but there were counterrevolutionary gangs throughout the country—we estimate there were more than five thousand bandits, in small bands in various places."[14] Víctor Dreke, a veteran of Cuba's wars in El Escambray and the Congo, lends a few more clues: "There was great unity [among the columns of the Movimiento 26 de Julio in Santa Clara province before 1959]. Without this unity, the revolution would not have been possible. Such unity has been lacking in some other revolutions [but not ours]. . . . The only ones who didn't agree to Che's leadership were those in the Second National Front of the Escambray. The majority of them, or many of them, later became bandits or abandoned the country."[15] Silenced in Dreke's explanation is the key reason for the peasant uprising: rejection of communism and anger over Che Guevara's willingness to include and reward Communist Party members with official rank in rebel columns during the last few months of the war against Batista. Until that point, Communists had withheld formal support. Moreover, their long and complex history as occasional allies of Batista made them not only suspect but abhorrent to liberal democratic members of the Movimiento 26 de Julio.

In fact, according to a right-wing exile version of the "bandit" movement, the vast majority of the rebel leaders, most of them larger landowners and small businessmen, did abandon the fight in the first year after the failure of the U.S. invasion at the Bay of Pigs.[16] However, the impoverished peasant rebels who stayed behind and continued to struggle infused their action with a meaning that told the story of counterrevolution from below. This is the story that Fuentes wanted to tell.

Fuentes wrote two collections of short stories based on his experiences in accompanying the revolution's armed forces while they fought the war. Although both were critically acclaimed in Cuba, only one, *Condenados de Condado* (The Condemned of the Condado Cemetery) was published there in 1968 by Unión de Escritores y Artistas (the Union of Artists and Writers of Cuba, UNEAC). The other, *Cazabandido*, was published in Uruguay, although allegedly widely read in Cuba. Fuentes's reputation as a writer officially sanctioned by the revolution had been well established prior to these works through the appearance of a number of his journalistic chronicles in all of Cuba's major government newspapers and magazines, including *Granma*, *Verde Olivo*, *Hoy*, and *Bohemia*. Despite their initially enthusiastic embrace among literary and political circles in Cuba, both *Condenados de Condado* and the gripping *Cazabandido*, named after revolutionaries' shorthand for the campaign, were officially banned. Strangely, neither collection of stories seems to break in any obvious way from a simple narrative of military combat against an implacable enemy. Nonetheless, the curious acceptance of the nonfictional *Nos impusieron la violencia* and the official rejection of Fuentes's fictional works, *Cazabandido* and *Condenados de Condado*, reveals an important tension between memory and countermemory. This tension defines the historical consciousness of the revolution as a collective and dynamic process of control, cooptation, and complicity, rather than one of simple terror imposed by a totalitarian dictatorship that enjoyed no popular legitimacy.

Cazabandido, like *Condenados de Condado*, features characters on both sides of the revolutionary and counterrevolutionary divide whose commonalities—of action and reaction, attitude and values—unite them more than their supposed ideological distinctions should imply. In particular, none of the revolutionary characters strike the reader as heroic. More important, the means by which they determine a peasant's identity as a "bandit" appear ill-defined and hauntingly arbitrary. For example, *Condenados de Condado* offers scenes of revolutionary raids into peasants' homes: "'Bandit?' asked the bandit hunter when he discovered that figure standing beneath the roof. 'You are a bandit,' he said to him, and charged his AKA rifle; the rest scattered. The man who lived there did not move. 'Advance so that I can identify you!' . . . 'I am good people,' replied the old man."[17] Another story whose title, "Al Palo," referred to revolutionaries' nickname for their gun, focuses on the nonideological desire of a government soldier to take a "bandit"/rebel's life as a personal trophy. Entering a bar filled with army comrades, the solder thinks to himself: "Here all of the [bandit] hunters tell stories about their killings, between sips, between open boxes of stinking dried beef and tubs of lard covered with persistent and noisy flies, and since I have never had a killing, I draw close to the ear of the commissary Iglesia and I whisper: *I want to be a member of the execution squad, I want to kill a bandit, you understand?*" In response, the other bandit hunters mock his bloodlust, eventually killing him, a comrade, out of sheer disgust.[18]

Featuring a title whose oral pronunciation plays with two potential meanings, "Hunt for the Bandit" and "Home of the Bandit," *Cazabandido* ventures far into the related inner worlds of bandit and revolutionary alike, postulating a connection. A gallery of photographs in the middle of the book shows images of armed, uniformed peasant children recruited to fight the bandits, a picture of Eloy Gutiérrez Menoyo at the time of his capture, and a typed letter from a bandit leader ordering the execution by hanging of a progovernment peasant. The letter ends with the slogan "Cuba, yes, Communism no!" The identification card of the bandits shows the U.S. flag and the Cuban flag over the phrase, "God, Fatherland and Freedom."[19]

In addition, the narrative also included intimate portraits of some bandit leaders, such as Pity Hernández, an earnest young man, who like the bandits in the photographs appears no more threatening than the average illiterate

During the early 1960s, it was a well-known and uncritically accepted fact, often highlighted in the state media, that the Cuban government trained boys as young as twelve for service in national militias. Apparently disturbed by this, Norberto Fuentes included this photograph in his short story collection *Cazabandido*.
Source: Norberto Fuentes, *Cazabandido* (Montevideo, Uruguay: Arca Editorial, 1970).

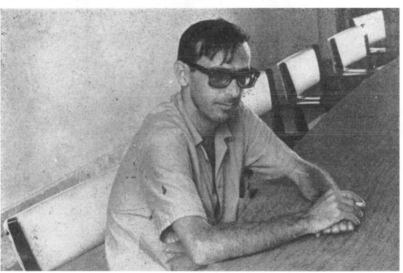

The son of exiled Spanish socialists, and a former war hero in the struggle against Batista, Eloy Gutiérrez Menoyo became a principal leader of efforts supported by exiles and the CIA to incite peasant rebellion in the Escambray mountain range. Shortly after his capture by government forces, he consented to an interview with Norberto Fuentes. Source: Norberto Fuentes, *Cazabandido* (Montevideo, Uruguay: Arca Editorial, 1970).

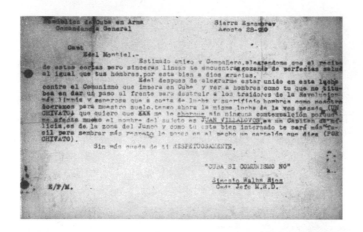

Norberto Fuentes supplemented his novel with a letter from one
"bandit" officer to another, in which the former urges the execution
by hanging of a captain in the Revolutionary Police. The officer also
orders his comrades to place a sign on the man's chest reading
"Por chivato" (For being a government agent). The officer then
signs off under the slogan "Cuba Yes, Communism No."
Source: Norberto Fuentes, *Cazabandido* (Montevideo, Uruguay:
Arca Editorial, 1970).

Counterrevolutionary rebel forces carried identification cards
like this one, which showed the U.S. and Cuban flags under the
rubric "Revolutionary Unity" or "U.R." and the slogan "God,
Fatherland and Freedom." Source: Norberto Fuentes, *Cazabandido*
(Montevideo, Uruguay: Arca Editorial, 1970).

peasant the revolution was meant to save. The book closed with a section titled "Fichero" (Catalogue). Here the author offered summary commentaries on topics such as the "Customs of the Bandits" and the "Customs of the Revolutionary Militias." Readers discovered that differences between them did not lie in the color of their uniforms (olive green) or choice of headgear (berets), which were the same in both cases, but in such minor foibles as their choice of hairstyle and the length of their beards (short versus long). The spiritual beliefs of the enemies differed only by shades; they were not white and black: while the bandits carried Catholic religious medals around their necks, the militiamen wore protective santería-inspired necklaces, "so packed with beads made of seeds that they came to weigh upward of five pounds each."[20]

In short, Fuentes constructed the rebels as typical peasants rather than bandits, the revolutionaries as typical peasants rather than heroes. He depicted counterrevolutionaries as humans whose idealism was potentially no more profound or more pragmatic than that of revolutionaries who called themselves bandit hunters. Importantly, Fuentes insisted that the counterrevolutionaries whom the state killed were humans, while the state's official language, press coverage, and exhibits at the "Museum of the Movement against the Bandits" in Trinidad insisted that they were not. Indeed, the use of the term "bandit" to describe the counterrevolutionary rebels is itself historically significant: members of every revolutionary movement organized in Cuba since 1868 were labeled bandits by their enemies and detractors. The Movimiento 26 de Julio was no different, since Batista's forces also labeled Fidel's followers "bandits." At the same time, Fidel's forces regularly executed peasant spies (*chivatos*) and common criminals as bandits during the guerrilla struggle in the Oriente Mountains.[21]

Today, El Escambray is better known internationally for its long tradition of popular theater than for its painful history as the site of a major civil war. As a founder of the Grupo Teatro Escambray explained to a U.S. scholar in 1996, "We chose this region for our work in 1968 because of its history and because the local people were receptive and understood that we, as theatre people, could help them with their own plans for change."[22] Such narratives obscure the complexities of the conflict as well as its aftermath. Having promised to make El Escambray Cuba's "most revolutionary region," Fidel apparently decided that the best means to achieve this was to empty the mountain range of most of its population, converting the area into a national park and military zone.[23] Yet, it was not the physical annihilation of unsympathetic and openly hostile peasants that the government sought but a forcible translocation and collective silencing of the story that they might otherwise tell.

Beginning in 1971, the government systematically rounded up thousands of male peasants in the region near Trinidad who had been known rebels or rebel sympathizers and transferred them to prison colonies in the provinces of Pinar del Río and Ciego de Ávila. Most of the men had already completed prison sentences and were living in permanent probation. After their transfer, these men spent the next four years working in agriculture and building extensive housing complexes that became the residential centers of three new towns: Sandino and Antonio Briones Montoto, in Pinar del Río, and a settlement called Miraflores, in Ciego de Ávila. In 1975, their families were allowed to join them, creating what local Cubans of the area called "pueblos de presos," that is, towns of former political prisoners cut off from the region and roots of a counterrevolutionary history. Only in the 1990s were the peasants, now old men, and their extended families allowed to move freely outside the towns without day passes. Many of them returned to Santa Clara. Others sought asylum in the United States, more than thirty years after most wealthier, educated leaders of the movement had abandoned them and the struggle for life in Miami.[24]

In my experience, visits to these towns were not restricted in the 1990s, if they ever were. Although they are now mostly empty of *presos*, Briones, when I visited it for the first time in the mid-1990s, was a town filled with aging, illiterate, and defeated former rebels anxious to talk. All claimed that their alliance with the CIA was minimal and any allegiance superficial or self-serving. At the time, I carried no tape recorder nor was I interested in the history of the period. But I could not escape the memories of the men I met in any conversation.

Fearful that they would lose their coffee farms and that communist policies would limit their rights to sell their surplus for market, the survivors of this conflict shocked me with their condemnations of those they saw as the real traitors. "U.S. imperialism and bourgeois cowardice are responsible for our plight," one man told me. Another, now living in Miami, described his purpose in this way:

> We wanted to topple [*derrocar*] the government, but only to save our coffee farms and because the Communists were atheists. You see, our wealth was not in land—we didn't own enough—but in the [coffee] bushes, and they

couldn't find a way to expropriate our bushes according to their own laws. So they knew we would go on selling our coffee in the region, even if we did it illegally. We had to be enemies because we *could* not conform [*no podíamos conformarnos*]. I was poor, but I wouldn't be grateful. I never went to church in my life and I lived in a wooden house with a dirt floor, but my values were not theirs. Before they took me here, to Briones, they took us first to that stadium in Santa Clara. That's when they said what my rights were: "You in this country have no other right than the right to work." [*Ustedes en este país no tienen derecho a nada más que al día de trabajo.*] I had already worked every day of my life. How could they tell me that my only right was the right to work? Did they know what it meant to work? I wanted to work, for me and my family, my *patria*, not for them, not for the Americans, not for anybody. We were revolutionaries, not counterrevolutionaries. That's just what they say.[25]

Populated by ghostly reminders of an experience whose story remains elusive, the towns are monuments to struggle, reminding Cubans that revolutionary and counterrevolutionary conflicts were not just political or ideological but personal, fratricidal, and profoundly nationalist battles fraught with pain. Competing claims to that pain and the moral righteousness of the struggle for liberation that engendered it inform the militarized political culture of post-1959 Cuba, as well as the structures of state control that dictate the rhythm of everyday life.

Assessing the Impact of the External Counterrevolution on the Revolution from Within

On a regular basis since 1959, the effects of counterrevolution and Cuban state responses to any attendant internal questioning of its authority took on predictable patterns of increasing limitations on individual rights, the elimination of all organizations or activities not controlled by the government (ranging from ethnic mutual aid societies to chess clubs, for instance), and an ever-widening set of demands for public participation in collective acts to demonstrate conformity and support for government policy and leaders. Most commonly, the Cuban state increasingly preferred to jail, "rehabilitate," and even relocate its opponents and potential opponents rather than annihilate them.

Launched with the passage of the first preemptive counterrevolutionary laws in July of 1959, the legalistic and bureaucratic nature of the state's judicial apparatus for curtailing and confining dissent remains nothing short of surprising. When combined with new revisions to the Code of Social Defense, these laws made certain that no one could ever challenge Fidel's power using the legal conditions that had favored Fidel Castro's own revolutionaries under Batista. For example, the Revolution's Code of Social Defense eliminated the category of political prisoner, defining all convicted opponents of the revolutionary state as "common delinquents." It also prohibited any tactics of passive resistance, whether at the collective or individual level, as a means for demonstrating dissent. These included work slow-downs, stoppages, and, of course, labor strikes.[26] Thus, long before the adoption of state communism would justify the elimination of workers' right to organize or strike independently of state control, fighting the counterrevolution produced laws that ended the basic labor rights of workers for political rather than economic reasons.

As I examine in some detail elsewhere, isolating critics, skeptics, and potential nonbelievers in the uncontestable "goodness" of the revolution's policies has most often involved discrediting people publicly, disciplining them through a variety of coercive forms. It has also included the institutional imposition of mandates for public and private behavior that involved surveillance and encouraging fellow workers, neighbors, and classmates to denounce those suspected of harboring "doubts" in return for potential material or symbolic rewards. Beginning in the 1960s, public culture and performance of one's ideological compliance with the state were the fields in which the state policed citizens' collective "support" of their leaders' vision and conformity with such mandates as attending mass rallies, fulfilling labor demands (both paid and unpaid or "voluntary" labor), as well as standards of personal austerity and self-denial. Perhaps most disturbing for the social and sexual conservatism they implied, these standards entailed harassment of Cubans on charges of "ideological diversionism" for such transgressions as wearing their hair long, listening to the Beatles, expressing solidarity with black liberation movements, or possessing a cultural sensitivity not in tune with militarized, homophobic criteria for defining masculinity. Meant to reflect and confirm the legitimacy of a generalized austerity produced by a frequently mismanaged, often disastrous state economy in the 1960s through the mid-1970s, these standards of personal austerity in dress and lifestyle emerged as significant factors in distinguishing the truly "revolutionary" from the *blandengues* (weak softies), *desmoralizadores* (discouraging doubters), and, of course, any clandestine *gusanos* (passive or active opponents to the revolutionary regime).[27] By 1967, Raúl Castro had launched "the Revolutionary Offensive," a set of policies meant to render a citizen-by-citizen accounting of who supported the government and how. Not only did the Cuban government then mandate membership in mass organizations as a prerequisite to participation in the state-controlled economy and educational institutions, it also increased its control over those mass organizations, including workers' unions.[28]

In response to international critics of these policies, Cuban officials have repeatedly cited the humanitarian ideals and successes of state-directed socialism as a means of securing citizens' basic needs and the implausibility of achieving egalitarianism in the face of unregulated, uninhibited individual pursuits of social and material comfort. By comparison, their response to local critics has generally been much more precise and strikingly less forgiving. Labeled counterrevolutionaries, ideological deviants, or simple traitors, famous critics such as Carlos Franqui, Reinaldo Arenas, José Aldao, Heberto Padilla, Virgilio Piñera, Walterio Carbonell, Ana María Simó, René Ariza, José Aldao, Guillermo Cabrera Infante, Vladimir Roca, and Marta Beatriz Roque, as well as hundreds, probably thousands, of relatively unknown citizens, have been consistently purged from state institutions and subjected to various forms of internal exile, forced reeducation through programs of "productive labor," and official condemnation. Others have been silenced through socially legitimated methods of collective intimidation, carried out by mass organizations like the ubiquitous Committees for the Defense of the Revolution, and long prison terms. Importantly, the pre-1959 progressive politics of these intellectuals' ideological orientation did not save them from repression. On the contrary, having a pre-1959 personal history of active opposition to political corruption and dictatorship invited greater suspicion and scrutiny from Fidel's trusted inner circle. For example, despite the fact that the most politically caustic of his plays were published and produced *before* 1959, Virgilio Piñera's theatrical parodies of paternalistic *caudillos* quickly made staging them a counterrevolutionary taboo *after* 1959: apparently, officials found it too easy for audiences to confuse the self-appointed messiahs and self-deceiving protagonists of Piñera's absurdist plays with Fidel Castro himself. That Piñera was also known to be homosexual only hastened his descent into domestic obscurity, despite continuing international fame.

However, with the exception of Piñera, the majority of intellectuals named above were once committed revolutionary intellectuals and Marxist in their orientation. Although most were not Communist Party members, those who were (such as the black radical Walterio Carbonell and Vladimir Roca, the son of Blas Roca, the Cuban Communists' principal ideologue since the 1930s), or had once been before 1959 (such as Carlos Franqui), abhorred Soviet models for change and defied the authority of Fidelismo without forsaking socialist ideals. All were eventually denounced as traitors, *anti-sociales*, and even given the label of "ex-Cubanos."[29]

Charges of betrayal—of Cuba, the revolution, and history itself—have come to define and create the basis for a shared, conflicted, and combative *Cubanidad* that does not apply only to Cubans in Cuba. On the contrary, if criticism and contestation of the political authority of Fidel Castro has elicited visceral condemnation or overt repression within Cuba, expressing cynicism about the intentions of exiled Cuban leaders, promoting dialogue with the Castro regime, or endorsing the reestablishment of relations with the United States could have similar or far worse consequences among exiles abroad. During the 1960s and 1970s, counterrevolutionary activists and U.S. intelligence forces launched a well-documented campaign of psychological warfare, overt violence, economic sabotage, selective assassinations, and terror tactics that included the bombing of a Cuban airliner in which over a hundred Cuban athletes died. Targets of these strategies included not just island Cubans or the Cuban system in general, but outspoken members of the Cuban exile community who called for reconciliation and the normalization of relations between Cuba and the United States.[30]

Deeply rooted in the culture of exile are the related beliefs that Cubans resident on the island desire to be rescued by their more fortunate brethren in the United States and that "the real Cuba is *aquí*, here, as opposed to the morally degraded Cuba *allá*, there." According to this logic, it is the responsibility of exile Cubans "to continue *la lucha* to 'save' Cuba *de allá*," often by any means necessary.[31] The fact that most Cubans in the United States demonstrate little interest in returning to Cuba after the hypothetical fall or death of Castro reveals how deeply contradictory their support for exile groups' ideological mission can be and how ultimately self-serving and paradoxical their goals of "freedom" for Cuba are.[32]

On the other hand, Cuban officials and the state-run media daily demonize Cuban exile organizations in terms that evoke little analysis of their origins, diversity, or intentions, calling them "the Miami mafia." That some exile organizations work toward moderation and dialogue with Cuba is a point often obscured. For instance, during the 1999–2000 international

IMITACION   *por Chago.*

As early as 1960, the Cuban state press began on a regular basis to equate U.S. imperialism and capital with Nazism and Hitler's Third Reich. Here President John F. Kennedy is depicted as an admirer of Hitler. Source: *Bohemia* (Cuba), May 21, 1961, 11.

custody battle over Elián González, a six-year-old survivor of his mother's failed attempt to escape with him to Florida, Fidel reportedly characterized Cuban American National Foundation officials as potential murderers, saying that they would rather kill the six-year-old than see him returned to his father in Cuba.[33] "This is the Struggle of the Truth against the Lie," announced the headlines of *Granma*.[34] Parallel sentiments were voiced in Miami as well, where exile supporters of Elián's "right to stay" ironically argued that the only "true" Cuba could be found in the United States.[35] Moreover, both sides have regularly accused the other of being Nazis, admiring Hitler, and espousing fascism.[36]

Historically, the diligence of Cuba's state press in disseminating detailed accounts of the attitudes, policies, and demands of exile organizations has not been matched by similar interest in providing critical investigations of the everyday realities of life in Cuba. Triumphalist reports on the commitment of workers to increasing production or efficiency flood televised news broadcasts in Cuba. Constant celebrations of the revolution's now-deteriorating advances in healthcare, infrastructure, and education replace

In recent years, roadside billboards denouncing George Bush's antiterrorism campaign and U.S. democracy as just another form of Nazi fascism have become commonplace features on Cuba's national highways. Photograph by the author.

debates on state policy making, let alone such social issues as Cuban racism, the return of poverty to certain neighborhoods, the rise of freelance prostitution, alcoholism, teenage pregnancy rates, or even the feelings of Cubans toward foreigners. It is hard to find any news that is not written in a highly editorial fashion. As one Cuban recently remarked to me while waiting for a bus in Old Havana and noticing my copy of *Granma*, Cuba's national newspaper and organ of the Communist Party: "Last night, someone killed another guy with a knife in my neighborhood, just so he could steal his bicycle. Maybe that doesn't happen every day in Cuba, *compañera*, maybe our crime here doesn't even compare with what you have in the United States. But reading *Granma*, you would think there was *no* crime in Cuba at all or that there is no interest in doing anything about it—and that is a dangerous way of thinking." Adding that he thought crime was on the rise either because of the return of capitalism to Cuba in the 1990s, or because of "declining moral values in general," he stated flatly, "I want *Granma* to investigate the causes of crime and report on crime, not pretend it doesn't exist and that things are always great."[37]

For Cuban officials, reporting on crime does not today constitute a pressing matter any more than it did in past decades. Historically, the role of the media, writing, and general self-expression is circumscribed by the need to prevent counterrevolutionary exploitation of weakness, whether of a spiritual, ideological, or structural nature. Fidel Castro is customarily credited with establishing this principle in 1961, when he addressed concerns among journalists, writers, and artists about the degree and nature to which freedom of thought, expression, and dissent would be allowed, encouraged, or tolerated in revolutionary Cuba:

> The great concern of all should be the Revolution itself. . . . Or do we believe that the Revolution is not in danger? What should be the first concern of every citizen today? Should it be the dangers, real or imaginary, that might threaten the creative spirit, or the dangers that might threaten the Revolution itself? . . . We believe that the Revolution still has many battles to fight, and we believe that our first thought and first concern should be: What can we do to assure the victory of the Revolution? That comes first, the Revolution itself, and then *afterwards*, we can concern ourselves with other questions.[38]

Today, Fidel Castro's forty-nine-year-old exhortation to unity premised on the notion that issues of individual expression and ideological pluralism might be considered "afterwards" seems both romantically naïve as well as tragic.

By 1987, Castro unequivocally defied his own prediction by arguing against any possibility of establishing checks and balances on the Communist Party's monopoly on power and decision making: "Nobody should imagine that somebody on his own can write an article judging the state, the party, the laws, but especially the party. We want broad information, but . . . nobody can assume the prerogative of judging the party. This should be very clear. Ours is not a liberal-bourgeois regime."[39] At the same time, Article 144 of the revised 1987 Penal Code raised minimum sentences for "offending the dignity of any public official" from previous levels set by Article 160 of the 1979 Code. According to the new provisions, those convicted faced three to twelve months for criticizing lower-level leaders, and from one to three years for criticizing leading state and party officials in a public manner.[40]

Importantly, the tightening of legal provisions overseeing such crimes against the state as public indictments of party leaders must be placed in the context of radical changes taking place in the Soviet Union during this period. Gorbachev's warming of relations with the United States under the Reagan administration, a government that had consistently demonstrated that it was anything but friendly toward Cuba, signaled not only impending danger to Cuba, but betrayal. Thus, in rejecting Perestroika "as another man's wife," the revolutionary leadership offered official and symbolic justifications for excoriating any similar philosophy through its own publications and the sudden elimination of longstanding Soviet magazines such as *Sputnik* from state kiosks.[41] So dangerous did the appeal of Perestroika seem to Cuban officials that some of Cuba's most stalwart party leaders like Carlos Aldana, a party militant since 1963 and a member of the Central Committee since 1973, found themselves purged from its ranks for having become, according to Aldana's confession, "Perestroika fans and Gorbachev fans."[42]

Even more dramatic was the televised trial, conviction, and execution in 1989 of the decorated and popularly revered veteran of the Angolan War, General Arnaldo Ochoa, on the charges of drug trafficking and other crimes related to the subversion of the Cuban state. Coming on the heels of the first Bush administration's military invasion of Panama, meant to capture and thereby silence President Manuel Noriega, a long-time CIA contact for the funneling of drug money to the Contras, Ochoa's trial seemed orchestrated to erase the evidence of Cuban government complicity in drug trafficking (possibly a strategy of increasing state revenues at a time of declining Soviet subsidies). Adding to this sense, Ochoa's oddly enthusiastic confession of guilt appeared to imply that he had consciously taken the fall for the Cuban government in order to eliminate any pretext on which the Bush administration might attempt to invade.[43]

However, Ochoa's strangely humiliating, inarticulate defense of himself in the televised trials, in which he appeared drunk or drugged, struck most observers as so uncharacteristic as to border on the politically ridiculous. Not since the highly publicized 1971 "self-criticism" of Heberto Padilla, a Cuban writer accused of crafting counterrevolutionary poetry, had a public proceeding in Cuba elicited so much international response and condemnation.[44] After Ochoa's execution by firing squad, the Cuban government went out of its way to translate trial transcripts into multiple languages and distribute them to foreign embassies and international organizations, a move that only added fuel to the fires of suspicion. Around Havana, many

Cubans reportedly manifested their solidarity with Ochoa by anonymously writing on walls "8A."[45] The number and letter, pronounced together in Spanish, sound out his name, *Ocho-A*, a thinly disguised signpost of solidarity with Ochoa as the sacrificial lamb of a self-serving state for whom former heroes of socialist internationalism quickly become expendable embarrassments.

Given the very real possibility that Ochoa *was* engaged in drug trafficking, it is likely that the Cuban government may never have condoned his actions, but attempted to put a very public halt to them because of fears generated by the Panama case. If this was so, Ochoa's shameful condition on national television only speaks to the extent of Cuban officials' paranoia regarding the need to discredit Ochoa in all respects, as a man, as a citizen, as a beloved soldier, and most important, as a revolutionary. In the eyes of the public, Ochoa's condition at trial was meant to transform him from a patriotic hero into the "antisocial" element and *escoria* (scum) that the revolution traditionally accused Cubans who tried to leave Cuba of being, especially in the 1980 Mariel boatlift. Ochoa was allowed to retain no shred of masculine honor precisely because the legitimacy of the revolution's foreign policy in Africa for decades, as well as its international and domestic image, depended on it. Essentially, the revolution represented itself as a zero-sum game, a testament to the ideal of total human commitment and the goal of altruistic self-sacrifice for the sake of ideological perfection as a nation. Unfortunately for Ochoa, the Cuban state's rescue of this ideal, at a time of Soviet betrayal, economic decay, and political uncertainty, cost him his life.

The subsequent departure of Lisandro Otero to exile in Mexico proved equally surprising. As the founding president of UNEAC, the head of the cultural wing of Cuba's diplomatic legation to the Soviet Union for many years, and a Communist Party militant at the helm of the Consejo Nacional de Cultura (National Council of Culture) in the late 1960s, Otero was responsible for carrying out a series of traumatic public purges against homosexual and religiously active intellectuals who worked at the Biblioteca Nacional José Martí. Otero was also at the center of the internationally scandalous imprisonment of Heberto Padilla, whom UNEAC stripped of a prize for his book of poetry shortly after the same organization had awarded it.[46] As such, Otero had nothing in common with the hundreds of thousands of Cubans who had left the island in earlier moments. Once in Mexico, Otero professed a rejection of both the U.S. model of capital-ism, as based on "absurd" and "uncontrolled consumption," and of Soviet-directed models of socialism, as "despotic." Neither had ended poverty and inequality, political or social, in the world. "Conflicts will continue as long as inequities persist because Western-style democracy does not guarantee any social equilibrium."[47] Moreover, Otero defended the need for one-party rule in the early phases of the revolution when its enemies openly conspired against it. However, he claimed that such a time had ended, that Cuba's leaders had manipulated counterrevolutionary fears as an excuse to main-tain themselves in power, and he suggested that the path was now clear for older revolutionaries to let the Cuban citizenry consider a variety of politi-cal options for themselves.[48] Not surprisingly, Cubans were left to wonder how a man who had personally repudiated thousands for leaving the island and, as part of his role as a major figure in UNEAC, marginalized Heberto Padilla for poetically criticizing the state, could not only leave himself, but endorse views long equated with counterrevolutionary thought.

These examples illustrate the degree to which Cuba's established politi-cal culture surged toward crisis in the midst of a global as well as a local reevaluation of communism with the end of the cold war. But they also demonstrate the resilience of the Cuban state in the face of its own offi-cials' counterconversions and policy reversals. If arbitrariness, selectivity, and insecurity had characterized state repression in the past, these principles found new meaning and new expression as the government itself began to adopt formerly counterrevolutionary positions without bothering to admit that that was what it was doing. The greatest evidence of this emerged not only with the espousal of procapitalist reforms in the early 1990s, but also in the official embrace of formerly counterrevolutionary exiles who returned to Cuba as tourists.

Thus, state officials who had once organized mass rallies to condemn Cubans who wanted to leave and intimidated them through "repudiation committees" (*comités de repudio*) in their workplaces and homes, now re-placed the discourse of rejection that had once scarred generations with a discourse of welcome.[49] By contrast, in April 1980, when tens of thou-sands of Cubans had crowded into the grounds of the Peruvian embassy demanding political asylum, the headlines of *Granma* had screamed "¡Que se vayan los vagos! ¡Que se vayan los lumpens! ¡Que se vaya la escoria! Como en la Sierra, como en la invasión, como en la guerra, como en Girón. ¡Sin tregua! [The lazy ones must leave! The lumpen must leave! The scum must leave! As it was in the Sierra, during the invasion, during the war, as it was during the Bay of Pigs. Without quarter!]"[50] Back then, the official press had published pictures of smiling Cubans holding defiant signs that condemned those who left in the Mariel boatlift as delinquents, *gusanos* (worms), and ungrateful sloths.[51] However, in the 1990s, the Cuban government's espousal of tourism and its relaxation of visa policies meant that more Mariel-era Cubans were returning to Cuba on a regular basis than ever before. Defining and enforcing counterrevolution, stripped now of any of the ideological criteria related to communism, became a matter of loyalty to the established leadership alone. Those willing to tolerate Fidel, even if they opposed him, were rewarded with equal toleration. For Cubans, the fact that the revolution had come to depend on the wealth of the counterrevolution for its very survival seemed nothing short of surreal.

Given that Cubans who left had once been likened to Pinochet, it is not surprising that many of those who stayed came to view their leaders as hypocrites.[52] As one Cuban told a reporter for *Foreign Affairs* magazine in 1996: "[Before,] you spat at the person leaving for Miami. You jeered at those who joined the Mariel boatlift. Nowadays, though, you greet a returning person like a king and wait anxiously for his arrival because the money he brings can change everything for you."[53]

Before he was himself purged on charges of aiding the counterrevolution through disloyalty, Cuba's minister of foreign relations and former rising star Roberto Robaina responded to these concerns by championing the cause of Cuban youth during his tenure as secretary general of the national Organization of Communist Youth. In the early 1990s, Robaina famously castigated the party for inundating Cubans with an unceasing barrage of sameness in the face of historical contradiction and ideological hypocrisy: "If we don't change the way that year after year we transmit those [revolutionary] ideas, a kid who is born today will be bored to death of so many marches with torches."[54] Repetition of the same slogans, the display of the same icons and such bizarre sights as the use of stencils in government signs meant to look like popular graffitti had undoubtedly taken their toll on the faith and outlook of Cuba's youth, a group constituting more than half the population by the early 1990s.[55] Testifying to this, the 1992 Report of the Sixth Congress of the Union of Communist Youth warned, "[The youth] are wavering. They simply have stopped believing or consider it impossible to resist and triumph. . . . They are the ones who criticize all . . . . One hears them say that everything is going wrong, that they are tired . . .

that we have spent thirty years saying that we are in the worst moment [of the revolution]."[56] Young Cubans, repeatedly told that things could only get better under socialism and Fidel, found that things were apparently getting worse.

Robaina's alleged advice to foreign diplomats negotiating trade deals with Cuba formed the basis for his dismissal from the Communist Party and public life. Accounts in the Mexican, Venezuelan, and Spanish press stated that charges against Robaina, primarily circulated among Cuba's party militants in a videotape of the party's disciplinary session, included comparisons to Carlos Aldana, the fan of perestroika. Robaina, like Aldana, was using the changing international context as an opportunity to court foreign supporters in his bid to place himself in line for rule after the death of Fidel. In particular, Raúl Castro, chief of Cuba's armed forces and Fidel's younger brother, allegedly remarked, "By any chance, did you receive a message from Fidel detailing how you were to guide [the Spanish minister of foreign relations, Abel Matutes] on how to deal with the problem of the counterrevolutionary bands? You gave advice to Matutes on how he should treat that issue with Fidel. . . . One *speaks* to the enemy, Robaina, one doesn't give him advice. . . . I am not going to allow people like you to screw this revolution three months after the oldest of us disappear."[57]

Yet, despite the reemergence of such high-profile cases of individual repression in the nearly two decades since Fidel announced that the post-Soviet age in Cuba would be known as "The Special Period in a Time of Peace," many Cubans have had the courage to reassess and reassign the charge of counterrevolution on their own, thereby attempting to redirect the political culture of Cuba toward greater citizen participation and the allowance for critique. Some, like Marta Beatriz Roque, garnered international attention when they were arrested in 1997 for publishing a manifesto titled *La Patria es de todos*, together with other high-profile dissidents such as Osvaldo Payá, a Catholic and former political prisoner; Elizardo Sánchez, repeatedly nominated for the Nobel Peace Prize; and Vladimiro Roca, a former Cuban air force pilot and the son of the Communist Party founder Blas Roca. These dissidents ironically placed Fidel Castro in the same category as militant exile groups, accusing both of rejecting dialogue in order to maintain their respective monopolies on power.[58]

But even these dissidents have fallen into the historical trap of relying on foreign allies such as former president Jimmy Carter to make their case for them before the Cuban state. Thus, their charge that revolutionary leaders have betrayed the revolution by espousing counterrevolutionary principles of inequality and capitalist policies is less than convincing. Indeed, it was not Osvaldo Payá, the Varela Project's organizer, but President Carter who presented the Varela Project to Cuban leaders on a goodwill visit to Havana in May of 2002. A petition originally signed by over eleven thousand Cuban citizens calling for democratic pluralism and elections in Cuba, the Varela Project was based on provisions outlined in the 1975 Cuban Constitution that allow Cubans to present petitions for popular referenda on issues not debated in the National Assembly. Organizers of the Varela Project continued to collect signatures, reaching over fourteen thousand by October, despite alleged government intimidation tactics that included the expulsion of students from national universities for signing the petition.[59] In response, the Cuban government mobilized a mass drive for a counterpetition that ultimately was said to have gathered 7.6 million signatures calling on the National Assembly to sponsor a referendum making Cuban socialism and one-party rule "irrevocable." The referendum passed and a few months later the Cuban state announced that 97.6 percent of eligible voters had approved a slate of uncontested candidates for the National Assembly.[60] Once again, the state ensured that proof of popular unanimity behind it was readily available and its leaders' right to rule undeniable.

Comparatively speaking, many critics of Cuban state policies or one-party rule, like the organizers of the Varela Project, do not appear so much as "dissidents" as simple "dissenters." Looking to reform the political system from within and take positions that defy the authority of both U.S. imperialists and exiled counterrevolutionary activists, these activists include Eloy Gutiérrez Menoyo, a former general of the Segundo Frente del Escambray in Santa Clara province who spent years in prison for deserting the revolution, founding the terrorist group Alpha 66, and organizing an expeditionary force to support rebels in El Escambray during the early 1960s. Official historical accounts of the revolution characterized Gutiérrez Menoyo as a traitor whose laziness in combat during the struggle against Batista earned him the nickname of *comevaca*, or cow eater.[61] After a brief return visit to Cuba, however, Gutiérrez Menoyo took the shocking step of requesting permission to live in Cuba from the Cuban government. In an equally bizarre move, the state granted him permission. Gutiérrez Menoyo then organized a group there called The Progressive Arch, which he has headed ever since.

In short, Gutiérrez Menoyo represents, much like Lisandro Otero, evidence of the degree to which counterrevolution has so embedded itself into the political culture of Cuba as to reverse the revolution's original logic and trends: once applied to the state's opponents and potential opponents in ambiguous and self-serving ways, counterrevolution has become a slippery discursive field within which the state and its critics engage each other in a largely nonviolent struggle for power, if not legitimacy. Rather than marginalize former traitors such as Gutiérrez Menoyo or the *escoria* of the Mariel boatlift, the state increasingly attempts to coopt them. Whereas life as an enemy of the revolution was once impossible in Cuba, today it is seems entirely compatible with the myth of unanimity: so long as dissidence is silent or controlled, its existence does not undermine but *reinforces* the state's contention that only a insignificant number of Cubans contest their leaders' right to rule and demand change.

For the same reason that very few Cubans found out about the many famous cases of defection or imprisonment of former revolutionaries that rocked the 1960s, most Cubans have little knowledge of Gutiérrez Menoyo's group or that of any other dissidents: they simply have no access to any means of mass communication outside the government's own state press. While dissidents rely on the international media to make their voices heard worldwide, the vast majority of Cubans have little or no idea of what they say. Inevitably, protestors' dependence on external forces critical of the revolution, rather than native forces within it, makes them by default just as counterrevolutionary as any group for the purposes of the Cuban state.

On a practical level, however, leading dissidents' presence *in* Cuba implies their unwillingness to play by the rules of the past and their desire to pursue change in defiance of the U.S.-exile alliance. In May 2004, for instance, Gutiérrez Menoyo, Sánchez, and other dissidents joined Cuban government officials in condemning Bush's 2004 severe tightening of the U.S. embargo, including provisions for the distribution of millions of dollars in "economic assistance" aid to island dissidents. Gutiérrez Menoyo said that U.S. plans "are a hair-raising effort to meddle" in Cuban affairs; Osvaldo Payá, principal organizer of the Varela Project, stated, "it is not appropriate or acceptable for any force outside Cuba to try to design the Cuban transition process."[62]

In some ways, the relative independence of these dissenters' discourse and the tactics involved in their campaign do seem to distinguish them in the minds of Cuban officials from the traditional exile ranks of the counter-revolution. Undoubtedly, for this reason, their voices are still being heard.[63] That the state media avoids covering their activities at all may actually assist these local forces in remaining outside the imperialist-counterrevolutionary camp and forming part of an internal, indigenous "antirevolution revolution." So far, their peaceful methods invite toleration from a government long reluctant to repress dissenters with the same kind of violence and terror tactics on which Latin American military regimes have traditionally relied.

Today, achieving an "antirevolution revolution" through internally driven insurgency or organized armed rebellion is highly unlikely. The notion that Cubans find themsevles *entre la espada y la pared* (between the sword and the wall) is not only taken for granted, it is widely understood to explain the stagnancy of Cuba's condition. "Aquí no pasa nada" (Nothing ever happens here) is a phrase on which Cubans regularly rely in their daily conversations. With it, Cubans capture and publicly disseminate a coded sense of frustration with the unchallenged legacies of a state that continues to propagate a myth of unanimity and an image of having enjoyed a serene rather than a tumultuous historical past. Ironically, this myth and image developed out of the state's very process of policing Cuba's cultural space and brutally repressing a highlands community of resistant peasants. In both cases, the government carefully constructed a strategy that diminished, quieted, and ultimately silenced any specific knowledge of the revolution's un-armed and armed critics by serving, in the case of certain forms of cultural expression such as film, as a coopting patron, and by erasing, in the case of peasant insurgents, the living evidence of their activities through forced translocation.

The Agony of Antigone

Caught between a revolutionary government that defined itself as fighting an eternal, moral war for self-preservation and the U.S.-exile campaign to overthrow not only Cuba's leaders but reverse changes in the island's economic life, the Cuban people, like El Escambray's peasants, have had to recalculate and redefine regularly the nature of their witness under the revolution. So central did denial of *any* popular opposition become to the state's own discourses of unanimous support and legitimacy that leaders increasingly found it easier to diminish or deny the relevance, origins, and meaning of popular resistance, doubt, and dissidence than to discuss them. Thus, Cuban citizens, like López Oliva's vision of Antigone, appear to gaze defiantly outward from a position of isolation that is both internally and externally imposed.

One of the last remaining states to pledge allegiance to communism in the world, the Cuban state is today as dependent for its survival on attracting foreign tourists and deepening foreign investment as that of any other nation of the Caribbean. Still, as López Oliva advised U.S. visitors to his studio in 2003, what appears real inside Cuba only makes sense and becomes real when viewed from the inside looking out. With no financial district, high-rises, drug lords, armed criminal gangs, fancy residential areas cordoned off by gated security systems, or any readily apparent shantytowns, Cuba's dilapidated and overburdened cities are isolated from the realities of Latin American urban life in ways that seem both shocking and complete. The strange, ancient beauty of Havana, even the contradictory symbols of official commitment to socialism in the midst of foreign-directed capitalism, are as much a testament to the exceptionality of the Cuban Revolution as they are to the resilience of the enemy lurking at its door. How Cubans may one day define this enemy themselves and reassess the legacies of the revolutionary government's actions in combating it is anyone's guess. Still, as this essay has shown, the greatest paradox in Cuba's revolutionary/counterrevolutionary history may not lie in the relationship between Cuba's internal reality and any enemy abroad, but in the state's relationship to its citizens and a coopting political culture that remains as steeped in national idealism as in legacies of fear.

Notes

1. For detailed discussions of Miami's exile elite and its dependence on stagnant U.S. policies, see Robert Levine, *Secret Missions to Cuba: Fidel Castro, Bernardo Benes and Cuban Miami* (New York: Palgrave, 2001); Lillian Guerra, "The Alliance of George W. Bush and Fidel Castro? Reassessing Perceptions and Consequences of U.S. Policy in Cuba," *Yale Journal of International Studies* (Winter–Spring 2006): 146–63; and Lillian Guerra, "Elián González and the 'Real Cuba' of Miami: Visions of Identity, Exceptionality and Divinity," *Cuban Studies/Estudios Cubanos* (2007): 1–25.

2. Adventure Divas, *Cuba: Paradox Found*, documentary film, Public Broadcasting System (2000); and Alan Richman, "Not Much of a Man in Havana," in *Fork*

It Over: The Intrepid Adventures of a Professional Eater (New York: Harper Collins, 2004), 113–23; originally published in *Gentleman's Quarterly*, December 1999.

3. Richman, "Not Much of a Man in Havana," 114–15.

4. "Castro's Evil Plot to Terrorize Our Beaches! Cuba Launches Shark Attack on U.S.!" *Weekly World News*, September 4, 2001, 1.

5. Lillian Guerra, "'To condemn the Revolution is to condemn Christ': Radicalization, Moral Redemption and the Sacrifice of Civil Society in Cuba, 1960," *Hispanic American Historical Review* 89, no. 1 (February 2009): 73–110.

6. Fidel Castro, "Conversión de otro cuartel en escuela," *Obra Revolucionaria*, no. 5 (January 28, 1961): 6.

7. Ibid.

8. Felipe Pérez Roque, *Address of the Cuban Minister of Foreign Affairs to the 57th Session of the UN Human Rights Commission*, Geneva, Switzerland, March 27, 2001.

9. For example, Néstor Almendros and Orlando Jiménez-Leal, *Conducta impropia* (Madrid: Editorial Playor, 1984), esp. 97–100; Emilio Bejel, *Gay Cuban Nation* (Chicago: University of Chicago Press, 2001), 95–112; Ian Lumsden, *Machos, Maricones and Gays: Cuba and Homosexuality* (Philadelphia: Temple University Press, 1996); and Allen Young, *Gays under the Cuban Revolution* (San Francisco: Grey Fox Press, 1981).

10. For example, Raúl Castro, "El diversionismo ideológico, arma sutil que esgrimen los enemigos contra la Revolución," *Verde Olivo* (July 23, 1972): 4–15; Leopoldo Ávila, "Las respuestas de Cain," *Verde Olivo* (November 3, 1968): 17–18; and Leopoldo Ávila, "Anton se va a la guerra," *Verde Olivo* (November 17, 1968): 16–18.

11. Joanna Beth Swanger, "Lands of Rebellion: Oriente and Escambray Encountering Cuban State Formation, 1934–1974," Ph.D. diss., University of Texas–Austin, 1999.

12. Norberto Fuentes, *Condenados de Condado* (Barcelona: Seix Barral Editores, 2000), 14–15; originally published in Cuba, 1968.

13. Fuentes, *Nos impusieron la violencia*, prologue by Carlos Aldana (Havana: Editorial Letras Cubanas, 1986), 57. See also the analytically barren book of revolutionary soldiers' baroque testimonies by Crespo Francisco, *Bandidismo en el Escambray, 1960–1965* (Havana: Editorial de Ciencias Sociales, 1986).

14. Quoted in Mary Alice Waters, *From the Escambray to the Congo: Interview with Víctor Dreke* (New York: Pathfinder Press, 2002), 112.

15. Ibid., 77–78.

16. Enrique G. Encinosa, *Escambray: la guerra olvidada* (Miami: Editorial SIBI, 1988).

17. Fuentes, *Condenados de Condado*, 79. Translation mine.

18. Ibid., 85–86.

19. Norberto Fuentes, *Cazabandido* (Montevideo: Area Editorial, 1970), photographs nos. 8, 9, 12 and 16.

20. Ibid., 168–69.

21. Andrew St. George, "Inside Cuba's Revolution," *Look* 22 (February 4, 1958): 24–30.

22. Judith Rudakoff, "R/Evolutionary Theatre in Contemporary Cuba: Grupo Teatro Escambray," *Drama Review* 40, no. 1 (Spring 1996): 78. See also Rafael González Rodríguez and Christopher Winks, "Teatro Escambray: Toward the Cuban's Inner Being" in the same issue, 98–111.

23. Jesús Orta, "Vamos a convertir al Escambray en la región más revolucionaria de Cuba," *INRA: Revista Mensual Ilustrada* 2, no. 4 (April 1961): 20–24.

24. Telephone interview with anonymous informant, January 17, 2005.

25. Taped interview with Norberto Hernández, December 18, 2000, Miami, Florida; and personal diary entry, November 20, 1996, Briones, Cuba.

26. Comisión Internacional de Juristas, *El Imperio de la ley en Cuba* (Geneva: La Comisión, 1962), 131–36.

27. Lillian Guerra, *Visions of Power: Revolution and Redemption in Cuba, 1952–1972* (Chapel Hill: University of North Carolina Press, forthcoming).

28. Roberto E. Hernández and Carmelo Mesa-Lago, "Labor Organization and Wages," and Rolland G. Paulston, "Education," in *Revolutionary Change in Cuba*, ed. Carmelo Mesa-Lago (Pittsburgh: University of Pittsburgh Press, 1971), 209–49, 375–97; Marifeli Pérez-Stable, *The Cuban Revolution: Origins, Course and Legacy* (New York: Oxford University Press, 1993), 61–81, 99–135.

29. Guerra, *Visions of Power*; Néstor Almendros and Jorge Ulla, *Nobody Listened/Nadie escuchó*, Cinematica-Condor Media Productions, 1989.

30. For the violent nature and policies of the alliance between the U.S. government and radical Cuban exiles, see Levine, *Secret Missions to Cuba*; Peter Kornbluh, *Bay of Pigs Declassified: The Secret CIA Report on the Invasion of Cuba* (New York: New Press, 1998); James Blight and Peter Kornbluh, *The Politics of Illusion: The Bay of Pigs Invasion Re-Examined* (Boulder, Colo.: Lynne Rienner Publishers, 1998); Jesús Arboleya, *The Cuban Counterrevolution*, trans. Rafael Betancourt (Athens: Ohio University Center for International Studies, 2000); Thomas C. Patterson, *Contesting Castro: The United States and the Triumph of the Cuban Revolution* (New York: Oxford University Press, 1994); *CIA Targets Fidel: Secret 1967 CIA Inspector General's Report on Plots to Assassinate Fidel Castro* (Melbourne: Ocean Press, 1996); Warren Hinckle and

William Turner, *The Fish Is Red: The Story of the Secret War against Castro* (New York: Harper and Row, 1981); Sandra H Dickson and the University of West Florida, *Campaign for Cuba*, PBS Video, 1992; and Howard Dratch and Allan Francovitch, *Inside the CIA: On Company Business: Part 1—The History*, MPI Home Video, 1990.

31. Miguel de la Torre, *La lucha por Cuba: Religion and Politics on the Streets of Miami* (Berkeley: University of California Press, 2003), 105.

32. Ibid., 76–77.

33. "La mafia de Miami y sus acólitos: son capaces de matar al niño antes de devolverlo sano y salvo al país," *Juventud Rebelde: Diario de la Juventud Cubana*, March 27, 2000, 1.

34. "Esta es la lucha de la verdad contra la mentira," *Granma: organo oficial del Comité Central del Partido Comunista de Cuba*, March 28, 2000, 1.

35. Guerra, "Elián González and the 'Real Cuba' of Miami."

36. Jorge Mas Canosa, "Radio Martí aumentará las posibilidades de la libertad en Cuba," and "Razones para no reconocer a Castro," in *Jorge Mas Canosa: en busca de una Cuba libre: Edición completa de sus discursos, entrevistas y declaraciones, 1962–1997* (Coral Gables, Fla.: North-South Center Press, University of Miami, 2003), 1:421, 1:398; for early examples in the revolution, see Nuez, "El fascismo en U.S.A.," *INRA: Revista Mensual Ilustrada* 3, no. 2 (March 1962): 94–95; and "En Cuba," *Bohemia* 53, no. 21 (May 21, 1961): 71.

37. Notes from personal diary entry, Havana, June 16, 2004.

38. Fidel Castro, "Words to the Intellectuals," in *The Revolution and Cultural Problems in Cuba* (Havana: Ministry of Foreign Relations, 1962), 13. Emphasis added.

39. Quoted in Pérez Stable, *The Cuban Revolution*, 163.

40. Código penal de Cuba, art. 144 (1987), published in *Gaceta Oficial de la República de Cuba* 85 (December 30, 1987) and quoted in *Código Penal de Cuba: Revista Cubana de Derecho* 15, no. 27 (April–December 1986).

41. Quoted in Carolee Bengelsdorf, *The Problem of Democracy in Cuba* (Oxford: Oxford University Press, 1994), 135; see also 134–54; and Abel Enrique Hart Santamaría, *Delitos contra la seguridad del estado* (Havana: Editorial de Ciencias Sociales, 1988), esp. 100–173. The unexplained elimination of the periodical *Sputnik* was a memorable event in the minds of most Cubans, a fact they attribute to its investigative reporting on the atrocities committed by Stalin and other human rights violations of Soviet regimes that had previously warranted little if any discussion in Cuba.

42. See transcript of Foreign Broadcast Service—Latin America (*FBIS-LAT-92-03*), January 6, 1992, 1–9.

43. "Opening Remarks by Division General Arnaldo Ochoa Sánchez to the Military Court of Honor," in *End of the Cuban Connection* (Havana: Editorial José Martí, 1989), esp. 55–60.

44. Lourdes Casal, *El caso Padilla: literatura y revolución en Cuba. Documentos* (Miami: Ediciones Universal, 1971), and Heberto Padilla, *Fuera del juego: Premio Julián del Casal 1968. Edición conmemorativa, 1968–1998* (Miami: Ediciones Universal, 1998).

45. A documentary film was later made that includes clips from the televised sessions of the trial. See Orlando Jiménez-Leal, *8-A Ochoa*, Meridian Video, 1992, 1996; and Orlando Jiménez-Leal, *8-A: La realidad invisible* (Miami: Ediciones Universal, 1996).

46. Guerra, *Visions of Power.*

47. Lisandro Otero, *La utopía cubana desde adentro: ¿Adónde va Cuba hoy?* (Mexico City: Siglo Veintiuno Editores, 1993), 28.

48. Ibid., 62–63.

49. For discussion of the Cuban government's attitude toward later waves of migrants, such as those who left in the Mariel boatlift in 1980, see María de los Angeles Torres, *In the Land of Mirrors: Cuban Exile Politics in the United States* (Ann Arbor: University of Michigan Press, 1999), 105–9.

50. For example, see "Declaración de la Central de Trabajadores de Cuba," *Granma* 16, no. 85 (April 8, 1980): 1; and "Comunicado de los CDR. ¡Cada cuadra una trinchera de la Revolución!" *Granma* 16, no. 87 (April 10, 1980): 1.

51. For photographs of the mass rallies with clearly visible signs and comités de repudio, see *Granma* 16, no. 86 (April 9, 1980): 1; *Granma* 16, no. 89 (April 12, 1980): 1, 3; *Granma*, 16, no. 93 (April 16, 1980): 1, 3; and "¡Coraje, disciplina, organización, en la Marcha del Pueblo Combatiente!," *Granma* 16, no. 96 (April 19, 1980): 8.

52. "Hay gran afinidad entre Pinochet y estos elementos," *Granma* 16, no. 86 (April 9, 1980): 3.

53. David Rieff, "Cuba Refrozen," *Foreign Affairs* 75, no. 4 (July–August 1996): 62.

54. Carlos Lage Dávila, Jorge Lezcano, and Enrique Martínez, "Queremos formar una juventud que piense con cabeza propia: Entrevista a Roberto Robaina, Secretario General de la Unión de Juventudes Comunistas de Cuba," in *¿Cuba? Sí, como no: No nos resignamos a vivir sin patira*, ed. Carlos Lage Dávila, Jorge Lezcano, and Enrique Martínez (Madrid: Partido Comunista Popular de España, 1993), 195.

55. Ibid., 190–93.

56. *Informe al Congreso* (Havana: Unión de Jovenes Comunistas, 1992). The copy I reviewed of this document lacked pagination.

57. Original text: "¿Acaso tú recibiste un mensaje de Fidel para orientar [al Ministro de Asuntos Exteriores de España, Abel Matutes] de cómo debía abordar el asunto

de los grupúsculos contrarrevolucionarios? Tú aconsejaste a Matutes de cómo debía desenvolverse en este asunto con Fidel. . . . Se habla con el enemigo, Robaina, pero no se le dan consejos. . . . No voy a permitir que gente como tú jodan esta revolución tres meses después de que desaparezcamos los más viejos." Quoted in Mauricio Vicent, "Expulsado Roberto Robaina," *El País*, reprinted in the electronic magazine, *Desafíos: Órgano Oficial de la STC (Solidaridad de Trabajadores Cubanos)* 11, no. 61 (September–October 2004), http://webstc.org/stc7.htm. See also Gerardo Arreola, "Mantuvo 'estrecha amistad' con Mario Villanueva Madrid, Asesgura" *La Jornada*, July 31, 2002; and Juan Tamayo, "Cuba Says Tourism Shake-Up Not Related to Corruption, Robaina," *Miami Herald*, June 11, 1999.

58. Elizardo Sánchez Santa Cruz et al., *La Patria es de todos: voces de la disidencia cubana*, ed. Federico Campbell (Mexico City: Ediciones del Milenio, 1998).

59. "Spanish Daily Details 'Unprecedented' Atmosphere in Cuba after Carter Visit," BBC Monitoring, May 18, 2002; Anita Snow, "Fidel Castro says Government Will Respond to Petition Effort in 'Due Course'," Associated Press, October 10, 2002; David González, "Cuba Can't Ignore a Dissident It Calls Insignificant," *New York Times*, October 13, 2002, 4; and "Cuban Opposition Cites Coercion against Members of Varela Project," BBC Monitoring, December 3, 2002.

60. Anita Snow, "Cubans Asked to Declare Castro Socialism 'Untouchable' in the Future," Associated Press, June 14, 2002.

61. See "Índice onomástico" in Instituto de Historia del Movimiento Comunista y de la Revolución Socialista de Cuba anexo al Comité Central del PCC, *El pensamiento de Fidel Castro: selección temática* 1, no. 2 (January 1959–April 1961): 792.

62. "Cuban Dissidents Slam U.S. Steps to Topple Castro," Agence France Presse, May 11, 2004.

63. David González, "Cuban Dissident Ends Tour Hopeful of Democratic Reform," *New York Times*, January 18, 2003, 6.

PART THREE   *The Weight of the Night*

The Furies of the Andes

Violence and Terror in the Chilean Revolution and Counterrevolution

PETER WINN

For roughly one thousand days, from 1970 to 1973, the Chilean Left tried to pioneer a nonviolent road to a democratic socialism under the leadership of an elected president, Salvador Allende. This *vía chilena* attracted the attention of foreign friends and foes out of all proportion to Chile's small size and peripheral location, and it has retained an outsized historical resonance ever since. Yet Allende's brief peaceful revolution ended in the most violent coup and most repressive military dictatorship in Chilean history—a coup and terror justified in large part as a response to the "climate of violence" allegedly created by Allende's Popular Unity government. Moreover, this accusation that the ostensibly nonviolent vía chilena was in reality a violent "communist" revolution like the Russian or Cuban Revolutions has remained a mantra of its rightist and centrist opponents in the battle over historical memory that has continued to this day. The violence/nonviolence of the Chilean Revolution/counterrevolution, therefore, remains a central historical debate.

The supposedly inherent violence of revolutions has been an essentialist staple of antirevolutionary political propaganda and historiography since the "classic" English and French revolutions of the precommunist era. More recently, historians of Europe who are sympathetic to revolutionary goals have felt obliged to confront the issue of violence and revolution, even if they have argued that revolutionary violence was a response to counterrevolutionary violence and that the furies of revolution in France and Russia were "manifold and dialectical."[1]

In the case of the Chilean Revolution, however, counterrevolutionary violence was met by revolutionary restraint and, as in ancient Greece, the furies of the Chilean Andes were "one-sided." Chilean revolutionaries were as self-conscious as Russian revolutionaries about the historical precedents of the revolutions that preceded them. But, in the case of Chile, the importance of the historical analogy was to define *difference*, not to claim similarity: the uniqueness of "the Chilean road to socialism" as a democratic and nonviolent revolutionary process. In great part, this stress on the *non*violence of la vía chilena was to avoid the revolutionary terror that had tarred the reputation of its communist predecessors in Russia and in Cuba. As Allende explained to me in an oral history interview in 1972: "Millions of people in the world want socialism, but don't want to have to pay the terrible price of civil war in order to obtain it." He was well aware that many leftists were convinced that this was impossible. As a good Marxist, he legitimated his stance by reference to Marx's belief that in countries with advanced democratic institutions and traditions, like England, it might be possible to reach socialism peacefully. No one had yet been able to do that, stressed Allende, but he believed that it was possible in Chile. His ambition was to become the first leader to lead his people to the promised land of socialism along that preferred peaceful path.[2] Throughout the Chilean "revolutionary process" of 1970–73, this ideology of peaceful, democratic revolution would act as a restraint on revolutionary violence.

Despite the final image of Allende firing the gun Fidel Castro had given him, defending his presidential palace against the attacking counterrevolution on the day of the military coup, until the day of his death Salvador Allende remained on that path. La vía chilena was conceived as a peaceful political road to a democratic socialism. This meant persuading a majority of Chileans to vote for socialism by the end of Allende's projected six-year term as president. In order to do that, it was necessary to convince Chileans that a peaceful revolution was possible, even "a revolution with meat pies and red wine"—that is, a revolution without sacrifice. Allende and the other Unidad Popular (Popular Unity) leaders were convinced that a majority of Chileans would never vote for a revolution characterized by collective violence and state terror.

What gets lost in the retrospective analyses of the Chilean Revolution—analyses viewed through its violent end in the coup of 1973—is how successful this nonviolent revolutionary model seemed to be during Allende's first year in office. The socialization of large-scale private property by congressional expropriation, market purchase, or executive decree had been so successful that in the November 4, 1971, speech celebrating the first anniversary of his inauguration Allende could proclaim: "We control 90 percent of what were the private banks. . . . [M]ore than seventy strategic and monopolistic enterprises have been expropriated—intervened, requisitioned or acquired by the state. We are *owners*! . . . We are able to say *our* copper, *our* coal, *our* iron, *our* nitrates, *our* steel; the fundamental bases of heavy industry today belong to Chile and the Chileans."[3] La vía chilena could also boast the most extensive and rapid land reform without a violent revolution—so sweeping and so fast that Chou En-lai warned Allende that he was going *too* fast—an agrarian reform that would be completed in eighteen months, instead of six years as originally projected. To these dramatic structural changes the Chilean Revolution had added worker participation in the management of the socialized enterprises, a massive distribution of income, significant legal reform, and expanded housing, health, education, and social security programs.

Together with the control of inflation and the reduction in unemployment, these "revolutionary advances" along the democratic road had won the Popular Unity a rapid increase in popular support, from the 36 percent who had voted for Salvador Allende for president in September 1970 to the 50 percent who voted for Popular Unity candidates for mayor in April 1971. The Popular Unity interpreted this quantum jump in leftist votes to an historic high as approval of its vía chilena, as a mandate for an accelerated advance toward socialism and as a sign that they might be able to secure an electoral majority for socialism even *before* Allende's presidency was over, using a constitutional plebiscite to create a new unicameral assembly with a leftist majority that would then legislate a democratic transition to socialism. In other words, a year into la vía chilena, a nonviolent road to socialism seemed not only feasible but well advanced, and more easily and rapidly than even the revolutionary leaders themselves had initially believed possible. There seemed no reason to consider any other revolutionary strategy.

During the year that followed, the emergence of economic dislocations, the increase in social conflict, and the loss of political momentum slowed the revolutionary advance and threatened to reverse its gains. But even on the defensive, the Chilean revolution kept to its peaceful road, despite counterrevolutionary plots and violence. In the face of numerous coup plots, Allende assumed both the dignified stance of civic outrage and the persona of the innocent victim, expressing a confidence he may not have felt in the loyalty of the Chilean armed forces. In those moments, his tendency was to present himself as the constitutional Chilean president, and not as the revolutionary leader. Allende might wrap himself in the flag of revolutionary nationalism, as when the covert intervention of the International Telephone and Telegraph Corporation (ITT) to prevent his inauguration was revealed in 1972. He might utilize that counterrevolutionary plot as a justification to expropriate the property of a hated foreign "monopoly." But, unlike earlier revolutionary leaders, he did not use this revelation of a foreign conspiracy to mobilize personal attacks on Americans or their Chilean collaborators. Moreover, even his attacks against property rights utilized legal instruments, not the force of arms or collective violence to accomplish their objectives.

The Right Takes to the Streets

As the counterrevolution shifted its attacks from the halls of Congress to the streets of Santiago in mid-1972, in increasingly violent political protests spearheaded by opposition students and neofascist strong-arm squads seeking violent confrontations and political martyrs, the Allende government tried to use the police to control the situation. In the end, the Communist Party mobilized its own student and youth groups to counter "the fascists." Yet, even then, revolutionary violence was defensive. It did not exceed the level of counterrevolutionary violence, nor did it take advantage of that opportunity to use violence to force a revolutionary breakthrough. As a result, there would be no "September Days" in the Chilean Revolution.

The same was true during the 1972 "October Strike," a Sorelian general strike (so called after Georges Sorel, the French philosopher who advocated displays of class power as mechanisms of change) *by* the bourgeoisie to demonstrate their power to cripple the economy and set up the conditions for the violent ouster of the Allende government by a military coup—in other words, a strike to rule. In the face of widespread lockouts, transport stoppages, and professionals' strikes, backed by a paramilitary threat of force, Allende called on the workers to defend their revolution from paramilitary attack, keep their enterprises running, and mobilize to produce and distribute essential commodities. But he pointedly did *not* encourage them to assault the perpetrators of these attacks on their workplaces, living standards, and revolution. Moreover, when the conflict escalated, Allende did not put himself at the head of a radicalized revolution and ride it to a revolutionary breakthrough that might involve collective violence. Instead, he brought the armed forces chiefs into his cabinet and brokered a truce that would calm the conflict and return the contest between revolution and counterrevolution to an electoral path.

When the midterm congressional elections of March 1973 confirmed the civilian stalemate, the counterrevolution started banging on the barracks doors for a violent ouster of the Popular Unity government and the reversal of its revolution. At the end of June, Allende was confronted by the *tancazo*, a dangerous coup attempt headed by a key Santiago armored regiment, which claimed a score of lives. In response, Allende called on the workers to occupy their factories, but did not call them into the streets to defend the revolutionary government or attack its enemies, relying instead on General Carlos Prats, the army commander, to suppress what was then spun as a localized mutiny by a rogue officer. Allende also refrained from vetoing the "Ley de Armas," which gave the armed forces the right to raid factories, farms, shantytowns, and institutions to search for "illegal arms," and urged his supporters to tolerate these often arbitrary and coercive searches during the months leading up to the coup of September 11, 1973.

As the armed forces became more politicized by the counterrevolution and less reliable as guardians of the constitution, Allende did rely more heavily on his personal bodyguard of political comrades, the so-called GAP (Grupo de Amigos Personales), a shift that the desertion of his official carabinero guard on September 11, 1973, would justify. They carried the light arms that might prevent an assassination attempt or delay mutineers, but not the heavy guns that might deter or defeat a military coup—or spearhead a revolutionary offensive. This was true as well of the weapons allegedly found stockpiled in Allende's presidential palace and residence after the coup.

The Left Responds

Even during the military coup, Allende did not call on his supporters to defend his government and their revolution, asking them instead to remain in their workplaces and wait for instructions—orders that never came. Instead, he offered himself as a sacrifice for the revolution, proclaiming in his last radio broadcast that morning—"I will pay with my life for the loyalty of the people"—and offering as consolation the Marxist faith that the future would belong to Chile's workers, "that history is ours and is made by the people." In the end, he was the Chilean president who considered civil war the worst disaster that could befall a nation, not the revolutionary willing to run any risk for his cause. Rather than risk the evil of civil war, Allende chose to become a revolutionary—and republican—martyr, whose death would validate his life's work as a democratic revolutionary and deny legitimacy to Pinochet's violent counterrevolution.

If we broaden this analysis to the parties of the Popular Unity, there is some difference of discourse, but little difference in practice. The Communist and Socialist Parties had long had small security forces, largely to act as bodyguards for their leaders and to keep order at demonstrations and marches. But the Moscow-line Communists were Allende's chief political supporters within the governing coalition arguing for revolutionary restraint, although they would mobilize their supporters to defend their revolution against violent attacks by "fascist" civilian paramilitary squads.

The Socialists, whose party had emerged out of the defeated fight for the twelve-day Socialist Republic of 1932—which had begun with a military coup by the air force commander—had preserved armed struggle in their founding myth, along with the search for "red generals." The redefinition of the Socialists as a Marxist-Leninist party in 1967 added a Cuban revolutionary update to this mythology with an explicit endorsement of armed struggle. Moreover, during 1973, as the revolutionary advance stalled and the counterrevolution grew in strength and violence, the head of the Socialist Party, Carlos Altamirano, argued for the need to leave la vía chilena for the route of mass mobilization that he acknowledged might lead to armed confrontation. By mid-1973, leaders on the left wing of the Popular Unity, like Altamirano, began to warn that armed confrontation between the forces of revolution and counterrevolution was inevitable and that the revolutionaries had to prepare for it. This was a position long held by the MIR (Revolutionary Left Movement), the Guevarist group to the left of the Popular Unity, which increasingly allied itself with the left wing of the governing coalition.

But this "revolutionary" left wing did not dominate the Popular Unity, as its decisive defeat at the key June 1972 Lo Curro meeting of the governing coalition on revolutionary strategy demonstrated—and as Allende's rejection of their demand that he "arm the people" in the wake of the tancazo a year later confirmed. Moreover, although the left wing of Popular Unity—composed principally of left Socialists and allied with the MIR, which was not a part of Popular Unity—were pushing in mid-1972 for a radicalization of the revolution from below through mass mobilization, they did not press for "arming the people" until after the October Strike, and even then as a defensive strategy that was never really implemented.

Last, although the chief leftist parties of the Popular Unity—the Communists and Socialists—acquired a limited amount of small arms and trained a restricted number of their activists in their use, their purpose was always defensive and the arms and numbers involved were too small to make a difference in a military coup, as the suicidal effort of the Socialist Youth to defend the presidential palace from the surrounding government office buildings on September 11, 1973, demonstrated. The intended role of these party security forces was to counter rightist civilian paramilitary forces, which they did successfully during the increasing violent street fighting during the weeks leading up to the coup. Even the MIR, the revolutionary movement to the left of Popular Unity, which had talked longest and loudest about the need to prepare for the inevitable violent confrontation between revolution and counterrevolution, seemed singularly unprepared when the coup took place, with activists waiting on street corners for guns and orders that never arrived.[4] In short, whether the focus is on Allende, on the parties of his governing coalition, or on the left wing of Popular Unity or on the movements to its left, the overwhelming impression is one of revolutionary restraint, even in the face of growing counterrevolutionary violence. The reluctance to unleash collective revolutionary violence was manifest among the leaders of the Chilean Revolution.

"A Climate of Violence"

Yet, despite this revolutionary restraint and commitment to Allende's peaceful road, counterrevolutionary violence and the military coup and terror were justified by claims that the revolutionaries had created a "climate of violence." To a great extent this was part of a disinformation campaign that played on the trope of violent revolutionaries. This campaign had begun in earnest during the 1964 presidential election, with funding and technical assistance from the CIA. That "campaign of terror" was intended to frighten Chileans into not voting for Allende and featured ads in which anxious children stared at a closed door above a caption that warned: when Communists come to power, fathers disappear. (Ironically, it was when the *counter*revolutionaries came to power a decade later that fathers were "disappeared" in Chile.) This oblique reference to Stalinist Russia was complemented by another ad warning that if Allende were elected Chilean children would be sent to Cuba. The endless repetition of these tropes had a profound impact, however, independent of their validity.[5]

Although a revival of the campaign of terror in the 1970 presidential elections was unable to prevent the election of Salvador Allende, the trope of revolutionary terror remained and served as a base for the counterrevolution to build an attack on the sincerity of the Popular Unity's proclaimed commitment to peaceful change. When the feared Allende presidency brought neither the disappearance of fathers, nor the export of Chilean children to Cuba, the counterrevolutionary strategy was compelled to shift. Increasingly, the strategy was to accuse the revolutionaries of creating "a *climate* of violence" and to use what I have described elsewhere as "the revolution from below" as proof of its claim.[6]

The key to the revolution from below and the charge that he was promoting a climate of violence was Allende's promise not to use the security forces against "the people"—unlike his predecessors. Freed from the fear of police violence, workers, peasants, and homeless *pobladores* increasingly took the revolution into their own hands, creating a veritable revolution from below, which accelerated and extended Allende's revolution from above. The key tactic was the *toma*, or seizure—whether it was a *toma de sitio* of vacant suburban lands by homeless squatters, a *toma de fundo* of a landed estate by its peasants, or the *toma* of a factory by its workers. By 1972, the toma had come to symbolize the revolution from below to its supporters—and the Chilean Revolution as a whole to its opponents.

The Revolution from Below: The Tomas

Tomas de sitio by homeless urban squatters had been common in Chile since the massive rural migration of the 1950s. They were usually peaceful actions that depended on public sympathy and political support to avert police repression and eviction, which were rare but still punctuated the struggles of the homeless during that era, as in the 1969 massacre of pobladores in Puerto Montt under President Eduardo Frei. Although many of these tomas were organized by political groups or their mass fronts, the dominant trope in these suburban tomas was that of the innocent victim, such as the young girl killed by the police in the toma of Herminda de la Victoria in

1967. In the wake of Allende's election, a record number of tomas de sitios took place, but they were generally nonviolent occupations of empty lands and lots.[7]

What changed in 1970 was the *image* of the suburban toma de sitio and the *discourse* surrounding it. In part, this was due to the revolutionary spin now given by the Popular Unity to homeless squatters seizing vacant suburban lands. For the most part, however, it was a result of the entry of the MIR into the organization of suburban tomas. The MIR had been founded as a clandestine Guevarist guerrilla movement during the preceding decade, but after Allende's election belied their prediction that he could not win, they began to organize an above-ground "revolutionary" mass movement. Because Communist and Socialist strength among industrial workers limited their advance within the "working class," the MIR focused its efforts instead on the unorganized peasants and rural migrants. The squatter settlements that they controlled, such as Nueva La Habana, were among the best organized and most orderly in Chile, with internal security providing protection from crime and even domestic violence, and with their own "people's courts" to resolve internal disputes peacefully. But the external image that the MIR projected through its Revolutionary Squatters Movement was an aggressive one of combative revolutionaries who in public demonstrations paraded down the main streets of Chile behind the MIR's red-and-black banner chanting: "¡Pueblo! ¡Fusil! ¡MIR!" Although the "guns" they carried were wooden or cardboard toys, the image of aggressive violent revolutionaries they projected reinforced the trope of revolutionary violence—and in turn was used by the counterrevolution to persuade Chileans that revolutionary violence was an imminent/immanent threat.

It was a working misunderstanding that served the purposes of both extremes of the Chilean political spectrum. For the MIR, it helped project their movement as a "revolutionary" alternative to the "reformist" parties of the Popular Unity. But, it also helped the counterrevolutionary Right persuade the Center that Allende and his vía chilena were creating a climate of violence. Although the suburban tomas and squatter settlements of the Allende era were nonviolent, the image that was publicized and magnified by the rightist media was one of a revolutionary violence close to the residences of the wealthy and the middle class. Significantly, the Pinochet dictatorship would forcibly remove squatters from these Barrio Alto shantytowns and resettle them in poorer shantytowns on the other side of Santiago, creating a socially segregated city.

Tomas de fundos by their resident peasantry were less common before 1970, although not unknown. But the geometric increase in such land seizures after Allende's election gave the phenomenon a new saliency to both the revolution and the counterrevolution. The tomas began in the south of Chile, where the Mapuches (Chile's largest surviving indigenous group) moved the fences back to where they had been a century earlier, before their lands were taken by European immigrants backed by the Chilean state. When these tomas succeeded, the tactic spread north through Chile's fertile Central Valley. The tomas themselves were not violent. There were no personal attacks on the land owners or managers, such as took place in the Bolivian and Mexican revolutions. Nor was there destruction of the fundo's property, which its new possessors wanted to preserve for their own use.

For the most part, the tomas de fundos were of large landed estates slated for expropriation under the agrarian reform law of 1967, which the centrist Christian Democratic government of Eduardo Frei had only partially implemented. After Allende's election, rural workers began seizing their fundos to make sure that the government would expropriate them this time, and to prevent the landowner from removing livestock and equipment before that legal expropriation process took place. By mid-1972, virtually all of these tomas had been transformed into legal expropriations.

Where violence did occur, as in the Mapuche south, it was when the old landowners employed armed paramilitary groups to try to retake the disputed lands, which the peasants defended with whatever primitive weapons they had. The victims of this violence tended to be the peasants who were defending their tomas. These land seizures, however, were "illegal" acts that violated the property rights of the owners, which the Right equated with violence. Such *retomas* were often justified as efforts to implement judicial decisions ordering the eviction of peasant squatters that the Allende government refused to allow the security forces to enforce; but they were illegal acts of violence undertaken by self-righteous property owners.[8] In general, however, the tomas de fundos were not violent, nor did they lead to violent retomas.

Once again, the image of these rural tomas was more violent than their reality. Here too, the rightist media exaggerated the violence, but the revolutionaries led by the MIR played into the rightist media campaign that made rural tomas a mainstay of their trope of violent revolutionaries. Once again, the MIR targeted areas and groups that had not yet been mobilized by leftist political parties for its Revolutionary Peasant Movement, and played an important, but often exaggerated role in the tomas of the south, including the Mapuche tomas that detonated the first wave of Allende-era rural tomas. As with their urban squatters' movement, the MIR tried to give its peasant movement a combative "revolutionary" image that it hoped would win converts from the movements organized by the "reformist" Popular Unity parties. The rightist media seized on images of armed peasant tomas and demonstrations to support its claim that the Popular Unity had created "a climate of violence."

Moreover, the reality was that every toma did have to guard against the possibility of a retoma, so peasants used whatever means they had to create a defense, including projecting an image of having the determination and the means to resist a retoma in order to discourage the old owner from attempting one. The first rural toma I observed, in Melipilla near Santiago in March 1972, was typical in its outward face of young male peasants blocking entry to their fundos with pointed sticks and an ancient fowling piece behind "barricades" of felled trees. It was a defensive stance, an image of "armed" activists ready for violence—even though they told me they hoped that violence would never happen and they did not threaten anyone who did not try and force their way past them onto their farm. Equally significant, in this highly conservative zone where landowners from some of Chile's leading families had estates—and had held meetings the month before that the government charged planned counterrevolutionary conspiracies—a local judge had ordered the arrest of peasant leaders, whose followers then organized a "sit-in" in the court building and demonstrated in protest outside in what the rightist media portrayed as a violent toma of the local courthouse.⁹ Once again, a movement that was not in itself violent was used by the counterrevolution to project the argument that the Popular Unity and its vía chilena promoted a "climate of violence."

Tomas of suburban and rural lands had a history in Chile to guide their protagonists and ease their acceptance by the public. Seizures of factories by their workers, on the other hand, were a new departure, which began with the Yarur textile mill in late April 1971, and spread rapidly through the textile industry and then to other industrial sectors. Yet, despite their novelty and their leaders' lack of experience, these industrial tomas were also nonviolent, as the emblematic example of Yarur demonstrates. Before the toma, the only sign of violence at the Yarur mill was when a counterrevolutionary union officer brandished a pistol and warned that he would shoot anyone who tried to seize the factory, which was the ground for his censure and ouster by the union assembly. During the toma itself, the revolutionaries were careful not to be violent, despite the factory's history of repression that included violence—such as the personnel chief running over strikers with his automobile in 1963 or the factory guards shooting strikers. In 1970, the revolutionaries utilized the factory's private guards to police the grounds, but posted a few dozen revolutionaries in strategic places (such as the warehouses) to prevent looting or arson. Several loyalists to the old owners chose not to appear at the factory after its toma to reclaim their positions, but there were no reprisals against those loyalists who did—and no physical violence even against those loyalists who had committed violence themselves in the past. I have compared the toma of Yarur to the fall of the Bastille in the French Revolution, and a government official who was there compared it to the taking of the Summer Palace in the Russian Revolution, but their new revolutionary empowerment led the Yarur workers to celebrate their liberation peacefully, not to seek violent revenge on their old oppressors.[10]

Nor did this revolutionary restraint disappear when the counterrevolution turned violent. During the October Strike of 1972, Yarur workers mobilized to defend their factory (by then known as Ex-Yarur) against a paramilitary attack similar to the one that had burned down the other Yarur mill at Chiguayante in the south, but their weapons consisted of sharpened pointed sticks, not guns or bombs, and were intended to defend against counterrevolutionary violence and not to impose a terror of their own. During the August 1973 replay of the October Strike, an Ex-Yarur truck was firebombed by counterrevolutionary terrorists. The response of the Ex-Yarur workers was to take an undamaged truck, fill it with fashions designed by the workers and place a sign on it saying: "Here is the work of the workers," while the sign on the damaged truck read: "Here is the work of the fascists." They paraded both in the September 4, 1973, demonstration that commemorated the third anniversary of Allende's election, a didactic display of nonviolent revolutionary virtue.[11]

The Revolution from Below: The cordones industriales

On the day of the coup itself, the leaders of Ex-Yarur decided that with only a few watchmen's pistols to defend the factory, flammable stocks of cotton and chemicals, and an artillery base across the street, resistance was not only futile but dangerously irresponsible, a decision ratified by the last general assembly of the workers of Ex-Yarur. Although the resistance of a handful of factories such as Sumar and Elecmetal got all the publicity, the Yarur's lack of weapons and decision not to resist was much more typical. Most Chilean workers were prepared to defend their factories against attacks by civilian paramilitary groups, but not against the Chilean armed forces. As one left-ist Ex-Yarur leader—a "hero" of its "liberation"—told me on the eve of the coup: "If I had thought that Allende would lead us into a civil war, I would never have voted for him."[12]

The resistance of Sumar to the coup was a special case because it was where the security apparatus of the Socialist Party retreated and decided to make a stand, with the help of the nearby *población* of La Legua and its Communist Youth organization.[13] Resistance at Elecmetal, on the other hand, needs to be contextualized within an account of the *cordón industrial* to which it belonged. The cordón industrial became the urban heart of the counterrevolutionary case that the Chilean Revolution had created a cli-mate of violence that justified a violent counterrevolutionary response.

Once again, the rhetoric was more violent than the reality. The cordón industrial was an original Chilean response to the confining conditions fac-ing the Chilean Revolution in 1972, when the easy advance of la vía chil-ena was over and Allende's legalistic democratic road to socialism seemed blocked. The cordón was a territorial organization of an industrial belt that transcended the craft lines that divided Chilean labor unions and allowed larger factories to help smaller factories organize and socialize. It was no accident that Cordón Cerillos, in Santiago, was formed in June 1972, the same month in which the Popular Unity Left was defeated at the Lo Curro meeting of the governing coalition, along with its strategy to break through these confining conditions by setting aside the original strategy of alliance with the middle class and radicalizing the revolution by mobilizing a Lenin-ist class alliance of workers and peasants from below. The cordón industrial was the response of the Popular Unity Left to this defeat and to the critical juncture they saw the revolution as confronting.[14]

Most cordones industriales, however, were formed in response to the "bourgeois" October Strike late in 1972, and they played key roles in the successful effort to stop that counterrevolutionary offensive, helping the workers locked out of smaller factories in their areas to occupy them and keep their production going, while organizing the distribution of es-sential goods and services in their area and defending their "territory" from counterrevolutionary sabotage and attacks. In the process, the cordones industriales helped the workers of hundreds of smaller enterprises to seize them and convert them to worker self-management. Although part of the accord that ended the October Strike provided for the return of enterprises occupied during the lockouts, many that were within a cordón industrial were not returned. As the cordones defended these tomas and Allende was unwilling to order the security forces to evict the occupying workers by force, they remained under worker control, a process that was repeated during the tancazo mutiny in June 1973 and again during the August 1973 repeat of the October Strike. As a result, over five hundred enterprises were in the hands of their workers by the coup of September 11, 1973, compared with the ninety-one enterprises on the official list to be nationalized.

With the cordones industriales too, however, their rhetoric was more "revolutionary" than their reality and their image more violent than their practice. The cordones reflected the Popular Unity Left's strategy of mobilization from below and their success during the October Strike led some in the Left faction to fantasize about the cordones as Chilean "soviets in embryo." It was a revolutionary fantasy. The cordones in Santiago did form a city-wide coordinating committee and created some links with suburban and rural county councils that included peasants and pobladores. But, unlike Russia in 1917, there were no soldiers or sailors in the cordones and no "people in arms." Moreover, as mass mobilization shifted from class struggle to partisan electioneering in the run-up to the March 1973 congressional elections, the cordones lost their dynamism and direction. At the same time, the refusal of the Communists to participate in the cordones—which they identified with political rivals and opposed as weakening the labor unions they controlled—limited their appeal and legitimacy. The tancazo offered an opportunity for the cordones to regain their momentum, but when Allende refused to "arm the people" they became demobilized once again. The result was an outward presentation that was more violent than their behavior. The cordones did mobilize their adherents to defend their territories from paramilitary attacks or retomas, but these mobilizations were purely defensive and depended on numbers, not guns. After the tancazo, a few factories in the most combative cordones—especially Cordón Vicuña Mackenna—did begin to accumulate a few defensive weapons. Most of these were small arms, with the exception of the metal works of Madeco, which produced a few of what the rightist media would dub *tanquetas*, but which were really armored forklifts.[15]

More typical was the behavior of Cordón O'Higgins, whose territory included the parade ground for the annual September 19 Independence Day military parade. The night before the coup the executive committee of the Cordón O'Higgins met to decide what measures to take the day of the parade. The meeting began with a show of unity: given the critical juncture the Communists had decided to integrate their members into the cordón—an indirect recognition that it was potentially the most powerful local organization that Chilean workers had developed. When the meeting was warned that a military coup was likely to take place before September 19, the "revolutionary" factory leaders present acknowledged that possibility, then went back to discussing what kind of signs should be carried at the military parade, deciding on signs that stressed prophetically: "Soldiers! Don't fire on your brothers!" The next day the coup took place, and the Cordón O'Higgins was unprepared to resist it. During the days that followed, the military reduced the cordones that did resist one by one, later commenting that their resistance was much lighter than they had expected. Interviewed after the coup, surviving leaders of the cordones explained that they were prepared to combat civilian paramilitary squads, but had neither the arms nor the training to fight the Chilean army—nor with rare exceptions did they attempt to do so.

Like the rest of the revolution from below, the cordones industriales were not as violent as their rhetoric or their image in the rightist media. This image of violence began with the media presentation of their tomas as the violent expulsion of owners from their property, to the image of the cordones armed to defend these "illegal" seizures, to the precoup image of the cordones searched by the military for hidden "illegal" arms, to the postcoup image of the cordones resisting the armed forces with "tanquetas" of their own manufacture. These fabricated images of "illegal" revolutionary violence then enabled Pinochet to label them "Cordons of Death" that required military intervention and justified the counterrevolutionary terror that followed.[16] In the end, the cordones industriales were neither the embryonic soviets of leftist dreams nor the extremist army of rightist nightmares. They were arguably the most revolutionary institution produced by the Chilean Revolution, with all the limitations and contradictions that that implied. Yet, they were also key constructions in the rightist "proof" that Allende, by design or by weakness, had promoted a climate of violence in Chile.

The single act that was most responsible for consolidating the trope of violent revolutionaries and fixing the image of a climate of violence under Allende, however, was the mid-1971 assassination of Eduardo Pérez Zujovic, interior minister in the Christian Democratic government of Eduardo Frei, by a previously little-known leftist guerrilla group, the VOP (Vanguardia Organizada del Pueblo), which judged him responsible for the massacre of pobladores in Puerto Montt in 1969. The enraged Christian Democrats gave Allende three days to bring the killers to justice. He met their deadline, but that did not mollify their leaders or lessen the shock of their followers. Moreover, in the shootout that crushed the VOP, those who could have clarified the killing died. I have never been satisfied with the official story. The timing of the assassination was suspicious—at a moment when the centrist Christian Democrats were deciding whether or not to ally with the Right. Moreover, the VOP was a shadowy group without the MIR's links to social movements or mass politics, one of whose leaders I know from my own research had been the rightist head of a factory security force a few years before. The possibility of an assassination plotted by counter-revolutionary provocateurs to tar the revolution and persuade the Christian Democrats to ally with the Right cannot be ruled out. Yet, whatever the truth of these claims, the VOP assassination of Pérez Zujovic branded the Chilean Revolution with the mark of Cain. Here Chilean revolutionaries, albeit an extremist splinter group outside the revolutionary mainstream and opposed to la vía chilena, seemed to have crossed the line into terror, as French and Russian revolutionaries had done before them.

But, in reality, the Pérez Zujovic assassination was the exception that proved the rule: the Chilean Revolution was a nonviolent process, even in the face of rightist provocations. There were no show trials and executions—as in the French, Russian, and Cuban Revolutions—even for captured coup plotters with foreign ties. International politics were as important for Chile as for France and Russia, but did not lead to a more radical or violent Chilean Revolution, despite an invisible U.S. blockade that was crippling the Chilean economy and revelations of U.S. involvement in counterrevolutionary plots—the kind of foreign intervention that had helped radicalize the Cuban Revolution a decade before. Nor were the revolutionary responses to economic crisis—price controls, food rationing, and property confiscation—accompanied by revolutionary terror as in earlier revolutions. On the contrary, they were handled in ways that epitomized the legalistic, bureaucratic character of la vía chilena, reinforced by a restrained popular mobilization. The U.S. copper mines were expropriated by a unanimous vote of the Chilean Congress. The agrarian reform utilized a Frei-era law. The banks were acquired by using a stock market takeover strategy—and the legal power of the CORFO, the Popular Front–era government development corporation, to buy and sell shares. Factories like Yarur might have been taken over by their workers, but their incorporation into the public sector utilized longstanding executive decree powers to take over indefinitely the administration of enterprises producing basic necessities whose production was threatened by the policies of their private owners or where production was threatened by an insoluble labor dispute.

The defensive stance and legalistic restraint of the Chilean revolutionaries is clear even in the historical precedents on which they drew. The most common historical analogy Chilean revolutionaries used was to label their enemies "fascists," a clear reference to the Second World War or the Spanish Civil War—references that explained the violence of the Chilean counterrevolution in different terms. The analogy was often to the Russian victory over Nazi Germany against long odds and in the face of superior armaments—although the fascist victory in the Spanish Civil War would prove the closer analogy. Either way, the image was one of revolutionary defense against counterrevolutionary political violence, and the message was revolutionary restraint, not revolutionary collective violence—distancing Chile from the Cuban, Russian, and French Revolutions.

What underscored the Chilean Revolution's difference from the Cuban, Russian, and French Revolutions was the limited radicalization of the Chilean Revolution at critical junctures. The national majority for the Popular Unity candidates in the April 1971 municipal elections did lead to a radicalization of the revolutionary process. Most of the gains of the revolution that I cited earlier were made during the revolutionary advance that followed, but it is striking how nonviolent that advance was, despite the speed and scope of "the changes."

The End of La Vía Chilena

The surfacing of armed counterrevolution in the "March of the Empty Pots" of December 1971, where mostly female demonstrators were "guarded" by armed neofascist squads, brought this period of revolutionary advance to an end. But it posed an opportunity to radicalize the revolution and escalate the violence by "retaking" the streets and forcing a new revolutionary breakthrough of confining conditions. What is striking is not only did this not take place, but it was never even attempted; moreover, this was a conscious decision of the revolutionary leadership, a decision ratified in the Popular Unity's summit meeting in February 1972 at El Arrayan. One of the meeting's major decisions was to accelerate the agrarian reform so that it would be completed in eighteen months instead of six years. But this was a strategy to *avert* the escalation of violence by eliminating some of its pressure points, defusing the revolution from below by accelerating the legalistic revolution from above. It was not a decision to radicalize the process.

By mid-1972, the Popular Unity Left was proclaiming the exhaustion of la vía chilena and the need to shift revolutionary strategies to a more orthodox one of mass mobilization of a class alliance of workers and peasants, giving up on the chimera of an alliance with the middle class and a deal with the Christian Democrats. In effect, it was an argument for the revolution from above putting itself at the head of the revolution from below. Yet, this position was defeated at the Lo Curro Popular Unity summit meeting of June 1972, which ousted the cabinet ministers who embraced that strategy and instead endorsed the moderate Popular Unity (principally Communists and moderate Socialists) strategy of containing the revolution from below and negotiating a compromise with the Christian Democrats that would consolidate most of the advances made in return for freezing further advances. In effect, this was a strategy for preserving a truncated version of la vía chilena. Significantly, despite the repeated failure to secure that deal with the Christian Democrats, this would remain the dominant Popular Unity strategy during the year of escalating violence that followed. The night before the coup, Allende postponed for a fatal twenty-four hours calling the plebiscite that might have averted the military takeover, in large part because he was waiting for a Christian Democrat agreement on it that never came. That was because the Christian Democrats had already joined the counterrevolution and did not want to avert the coup. In the political imagery bequeathed by the French Revolution, if the Popular Unity moderates were the responsible Girondins of the Chilean Revolution and the Popular Unity Left its Jacobins, what is striking is the continuing triumph of the Chilean "Girondins" in circumstances that in France would have produced a Jacobin victory.

This explains why the critical junctures that in the French, Russian, or Cuban Revolutions might have served to mobilize revolutionary violence to defeat the counterrevolution and to radicalize the revolution were not used for those purposes in Chile. The most important was the October Strike of 1972, which the revolution from above could not contain and was thus forced to mobilize the revolution from below to stalemate. At the same time, the revolution from below used the opportunity to advance the revolutionary process through the seizure of workplaces and the formation of cordones industriales, which took control of entire areas of cities and organized self-defense, as well as production and distribution—emerging as what the Popular Unity Left hailed as "soviets in embryo." It was precisely that prospect, along with the escalating violence it would produce, that led Allende to negotiate an electoral truce with the counterrevolution and bring in the armed forces to guarantee and police it. In other words, faced with the choice of navigating a vía chilena that was now so constricted as to seem blocked to most observers, or putting himself at the head of a surging revolution from below and trying to use its momentum to force a revolutionary breakthrough, Allende chose to reaffirm his original strategy and impose that choice on his coalition.

Counterfactual history is a perilous pursuit and it is likely that taking that alternative route might have led not to a revolutionary breakthrough but rather to an earlier coup and even more deadly confrontation. It is clear that neither Allende, nor his military chief, General Prats, had much faith in "the people in arms" as a counter to the Chilean armed forces. And it can be argued that September 11, 1973, proved them correct. During the next major crisis/opportunity—the tancazo of June 1973—when the Socialist chief, Carlos Altamirano, demanded that Allende "mobilize the masses" to defeat the counterrevolution, Allende's withering response was: "Compañero. How many 'masses' equal one tank?"[17] But, the point here is that Allende did *not* take advantage of these critical junctures—or others where the U.S. role in the counterrevolution was revealed—to radicalize the revolution and mobilize and arm his supporters, as Cuban, French, and Russian revolutionary leaders had done in comparable circumstances; and second, that Allende and the moderates were able to impose these choices on the revolutionary coalition.

There would be no Chilean "Red Army" or "levée en masse." The only branch of the security forces that Allende was able to transform into a revolutionary instrument was Investigaciones, the Chilean FBI, but it was too small in numbers and in the caliber of its weapons to make a difference on September 11, 1973. It was Pinochet who commanded on that other "9/11" the conscript national army created with the universal military service that was a legacy of the French Revolution to Latin American republics, refracted through the hierarchical Prussian traditions of Chile's officer corps, with their Germanic training. Unlike Castro in Cuba, Allende did not have the power to destroy the Chilean army, which had not been defeated militarily, was not imploding internally, could not be charged with treason to the nation, and had a strong sense of institutional loyalty and autonomy. So Allende, through General Carlos Prats, the army's constitutionalist commander after the assassination of General Schneider by neofascist kidnappers, concentrated on maintaining the loyalty of the armed forces to him as Chile's constitutional president.

In order to assure their loyalty, Allende promised to respect the autonomy and political neutrality of the armed forces. He also sought to win the support of the military by giving them the salaries and weapons they wanted and allowing a record number of officers to go to Panama and other U.S. bases for special training. Allende tried as well to increase their sympathy with his revolutionary process by involving them in his government's development programs. Most of these measures backfired: the United States used the training to instill the national security doctrine in Chilean officers and to train them for the counterrevolution, even to communicate to them U.S. support for a military coup.[18] And the experience of a messy revolutionary process replete with inefficiency, partisanship, and "disorder" convinced the officers who participated in it that the military could run the country better than civilians.

Most of all, however, Allende's efforts to maintain the loyalty of the army failed because of the pressures from civil society and the political class that politicized the officer corps and in an increasingly counterrevolutionary direction. This became clear when Prats was forced out by his generals in August 1973, following protests around his house by their wives. It became evident that Allende had depended too much on Prats and his ability to control his officer corps. This made Prats a central target of the counterrevolution before the coup and a major assassination target of the Pinochet dictatorship. Ironically, it was Prats who recommended to Allende that he should name Pinochet as his successor, mistakenly considering his leading subordinate to be an apolitical constitutionalist who had the respect of the officer corps that Prats himself had lost by mid-August 1973. A fortnight later, Pinochet led the military coup that ousted Allende—and the counterrevolutionary terror began.

In sum, what is striking—given the escalating war of words, the social tensions, the political polarization, and the ostensible "climate of violence" they created—was how *limited* the political violence was during the Allende era. Even if one accepts as an upper bound the uncritical catalogue of ostensibly violent acts published by a rightist, Opus Dei think tank to justify the coup and its violence,[19] the number of acts of "violence" of all kinds was only a couple of hundred over three years—and most of these were acts of "violence" against *property*, not *people*, including nonviolent sit-ins in government buildings. Moreover, despite the escalating confrontations of 1972–73, only one hundred Chileans died from political violence during the Allende era and this includes the twenty-two killed during the tancazo, the counterrevolutionary army mutiny of June 1973. In fact, three times as many Chileans lost their lives as a result of counterrevolutionary violence during the Allende epoch than from revolutionary violence. Last, these pre-coup deaths from political violence pale by comparison with the lives lost and destroyed by the most violent coup in Chilean history and the brutal and bloody counterrevolutionary dictatorship that followed.

The Counterrevolution in Power

During the days, months, and years that followed the military coup of September 11, 1973, more than three thousand Chileans were killed by this counterrevolutionary violence, most of them detained and "disappeared" in secret without any legal proceeding. Equally significant, but less well known outside Chile, is that at least twenty-eight thousand—and probably more than fifty thousand—Chileans were "detained" and tortured in this counterrevolutionary terror, a trauma so profound that Chileans are only beginning to confront it three decades later.[20] This dark night of counterrevolutionary terror would last for sixteen years, eleven of them supposedly under "the rule of law," when the "internal war" that justified the initial state terror was officially over.

But counterrevolutionary violence began long before September 11, 1973. It cast its shadow over the Chilean Revolution from the very start, creating the very "climate of violence" that the counterrevolution then used to justify the military coup and the terror that followed. With the support of the United States, whose plots to block Allende's inauguration included a violent "Track II," after Allende was elected in 1970, neofascist conspirators murdered the constitutionalist armed forces commander General René Schneider. This unaccustomed political violence prompted a revulsion in Chile that assured Allende's inauguration and the succession as armed forces commander of another constitutionalist, General Carlos Prats, but it was a harbinger of things to come.

During the three years that followed, counterrevolutionary violence would claim dozens of lives. Some were Mapuches or Chilean peasants killed while resisting efforts to retake rural properties by armed rightist groups contracted by the old landowners in 1970 and 1971. Others were students or leftist youths shot in the street fighting of 1972 and 1973 with armed neofascist squads. Still others were workers murdered for trying to distribute food and other necessities during the October 1972 and August 1973 strikes, or innocent bystanders struck by bullets during the tancazo of June 1973. But the victims also included the politically prominent, such as Allende's aide-de-camp, the naval captain Arturo Araya, who was assassinated while trying to promote a dialogue with the navy.

For a year following the Schneider assassination, the counterrevolution was on the defensive, with its violent side mostly manifested in rural Chile, in attacks on Mapuches and peasants who had seized control of landed estates. When it reappeared in December 1971, it was as armed paramilitary squads protecting the mostly upper- and middle-class women in the March of the Empty Pots, where their appearance created almost as much shock as the Schneider assassination. Both heralded intensified counterrevolutionary violence; both seemed "un-Chilean," at odds with the country's traditions and self-image. During the months that followed, as the counterrevolution shifted from the halls of Congress to the streets of Santiago, neofascist squads escalated street fighting from fists to stones and then to guns. Significantly, whenever the possibility of a negotiated solution to the polarized Chilean conflict arose, a violent confrontation undermined it and polarized politics still further. During the October Strike, counterrevolutionary violence reached new levels: trucks that continued operating had their tires punctured or their cabs sprayed with bullets; factories and stores that remained open were attacked and industrial plants were burned down. The election campaign of 1973 quieted the violence for a few months, but when the March congressional balloting confirmed the civilian stalemate, opposition politicians began banging on the barracks doors and demanding a military coup. The first attempt in that direction—the June 1973 tancazo—claimed a score of victims, including the deliberate shooting of a Swedish photographer.

In the months following, the armed forces became increasingly involved in the violence that they were charged to prevent. Some of it was symbolic violence, as in the raids on factories, shantytowns, and universities ostensibly in search of "illegal arms," but in reality to accustom their troops to treating Chileans like themselves as enemies in an internal war. Other armed forces violence was all too real. During the August 1973 opposition "strike," Chile was terrorized by electricity blackouts caused by explosives blowing up the main power lines pylons. Everyone assumed that paramilitary groups such as Patria y Libertad were responsible, and a Communist Youth delegation met with Allende to insist that he "take a hard line with the fascists." They were stunned and silenced when Allende told them that it was the Chilean navy and not civilian neofascists who were responsible for these "terrorist acts." These acts of violence forced Allende to declare states of emergency in many provinces, with the local military commander taking control of the government. Together with the arms raids and terrorist attacks by the armed forces, this "creeping coup" prepared the way for the violent military coup of September 11, 1973. If there was a "climate of violence" in Chile, it was because the counterrevolutionaries had consciously created it during the preceding three years.

But the way to the military coup and counterrevolutionary violence had also been prepared by a century and a half of Chilean history, some of which served as explicit precedents for Pinochet's counterrevolution. The model for his authoritarian regime, he claimed, was created in the 1830s by Diego Portales, generally regarded as the founder of the Chilean state. Portales was a pessimistic conservative, who wrote to a friend in 1832 that "the social order in Chile is maintained by the weight of the night." By this he meant the passivity of the "ignorant" masses, which allowed Chile's elites to rule the country as they saw fit. Portales warned that should this cease to be the case, "we will find ourselves in darkness and without any power to contain the rebellious aside from the methods dictated by commonsense or those which experience has proven useful"—methods that he defined elsewhere as "the cake and the stick."[21] When the "weight of the night" began to be lifted by increasingly rebellious workers at the turn of the twentieth century, the stick was more apparent in the response of Chile's elites than the cake. Not for nothing is the national motto "By reason or by force."

It was among the nitrate miners of the north of Chile that working-class movements on a scale that alarmed the elites first emerged at the turn of the twentieth century, when regional organizations and general strikes paralyzed the nitrate exports on which the Chilean government depended for its revenues. Significantly, it was against those miners in 1907 that the Chilean state unleashed violence on an unprecedented scale. For years, miners who labored under oppressive conditions (that included corporal punishment) for mostly foreign companies that paid them a pittance in tokens they could only redeem at the company store had protested their exploitation by companies whose own profits averaged 20 percent annually. When their local organizations coalesced into a regional organization, the *mancomunal*, which called a successful general strike in 1907 centered on the nitrate port of Iquique, the elite response was to massacre perhaps three thousand miners and their families—roughly the same number killed under Pinochet, but out of a far smaller Chilean population and in sixteen minutes, not sixteen years. This didactic use of violence to counter what the elites saw as a revolutionary threat set back the Chilean labor movement for a decade, but it removed the "weight of the night" from the Chilean working class.[22]

What most concerned Chile's conservative elite, however, was that the rural laborers on their estates should remain obedient workers and loyal clients, assuring also that these rural constituencies would be safe conservative congressional districts. For a time they were able to maintain this arrangement. During the 1930s, when Chile was the most depressed nation in the world, Portales's "cake" was offered to urban workers by worried elites, who agreed to a labor code legalizing unions and strikes, although subject to strong government regulation. But when rural workers tried to organize and strike in the elite's agrarian preserve, the elite response in 1934 was another massacre—of more than one hundred peasants in southern Chile. Within a local context of intensifying elite abuses and growing peasant organization and militancy, this massacre sparked the Ránquil peasant rebellion and, in response, the murder of its peasant leaders, before order—and the weight of the night—was restored to rural Chile once more.[23] This didactic use of violence made its political point: the center-left Popular Front exempted rural labor from its reforms, postponing rural unionization for another three decades, while guaranteeing conservative elites both a docile labor force and a safe political base in Chile's "model democracy." These measures solidified the tripartite "three-thirds" division in Chilean politics among Left, Right, and Center, assuring that the status quo would suffer only marginal changes. In addition to these periodic displays of officially sanctioned violence, twentieth-century Chile also witnessed "recurrent declarations" of states of siege, delegation of "extraordinary authority" to presidents, and jurisdiction of military courts over civilians for "crimes against the internal security of the state."[24]

Yet, despite these periodic massacres and daily disciplining, the weight of the night was increasingly lifted off Chile's rural laborers as the twentieth century advanced, bringing public education, transistor radios, union organization, and competing political parties to the countryside. By 1970, Chile's rural workers had joined the nation's urban workers and suburban shantytown dwellers in the ranks of the "rebellious" who elected Salvador Allende on a platform of a democratic peaceful revolution. Neither the conservative stick nor the reformist "cake" of the centrist Christian Democrats had proved sufficient to stop their rebellion, which developed into a revolution from below.

Finding themselves in the social and political "darkness" that Portales had prophesied, and "without any power to contain the rebellious," Chile's conservative elites turned counterrevolutionary and conjured up the violence and terror that "experience had proved useful." The result was the escalating violence of an undeclared civil war, culminating in a counterrevolutionary military coup that would loose a terror such as Chile had never seen, yet one in line with elite responses to past challenges from below, and citing Portales as its inspiration.

In Chile, then, the furies were loosed when the social hierarchy was challenged from below, to punish the transgressions of rebellious *rotos*—literally "broken ones"—as the Chilean elite has traditionally referred to their lower class. Within the fictive family of the paternalistic rural estate, such rebelliousness amounts to parricide, which the Greek furies traditionally punished. But in Chile such disciplining reflected the elite's determination to defeat challenges to a social hierarchy that the elite viewed as both "natural" and necessary. Their violent response was not only meant to punish those who had challenged this "natural" social order, but also as a didactic violence to discourage those who might be tempted to challenge it in the future.

The belief that such transgressions justify terrible revenge underlies the counterrevolutionary violence and terror of the Pinochet dictatorship. One example is gender role transgressions: at Villa Grimaldi, where the

Dirección de Inteligencia Nacional (DINA) operated its most notorious torture chamber, male torturers subjected female prisoners to special sexual tortures, from rape to electrodes in the vagina, because they "rejected the fact that women were involved in politics, because women should be at home," testified a Villa Grimaldi survivor. "To them it was very offensive that women should be involved in other things, a break with the past. That made them very angry . . . [so] they wanted to make us feel like prostitutes." "We had transgressed, so we had to be punished," added her cellmate. "It was our fault that we were there."[25] In Chile, as in France or Russia, the rage of the furies at such transgressions turned violence into terror. But it was the *counter*revolution, not the revolution, which loosed the furies and created this terror.

In Chile, the terror began the night before the coup in army barracks and naval vessels, targeting soldiers and sailors who could not be relied on to overthrow the elected government. It exploded on the day of the coup in the attack on the presidential palace that began with tanks, continued with airborne rockets, and culminated in the storming of La Moneda that ended in the death of President Allende and the capture of those who had remained with him, most of whom were taken to the base of the Tacna Regiment and executed there.

The counterrevolutionary violence continued during the days that followed in the attacks on the cordones industriales, shantytowns, and university campuses, as well as on mines and farms. It was accompanied by a terror announced in calls for Chileans to anonymously denounce "subversives" and by dragnet searches of residential complexes, interrogations of workers, a strict nightly curfew, and bans on gatherings of more than three people.

The tens of thousands of people "captured" in the attacks and raids of the postcoup period were taken to sports stadiums, such as the National (Soccer) Stadium in Santiago, where they were interrogated, usually tortured, and sometimes executed, as the public martyrdom of the singer Víctor Jara and the private death of a U.S. student, Frank Teruggi, attested. Some of those who survived the stadiums were released, taking the terror with them and spreading its didactic message; others were sent to concentration camps in abandoned mines in the burning northern deserts, or in frozen Antarctic wastelands like Isla Dawson, where torture and interrogation continued. In the cities, the nightly sounds of gunfire after the curfew testified to the continuation of counterrevolutionary violence during the weeks and months following the coup. So did the bodies bumping against the shores of the Río Mapocho in downtown Santiago each morning, most of them young men from the shantytowns upriver, their hands tied behind their backs with barbed wire, sometimes headless, or with bodies with multiple bullet wounds.

In the countryside, where there were no embassies and no foreign journalists, the terror may have been even worse. Mapuches in particular were targeted.[26] In the provinces, even those who had survived military trials were not safe. A few weeks after the coup, Pinochet sent a team of officers to provinces whose commanders were suspected of "leniency," to review all sentences. This "Caravan of Death," as it became known, left a trail of executions in its wake.[27]

Since the coup, I had been sending information on human rights violations in Chile back to the office of Senator Edward Kennedy, then a leader in the defense of human rights in the U.S. Congress. In early December, a Chilean army colonel whom I did not know approached me at a press conference cocktail party and declared: "Senator Kennedy can relax now. We have moved from 'la matanza masiva a la matanza selectiva' [from 'massacres to selective slaughter']." I began hearing reports of the systematization and computerization of the repression, of the formation of a Chilean "Gestapo" (referring to the DINA), of a selective slaughter, like Operation Phoenix in Vietnam, that targeted political cadres and local social movement leaders who might lead future resistance. The counterrevolutionary violence became less visible, but the terror continued, moved now to secret torture centers like Villa Grimaldi. By then, the terror had been internalized and a population accustomed to living in liberty had been disciplined. The counterrevolution had consolidated itself through violence.

This counterrevolutionary violence had so exceeded Chilean norms and expectations that it shocked many Chileans who had initially supported the coup. Outside Chile, the Pinochet dictatorship came to symbolize counterrevolutionary state terror in a region notorious for it. The military junta might be a de facto "regime of force," but even the Pinochet dictatorship felt the need to justify its violence and terror.

At bottom, its justification was based on the trope of revolutionary violence that the counterrevolution had carefully constructed during the preceding three years of the Chilean revolutionary process. The initial military communiques and censored media coverage redefined Allende supporters as "subversives" and portrayed their defense of the elected constitutional government as illegitimate, a violation of the armed forces' monopoly of coercive force. It was as if the Chilean army, not the Chilean constitution, had the right to define what was legal and illegal conduct. The metaphor was "internal war" and the junta left no doubt as to who had right—as well as might—on its side.

Yet this was not enough to persuade Chileans who might have supported the "soft coup" that most Chileans expected but were skeptical of the need for such "un-Chilean" counterrevolutionary violence. In the days following the coup, the censored television repeatedly showed images of "illegal arms" the military claimed to have found in both the presidential palace and Allende's residence. What the press was shown were small caches of small arms, probably intended for Allende's personal bodyguards or the Socialist Party (as defensive weapons against paramilitary attack), certainly nothing like the weapons needed to equip ten battalions, as the junta later claimed. The purpose of this disinformation campaign became clear on the first day that Chileans emerged from the seventy-two-hour curfew imposed by the junta to a world pockmarked by bullets and policed by bayonets. General Oscar Bonilla, the most political of the coup plotters, announced the "discovery" of a leftist plot to assassinate the top military officers on the day before Chilean Independence Day and the annual military parade, using Cuban arms and ten thousand foreign extremists. It was us or them, he argued, articulating what would become the central justification for the counterrevolutionary terror.

A week later, Federico Willoughby, the junta's press secretary and a CIA asset, revealed the "discovery" of an even wider-ranging conspiracy that he called "Plan Z."[28] During the days and weeks that followed, seemingly daily "revelations" amplified Plan Z with alleged war plans, assassination lists, weapons caches, training camps, and logistical support for a massacre of military, political, and social leaders whose goal was to destroy Chile's democracy and replace it with a leftist dictatorship. At bottom, it was the reverse of what the military coup plotters had done to the elected leftist government and its supporters. This "discovery" was intended to justify that counterrevolutionary violence and the continuing counterrevolutionary terror.

None of the foreign correspondents believed Plan Z. Everyone knew it was a fabrication, and most thought the CIA had a hand in it. Moreover, as it grew in scope, Plan Z became less and less believable. By the time it morphed into an ostensible plot to murder Allende by left Socialists—perhaps playing on the trope of revolutions consuming their own children—and was bound into the White Book (*Libro Blanco*) of leftist perfidy, no one in the press corps took it seriously, not even journalists for the pro-junta newspapers who had to write positive articles about it.[29]

Within the public at large, however, it was a different story. There, the Big Lie began to have its effect. The repetition of charges and media images of "illegal arms," the daily "discovery" of new plots and their revelation by military commanders around the country led to increased credibility, not growing incredulity. In part, this reflected the prestige of the Chilean armed forces as "honest" and "correct"; in part, it stemmed from the isolation of most Chileans from any other source of information in a country where every newspaper, every radio broadcast, every television show was censored. But it also reflected the psychological effects of the tensions and trauma Chileans had lived through, from an attitude akin to the expression "Where there's smoke, there's fire," to the cognitive dissonance of wanting to believe that what they had endured and were living through was justified. This was particularly true for centrist Christian Democrats or largely apolitical Chileans, or those who had felt traumatized by the "climate of violence" or food shortages under Allende and wanted a return to "order." By December 1973, I noticed that many who had been skeptical initially, had begun to refer to Plan Z as if it were a fact—something that rightists still do in Chile today. In other words, the fabricated evidence of revolutionary violence/terror was used to justify an otherwise unjustifiable counterrevolutionary violence/terror, building on the trope of revolutionary violence and communist terror that stretches back to the French, Russian, and Cuban Revolutions—despite all the efforts by the Chilean Revolution to avoid revolutionary violence and differentiate itself from those earlier revolutions.[30]

If the objective of the coup was to overthrow the Allende government and install a military regime, the counterrevolutionary violence of the coup and the terror that followed were unnecessary. No unit of the Chilean armed forces fought in defense of the elected constitutional government, so the plotters were not faced by a civil war with an unknown outcome that might have justified such extreme measures, but rather a military coup whose outcome was never in doubt. At most, the Popular Unity strategy was to use their weapons to try to hold out until loyal military units could rescue them, as had happened in the tancazo. Once the armed forces succeeded in imposing unity within their own ranks, they had nothing to fear militarily. The counterrevolutionary terror they unleashed was both unnecessary and unjustified by anything that the Left had done, was capable of doing, or had planned to do.

How then can we explain the scope and intensity of this counterrevolutionary terror? One explanation is suggested by a comment that a Chilean army major made to me a few weeks after the coup: "We have to crush them now so that we can let up later." It was military strategy applied to counterrevolutionary politics, which explained as well the targeting of political, labor, and neighborhood leaders who had the capacity to organize future political resistance and the organized working class, peasants, and shantytown dwellers, who could form the base for such resistance. Terror might not be needed to oust Allende and install a military regime, but it was required to consolidate that military dictatorship and to carry out a counterrevolution that would reverse the changes of the Allende revolution and take away what it had done for workers, peasants, and shantytown dwellers, from material benefits and organization to dignity and empowerment. The Chilean Revolution might not need to resort to violence to carry out confiscations of private property, as was the case in the French and Russian Revolutions, but the counterrevolution clearly thought that it had to use terror to reprivatize those properties and discipline workers, peasants, and shantytown dwellers who had gotten out of hand and threatened the social order.

There was also a less rational element in this counterrevolutionary violence, particularly on the day of the coup and during the chaotic days that followed. In those first days of the counterrevolution, every army officer was his own judge—and executioner—and counterrevolutionary paramilitary units operated freely as death squads. Equally fierce was the anger of the counterrevolutionary elites I interviewed at the "treason" of elite leftists like Carlos Altamirano or Oscar Guillermo Garretón, or at the temerity of lower-class *rotos* in challenging their place and in trying to turn the "natural" social order upside down. Significantly, the counterrevolutionary terror in rural areas targeted at peasant and Mapuche leaders was among the worst in Chile.

It was here that the furies seemed hard at work. Whereas ideology acted as a restraint on revolutionary violence, it seemed to have fueled *counter-*

revolutionary violence. Anticommunism encouraged Chilean rightists to believe that they were engaged in a war between good and evil, in which the fate of their families and their country hung in the balance. This struggle was given a religious dimension by ideological portrayals of it as a fight to defend Christian civilization against atheistic communism. It was wrapped in the flag of nationalism by an ideology that identified its cause with patriotism and the internal enemy as betraying the nation to international subversion. Interest was added to ideology and transmuted into a defense of private property as if it were a sacred value as natural as motherhood. The various aspects of this ideology were synthesized in the slogan "So that Chile continues to be Chile"—although this war cry also reflected the elite's visceral reaction to the revolutionaries' challenge to the old social hierarchy and politics of deference, which their furies would punish with a vengeance. Together, these dimensions justified an escalating counterrevolutionary violence leading up to the coup.

Ideology also informed military cultural violence after the coup, with its enraged overreaction against the cultural changes of the preceding decade. The public execution of Víctor Jara, the most popular singer-songwriter of the leftist "New Song" movement, expressed this rage and determination to reverse this cultural revolution. The purging of universities and libraries, the censorship of publications and mass media, and the burning of books were steps in the same counterrevolutionary direction. The sacking of the homes and art collection of the Nobel laureate Pablo Neruda, the order to the National Library to destroy its archive of leftist newspapers, the removal of foreign revolutions from educational curricula, were all acts of an ideological or cultural iconoclasm. For the next fifteen years Pinochet would try to maintain Chile in intellectual and cultural isolation, keeping out "subversive" foreign books and performers, and censoring those that were permitted. This Chilean cultural counterrevolution was xenophobic as well as iconoclastic.

This demonizing of the "foreign" underscores the importance of international factors in helping to explain revolutionary/counterrevolutionary violence and terror. In Chile, there was no foreign war or "invasion," but the cold war and invisible foreign threats were used as a functional equivalent by the counterrevolutionaries—although not by the revolutionaries. Allende might decide *not* to use revelations of U.S. covert warfare to radicalize his revolution—as Fidel Castro had done in Cuba with the U.S.

covert intervention there a decade before—but the junta would use the fabricated threat of Cuban intervention to justify its own counterrevolutionary violence.

The trope of Cuban violence, terror, and subversion was everywhere after the coup, helping persuade Chileans of the need for counterrevolutionary terror. The "illegal arms" discovered were ostensibly "Cuban arms." The mythic "guerrillas" captured were supposedly "Cuban-trained." The "ten thousand foreigners" who allegedly were to have executed Plan Z were also claimed to be Cubans or Cuban-trained. Even before the coup, as part of the disinformation campaign of the U.S. covert war against Allende, the CIA had fabricated documents "proving" that Allende was betraying Chilean military secrets to Cuba. These were circulated to apolitical army officers as part of a campaign to persuade them that Allende had to be ousted and the army had to abandon its traditional constitutional neutrality.[31] This demonizing of Cuba as "*the* enemy" may help explain what led the Chilean army to mount a military assault on the Cuban embassy after the coup, in total violation of international law and diplomatic norms.

The U.S. promotion of the "National Security Doctrine," with its expanded armed forces' mission justifying military political intervention and social control in the name of national security and anticommunism, also played an important role in encouraging the Chilean counterrevolution. So did the diplomatic, financial, and logistical support that the U.S. government, led by Richard Nixon and Henry Kissinger, gave to the junta, with full knowledge of its counterrevolutionary violence and terror.

Recently declassified documents have confirmed the involvement or complicity of the U.S. government in the events leading up to the coup and its violent aftermath. Significantly, the first political killing of the era—the assassination in October 1970 of General René Schneider, the constitutionalist army commander—was promoted by the CIA, which recruited, paid and armed the killers.[32] The 1973 coup was set up by a three-year covert U.S. intervention, which included deliberate efforts to "destabilize" the Allende government and to promote a military coup. During this time, Washington imposed an "invisible blockade" to "make the economy scream," funded opposition media, political parties, and social movements (including groups known to be planning political violence), and provided expert advice to the Right in the increasingly violent discourse of the psychological war known in Chile as "the campaign of terror." In addition, the CIA drew up lists of Chileans who were to be arrested in the event of a coup, and the U.S. army assured Pinochet that if he led a coup the U.S. government would support him. As late as 1976, Kissinger would go out of his way to praise Pinochet and reassure him of U.S. support during a meeting ostensibly devoted to protesting his dictatorship's notorious human rights abuses. There are also growing indications that the U.S. role in counterrevolutionary violence in Chile—from the events that led up to the coup to the terror that followed it—was greater than just complicity and diplomatic obfuscation.[33]

International politics also loomed large in the use of historical analogies by Chile's counterrevolution. "The importance of precedent" to explain "the monstrosity of violence" that Arno Mayer points to in the Russian and French cases was also present in Chile, but to justify *counter*revolutionary violence.[34] I have already commented on the military's use of the trope of revolutionary violence to justify their own violence, and their explicit referencing of the Cuban Revolution, along with the implicit reference to the French and Russian Revolutions. Less well known is the counterrevolution's use of historical precedents for *counter*revolutionary terror, such as the letters and flyers left in the mailboxes and door transoms of leading leftists during the weeks before the coup with the chilling message: "Djakarta se acerca"—"Jakarta is Coming." This was a pointed reference to the massacre of two hundred thousand leftists in the wake of the 1965 military coup in Indonesia that overthrew Sukarno, another constitutionally elected "socialist" president. The military coup and counterrevolution in Brazil provided another historical precedent, one that Chilean counterrevolutionaries not only cited as a legitimating precedent, but actually traveled to Brazil to study and learn from, at a special institute set up by Brazilian counterrevolutionaries for that purpose.[35]

What all this points to is what the Chilean Revolution may have lost in clinging to its democratic road. Its unwillingness to loose the furies of revolution is part of the explanation of why the French and Russian Revolutions succeeded in defeating their counterrevolutions while the Chilean Revolution did not. Instead, it was defeated by a counterrevolution that was willing to loose *its* furies, while the revolutionaries restrained their own—although given the "correlation of forces" the outcome of a more Jacobin or Leninist strategy might have been the same or worse.

In Chile, it was the counterrevolutionaries—not the revolutionaries—who utilized political violence and state terror as a conscious strategy. In the face of this violent counterrevolution, the determination of Allende and the bulk of the Popular Unity to keep to the nonviolent road to socialism may have doomed that strategy to ultimate failure—and condemned Chile to suffer the darkest night of political violence in its history.

Notes

1. Arno J. Mayer, *The Furies: Violence and Terror in the French and Russian Revolutions* (Princeton: Princeton University Press, 2000), xvii.

2. Salvador Allende, interview, July 1972, Santiago.

3. Quoted in Peter Winn, *Weavers of Revolution: The Yarur Workers and Chile's Road to Socialism* (New York: Oxford University Press, 1986), 227–28.

4. See Franck Gaudichaud, *Poder popular y cordones industriales: testimonios sobre el movimiento popular urbano, 1970–1973* (Santiago: LOM, 2004), 265, 285.

5. United States, Senate, Intelligence Committee, Staff Report, *Covert Action in Chile, 1963–1973* (Washington, 1975), 7–8, 15–17, 21–23. A CIA report concluded that this covert U.S. intervention gave Allende's centrist opponent a majority on the first round.

6. Winn, *Weavers of Revolution*, chaps. 10–16, especially 139–43.

7. See Mario Garcés, *Tomando su sitio: el movimiento de pobladores de Santiago, 1957–1970* (Santiago: LOM, 2002).

8. See, for example, Florencia Mallon, *Courage Tastes of Blood: The Mapuche Community of Nicolás Ailío and the Chilean State, 1906–2001* (Durham: Duke University Press, 2005), 92–113.

9. I am indebted to Ian Roxborough for sharing with me this result of his as yet unpublished research on the agrarian reform in Melipilla.

10. Winn, *Weavers of Revolution*, chaps. 13–16.

11. Ibid., especially 236 and 244.

12. Ibid., especially 243.

13. Mario Garcés and Sebastián Leiva, *El golpe en La Legua: los caminos de la historia y la memoria* (Santiago: LOM, 2005).

14. Gaudichaud, *Poder popular y cordones industriales*, 106, 119, 127, 242–43, and 264–66.

15. Ibid., 301–45.

16. Augusto Pinochet, *The Crucial Day* (Santiago: Ed. Renacimiento, 1982), annex 8, "The Cordons of Death," 203–33.

17. Orlando Letelier, interview, September 1976, New York. It is a well-known story that I have heard related in roughly the same way from multiple sources.

18. See, for example, Peter Kornbluh, ed., *The Pinochet File: A Declassified Dossier on Atrocity and Accountability* (New York: New Press, 2003), 94–97, 141–49.

19. The most elaborate effort to catalogue political violence in Allende's Chile is in Patricia Arancibia Clavel, María de los Angeles Aylwin Ramírez, and Soledad Reyes del Villar, *Los hechos de la violencia en Chile: del discurso a la acción* (Santiago: CIDOC/ Universidad Finis Terrae, 2003).

The book is a propaganda volume in the guise of serious scholarship. Arancibia, the primary author, is a rightist journalist and head of the archive created by the Opus Dei Universidad Finis Terrae to contest the historical memory of Chile's recent history. Her brother was a DINA agent imprisoned in Argentina for masterminding the 1974 assassination, in Buenos Aires, of General Carlos Prats and his spouse, an act of political violence the book does not mention.

The book lists 708 "incidents" of violence during the Allende presidency, but this number is so inflated that I was forced to recalculate it using Arancibia's own data— largely drawn from the press of the era—which is too ambiguous to yield more than a rough estimate. I set aside from the author's politically self-interested categories what she calls "incidents without violence": searches by the security forces ostensibly for arms but where no violence took place other than that perpetrated by the security forces. I also set aside nonviolent "attempts against public order," a vague category that includes any challenge, however nonviolent—such as an unauthorized demonstration—to the security forces. I also removed supposed acts of violence against the security forces claimed by General Manuel Contreras, formerly the head of the DINA, in his tendentious and sourceless *La verdad histórica: el ejercito guerrillero* (Santiago: Ed. Encina, 2000).

When these dubious "incidents" are removed, the list of acts of violence during the 1970–73 Allende era is reduced to roughly two hundred. I had to go further in reanalyzing Arancibia's data, as she does not distinguish between *kinds* of violence. For her there is no difference between a murder and a nonviolent sit-in a government building, or a murder and an act of squatting on an empty suburban lot. When "violence" against property is disaggregated from the list, it becomes clear that the overwhelming majority of "incidents" between 1970–73 targeted property, not people. Her undifferentiated category is a statement of the values that informed the study—and the counterrevolutionary violence of the Allende era. Arancibia's stress on property reflects the neoliberal values that informed the Pinochet era.

There was, however, a significant shift over time in the frequency and character of the violence. During the revolutionary advance of 1970–71 there were far fewer acts of violence and a higher percentage of them were tomas of property. During the deepening struggle between revolution and counterrevolution of 1972–73 that culminated in the violent military coup of September 11, 1973, the number of violent acts increased and a higher percentage were directed at people. The numbers of dead, wounded, and arrested grew markedly, along with the multiplying and intensifying street confrontations between revolutionaries and counterrevolutionaries. The confrontations were generally provoked by the counterrevolutionaries seeking to create a "climate of violence" that would destabilize Chilean democracy and justify a military coup. Significantly, counterrevolutionaries were responsible for more than three times the number of violent acts against people (or attacks against property with bombs or guns that sought to injure or risked injuring people) than revolutionaries.

Despite the escalating confrontations, relatively few Chileans died from political violence during the Allende presidency. The number killed is roughly one hundred, and this includes the twenty-two killed during the *tancazo*, the counterrevolutionary army mutiny of June 1973, the largest single cause of deaths from political violence during the Allende years. Disaggregating this figure, the political violence of counterrevolutionaries caused nearly three times the number of deaths as that of revolutionaries. Even General Contreras claims that only eleven members of the security forces were killed during the Allende era, and not all of these were killed by revolutionaries.

In short, whether the measure is numbers of violent acts or deaths from political violence, the numbers during the Allende era were low by comparison to the political violence during the Pinochet dictatorship, and to the numbers claimed by the "climate of violence" propaganda of the right. Moreover, the majority of violent acts and deaths perpetrated during the Allende era were by *counter*revolutionaries, not revolutionaries. It is all the more ironic that this violence was then used by the counterrevolution to justify the violent military coup in September 1973 and its even bloodier aftermath—and it continues to be used to justify the coup today.

20. Chile, *Informe de la Comisión [Valech] Nacional sobre la prisión política y la tortura* (Gobierno de Chile, Ministerio del Interior: Santiago, 2004); Elizabeth Lira, interview, July 2007, Santiago.

21. Brian Loveman, *Chile: The Legacy of Hispanic Capitalism*, 3rd ed. (New York: Oxford University Press, 2001), 4–5. See also Alfredo Jocelyn-Holt, *El peso de la noche: nuestra frágil fortaleza histórica* (Buenos Aires: Ariel, 1997).

22. Some recent estimates of the number of victims are closer to one thousand. See, for example, Eduardo Deves, *Los que van a morir te saludan: historia de una masacre, Escuela Santa María de Iquique, 1907*, 3rd ed. (Santiago: LOM, 1997). See also Lessie Jo Frazier, *Salt in the Sand: Memory, Violence and the Nation-State in Chile, 1890 to the Present* (Durham: Duke University Press, 2007).

23. I am indebted to Thomas Klubock for sharing his unpublished research on Ránquil; also see his contribution to this volume.

24. Loveman, *Chile*, 3.

25. Statements by Marysa Matamala and Nubia Becker, quoted in Peter Winn, *Americas: The Changing Face of Latin America and the Caribbean*, 3rd ed. (Berkeley: University of California Press, 2006), 340. I have restored here a part of the interview omitted in the book.

26. See, for example, Mallon, *Courage Tastes of Blood*, chap. 5.

27. See Patricia Verdugo, *Chile, Pinochet and the Caravan of Death* (Miami: North-South Center Press, 2001).

28. For the CIA role, see United States, Senate Intelligence Committee, *Covert Action in Chile*, 40.

29. Chile, Secretary General of the Government, *Libro Blanco del cambio de gobierno de Chile: 11 de septiembre de 1973* (Santiago: Ed. Lord Cochrane, 1973).

30. For an excellent account of this process, see Steve Stern, *Battling for Hearts and Minds: Memory Struggles in Pinochet's Chile, 1973–1988* (Durham: Duke University Press, 2006), 35–36.

31. United States, Senate Intelligence Committee, *Covert Action in Chile*, 38.

32. Kornbluh, *The Pinochet File*, chaps. 1–2.

33. Ibid., chap. 4.

34. Mayer, *The Furies*, 14.

35. Marlise Simons, "The Brazilian Connection," *Washington Post*, January 9, 1974.

A Headlong Rush into the Future

Violence and Revolution in a

Guatemalan Indigenous Village

CARLOTA MCALLISTER

To write about revolution in Guatemala is to write about twentieth-century Latin America's bloodiest armed conflict. Rapacious agrarian capitalism, combined with systemic Ladino (nonindigenous) oppression of the Mayan majority, made Guatemala fertile terrain for struggles for radical change, but also made those struggles exceptionally punishing to fight. Beginning in 1944, a series of left movements attempted to seize power to address Guatemala's inequities, first by winning elections, and then with armed force, after a U.S.-backed military coup overthrew President Jacobo Arbenz for enacting overly progressive policies in 1954. One by one, however, these movements succumbed to ruthless counterrevolutionary forces in a civil war that took the lives of over 200,000 civilians.[1] The violence culminated in the early 1980s, when the army went on a sweeping scorched-earth campaign through the heartland of insurgent support in the mostly indigenous western highlands. In a terrible irony, therefore, the great majority of the victims of the war in general and the scorched-earth campaigns in particular were the poor, rural Mayans who should have been best served by a revolution.[2]

Contemporary Guatemalan political discourse deploys what Charles Hale calls a *dos demonios* (two demons) narrative—the two demons being the army and the guerrillas—to frame this entanglement of Guatemala's revolutionary projects with its history of genocidal violence.[3] The narrative casts Mayans as the mute and terrified cannon fodder of an internecine conflict among trigger-happy Ladinos over an ideology—communism—that had little relevance to their communitarian lives, and blames the violence on racial prejudice rather than political conflict.[4] "Powerfully ascendant" across much of the political spectrum, including among many Mayan intellectuals,[5] this narrative not only dismisses the Left's claims to serve Mayan interests, but effectively charges the guerrillas with complicity in the genocide by suggesting that these false claims are what "provoked" state violence.

There is justice in the charge that guerrillas failed to adequately represent Mayans: the same groups that claimed "the indigenous question" as the centerpiece of their revolutionary program were led, almost exclusively, by Ladinos. But to treat the Guatemalan state and its armed opposition as equally guilty of genocide is not only to ignore statistics showing that state forces committed 93 percent of wartime human rights violations and guerrillas only 3 percent, but also to occlude the phenomenon of Mayan participation in Guatemalan leftist groups, including armed ones.[6] Since the civil war has ended and the need to conceal subversive pasts has become less pressing, new accounts of the war have begun to reveal the magnitude and diversity of this indigenous leftism, undermining images of Mayans as simple victims of a conflict they didn't understand.[7]

The dos demonios narrative, however, speaks more to the present than the past. The demonization of Guatemala's armed Left and its adherents participates in a long tradition of seeing the revolutionary enterprise as mere senseless violence cloaked in high principle, a tradition that currently has the upper hand on the revolutionary tradition it opposes. Both traditions share a "historicophilosophical" concept of revolution as a law of historical motion which dictates that the future will always be radically different from the present and that the task of the present is that of mastering the future.[8] Revolutionaries since Robespierre have accepted the responsibility for advancing the future in a revolutionary direction that this law entails, and with it the legitimacy of using any means necessary, including violence, to bring this future about.[9] Critics of revolution, in contrast, argue that the revolutionary appeal to history to legitimate violence exposes a fatal contradiction at the heart of the revolutionary cause. As Hannah Arendt argues, this embrace of necessity negates the revolutionary goal of freedom, transforming revolutionaries into what she calls "the fools of history."[10] Mayans who lay claim to a revolutionary past in contemporary Guatemala risk finding themselves trapped in this argument and taking the blame for a foolish misreading of the future that awaited Mayan people.

Recovering the Mayan revolutionary past, therefore, requires historicizing the workings of the concept of revolution in Guatemala's revolutionary struggle rather than allowing it to frame that struggle. Arendt herself hints that the centrality of violence to revolutions may be practical as much as ideological, for in doing away with the old order, revolutions also abolish the distinctions between legitimate and illegitimate uses of force it once upheld, posing a special "problem of beginning" in which every action to found a new order is necessarily violent.[11] Arno Mayer further notes that the lifting of constraints on revolutionary violence also liberates counterrevolutionaries to use any means necessary to prevent the revolution from establishing itself, effectively placing the revolution's future in jeopardy at the very moment when that future finally becomes possible.[12] The struggle to determine which acts of violence may be considered legitimate and which illegitimate is in fact constitutive of revolution's particularity as a political event. Revolutionary violence and chaos are thus better understood as markers of the essential contingency of revolution, the "headlong rush into an indeterminate but exigent future" that it entails, than as symptoms of revolutionaries' delusions of necessity.[13] Here I will follow the traces of this headlong rush through the past of a Maya-K'iche' village called Chupol to argue that indigenous revolutionary mobilization in Guatemala generated enormous violence not because it was foolish or unnecessary but rather because it seriously threatened the old order, including Ladino racial privilege.[14]

Chupol's recent history is a paradigm of the vicissitudes of Mayan revolutionary mobilization. In the early 1980s, after more than a decade of increasingly radical community organization, it became a stronghold of support for Guatemala's largest guerrilla group, the Guerrilla Army of the Poor (Ejército Guerrillero de los Pobres, or EGP). From 1981 to 1983, the Guatemalan state punished Chupolenses for this militancy with every mode of repression at its command—massacres, kidnappings, rapes, bombardments, and forcible displacement. Chupolenses now refer to this period as *el ochenta* or "eighty," and consider el ochenta, as they told me repeatedly, a "crime." What gives el ochenta its criminal character, however, is as much the destruction of the revolutionary hopes Chupolenses had formed as the repression they experienced. Juxtaposing Chupolense accounts of how their rush into the future was arrested with accounts that deny such a movement ever took place, I seek to recover the possibility of Guatemala's indigenous revolution from the violence that foreclosed it.

The Guerrilla Army of the Poor
and the Committee for Peasant Unity

A centerpiece of the dos demonios narrative is the argument that modernizing initiatives, implemented after 1954 by the Guatemalan state, American and European foreign aid agencies, and especially the modernizing and revitalizing Catholic Church, had eliminated Mayan motivations for participating in revolution by gradually but significantly improving conditions in highlands communities.[15] Wooing rural hearts, minds, and souls away from the temptations of communism was certainly the stated goal of these initiatives, whose planners, religious as well as secular, recognized the abysmal poverty in which most Mayans lived as a potential source of political unrest. Modernization's successes, moreover, were real. By the late 1960s, Green Revolution–style agricultural cooperatives and associations, credit and savings organizations, literacy initiatives, and programs for training community leaders, coupled with the Catholic Church's renewed attention to its indigenous parishioners, had profoundly undermined the material and symbolic bases of the quasi-caste system of racial stratification previously operative in rural communities.[16]

Within little more than a decade, however, many of the indigenous communities where modernizing initiatives had flourished were flocking to the very revolutionary movements modernizers had hoped to choke off. In particular, they joined the EGP, which at its height could claim some 270,000 supporters, including urban trade unionists, students, and intellectuals as well as poor Ladinos from rural areas, but above all indigenous villagers from the highlands departments of the Quiché, Chimaltenango, Huehuetenango, and the Verapaces.[17] The principal agent of this extraordinary mobilization was an organization called the Committee for Peasant Unity (Comité de Unidad Campesina, or CUC), which was baptized on April 15, 1978, at a meeting of the EGP's national leadership, and which quickly came to dwarf every previous Guatemalan indigenous political group. Pablo Ceto, a Maya-Ixil who was one of the CUC's founders, has described the CUC as a convergence of "two insurgent and clandestine movements"—the leftist insurgency, on the one hand, and the quincentenary resistance of indigenous communities to the Spanish invasion, on the other.[18] The story of this convergence suggests that, contrary to the dos demonios narrative, modernizers' attempts to mitigate demands for change in the context of a social order founded on racial inequality simply reproduced these demands in a racialized form.

From its inception, the EGP contemplated forming a mass organization that would include indigenous people. In the late 1960s, a U.S.-backed counterinsurgency campaign had quashed Guatemala's first major armed insurgency, the Rebel Armed Forces (Fuerzas Armadas Rebeldes, or FAR), by killing between 2,800 and 8,000 FAR supporters in eastern Guatemala and disappearing or assassinating hundreds of urban leftist leaders of different stripes. Survivors of this rout, including FAR veterans—notably the Ladinos Rolando Morán (the nom de guerre of Ricardo Ramírez) and César Montes (the nom de guerre of Julio César Macías), but also several indigenous former fighters—and members of persecuted youth, student, and Christian groups, regrouped in Mexico City in the early 1970s to form the EGP. Morán had long been critical of the FAR's *foquismo*, Che Guevara's theory that a small group or *foco* of guerrilla fighters could inspire a massive uprising among the oppressed with little more than their heroic example. The mostly Ladino younger members of the group were engaged in the debates then raging among Guatemalan intellectuals over how to account historically for Guatemalan indigenous distinctiveness; they felt that the FAR's failure to theorize racial discrimination separately from class oppression had also limited its gestures at consciousness-raising. United in the sense that the FAR's failings were political as much as military, this motley crew sought to elaborate a more sophisticated strategy for appealing to its potential supporters' deepest hopes and desires.

At a historical juncture marked by Che's death in Bolivia, the repression of the Prague Spring, and the rapprochement of China with the West, revolutionary inspiration for such an endeavour was scant. Only Vietnam, where an anticolonial and nationalist Marxist-Leninist armed movement was beating back the American empire despite severe logistical disadvantages and brutal repression, stood as a beacon of hope. Perceiving parallels between Vietnam, an agrarian country oppressed by both capitalism and American imperialism, and Guatemala, the nascent EGP took the Vietnamese struggle as its "point of reference," in César Montes's words.[19] Invoking the writings of the Vietnamese general Vo Nguyen Giap, the EGP dubbed its strategy "Popular Revolutionary War," or "the armed struggle and the political struggles of all poor people to take power and change our lives," as an EGP training manual explains.[20]

In Popular Revolutionary War, the role of the revolutionary organization is to "awaken, organize and lead the masses."[21] Leading the masses meant incorporating their interests and "characteristic instruments of struggle" into the organization, while simultaneously instructing them in the "political content of the struggle for power," until they ceased to see the revolution "as something alien, but rather as a part and a projection of their own aspirations."[22] The new organization thus aimed to straddle the boundaries between civilians and fighters as well as between legal and illegal forms of struggle, merging all Guatemala's poor people into a single revolutionary body with the EGP at its head.

In Guatemala, however, the majority of "all poor people" are indigenous. This principle holds still more strongly in the highlands, or what EGP strategists called the "mountain" (*la montaña*), whose rugged and historically marginalized terrain they imagined as providing the ideal conditions for constructing a "local revolutionary power" to serve as a territorial base for the revolutionary army's final assault on the state.[23] To recognize this relationship between poverty and indigeneity in Guatemala and the role it would play in shaping the organization's demands on the future, the EGP claimed indigenous people as the Guatemalan revolution's "special element."[24] An internal document explicating this claim, however, suggests that the EGP was uncomfortable with the division that indigenous distinctiveness threatened to introduce into the army of the poor. "To ground indigenous grievances in the revolutionary process it is necessary to abstract the most important contradictions from the complex situation and determine their character, always remembering that indigenous people are part of the global political, economic and social system."[25] While such grievances "refer to indigenous problems and must agree with their needs and preferably should be posed by them," they are also the "problems of all revolutionaries." The organization thus reserved the right to determine the form these grievances might take—including ruling out accusations of Ladino racism that did not take class differentiation among Ladinos into account.[26]

Armed with this ambivalent account of indigenous revolutionary potential, the EGP sought contact with indigenous people from the moment its first combatants crossed back from Mexico into Guatemala on January 19, 1972. By 1975, as the EGP founder, Mario Payeras, recounts in his testimony *Days of the Jungle*, the group's patient efforts had recruited some fifty mostly Maya-Ixiles to the struggle—representing, Payeras claims, a "multitude of peasants"—in addition to a number of Ladinos.[27] The EGP's success among Ixiles, however, came at some cost to its desire to ground its praxis in the interests and instruments of the masses. Finding that traditional community leaders and their thinking were "the first obstacle to the development of war," the guerrillas had instead selected those community members they considered "the firmest and most lucid" for revolutionary awakening.[28] Payeras hints that this top-down approach muddied the EGP's ability to recognize the relationship between the revolution and indigenous aspirations. "Popular pressure for action was great, but announcements of imminent combat also occupied a huge place in our preaching."[29] Even after the 1975 execution of two of the Ixil region's most notorious Ladino oppressors, in which the EGP made its existence public, Payeras can only confirm that Ixiles approved of the action by reading their minds: "When later we visited the Indians' isolated dwellings, many of them, especially the old ones, would take our hands and look us in the eyes for a long time, in a sign of gratitude and recognition."[30]

The official face of the Committee for Peasant Unity also reflected the EGP's ideological leadership. Thus, in its inaugural newsletter the CUC makes no explicit mention of indigenous grievances but rather describes itself as "an organization of all workers in the countryside, individuals, associations, leagues, committees, who want to fight valiantly to get rid of oppression, with our strength united with that of all the other exploited people of Guatemala."[31] Likewise, the CUC's first public act, a huge 1978 May Day demonstration in Guatemala City, symbolically joined indigenous peasant interests to those of urban workers in accordance with the EGP's vision of a single mass struggle. But the CUC's apparent conformity with EGP mass organizational strategy belied both its complex origins in the indigenous politics of the central highlands, and the shifts these politics produced in the EGP's own understanding of the role of its indigenous element.

By the mid-1970s, modernization's potential for transformation had reached its limits. Symptomatic of its exhaustion was the 1974 presidential election, which General Kjell Laugerud, the corrupt and alcoholic candidate preferred by the military hierarchy, stole from General Efraín Ríos Montt, the presidential candidate for the Christian Democratic Party, which was the first mainstream political party to actively recruit indigenous voters and candidates. The election of a number of indigenous Christian Democratic mayors did not soothe the sting of this snub. After the EGP's public emergence, the indigenous organizations formed to channel modernizing efforts found themselves subject to state repression if they expanded their demands or activities beyond modernization's narrow mandate. Tensions between popular expectations for change and military and elite unwillingness to accommodate them were further exacerbated by the earthquake of February 4, 1976. Measuring 7.5 on the Richter scale, the earthquake killed some twenty-seven thousand Guatemalans and left more than one million without homes, mostly in the indigenous communities around the earthquake's epicenter in Chimaltenango.[32] The scale of the destruction laid Guatemala's structural racism bare, while the national government's totally inadequate response to the emergency exposed its fragility.[33] The army, which seized donated goods and tried to sell them, added the insult of corruption to the injury of state incompetence.[34]

For indigenous communities affected by the earthquake, the way forward clearly did not pass through state channels. Relief efforts linked community leaders to new networks that included left-wing students and priests from the capital. A group of young Jesuits who had chosen liberation theology's "option for the poor" further entrenched these networks by organizing Bible study groups among the catechists who had led relief efforts in places like San Martín Jilotepeque in Chimaltenango and Santa Cruz in the Quiché. These groups began to advocate "structural changes, and assumed as a personal commitment the task of establishing some type of organization that would somehow respond to this need," which often prompted their expulsion from local parishes and dioceses and with it their increasing radicalization.[35] It is unclear how these groups, which joined together in 1977 to form the nucleus of what would become the CUC, first encountered the EGP: some members had likely met EGP members after the earthquake, while Jesuits like Enrique Corral and Fernando Hoyos, who eventually became EGP commanders, certainly did.[36] But the convergence between guerrillas and Mayans that Pablo Ceto pointed to was driven as much by indigenous community leaders as by the revolutionary organization.

The CUC, moreover, retained its autonomy from the EGP; neither the EGP nor the CUC considered CUC members to belong automatically to the EGP. This distinction was most clearly signaled in the CUC's voice. Articles in the organization's newsletter are written in a conversational style, quite unlike that of EGP literature, and use the first person plural or a local informal second person singular pronoun (*vos*) to articulate jargon-free analyses of indigenous concerns, like "they're kicking us out [of the plantations] because we're asking for our rights."[37] The former head of EGP mass organization, Gustavo Meoño, told me that this voice was intended to invoke that of indigenous people, so they would feel the CUC and its politics were their own.[38] Describing the organization's approach to the increasing problem of forcible army recruitment of young indigenous men to fight in the escalating civil war, he noted, "Now, organizations are fighting for 'conscientious objection.' But who in the communities understands 'conscientious objection?' The *agarradas para el cuartel* [roundups for the barracks], everyone understood that, and that's what we called it." He claimed that the organization's name was likewise chosen for its indigenous resonance: in most Mayan languages, the easily pronounced monosyllable CUC means "squirrel" (*kuk*), a wild but friendly creature.

Such linguistic gambits made the CUC what Meoño calls a "profoundly symbolic organization." What it stood for was the natural evolution of the previous decade's community organizing into a stance of indigenous unity against the state: "We defend ourselves together," CUC newsletters insisted.[39] The new organization gave the EGP its first access to indigenous communities on their own terms; in return, the EGP gave indigenous community leaders a strategy to extend their efforts at self-defense beyond their community's confines and toward the transformation of relations between indigenous people and Ladinos in the nation as a whole.

The Dog and the Stick: Articulating Historical Necessity in Chupol

Chupol is one of sixty-four rural *cantones* (cantons) or hamlets of the municipality of Chichicastenango, in the majority indigenous department of the Quiché. A village of some four thousand indigenous Maya-K'iche' speakers, Chupol lies about an hour and a half from Guatemala City, on the Inter-American Highway (as the Pan-American Highway is called in Central America), which bisects it. Soon after crossing into the Quiché, the highway begins to climb and twist until it sweeps around a large curve at kilometer 110, where Chupol's small church is visible to the left, on a bluff overlooking the highway. On Sundays, a large market, whose exclusively indigenous vendors and customers come from neighboring municipalities as well as other parts of southern Chichicastenango, spills down from the plaza beside the church onto the highway, slowing traffic considerably.

These features of Chupol's landscape—the highway, the church, and the market—are the physical traces of the village's participation in post-1954 modernizing projects.[40] At mid-century Chupolenses lived, like most highlands Mayans, in historically entrenched poverty and marginalization, forced by law and extralegal mechanisms into grueling and ill-paid seasonal labor on coastal export-crop plantations to supplement what they could grow on their small plots of land. But the highway's 1956 construction and the subsequent introduction of third-class bus lines granted Chupolenses rapid access to Guatemala City, allowing them to abandon plantation work for the much preferred alternative of informal commerce on the streets of the capital. In 1969, Chichicastenango's progressive parish priest further capitalized on Chupol's accessibility to build a church and market to bring revitalized Catholicism as well as opportunities for economic development to southern Chichicastenango. Chupol became a regional "center," as Chupolenses still proudly describe their home, for both commerce and ideas.

These modernizing initiatives also formed the man who brought armed struggle to Chupol, a prominent local catechist and cooperativist named Sebastián. Highly respected throughout Chichicastenango, Sebastián worked tirelessly throughout the 1960s and 1970s on church and agrarian initiatives to improve community well-being. He was best known for his leadership in organizing the construction of Chupol's church and market, as well as for his honest and ecumenical distribution of earthquake aid for southern Chichicastenango, which he directed out of the church at the behest of the parish priest. These successful experiences of community organizing moved Sebastián to reflect on the arbitrary nature of the inequities that characterized indigenous life.[41] "Here in the center we are all equal, no one is greater and no one is lesser, but all the people are the same," he noticed, contrasting this situation with that of Ladino treatment of indigenous people: "As though we weren't people! So that's when I understood that it's true, they haven't taken us into account. . . . As though one were worth more and the other less!" Participating in a 1976 Bible-reading workshop run by Jesuits in Guatemala City helped Sebastián develop these reflections further. Presenting compelling liberation theology readings of the stories of Moses and Jesus as liberators of their people, the Jesuits enjoined participants to follow these biblical examples in their communities.

Sebastián was soon presented with an opportunity to do so. In 1977, Manuel, a friend and fellow catechist from a nearby village, asked him to join an "organization." Sebastián protested that he already belonged to the Peasant Leagues (an agrarian association linked to the Christian Democrats). "Oh, but the Peasant Leagues," Manuel said, "They're doing long-term work. Who knows for when? But us, we're going to do some short-term work." Intrigued by this timeline, Sebastián joined the organization, which was one of the groups that formed the CUC.

Initially, he respected the new organization's semiclandestine nature, keeping its short-term plans secret from everyone but a few of his fellow leaders of previous local projects. Together, however, they grafted the CUC onto the networks he already commanded through his work with the church. Early CUC proselytizing was conducted in the familiar language of liberal Catholicism and developmentalism: "When we spoke about the CUC, the organization of the CUC, we didn't, shall we say, *identify* it as the CUC," one of the early inductees, Cristóbal, told me; instead they talked about God and biblical visions of justice. Likewise, early CUC projects worked toward such unthreatening goals as purchasing fertilizer or vaccinating chickens. Rather than explicitly enlisting Chupol's households for the coming revolution, therefore, Sebastián and his collaborators gradually wove a more revolutionary temporality into the fabric of community life.

As the CUC's command over Chupol solidified, Sebastián then began to organize activities that brought Chupolenses into increasingly overt clashes with government authorities, even those previously identified with indigenous interests. In 1979, the CUC organized a protest against the *agarradas para el cuartel*. One Sunday, when an army truck drove into Chupol's marketplace to carry its young men off to the barracks, a group of their mothers and wives emerged and drove the soldiers away with torches, sticks, and stones. Capitalizing on this small but symbolically important triumph of community self-defense, Sebastián and other CUC leaders led what they claim were several thousand followers to Chichicastenango to demand greater respect for indigenous residents of the municipality from Ladino municipal employees. The indigenous Christian Democratic mayor, Domingo Morales, responded by calling Sebastián to his office and asking him hostile questions: "Who's been counseling you? Why are you doing this work?" Worse still, Morales threatened to call in the state to police his own people: "I'm very sorry about this, but I'm going to send for one hundred soldiers, and everyone that is now gathered in the plaza, well, we'll shoot them."

Such frustrations of his peaceful demands for change primed Sebastián to decipher Manuel's next message, delivered some time in 1979. This time Manuel posed the problem in the form of a riddle:

I want you to analyze a little bit: what if there's a dog lying in the way, and we want to get that dog out of there? Are we just going to say, good dog, get out, go away? He won't pay attention. And if you kick him, he'll jump on you and bite you, and stay anyway. Instead, if we make a good stick, and we tell that dog to respect us and to get out of there, and he doesn't want to go, we'll get him out with blows. And if he wants to jump on us, we'll answer him back with blows. . . . Analyze this, analyze it, and afterward we'll talk.

After a few days' analysis, Sebastián visited Manuel, who introduced him to a Ladino, Juan Antonio. Juan Antonio confirmed what Sebastián had already guessed: the dog in the door represented oppression and the stick represented the armed struggle of the people to overcome oppression.

Sebastián missed the CUC's official founding, and insists that he did not know of the EGP's hand in the CUC or anything at all about armed organizations until he met Juan Antonio. The fact that Juan Antonio belonged not to the EGP but to a rival political-military organization called Our Movement (Nuestro Movimiento) supports Sebastián's disclaimer. Our Movement, like the EGP, was an offspring of the FAR: it emerged out of the FAR's Western Regional Front, which operated throughout the 1970s along Guatemala's southern coast and in the western highlands. In 1979, after a complicated series of schisms, the highlands section of the Front became Our Movement.[42] Like the EGP's founders, Our Movement's leaders sought contact with mass movements, and claimed the indigenous peasantry as the revolution's principal actor. Unlike the EGP, however, they refused to create or infiltrate mass organizations, maintaining the distinction between legal and illegal forms of struggle. Much more than the EGP, moreover, they respected the particularities of the "Indian question," refusing to subsume it under economic relations.[43]

At their meeting, Juan Antonio congratulated Sebastián on his hard work for his community, but said this "pacific struggle, not with arms," didn't go far enough. Juan Antonio explained that the struggle against the government and the rich required arms because the enemy already had them:

The government has three powers in its hands: military power, economic power, and the power of the media. . . . And what do we have? When we speak of military power, we mean it has the army, the tanks, the arms, the planes, the helicopters. And what do we have? So why did we lose the war of our ancestors with the Spaniards? You know there was a big war. They came to invade our territory. They came to fight with the Maya. And why didn't the Maya win? Do you think it's because they weren't strong enough? A man may be strong, but the enemy fights with arms in his hands.

Indifferent to the fact that it was a Ladino that invoked the defeat of "our ancestors," Sebastián credits this argument with convincing him to join the armed struggle.

By late 1979, therefore, there were two clandestine movements, Our Movement and the CUC, operating with essentially the same constituency in southern Chichicastengo. The overlap, according to Gregorio Chay, the member of the CUC National Committee then responsible for the area of Chupol, began to generate a dynamic that surpassed both organizations' capacities for containment and coordination: "Those most resolved to join the struggle were the communities organized by Our Movement. . . . From the CUC there was clarity that this system was oppressive, exploitative, that this system had closed off the roads of struggle, the roads to pacific and political solutions, and that we had to look for other ways and . . . the sole presence of the guerrillas motivated people immediately to seek us out, to seek out the guerrillas."[44] This indigenous clamor for a short-term solution, which was echoed throughout the southwestern highlands, gave the EGP and other insurgencies a sense of extraordinary political momentum.[45] By the beginning of the 1980s, therefore, indigenous communities were effectively claiming the vanguard position previously designated for them by Guatemala's revolutionary theorists.

Rushing into the Future: War comes to Chupol

In the wake of the 1979 Sandinista victory in Nicaragua, revolution seemed imminent throughout Central America.[46] In Guatemala, to which Jimmy Carter had suspended U.S. military aid in 1977 for human rights abuses, the corrupt and violent government of General Romeo Lucas García was in disarray after an extended bout of urban and rural strikes, general work stoppages, and riots.[47] In February 1980, a CUC-led strike of some seventy-five thousand plantation workers, the first such action in Guatemala's history, brought a halt to the sugar harvest and forced the government to raise the rural minimum wage by more than 200 percent.[48] The state responded by intensifying its persecution of its critics, in a campaign of murder of rural catechists, priests, community leaders, centrist politicians, union leaders, and students that culminated in the Spanish Embassy massacre of January 31, 1980. On that day, a delegation of CUC members from the Quiché, joined by members of the Association of University Students, peacefully occupied the Spanish Embassy to protest rural land seizures and selective killings. The police firebombed the building, killing thirty-nine people, including embassy officials and former high-level members of the Guatemalan government who happened to be present, and forcing the Spanish ambassador, who barely survived the incident, to take refuge in another country's mission.[49] Spain, which had been selling Guatemala military equipment, now broke diplomatic relations, leaving Guatemala with only such fellow pariahs as Israel, Chile, and Argentina for allies.

The total collapse of the regime's legitimacy, combined with the ferment in the highlands, produced a qualitative shift in the EGP's revolutionary strategy. The organization's first public response to the Spanish Embassy massacre was the Declaration of Iximché, the first guerrilla document to be written in an explicitly indigenous first-person voice. Released on February 14, 1980, this document invokes indigenous suffering to claim a separate space for indigenous people within the revolutionary army:

> The massacre in the Spanish Embassy is not an isolated case, but part of a chain of massacres. The suffering of our people comes from centuries ago. . . . To end all the evils caused by the descendants of the invaders and the *ricachones* [pejorative term for the rich], we must struggle in alliance with workers, peasants, students, squatters and other popular and democratic sectors, and strengthen our union and solidarity with ladinos, now that the solidarity of the popular movement with the indigenous struggle has been sealed with their lives in the Spanish Embassy. The sacrifice of these lives brings us, now more than ever, closer to a new society, to an Indian dawn.

Simultaneously, the EGP created a staging area for this Indian dawn, placing four new "guerrilla zones" under the command of Camilo, the nom de guerre of a FAR veteran whose EGP experience was largely military and whose political inclinations were decidedly triumphalist.

These zones stretched across the CUC's heartland: the departments of Chimaltenango and Baja Verapaz, parts of Suchitepéquez and Sololá, and the southern Quiché. According to the strategy of Popular Revolutionary War, to call an area a "zone" implies that guerrilla forces have reached equilibrium with enemy forces in the area. Guerrilla forces had yet to set up military operations in the new zones, but Camilo convinced the national leadership that the CUC's momentum in the region was sufficient evidence of the population's readiness for war. In agreeing, the EGP effectively eliminated the distinctions between the CUC and the EGP. The CUC's leadership did not object, at least not publicly: Gregorio Chay was only one of many CUC leaders who formally joined the EGP in this period.

The guerrilla zone with Chupol at its heart was dubbed the "Hanoi Guerrilla Zone." Given the EGP's admiration for Vietnam, this name hints at the role the organization hoped Chupol would play, as both secure center of operations and refuge for combatants in the coming war. Chupol was chosen for this role in spite of its rather vulnerable position on the Pan-American Highway: Chay, who was put in charge of the Hanoi Guerrilla Zone, claims that "the strategic importance of Chupol was not, shall we say, foreseen. If we developed our work there it was because we already had bases." Chupolenses learned of their community's new status when the organization announced that it would henceforth be known as the EGP rather than the CUC, disregarding a subsequent vote showing the community preferred the old name. As for Our Movement, Chay claims that Juan Antonio also willingly left his organization and joined the EGP, but Juan Antonio did not survive the war to corroborate this statement. A former member of another revolutionary organization insists that the EGP "took away Our Movement's bases as if they belonged to the enemy."

Through such forceful maneuvers Chupol came under what was effectively EGP rule. The EGP's organizational structure, composed of subgroups with different revolutionary tasks, was superimposed on community relations. The Local Clandestine Committee coordinated nonmilitary logistical support for the organization, including procuring food from the local population for combatants, finding women to cook it, securing lodging for combatants visiting the community, and similar matters. The Political Formation Team was charged with raising support for the revolutionary struggle: team members gave consciousness-raising talks but also enforced political conformity, as described below. Community defense was in the hands of the Local Irregular Forces (sometimes called Local Guerrilla Forces), patrols of ten adult men, trained in self-defense techniques and armed with whatever the community could provide, who took turns keeping watch for soldiers. Finally, a liaison committee, led by a Regional Director, dealt directly with the combatants operating in the area, providing them with military logistical support. Together these instances coordinated a large portion of the community's daily activities.

An infrastructure for military operations was also established, transforming the regional landscape. The EGP opened five military training camps within easy walking distance of Chupol, where young men from distant communities as well as locals could learn the art of guerrilla warfare. Clandestine Production Units—factories for making Klaymore mines and primitive 12-caliber rifles out of readily available springs and pipes for the use of the Local Irregular Forces—were also set up in Chupol and surrounding villages, and members of the liaison committee were shown how to make these munitions. Chupolenses also began to construct a printing press for EGP propaganda in a neighboring village, where one member of the liaison committee had property.

By late 1980, in short, the support structures for revolutionary war had been put in place in Chupol. All that remained was to convince Chupolenses to man them. This was the job of the Political Formation Team. Sometimes, the team's message was couched in the moral language of Catholicism. One woman told me the guerrillas came to her house to announce: "'We have to make a war because of the rich. We have no rights. God says we should.' My husband said, 'Where does it say that? I have a Bible and I can't find that part.' 'That is what the priest in Chichi says. We have to flatten the hills, straighten the roads. . . . Who does the work of making it straight? We do. Who twists it? The rich.'" On other occasions, the team naturalized the struggle by describing it in metaphors derived from peasant experience of the physical environment, arguing that fighting the state was just like cutting down a rotten tree or killing a predatory animal. In the final instance, however, anyone who refused to believe that war was coming was subjected to a taste of it. Many Chupolenses—including the woman I have quoted above—remember the Political Formation Team backing up its message with death threats. Such threats were not idle: in one particularly notorious incident among many, the Political Formation Team killed two holdouts at the height of market day, at the base of a large tree that still marks the market's entrance. Even EGP leaders felt these *ajusticiamientos*, or executions, spiraled out of control: Sebastián told me of a man from a nearby village who had to be restrained from murdering his own wife when she uttered a disparaging comment about the struggle.

Meoño argues that during this period "there were many people who, against their will, found themselves swept up in this dynamic." Participant accounts of the dynamic, however, suggest that the question of whose will it represented is in a deeper sense moot. Once the EGP and the community merged, the sense of historical necessity, which Sebastián had spent the late 1970s articulating for the community, acquired a life of its own, sweeping the organization and Chupolenses alike into what Meoño more accurately describes as a "vortex." Like Chay, Meoño tends to attribute the breathtaking swiftness of the mobilization of the area to indigenous communities' seizure of the revolutionary process: "The same massivity and generalization that the popular organizations, principally the CUC had, were now transferred to the EGP, in some communities from one day to the next." Rank-and-file Chupolense EGP members, however, tend to describe themselves as overwhelmed by the logic of revolution, saying that they joined the organization because they believed war was coming. "Why did we organize? Because a war was coming. Why was a war coming? Because we were asking for our rights. People were warned; they knew that if the soldiers came we should flee. Why? Because we are indigenes and we don't have rights," one man reasoned to me. Even a member of the feared Political Formation Team, albeit somewhat disingenously, described himself to me as simply acquiescing to the revolution's inevitability: "I went to a meeting and began to talk to them, what were they doing there? They answered that they were talking about the organization, that why don't we all get together, why has everything we've done been for the army's high command, for the rich, for the government. . . . They asked me if I would join the organization right then, and I said yes."

Whether they willed it or not, therefore—and those who willed it least undoubtedly survived in fewer numbers to tell of their desires—Chupolenses were soon spending most of their time in war-related activities. They participated regularly in EGP acts of sabotage along the corridor of the Pan-American Highway, making blockades out of trees, digging trenches, and laying Klaymore mines—acts that, as Meoño pointed out to me, required mobilizing a substantial workforce. In June 1981, they commenced the still more time-consuming construction of a series of earthworks modeled on the Vietcong's tunnels in Cu Chi outside Saigon, earning Chupol the approving epithet of "Vietnamese village" among the urban Left. An EGP member who had perhaps visited Vietnam showed Chupolenses how to dig both *buzones*—"mailboxes" in which to store arms, supplies, clothes, and themselves in case of enemy attack—and *trampas*, three-meter-deep "traps" lined with sharpened and fire-hardened wooden stakes, to impale unwanted visitors. Almost every household built its own *buzón*, its entrance commonly located inside the family *temascal* (a low, beehive-shaped steam bath), while trampas were dug at all major entrances to the village. Also for purposes of self-defense, Chupolense women were instructed to have water boiling at all times and keep ground chili peppers handy, to throw in the faces of any soldiers who might suddenly arrive.

EGP actions in the area also grew more aggressive: EGP communiqués reported that in June, July, and August 1981, numerous army convoys and patrols were bombed near Chupol and several military commissioners and army officers were executed in the area. On July 19, 1981, the EGP further upped the ante by incorporating the four guerrilla zones of the southwestern highlands into the Augusto César Sandino Guerrilla Front (FACS). To create a "front" was to declare that insurgent activities in the area of its operations were now explicitly military, a declaration that, like the earlier transformation of this area into guerrilla zones, did not reflect the EGP's true weakness on the ground. The new front was inaugurated on the second anniversary of the revolution in Nicaragua: its name and its slogan "Nicaragua venció; Guatemala vencerá" (Nicaragua triumphed; Guatemala will triumph), laid a clear claim to the Sandinista legacy of revolutionary success. To celebrate its imminent triumph, the EGP launched seventeen simultaneous attacks in the area.[50]

Chupolenses, who don't usually pay much attention to calendrical dates, universally agree that el ochenta began on August 15, 1981, less than a month after the establishment of the FACS. On that date, they say, the war arrived: a patrol of soldiers marched into the village, undaunted by the trampas, and proceeded to the printing press, which was still under construction. Caught off guard, the twenty-six people who happened to be working there, including several women and children, were kidnapped. As two witnesses who managed to escape later recounted, the soldiers brought the group to a local school and forced them to lie in a circle with candles at their heads, telling them they would die and burning them with cigarettes as they repeatedly kicked them. The next day, the soldiers drove their victims in a truck along the highway toward the north, killing one person every kilometer, and throwing the cadavers onto the road.

The failure of Chupolenses to predict when war would finally arrive did not diminish their sense that its coming was inevitable. Some believe the community's indiscretions had reached an unacceptable level: "People just couldn't keep their mouths shut," lamented a former Political Formation Team member. For others, the EGP's presence had become too obvious—a notion EGP war reports support. One man, who was fighting as an EGP combatant in the Ixil region at the time of el ochenta, told me that he heard that just prior to August 15, passing tourists had tried to take pictures of a funeral in Chupol. The mourners, unwilling to suffer such indignities any longer, threw stones at their abusers, who informed the army in Chichicastenango. A woman who was a child at the time told me a similar story, except that in her version, what provoked the tourists' report to the army was seeing the mourners at the funeral carrying AK-47s. For still other Chupolenses, however, the coming of war was so overdetermined that it was presaged in nature itself. Many insist that their animals behaved strangely in the days leading up to the war, and one couple remembers that on the eve of August 15, coyotes came into the patio of their house and fought. Another man noticed on a trip to Santa Cruz del Quiché that a nearby lake had dried up, a sign, he now feels, that war was imminent.

Their belief that war was inevitable, moreover, meant that organized Chupolenses had plans for what to do when it came, which they promptly followed, fanning out in previously determined groups to other organized villages more distant from the highway. Heads of families still peddling their wares in the capital or the coast were informed by friends of the war's arrival; imagining the conflict would be short, they left their goods in the city for safekeeping and returned to join their wives and children in hiding until the war was over. Likewise, younger men in the capital were told to wait it out there. Only a few families remained in Chupol, either because they were uninformed or because they had refused to heed the organization. None of them survived very long.[51]

The soldiers soon established a base in Chupol's church, digging trenches in the marketplace, and ringing this compound with tanks. At first they seemed reluctant to leave the church's safety, but soon army patrols were making regular excursions into the hinterland to find and kill or kidnap Chupolenses while planes overhead and tanks on the highway began to shell Chupolense hiding places. The soldiers also set up roadblocks to stop and search passing cars and buses, using masked informants and lists obtained under torture to identify "subversives" and bring them into the church for interrogation, something few people survived. Chupol now became a killing center, a place where dead bodies and burning fields were always visible by the side of the road and where travelers dreaded to pass.

Eventually, the military onslaught forced Chupolenses and their hosts into the high, cold mountains surrounding their villages, where they spent a year running from the army, sleeping out of doors under the rain, and eating what little food they could gather in the forest. Except for the highest-placed members of the liaison committee, they lost contact with the EGP. When the Guatemalan government offered an amnesty to guerrilla supporters in 1983, the EGP finally sent a message telling Chupolenses to surrender, as the organization could not guarantee their safety. Using whatever scraps of white and blue plastic they could find to fashion facsimiles of the Guatemalan flag, the survivors of this long ordeal went home to find their homes and crops burnt, their animals stolen, and their church still occupied by the army. The goods men had left behind in the cities, often representing significant capital investments, had likewise disappeared.

As a condition of their surrender, all adult men were forced to participate in civil armed patrols, organized by the army to "guard" rural villages against the guerrillas, which soon took over community political life. In many communities surrounding Chupol—although not, Chupolenses claim, in Chupol itself—these patrols enacted a new wave of terror, denouncing their neighbors to the army as subversives, or perpetrating massacres themselves. Even in the absence of violence, the patrols helped harden suspicions among neighboring villages and particularly against Chupolenses, whom outlying communities now blamed for the war. The army evacuated Chupol's church in 1985, but built a new base on the hill next to the church, where a platoon of soldiers is stationed to this day, in violation of peace agreements limiting the army's presence in Guatemala's interior. Gradually Chupolenses learned to make a new life in these circumstances, rebuilding their houses, restoring their fields, and returning to their commercial activities, but the echoes of el ochenta continue to sound in every aspect of their lives.

Interpreting el Ochenta

This brief survey of el ochenta and the history of organizing that led up to it suggests how thoroughly the experience of these events was structured by the revolutionary sense of historical necessity, not only for the EGP and the army that sought to destroy it, but also for Chupolenses themselves. It also shows how mistaken this sense was: the future revolutionaries imagined as inevitable turned out to be anything but that. What is at stake, then, in holding historical necessity accountable for the course Guatemala's revolution took, when it clearly did not possess the power to determine that course?

Questions about who bears responsibility for the war's violence are important, and they are ones Chupolenses themselves pose. All Chupolenses fear the army and blame it for the innummerable atrocities it committed against them to some degree, but many Chupolenses are also furious at the EGP. Some believe the organization provoked the army's wrath and brought the war upon them, just as the dos demonios narrative posits. Others accuse the guerrillas of abandoning Chupolenses in their hour of greatest need: as one man pithily argued, "They just fucked off [*se fueron a la chingada*]. What about 'Hasta la victoria siempre'?" (This EGP slogan, borrowed from Che Guevara, means "Always onward to victory.")

More surprising than these sentiments of anger, however, are those of the large number of Chupolenses who continued to believe in the possibility of victory even after el ochenta. Speaking of the violence, one man told me with extraordinary equanimity, "The thing is, the struggle is like that," before revealing that he had joined up again with the EGP "as soon as I could find them" upon returning to the community. It is also worth noting that Chupolenses were among the very first rural indigenous Guatemalans to join the human rights organizations that sprang up after the intensity of the violence lessened in the mid-1980s, a move that they describe as a continuation of the struggle for indigenous rights and against the state that the CUC and the EGP helped them initiate. Such complex and even counterintuitive political trajectories are poorly served by a framework that seeks to adjudicate the revolutionary past rather than historicize it.

Understanding these trajectories requires driving a wedge between the sense of necessity and the context in which it operated. To do so, I will make use of certain discrepancies between Chupolense and non-Chupolense accounts of what Chupolenses call el ochenta. These discrepancies are as follows. First, although Chupolenses are so peculiarly insistent on dating the beginning of el ochenta to August 15, 1981, Mauricio López Bonilla, a retired army colonel who fought in the campaign against the FACS, told me that the army did not actually arrive in Chupol until November of that year—a difference of several months.[52] Second, when I spoke to former members of the EGP leadership, who consider phenomena like el ochenta a "tragedy," in Gustavo Meoño's words, they blamed this tragedy on their own mistaken faith in the utopian possibilities that the "Vietnamese town" seemed to offer. Meoño, for example, told me that the EGP "shouldn't have overestimated people's capacities just because they were organized, because they were willing." But Chupolenses do not attribute the disaster of el ochenta to the insufficiency of their own capacities for revolution, but rather to the EGP's failure to enable those capacities.

One former Chupolense militant put the problem bluntly: "We were totally ready, resolved to do anything, but they didn't give us weapons."

The incommensurable vantage points from which Chupolenses, army officers, and the guerrilla leadership respectively participated in the war could explain these apparently trivial differences. Thus, the November date López Bonilla gave me refers to the launching of Task Force Iximché, a new form of counterinsurgency operation that combined infantry troops with heavy weaponry, armored vehicles, and air cover to wage what he called an "unstoppable offensive against the countryside." Although patrols of soldiers had indeed gone on earlier reconnaissance missions in the highlands, it was not until November 17 that the task force swept up from Guatemala City to occupy Chupol, in the first phase of the two-year string of massacres that would ultimately seal the guerrilla's defeat. Thus, el ochenta in the sense of the crushing of Chupolense revolutionary hopes did begin when López Bonilla claims. Similarly, Gustavo Meoño is right to accept that when the EGP took popular enthusiasm for revolution as a mandate for military action, it committed a dreadful error. El ochenta, in this sense, was indeed triumphalism's tragedy. Better situated to understand the national course of the war, in short, the army and the guerrillas can provide more authoritative accounts of its course than Chupolenses can. Privileging these accounts over those of Chupolenses, however, obscures the traces of the challenge el ochenta represented to such claims to authority.

López Bonilla acknowledges that an army patrol may well have arrived in Chupol on August 15, 1981, but he does not factor this date into his story about the army victory he tellingly describes as "unstoppable." During the summer of 1981, however, the army had not yet earned this characterization: the signs of governmental breakdown that the EGP had detected in 1980 were real, and by early 1981 a lack of both direction and intelligence had seriously weakened the army's strategy for counterinsurgency. Even López Bonilla described this pre–task force period to me as one of deep confusion and fear, recalling his experiences patrolling the highlands beset by the feeling that the enemy was all around and yet invisible and unknowable.

During the summer of 1981, however, a set of contingencies came together to place the army on a stronger footing. After U.S. military aid to Guatemala was withdrawn in 1977, Israel and Argentina had quietly begun to sell the Guatemalan military sophisticated electronic surveillance equipment and technologies as well as providing it with the training, honed in long years of counterinsurgent warfare, to make the most of its purchases.[53]

In June 1981, the military received a new boost when the newly installed Reagan administration in Washington restored military aid to Guatemala and immediately sent it a shipment of military trucks. On July 1, President Lucas García announced to the Guatemalan Congress that he was ready to cash out his government's investments in war: the Guatemalan news agency Inforpress reported that he "'was ready to go to all the extremes of the law' to prevent communism from winning in Guatemala."[54] On July 10, the army seized what a spokesperson called both the "general headquarters" and the "General Archives" of the guerrillas, which was in fact a safe house containing weapons and papers belonging to all four major insurgent groups.[55]

Such findings enabled the army to embark on "the analysis of our propaganda, our tactics and operative arts; the study of the internal documents and the resources they found in houses and camps, as well as the personal documents they seized," Mario Payeras recounts. They also revealed the locations of other safe houses, yielding more prisoners, who then gave up more names and locations under torture.[56] According to López Bonilla, it was only *after* the army gathered this intelligence that it began to understand the strength of insurgent organization in the countryside: the army patrol that arrived in Chupol on August 15 was searching for supporters of revolution without yet being sure where exactly they were located, or who they were. Evidence of broad-based revolutionary organization like Chupol's earthworks, which López Bonilla mentioned in particular, combined with the information from the safe houses, forced the army to profoundly rethink what it was doing in the highlands. This months-long process of reformulation of counterinsurgency strategy produced the "unstoppable" task forces with their mandate to commit genocide if that was what stopping the budding insurrection in the highlands required. When López Bonilla dates the commencement of the war against Chupol in November rather than August, therefore, what he elides is the possibility that in the period of army confusion and reflection represented by those months the balance of forces might have played out differently.

What Meoño's lament about the tragedy of Chupol omits is a still more heart-breaking story about how and why the revolutionary organization was unable to alter this balance. In EGP-organized indigenous communities, complaints about the EGP's failure to provide weaponry for its supporters like the one I have quoted here are common. As Mario Payeras's testimony makes painfully clear, logistical problems plagued the EGP from its inception, in part because Cuba, a conduit for funds and weaponry for many Latin American insurgent groups, disliked the EGP's Vietnamese-style mass organizational strategy and refused to support it.[57] EGP combatants did have guns, but EGP Local Guerrilla Forces, charged with their communities' self-defense, were instead trained for combat with wooden dummies of guns. The EGP told them that if they wanted the real thing, they would have to take it from the enemy themselves. Like the stake-lined booby traps Chupolenses built in their village, or the hot water and chili peppers women kept to throw at soldiers, this injunction seems pathetically unsuited to a war in which the enemy was armed with the most lethal weapons the military-industrial complex could produce, along with a documented willingness to use them against civilians. The best gloss one can put on EGP triumphalism in such circumstances is that the organization's leaders were appallingly naive about what it takes to overthrow a military state—the one Meoño gives it. But it is difficult to avoid the much worse conclusions of the dos demonios narrative.

The assumption that the EGP was in fact triumphalist, however, may not be entirely correct. The EGP founder, César Montes, who left the organization in 1981 after bitter fights with other members of the national leadership, suggested as much when he told me that the EGP did in fact have caches of arms that he himself had procured and buried in underground storage pits located not far from Chupol. Montes claims that his former comrades withheld these weapons from people like Chupolenses, not because they trusted too much in indigenous enthusiasms but rather because they didn't trust this enthusiasm *enough* to hand them such a precious resource. Disturbed by this allegation, I asked Enrique Corral, an EGP commander who worked near Chupol and remained in the organization until peace treaties were signed in 1996, to comment. He angrily dismissed this story as a calumny perpetrated by a disgruntled troublemaker, a characterization of Montes shared by many on Guatemala's Left.[58] But Meoño's claim that the EGP "overestimated" the capacities of indigenous people gives off a whiff of the kind of condescension toward indigenous contributions to the revolutionary process to which Montes refers. A comment Mario Payeras made about communities like Chupol in an interview contemporary with el ochenta reeks of it: "The enemy's escalation of repression . . . has been quicker than the ability of the organized masses to assimilate this truth—here we must remember the imbalance between objective and subjective forces—and implement the appropriate measures for self-defense."[59] Could it be that the EGP held so firmly to its analysis of this imbalance that it actually denied its supporters the means of implementing such measures?

Still another story I heard about these caches, however, suggests that the truth about how the EGP confronted this imbalance cannot be reduced either to revolutionary delusions or revolutionary cynicism. Another highly placed ex-EGP member, himself no fan of Montes, nonetheless confirmed his story about the weapons. "But they were totally useless!" he explained. "They were rusty and dirty from being buried, and besides, they were of different makes and calibers, because they had just been stolen from the enemy. We could have given people those weapons, but we could never have supplied them with the ammunition to use them." The image of these bulletless guns convincingly locates the EGP's failure in the realm of praxis rather than ideology: Chupolenses put their finger in the heart of the revolutionary wound when they complain that the logistically outmatched group simply could not manage to get useable arms into the indigenous hands that would have used them.

I draw attention to the details that army officers and guerrilla leaders omit from their retrospective accounts of what Chupolenses call el ochenta, not to excuse such logistical failures but rather to show how such omissions help foreclose the essential contingency of the revolutionary moment. The accumulation of events in which particular militants gave up particular pieces of information under particular techniques of torture, or in which the wrong sorts of weapons were stolen, is not one that revolutionaries or their enemies could have entirely predicted or controlled. The sense of historical necessity helped shape the struggles that determined the future of Guatemala's revolution, but it was incapable of shaping that future itself.

In Chupolense accounts of el ochenta, in contrast to those of López Bonilla or Meoño, it is precisely the uncertainty of the future that is foregrounded. For Chupolenses, August 15, 1981, marks the abandonment not only of their community but also of the structures that had given direction to their actions up until that moment. Men who came home from the capital after hearing that the war had come recall a profoundly uncanny arrival. "I got off the bus a little before Chupol," Tomás told me, "because I had been warned that the army was waiting for us there. The whole village was *silencio* [silence] and in my house only the chickens were crying, all the people were gone." Another man, José, spent two days hiding in his household's *temascal*, feeling sure he would never see his family again.[60] He found them by accident: while wandering in despair around the mountains, he suddenly entered a valley where two hundred people, including his family and neighbors, were sitting in utter silence. Women who left the village when the soldiers arrived experienced more terrifying scenes. Anastasia, for example, gave birth only hours before she was forced, in a state of deep disorientation, to escape by swimming across a river with her newborn on her back. Ana, only twelve years old when el ochenta happened, got separated from her family as they fled. She spent the next two days running through the forest, with bombs raining down around her, before she stumbled on someone who could tell her where her family had gone.

This violent rupture with the past also gave rise to further violence. In their refuge, Chupolenses answered to no authority but the guerrillas, who were not entirely sure how to begin administering entire indigenous villages. Gustavo Meoño claims that before the arrival of the task force the EGP had constituted a parallel state in the communities in hiding, performing weddings and registering births, as well as schooling children. Chupolense recollections of guerrilla rule, however, tend to emphasize its repressive functions. The Political Formation Team was given free reign over the villages, and its suspicions and felt need to ensure total solidarity increased proportionately. Such minor offenses as arriving late to one's lookout duties, Chupolenses remember, could lead to extravagant punishments like being tied to a tree to be found by soldiers. When guerrilla rule became unsustainable, however, the violence grew still worse. Chupolenses describe themselves during this period as being reduced to the state of animals: running from the soldiers through the high, cold, mountains; eating wild plants and roots; and taking shelter under trees or rocks, focused only on survival. Many are plagued by horrible memories of having failed their own children, spouses, or parents in this struggle to stay alive.

Mixed in with these horrors, however, Chupolenses recall el ochenta as a time of similar "pleasures of agency" to those Elisabeth Wood heard about from former insurgents in El Salvador.[61] Solidarity is first among these pleasures: any occasion on which sharing is demanded elicits extensive reminiscences about how unstintingly Chupolenses' neighbors gave of their food and their homes during el ochenta. Often Chupolenses lament that they are no longer as united, either with their neighbors or among themselves, as they were back then. Even memories of the bleakest times can sometimes be enlivened by threads of the joy of generous sociability. During a meeting intended to explain to members of a women's organization the implications of Guatemala's Truth Commission, for example, the speaker's mention of "forcible displacement" provoked participants to relive their experiences hiding from the army not in tragic but in comic mode. "Remember how we would call out when they would leave? Juana, Maria . . . Eu!," they mimicked, collapsing into collective laughter.

For men more than women, another saving grace of el ochenta is pride in their own ingenuity and courage in the face of the enemy. During one of many collective discussions about the extraordinary difficulties of their experiences in hiding, I asked the head of a household that had given refuge to hundreds of Chupolenses how he had managed to get food to feed them all. "I'm so glad you asked that!" he exclaimed, leaning forward eagerly to tell me about the footpaths and bypasses, known only to the indigenous residents of the zone, that he and others would take to get to the market in Chichicastenango and bring back their purchases. Other men told me about escaping from patrols of soldiers by lying to them, scolding them for their bad behavior, confusing them with clever casuistry, or even by relieving themselves by the side of the road as the soldiers passed, to appear unafraid. Stories about el ochenta in this heroic register are so common that it is hard to give credence to the argument that revolutionary mobilization in no way expressed the desires or hopes of people like Chupolenses.

Chupolenses are also nostalgic, however, about an aspect of el ochenta that speaks more directly to the tenets of the dos demonios narrative. They have fond memories of their intellectual and political exchanges with Ladino guerrilla leaders. After the organization's safe houses in the capital fell, urban insurgents from the EGP as well as other insurgent groups tried to escape repression by escaping to the organization's rural strongholds. Chupol's hinterland, imagined as liberated territory but with the added attraction of proximity to the capital, received a disproportionate number of these refugees: one former EGP member told me visiting Chupol became a kind of rite of passage for urbanites seeking to join the struggle in la montaña. At a mental health workshop where a group of survivors was asked to draw a mural representing their history, they drew the guerrillas as giants surrounded by the smaller stick figures of Chupolenses themselves, dutifully spelling out the acronyms of all the organizations to which these giants had belonged. Those who had greater contact with the visitors proudly recite their names, which include those of many leaders still prominent in the political party the former insurgency has become. These memories, like those of the man who asked "What about Hasta la victoria siempre?"

are sometimes tinged with a sense of betrayal. One woman told me of her encounter on the streets of Antigua, Guatemala, years after losing contact with the guerrillas but before peace made open contact safe, with a Ladino insurgent who had spent long stretches in Chupol: "We had children the same age; we had talked a lot. I looked at him out of the side of my eye and nodded. He nodded back and we walked right on. I have never seen him again, and I don't know his real name because all I knew was his pseudonym." The poignancy of the encounter nonetheless suggests the value she placed on this relationship and the fellowship it had provided.

Finally, even Chupolenses who now revile the insurgents ultimately find value in the opportunity el ochenta gave them to fight back. Despite their anger, many refuse to count el ochenta as an entirely failed endeavor, arguing that "at least Ladinos learned that we have to be respected, *que no nos vamos a dejar* [that we won't be pushed around]." The modest gain of reformulating their relationships with Ladinos is not all that Chupolenses hoped for when they turned their village Vietnamese. But if Guatemalan history is one of Ladino oppression of indigenous people, these new relationships represent a notable—arguably revolutionary—change.

Conclusion

The dos demonios narrative subscribes to a voluntarist model of revolution: Guatemala's revolution failed, it implies, because indigenous people never willed it to succeed. Timothy Wickham-Crowley, using a structuralist model of revolution that counters such voluntarism by showing revolutions succeed because of factors independent of participants' subjective goals, finds that Guatemala's 1980s insurgencies failed *in spite* of what he characterizes as their success in mobilizing indigenous support.[62] He convincingly shows that the strengths of the military regime that the insurgency sought to overthrow—its entrenchment in government, its tight links to the oligarchy, and its ferocious and well-funded anticommunist policies—in addition to specific measures the military took, precluded the formation of the cross-class coalitions that enabled revolutionary successes elsewhere in Latin America. The persistence of the dos demonios narrative, however, suggests that proving revolutionaries' subjective desires and purposes do not determine the course of revolutions does not dispense with the need to consider such desires and purposes. If revolution is both a historical process and a historicophilosophical concept, the revolutionary will to shape the future may depend on an illusion, but this illusion is constitutive of being revolutionary, and explains at least some of the actions revolutionaries take.

In Guatemala, the military's genocidal acts made the gap between revolutionary wills and revolutionary outcomes, between the metahistorical and historical dimensions of revolution, too wide for the insurgency to span. The past and present capacities for action of people like the Chupolenses were nonetheless formed in this gap, and continue to reside within it. Contemporary claims about what the Chupolenses wanted from revolution, or what revolutionary insurgents wanted from them, are voiced in the context of the counterinsurgency's victory and in tension with the order of poverty and structural racism that victory served to reestablish. In such a context, it is perhaps unsurprising that the violence that attended insurgent mobilization of indigenous people in Guatemala feels meaningless, or that revolution seems essentially alien to the Mayans it failed to empower as promised. Stripping this mobilization of meaning, however, renders the courage of indigenous revolutionaries who rushed into the future and the desires they brought with them invisible, and with them the counterrevolutionary violence that worked to stop this movement forward and thus to create and sustain these appearances. Recognizing Guatemala's indigenous revolution as a defeat instead of a nonevent keeps open the temporal and social breach it produced, and from which something unpredictable may yet emerge.

Notes

1. Guatemala's truth commission, the Comisión para el Esclarecimiento Histórico (CEH), found that 150,000 civilians had been killed and 50,000 disappeared during the war. Subsequent investigations have suggested that the true figures may be still greater. See *Guatemala: Memoria del silencio*, 12 vols. (Guatemala City: UNOPS, 1999), 1:23.

2. The CEH also found that 83 percent of wartime human rights violations were perpetrated against Mayans, and ruled that the Guatemalan state, in some areas and during certain periods of the war, had committed acts of genocide. Ibid., 1:25.

3. Charles R. Hale, *Más que un indio: Racial Ambivalence and Neoliberal Multiculturalism in Guatemala* (Santa Fe: School of American Research, 2006), 105.

4. For the academic formulations of this argument, see David Stoll, *Between Two Armies in the Ixil Towns of Guatemala* (New York: Columbia University Press, 1993),

and *Rigoberta Menchú and the Story of All Poor Guatemalans* (Boulder, Colo.: Westview Press, 1999), as well as Yvon LeBot, *La guerra en tierras mayas* (Mexico City: Fondo de Cultura Económica, 1996).

5. Hale, *Más que un indio*, 105

6. CEH, *Memoria del silencio*, 1:24.

7. Greg Grandin, *The Last Colonial Massacre: Latin America in the Cold War* (Chicago: University of Chicago Press, 2004); Beatriz Manz, *Paradise in Ashes: A Guatemalan Journey of Courage, Terror, and Hope* (Berkeley: University of California Press, 2004); Santiago Bastos and Manuela Camus, *Entre el mecapal y el cielo: desarrollo del movimiento maya en Guatemala* (Guatemala City: FLACSO, 2003); and Carlota McAllister, "Good People: Revolution, Community, and *Conciencia* in a Maya-K'iche' Village in Guatemala," Ph.D. diss., Johns Hopkins University, 2003.

8. Reinhardt Koselleck, *Futures Past: On the Semantics of Historical Time* (Cambridge, Mass.: MIT Press, 1985), 48.

9. Ibid., 53.

10. Ibid., 58.

11. Arno Mayer, *The Furies: Violence and Terror in the French and Russian Revolutions* (Princeton: Princeton University Press, 2000), 37.

12. Ibid., 87.

13. Ibid., 23.

14. This essay is based on seventeen months of fieldwork in Chupol, conducted during several periods over the years between February 1997 and January 2001, as well as on interviews with army personnel and former members of revolutionary organizations and on archival research. The primary method I used during fieldwork in Chupol was participant observation; I lived with a Chupolense family and took part in community activities, including those organized by different churches and popular organizations as well as more familial events. I also conducted a survey of twenty-five households, as well as numerous informal interviews and fewer formal interviews with Chupolenses and other actors. Only some of the latter are taped, in accordance with the expressed desires of my respondents. All comments attributed to Chupolenses within this essay come from interviews or conversations that took place during the time of my fieldwork. The names of my Chupolense interlocutors have been changed; the guerrilla and military personnel named here gave me permission to do so.

15. See Stoll, *Rigoberta Menchú*, and Le Bot, *La guerra en tierras mayas*.

16. For more detailed accounts of this process, see Ricardo Falla, *Quiché rebelde* (Guatemala City: Editorial Universitaria de Guatemala, 1978); Kay Warren, *The Symbolism of Subordination: Indian Identity in a Guatemalan Town*, 2nd ed. (Austin:

University of Texas Press, 1989); Douglas E. Brintnall, *Revolt against the Dead: The Modernization of a Mayan Community in the Highlands of Guatemala* (New York: Gordon and Breach, 1979); and Benjamin N. Colby and Pierre L. van den Berghe, *Ixiles y ladinos* (Guatemala City: Editorial José de Pineda Ibarra, 1977).

17. CEH, *Memoria del silencio*, 1:193.

18. Cited in Kajkoj Ba Tiul, "Movimiento Winaq, la controversia: ni a la izquierda, ni a la derecha," working paper prepared for the seminar "Izquierdas y construcción de orden democrático en Guatemala," organized by FLACSO Guatemala and the Friedrich Ebert Foundation, June 2007, 6.

19. Others saw these parallels as well: Marjorie and Thomas Melville—the former Maryknoll religious who left the order and got married, after helping to educate a number of the Guatemalan students who later become EGP founders—published a book called *Guatemala, Another Vietnam?* (Harmondsworth, England: Penguin Books) in 1971.

20. Ejército Guerrillero de los Pobres, "¿Cómo vamos a tomar el poder? Línea militar del EGP durante la guerra popular revolucionaria. Materiales de formación política, Nivel I," EGP internal document (1979), 5.

21. Ejército Guerrillero de los Pobres, "Línea de masas del EGP durante la guerra popular revolucionaria. Materiales de formación política, Nivel I," EGP internal document (1979), 4.

22. Marta Harnecker, "Un trabajo de masas para la guerra: entrevista con el comandante Rolando Morán," in *Pueblos en armas* (Mexico City: Ediciones Era, 1984), 78.

23. Ejército Guerrillero de los Pobres, "¿Cómo vamos a tomar el poder?" 16.

24. Ejército Guerrillero de los Pobres, "Línea de masas," 10.

25. Ejército Guerrillero de los Pobres, "Sobre las revindicaciones revolucionarias de los indígenas guatemaltecos," EGP internal document (n.d.), 1.

26. Ibid., 3.

27. Mario Payeras, *Los días de la selva* (Guatemala City: Editorial Piedra Santa, 1998), 121.

28. Ibid., 113.

29. Ibid., 121.

30. Ibid., 131.

31. Comité de Unidad Campesina, "Presentación," *Voz del Comité de Unidad Campesina: periódico informativo del CUC*, newsletter (1978), 1.

32. Michael McClintock, *The American Connection*, vol. 2, *State Terror and Popular Resistance in Guatemala* (London: Zed Books, 1985), 136.

33. Arturo Arias, "Changing Indian Identity: Guatemala's Violent Transition to Modernity," in *Guatemalan Indians and the State: 1540 to 1988*, ed. C. Smith (Austin: University of Texas Press, 1990), 243.

34. Ibid.

35. Diócesis del Quiché, *El Quiché: el pueblo y su iglesia, 1960–1980* (Santa Cruz del Quiché: Diócesis del Quiché, 1994), 107.

36. Le Bot, *La guerra en tierras mayas*, 148.

37. Comité de Unidad Campesina, "Los campesinos del CUC estamos cada día más organizados," *Voz del Comité de Unidad Campesina*, newsletter (1979), 4.

38. Interview with Gustavo Meoño, Guatemala City, July 1998.

39. Comité de Unidad Campesina, "Los campesinos del CUC," 5.

40. For a fuller account of this process, see my article "Rural Markets, Revolutionary Souls, and Rebellious Women in Cold War Guatemala," in *In from the Cold: Latin America's New Encounter with the Cold War*, ed. Gilbert M. Joseph and Daniela Spenser (Durham: Duke University Press, 2008).

41. Interview with Sebastián Morales, Chugüexá, Chichicastenango, March 1999.

42. The other half became the better-known Revolutionary Organization of the People in Arms (Organización Revolucionaria del Pueblo en Armas, or ORPA).

43. CEH, *Memoria del silencio*, 6:175–76; Mario Roberto Morales, *Los que se fueron por la libre* (Mexico City: Editorial Praxis, 1998), 48–49.

44. Interview with Gregorio Chay, August 1998, Guatemala City.

45. Hale, *Más que un indio*, 64

46. Mario Payeras, *El trueno en la cuidad: episodios de la lucha armada urbana de 1981 en Guatemala* (Mexico City: Juan Pablos Editor, 1987), 15.

47. Deborah Levenson-Estrada, *Trade Unionists against Terror: Guatemala City, 1954–1985* (Chapel Hill: University of North Carolina Press, 1994), 143.

48. Ibid., 167.

49. For a fuller account of this event, see CEH, *Memoria del silencio*, 6:163–82.

50. Ejército Guerrillero de los Pobres, *Compañero*, newsletter (1981), 21.

51. Of course, their deaths further restrict the sample of Chupolenses who might have told me that they did not wish to participate in the revolutionary organization.

52. Interview with Héctor Mauricio López Bonilla, Guatemala City, July 1998.

53. CEH, *Memoria del silencio*, 1:157.

54. *Inforpress*, no. 449, 6.

55. *Inforpress*, no. 451, 4; *Inforpress* no. 452, 6.

56. Payeras, *El trueno en la cuidad*, 84.

57. Interview with César Montes (Julio César Macías), Mexico City, October 2001.

58. Interview with Enrique Corral, Guatemala City, October 2003.

59. Mario Payeras, "El pueblo resistirá las pruebas: entrevista con Marta Harnecker," in *Los días de la selva* (Managua: Editorial Nueva Nicaragua, 1982), 16

60. José's is an interesting case: although his wife and his family were organized, as were virtually all his neighbors and friends, he had not been included in consciousness-raising efforts because, he believes, he had done military service in the past. His omission still irritates him, especially because he claims to have worked with an earlier revolutionary organization, probably the western front of the FAR, while performing his military service on the coast! Despite his omission, moreover, he remains deeply loyal to the idea of revolutionary organizing and always presents himself and his life story in revolutionary terms.

61. Elisabeth J. Wood, *Insurgent Action and Civil War in El Salvador* (Cambridge: Cambridge University Press, 2003).

62. Timothy Wickham-Crowley, *Guerrillas and Revolution in Latin America: A Comparative Study of Insurgents and Regimes since 1956* (Princeton: Princeton University Press, 1992), 250–51.

"People's War," "Dirty War"

Cold War Legacy and the
End of History in Postwar Peru

GERARDO RÉNIQUE

By any reckoning, the war that unfolded in Peru between 1980 and 1992 marked a modal shift in the experience of violence in Peruvian politics and history. Although the Peruvian state had previously used arbitrary detentions, killings, torture, exile, and deportation to discourage mass action and eliminate opposition leaders, during the 1980s war between the Partido Comunista del Perú (more famously known as Sendero Luminoso) and the Peruvian armed forces, "traditional" modes of repression gave way to harsher forms of exemplary and punitive violence aimed against civilian men, women, and children. Political terror claimed victims from popular or grassroots organizations, left-wing parties, and the general population. In a perverse and curious resemblance to the "dirty wars" that took place in the rural areas of other Latin American countries, "death caravans" run by the Peruvian military carried out rapes, tortured, executed, and disappeared not just alleged subversives and their relatives but also college professors and students; they also corralled peasant villagers into strategic hamlets and arbitrarily detained and harassed thousands of citizens, including large numbers of journalists and lawyers.[1] For its part, Sendero's tactics likewise went well beyond the established forms of class-based vindictive violence—including armed propaganda, bank "expropriations," sabotage, and occasional military engagements—through which the Peruvian Left had traditionally pursued its revolutionary aims. Instead, Sendero turned its violence against leaders of popular organizations, elected officials, priests and nuns, nongovernmental organization members, and state functionaries. Sendero cadres targeted, in short, all those who did not pledge allegiance to their "people's war."

Founded in the early 1970s during Peru's military reformist government (1968–80), Sendero had its origins in one of the several splinter Maoist groups created after the Sino-Soviet split of the late 1960s. Established as a militarized cadre organization, Sendero (which took its name from an early party newspaper) rejected electoral politics as "parliamentary cretinism" and "pacifism." Indeed, Abimael Guzmán—Sendero's ideologue and leader—dismissed all such forms of legal or peaceful struggle as symptoms of the "revisionism" he claimed dominated the rest of the Peruvian Left. In Guzmán's uncompromising brand of "scientific Marxism," violence functioned as a constitutive element of his social vision, serving as a guiding principle for political action, revolutionary praxis, and the reorganization of the "new society." In particular, Guzmán and his followers considered terror a sort of universal purging mechanism for ridding the world of the two evils—revisionism and reaction—that threatened the success of Sendero's people's war.[2]

Sendero's position must be contrasted to that of the rest of the Peruvian Left, most of which saw the democratic transition of 1979–80 as potentially allowing for the creative consolidation of the dramatic expansion of left-wing political hegemony that had marked both the early phase of the military government and the later popular struggle against the military dictatorship. Although the Peruvian Left was far from united, a majority of the parties joined with social and popular organizations to form the "revolutionary mass front" Izquierda Unida. The Izquierda Unida's objectives were "to respond to popular demands for a democratic process that come from the people, [and] to become the leading force of the different classes and sectors that make up the national popular bloc."[3] By the late 1980s, the Izquierda Unida had become the second largest electoral force. Yet the front's success at the polls also marked the beginning of its rapid decline, as left-wing parties proved incapable of accommodating their parliamentary agendas to the twin challenges posed by, on the one hand, Sendero's escalating armed struggle and, on the other, growing demands for more participatory and militant forms of struggle coming from their mobilized membership. Coinciding as it did with the international collapse of "really existing socialism" and a worldwide neoliberal ideological offensive, the crisis of the Peruvian Left took the form of an ever-widening split between those who favored a more centrist and conciliatory political strategy and those who were inclined toward mass mobilization and direct action. As sectarianism, opportunism, and antidemocratic practices—all problems that the Izquierda Unida had pledged to overcome—resurfaced among its rank and file, the Left became engulfed in bitter infighting that led to the eventual disintegration of the Izquierda Unida in the early 1990s.

In addition to the Izquierda Unida, the Movimiento Revolucionario Tupac Amaru (MRTA), an armed organization formed in 1984 in the tradition of the 1960s Movimiento de Izquierda Revolucionaria, conceived of itself as part of a front in which popular or grassroots organizations and political parties would combine political, electoral, and armed actions with mass mobilization. From Guzmán's perspective, however, since both Tupac Amaru and Izquierda Unida represented forms of ideological "revisionism" that ran counter to Sendero's idiosyncratic armed struggle, their members—as well as those of numerous grassroots and social organizations they represented—were declared "enemies of the people" and targeted for assassination.[4]

As an extraordinarily singular case in the history of Latin American guerrilla warfare, Sendero's "people's war" has attracted the attention of a wide range of political functionaries, analysts, academics, and observers. Their diverse interpretations of the causes, character, and motivations of the insurgents speak not only to the increasing political polarization in Peru but also to the ideological accommodations to neoliberalism, not just as an economic form but as a social imaginary to interpret the political conflict that took place among the Peruvian—and Latin American—intelligentsias of the post–cold war era. Initial efforts to explain Sendero's actions drew from both cold war anticommunist sensibilities and long-established contempt among *limeños* (residents of the capital, Lima) for the Andean indigenous highlands where Sendero was first founded, to describe an insurgency or "narcoterrorist mafia" fueled by "international agents" and financed by international drug lords.[5] Subsequent Senderologists, both in Peru and in the United States, drew on modernization theory, particularly that informed by Samuel Huntington, to interpret Sendero's insurgency as resulting from a generalized institutional breakdown and its ideology as a form of premodern political fundamentalism comprised of equal parts peasant millenarianism and doctrinaire Maoism.[6]

Left-wing parties and commentators also regarded Sendero violence as the product of its sectarianism, ideological extremism, and fundamentalist interpretation of Marxism, and after an initial brief hesitance a majority of left analysts characterized it as counterrevolutionary. Together with human rights organizations, however, the Left also carried on a relentless campaign against the brutal counterinsurgency of the Peruvian armed forces. Public intellectuals identified with the Left adamantly denounced the racist under-pinnings and motivations of the military campaigns.[7]

Despite their conflicting agendas and analytical frameworks, analysts from the Left and Right did overlap in placing the blame on Sendero for the genesis and propagation of the violence and terror that devastated Peruvian society during the 1980s and 1990s. Drawing on a dominant—albeit largely implicit—explanatory model in which violence is attributed to a totalitarian drive toward utopia or innate authoritarian tendencies, both left and right observers located the origin of Peruvian political violence not in the coun-try's highly exploitative and exclusionary social system but in the synergy that resulted from the fusion of Sendero's Manichean ideology to the iron will of its charismatic leader and founder.[8] In the case of Peru, the model offered an expedient formula through which responsibility for the extreme violence of the war could be attributed to the authoritarianism of the Sen-dero, as a force that was imagined to have developed independently of the equally lethal strategies and counterinsurgency doctrines embraced by the Peruvian military. Defended as a reactive response to Sendero provocation, analysts across the political spectrum tended to blame the brutal behavior of the Peruvian armed forces as a product of ethnic and racial prejudices and to the colonial mentality that haunts the Peruvian psyche.[9] By overstating the weight of ideological and subjective motivations, these accounts minimized the pivotal role played by the counterinsurgency in creating a situation in which the state used fear to normalize and further its own violence against both the armed insurgency and the growing popular resistance and po-litical opposition that emerged in response to President Alberto Fujimori's (1990–2000) neoliberal economic regime and authoritarian policies. Stud-ies carried out in the aftermath of the war likewise avoided in-depth exami-nations of the Peruvian armed forces' role in carrying out preventive and punitive violence, and its origins in the anticommunist national security doctrines of the cold war. In particular, they studiously avoided examining the actions of state security forces in relation to a longer history of the pro-motion of counterinsurgency tactics by foreign, mostly U.S., advisors dur-ing the "dirty wars" and "low-intensity conflicts" that took place in South and Central America in the two decades prior to the Sendero insurgency, including in Peru to combat a peasant rebellion in the 1960s. Although Pe-ruvian historians and sociologists acknowledge this prehistory of the 1980s war as contributing to the "modernization" of the Peruvian armed forces, they tend to cast the violence deployed against peasant leaders and organizations of the 1960s and 1980s as "reactive" responses to left-wing provocation. The "excessive" brutality that defined the counterinsurgency violence of the 1980s is explained away as an unconscious product of the soldiers' "colonial," racist, and ethnocentric mentalities.[10]

The shift by many left-wing academics from structural-historical modes of analysis to single-factor accounts that emphasize psychological factors or premodern "mentalities" to explain violence committed in the name of the state, or to interpretations that see counterinsurgent terror as merely a response to a left-wing utopianism that can be traced either to Castro or Mao, speaks to Peru's changing post–cold war intellectual and cultural sensibilities. Dispirited by the consecutive and cumulative political defeats suffered by the Latin American Left during the final decades of the twentieth century, and the delegitimation of socialism and developmentalism that came with the fall of the Berlin Wall, the democratic and progressive achievements of popular and revolutionary radicalism of the 1960s and 1970s have been either elided or grossly simplified in academic analyses and interpretations of recent Peruvian history.[11] In their stead a new pragmatic or functionalist politics took hold in which collective projects, utopian ideologies, and demands for systemic change were sweepingly—and somewhat arrogantly—dismissed as anachronistic, ill-conceived, and unproductive.[12] This shift has occurred to differing degrees throughout Latin America—represented in its most articulate and influential form by Jorge Castañeda's 1994 *Utopia Unarmed: The Latin American Left after the Cold War*—yet in Peru the appeals of pragmatism were heightened by the disillusionment bred by the split of the Izquierda Unida, the deepening economic crisis brought on by neoliberal reforms, and the escalating violence of Sendero's war itself. In this context, many Peruvians embraced the dystopic intellectual fashions of the post–cold war era as a means to distance themselves from the egalitarian utopias, party politics, and revolutionary aspirations which they themselves had once embraced but now dismissed as an "unnecessary and bloody affair," as historian Arno Mayer describes a similar reassessment of the place of revolution and political violence in European history.[13]

This dramatic retreat required a reconsideration of the role and centrality of revolution and socialism—indeed, of all radicalism and progressive thinking in general—to modernity and democracy. Just as the French Revolution has been recast as "the source of all purgatorial fires of the twentieth century" and revolutionary socialism redefined as the "apocalysm" responsible for the world wars of the twentieth century, recent writing in Peru has also pointed towards the New Left of the 1960s as the foundational moment of the country's most recent cycle of violence and terror.[14] Indeed, rather than situating the radicalism of the time in its historical context, as a result of successive political frustrations and in reaction to the state's increased capacity to silence dissent through repression, many analysts and academics go as far as to suggest that the origins of the 1980–92 violence should be traced back to a "cult to violence," which they claimed defined the New Left. By likening the revolutionary passions and utopian aspirations of Marxism to the zeal and intransigence of sixteenth-century European religious wars, former left-wing and progressive intellectuals by extension also condemn all radical and antisystemic positions as irrational and sinister.[15] Further extended, such a position unavoidably leads to an accommodation with the neoliberal present—not just as an economic form but its political one as well, as the role of the state becomes redefined not as either a mechanism for redistribution or a site of class struggle but a necessary bulwark against the kind of radicalism expressed by Sendero. Although by no means unique to Peru, the rewriting of this hopeful and radical decade has relied on a selective erasure of "certain traces of the past sedimented in common sense by the progressive gains of the 1960s."[16] Likewise, recent claims that Peru's 1960s revolutionary radicalism was a "mental construct" among "marginal groups" sustained on an "imagined scenario of absolute confrontation" not only suggest the irrationality of leftist thought;[17] they also constitute a creative rewriting of the political and social history of a country in which, as we will see, the most important social and political democratic transformations were spearheaded by left-wing and popular political organizations and mobilizations.

Oligarchic Domination, Democracy, and Violence

The subaltern democratic mobilizations that shook Peru during the 1960s revealed the legacy of colonial oppression and racism that lay at the heart of Peruvian historical and socioeconomic formations. Since the late eighteenth-century indigenous rebellions that preceded independence in 1821, the Peruvian creole elite have lived in fear of the popular classes. Together with a liberal emphasis on individual rights and private property, this racialized fear stood as the most important pillar of the exclusionary democracy that took shape over the first one hundred years of independence. Following independence, the evolution of capitalism deepened the "semifeudal" labor and land relations that defined the colonial state, exacerbating Peru's racial and geographical divide.[18] Separated from the majority of the Indian and mestizo population by skin color, class, and culture, the oligarchic coastal elites clung to their ideals of European civilization as a means to reaffirm what they perceived as their superior "white" origins. These racialized class divides were reinforced by the striking geographic and ecological differences between Peru's arid coast, with its creole cities, and the mountainous Andean highlands inhabited by Quechua- and Aymara-speaking Indians.

The export economies that integrated the Peruvian economy to the world capitalist market were based on coercion and outright violence. Labor regimes on both coastal sugar and cotton plantations and U.S.-owned mines combined wage labor incentives with the coercive recruitment and abusive control of a mostly indigenous seasonal labor force drawn from nearby communities that produced crops and wool for domestic and international markets. In the highlands, agricultural and livestock estates (haciendas) produced crops for local consumption, coastal markets, mines, and plantations, as well as wool for the booming export markets. Production on these haciendas relied on a variety of servile and unsalaried labor arrangements. Landlords exercised a highly personalized form of power known as *gamonalismo* based in equal measure on paternalism and an unrestrained use of violence. These landlords joined with merchants, labor contractors, elected authorities, and state officials to form dense and complex regional power networks. They were articulated to the central government through their membership in liberal state institutions where they held appointed and elected positions as judges, congressional representatives, senators, or even in some occasions as holders of the executive office or cabinet positions.[19]

This incongruence between the country's predominantly coercive and colonial labor regimes and the liberalism espoused by its political and economic elites defined the nature of Peru's oligarchic republic. Three characteristics defined Peruvian republicanism: (1) the political exclusion and domination of a majority indigenous population; (2) a model of capitalist accumulation closely intertwined with the extraction of noncapitalist rents; and (3) coercive forms of social and labor control. Peruvian oligarchic liberal traditions were built with an almost exclusive emphasis on free trade and extraeconomic modes of labor control, which made a mockery of liberal constitutional guarantees of individual rights and freedoms. Under these circumstances, power was exercised through cultural and political traditions and institutions based on the domination and marginalization of Peru's indigenous majorities. Without either social consensus or authority, oligarchic elites maintained their control through coercion and an ideology of *blanco-criollo* superiority.[20]

Up through the mid-twentieth century, subaltern intervention in politics was manifested through everyday acts of resistance, sporadic—and many times violent—protest, and occasional rebellions and insurrections. The first half of the twentieth century saw the emergence of mass politics—the birth of the Alianza Popular Revolucionaria Americana (APRA) and the Communist Party, union movements in the city and mining centers, and rural protest—which began the assault on what Alberto Flores Galindo and Manuel Burga have described as Peru's "aristocratic republic," in which politics remained an exclusive domain of oligarchic elites.[21] Although highly fragmented and localized, peasant mobilizations in different parts of the country combined common demands for land and rural education, and an end to servile relations of domination, unjust taxation, compulsory military service, and unpaid labor in road construction. Without the existence of mechanisms and institutions of political mediation and negotiation, however, landlord and state responses to subaltern defiance and rebelliousness continued to rely on violence and feudal forms of domination and labor exploitation. And by the start of the cold war—signaled in Peru with the 1948 military coup against the center-left elected government of José Luis Bustamante y Rivero—the militant threat of early twentieth-century social movements had been definitively diffused.

In the late 1950s, months before the victory of the Cuban Revolution, a massive peasant movement rocked the foundations of the Peruvian state and society, ushering in a crisis of legitimacy and hegemony that has remained unresolved until this day. In late 1959 *comuneros* (peasant villagers) in the central highland department of Pasco led simultaneous occupations of lands that had been unjustly appropriated by large haciendas or estates. Home to the most productive beef, wool, and dairy enterprises in the country, more than 90 percent of the agricultural and pasturelands in Pasco and other central Andean departments were controlled by a few families and private—national and foreign—corporations. By 1964 a majority of haciendas in the region had been affected by peasant "land recoveries." Using customary institutions and relations of communal authority as an organizational framework, villagers in the central Andes—with the support of village migrants in the capital city of Lima and surrounding mining centers and the participation of urban left-wing political advisors affiliated to the emerging New Left political formations—created federations and associations to coordinate their actions, defend their members, and negotiate with state authorities. At the same time, another center of peasant mobilization opened in La Convención y Lares Valley, located in the southern department of Cusco. There, indigenous tenants organized into "peasant unions" and conducted struggles demanding the abolition of non–wage labor regimes, the establishment of work contracts, and the creation of schools in the haciendas where they toiled.[22] In the department of Cuzco alone, during the early weeks of 1962 120 peasant unions occupied more than one hundred haciendas. From these two regions, rural unrest spread to other parts of the country as far as the northern coastal sugar plantations, to areas of colonization in the eastern part of the country, and other Andean provinces. Inspired by the Cuban Revolution and organizing under the slogan "Tierra o muerte: venceremos," more than 300,000 peasants, their families, and their communities participated between 1958 and 1964, in roughly four hundred recorded peasant-led agrarian land takeovers.[23]

A remarkable characteristic of the land takeovers in Pasco and other central Andean regions was the inverse relation between the animosity of the peasant invaders toward the landowners and the levels of violence displayed during these actions. The caution and restraint observed by the villagers stood in marked contrast to the behavior and attitudes of the police, landlords, and guards responsible for the initiation of virtually all the bloodshed associated with the land occupations.[24] Despite the lack of systematic statistics for peasant casualties in this pre–human rights era and the highly biased journalistic coverage of the agrarian conflicts, peasant deaths did not go unreported. There are, however, no reliable estimates of total casualties. Trained to deal with urban turmoil and crowd control, the national police antiriot unit was in most cases overwhelmed by the peasants. Despite their larger—and deadlier—firearm capacity, army troops were also equally ineffective.

In the departments of the southern Andes, particularly in Cusco, direct confrontations were more frequent and violent. Peasant deaths between 1950 and 1964 in this region alone were estimated at around three hundred. To confront land occupations, landowners, militants from the initially reformist and anti-imperialist APRA, which had turned pro-oligarchic after the Second World War, and local chambers of commerce members organized "white guards" and harassed peasant leaders and left-wing activists.[25] In response, peasant unions in the Valley of La Convención formed armed self-defense groups. Driven by the anger provoked by massacres, abusive behavior, or arbitrary detentions, peasant offensive actions generally targeted police stations in an effort to liberate unjustly detained leaders and union activists. Peasant readiness both to confront landlord guards and state security forces and to defend the recovered lands, however, may have played an important role in preventing an even greater escalation of state-led and landlord violence. Equally important in deterring state violence was the constant lobbying and pressure exercised by peasant supporters and their representatives on parliamentary representatives and local and national authorities.

Over the course of these two decades, Peru's peasantry emerged as an autonomous and independent political force in its own right. Their success depended in large part on their ability to combine old and new forms of organization, including corporate peasant or Indian communities, "peasant labor unions," broad-based regional organizations, political alliances, and finally the creation in 1963 of the Confederación Campesina del Perú. This confederation, which was created in a collaboration between peasant leaders and left-wing activists, along with the creation of the Confederación General de Trabajadores five years later, constituted a foundational moment in Peru's oppositional history.[26] Galvanized by the Cuban Revolution, students, workers, professionals, intellectuals, Christian youth groups, activists from the Partido Comunista Peruano, and left-wing dissidents from APRA coalesced around new parties and organizations committed to a revolutionary transformation of the country.[27] The convergence of subaltern resistance and socialist analyses and representations of Peruvian history and society sustained the emergence of a distinctive praxis at the center of the country's democratic struggles. Breaking with a long established pattern of rural conflict characterized by sporadic and relatively small-scale gains, the new peasant mobilizations forced the Peruvian state to enact legislation abolishing unpaid labor and declaring a limited land reform in the two most conflictive regions. Most of the contested lands, moreover, remained under de facto peasant occupation. Apprehensive landlords in many rural areas either negotiated concessions with their tenant-laborers and surrounding villages or, as happened in many cases, simply abandoned their properties. In the words of Peruvian historian Alberto Flores Galindo, the end of servile labor relations was an event of "seismic consequences." It implied both the collapse of seignioral (semifeudal) domination and the unraveling of the local power structures that sustained the oligarchic state.[28]

Land occupations also resonated within the mounting migrant working-class population in the capital city of Lima and other coastal urban centers. Starting in the early 1950s, rural-urban migration expanded dramatically in response to a renewed export "boom" prompted by the Korean War and an industrial expansion concentrated in Lima and other coastal regions. By decade's end, however, an economic recession turned the piecemeal occupation and formation of squatter settlements on empty lots into massive and well-organized occupations of public and private lands. By the mid-1960s these precarious urban settlements or *barriadas* housed more than 70 percent of Peru's urban population.[29]

The most important and critical support for the peasant struggle, however, came from the urban labor movement, which was in a process of renewal after almost a decade of repression, including persecution of union leaders and the prohibition of opposition political parties—both the Communist Party and APRA—during the dictatorial regime of General Manuel Odría (1948–56). Labor federations and workers' unions staged stoppages protesting government repression and expressing support for peasant demands and an end to nonwage labor. Wildcat strikes in the mining centers of the central Andes and occupations of sugar mills on the northern coastal plantations supported the peasant struggle, marking the beginnings of a new wave of intense labor mobilization. Deprived of basic rights by the repression of the previous eight years, labor unions represented an important vehicle for political participation—particularly for the newer sectors of the working class made up of recently migrated peasants. As the economic woes of the working class deepened and the bourgeoisie hardened its stance toward union demands, labor militancy rose accordingly. Between 1957 and 1962 the number of yearly strikes surged from 161 to 382. Led by a younger generation of left-wing organizers, labor mobilizations began to include more militant tactics including wildcat strikes, factory occupations, *marchas de sacrificio* (long walks of peasants and miners to the capital, Lima), takeovers of radio stations, and hunger strikes.[30] Labor unions, particularly those in the U.S.-controlled mining and oil industries, led an anti-imperialist mobilization calling for the nationalization of these strategic sectors. Workers' organizations were also central to regionalist movements that called on the government to compensate for the regional inequities caused by uneven capitalist development, a highly centralized political and fiscal structure, and the racialized disdain toward Indians and peasants on the part of limeño elites and the central state they controlled.

Taken as a whole, the worker and peasant protests of the 1960s add up to what was undoubtedly the most important democratic mobilization in modern Peruvian history. In hindsight, six aspects of this mobilization render it historically significant: (1) its far-reaching territorial scope; (2) its forging of a sustained peasant and urban worker alliance; (3) its articulation of a popular anti-imperialist nationalism; (4) the growing appeal of demands that transcended particular corporatist (that is, peasant or worker) interests; (5) a counterhegemonic realization of shared burdens imposed on these subaltern sectors by the exclusionary and racializing practices of Peru's ruling oligarchy; and (6) the emergence of an autonomous radicalized campesino-indigenous leadership.[31] In this respect, the 1960s struggles for land and the abolition of nonwage labor constituted what Neil Harvey describes, in reference to the much later Mexican Zapatista insurrection, as a struggle for "the right to have rights"—that is, to be recognized as an equal member of the political community.[32] By calling into question the colonial forms of labor exploitation and land tenure that still held sway in much of Peru, such demands posed a serious and sustained threat to oligarchic domination. Although this upheaval did not lead to either the radical alteration of the established government and class system, or to the establishment of a new revolutionary order, in the context of Peru's exclusionary democracy, it did mark the advent of a severe crisis of authority. Following the pattern described by Gramsci as the transition of the masses "from a state of political passivity to a certain activity," the demands voiced by Peru's peasant and worker mobilization of the 1960s, "taken together, albeit not organically formulated, add up to a revolution."[33] Seen from this perspective, the upheavals that gripped Peru in the 1960s, while refracted through the perceived success of the Cuban Revolution, were entirely domestic. Having emerged from an unsustainable model of exclusionary and highly exploitative development, mobilized Peruvian peasants and workers were but one front in a larger international constellation of antisystemic forces that sought to challenge not just national elites but the imperial and capitalist system that propped up those elites.

Cuba's radical solutions to long-seated problems of economic development, social justice, national sovereignty, and public health and universal education sharpened and emboldened nationalist, antioligarchic and democratic demands and expectations. The political legitimacy of the Cuban

Revolution, enhanced after its defeat of the U.S.-sponsored Bay of Pigs invasion, generated not only admiration but also a genuine interest in its domestic policies and transformations. In this respect, it is important to underline the fact that Cuba's influence over the Peruvian Left had as much to do with a generalized historical curiosity and a shared criticism borne out of similar experiences, as it did with a fascination with the supposed dogmatism of "foquismo."[34] In the decades after the triumph of the Cuban Revolution, the emergence of reformist and revolutionary organizations and the popularization of critical left social analysis also played an effective—and unexpected—part in undermining the traditionally conservative position of the three pillars of the oligarchic state: the Catholic Church, the academy, and the armed forces.

Revolutionary Left, Counterinsurgency, and State Formation

The surge in popular mobilization and organization was mirrored by a corresponding turn to the left among Peru's cultural and intellectual elites. Spurred by the success of dependency theory and the establishment and professionalization of the social sciences as autonomous careers, Marxism and socialism found fertile ground among intellectuals, academics, artists, and professionals. Socialist analyses, formulations, and prescriptions central to Peru's left-wing intellectual and political strategies were quickly incorporated into public discourse; and interpretations of Peruvian history, social science, and public policy were in one way or another shaped by socialist polemics and left-wing analyses. Among the more popular themes of academic analysis during this period were the consequences of imperialism for the process of state formation, class formation, systems of exploitation and social oppression, and the national problem and the nature of Peruvian identity. Popular organizations were also influenced in their strategies, goals, and desires by the critical discourse and thinking of socialist intellectuals.[35]

Left-wing cultural influence also left its imprint in the traditionally conservative Catholic Church. Marxist analyses and interpretations were particularly crucial to the development of liberation theology. Progressive members of the priesthood mobilized by its newly found "preferential option with the poor" gained prominence both among subaltern classes and within the church hierarchy, thereby undermining the influence of its most conservative sectors.[36] The dramatic transformation of the country's political and cultural landscape also had an impact on professional and middle sectors, who were frustrated with APRA's desertion from the reformist camp and its new-found alliance with the most recalcitrant sector of the oligarchy. The reformist and populist platforms of newly created parties emphasized the incorporation of subaltern demands and the defense of national sovereignty as central tasks in a postoligarchic order.

Concerns with development and national sovereignty also resonated with the younger ranks of the military. The academic activities of the Centro de Altos Estudios Militares led to the self-examination of the armed forces' role in society and its responsibility in generating the oligarchic crisis, producing what the former military officer-turned-progressive essayist and commentator Víctor Villanueva described as a "new military mentality."[37] Informed by theories of national development and counterinsurgency, the military developed what might be described as an internal security doctrine. According to this doctrine, the military recast their role to become protectors of the "internal order" against "domestic enemies." As a result, the armed forces shed their traditional role as guardians of the status quo to embrace a nationalist antioligarchic stance premised on the need to deter autonomous popular mobilizations and further advances on the left.[38] Confronted with an unabated peasant mobilization and escalating democratic demands in the context of a broader fear generated by the consolidation of the Cuban Revolution, along with a likely electoral victory of the presidential candidate representing oligarchic interest which military analysts feared would only lead to greater political polarization, the Peruvian armed forces staged a coup in 1962. This of course was not the first time the military had intervened in politics, but this coup signaled a turning point in Peruvian history. Unlike previous occasions, coup leaders did not represent specific factional interests but rather advanced an institutional consensus that the military needed to step in and impose a solution to the crisis of the oligarchic state, one that fused together national development and security objectives in a way that closely corresponded with John F. Kennedy's hemispheric prescription for the containment of Cuba's revolutionary "contagion."[39]

The new strategy of national state formation espoused by the Peruvian military resembled the "passive revolution" deployed by European conservative regimes to contain the spread of revolutionary fervor unleashed by the 1789 French Revolution.[40] With an industrial bourgeoisie organically linked to the interests of the oligarchy and thus unable to offer a solution to the crisis, and with the desertion of the most influential reformist party

(APRA) to the oligarchic camp, the only institution that could stem the Left and avoid a complete collapse of the state was the Peruvian military.[41] The dramatic and radical response of the Peruvian armed forces reached its climax with the military government of 1968–80. Informed by both the strategic concerns of development and internal security promoted by the Alliance for Progress, and their own conviction that the military should serve as the agent of modernization and civilization, the armed forces set out to create a new postoligarchic state.[42] Claiming as its main goals "the transformation of the structure of the state and the social, economic, and cultural structures"[43] of the country, as well as the establishment of a "noncapitalist" and "noncommunist" regime, the fiery antioligarchic and anti-imperialist rhetoric of General Juan Velasco Alvarado and calls for "participatory socialism" galvanized the popular imagination. Its nationalization of selected foreign oil and mining companies, and implementation of the 1969 Land Reform neutralized existing labor and peasant organizations, enlisted the support of the Communist Party and a number of left-wing intellectuals, and created its own corporatist mass organizations among workers, peasants, and shantytown dwellers.

Political and economic *dirigisme* in Peru, however, did not merely reflect cold war doctrine. It also built on traditions and theories introduced into the country by French military training officers between 1896 and 1940.[44] French training officers occupied key positions in both the Escuela Militar and the Escuela Superior de Guerra established in 1904 and modeled after their counterparts in France. Many of these individuals had served in colonial postings under the command of Joseph Gallieri and Hubert G. Lyautey, prominent strategists and theoreticians whose writings were highly influential in both the French and Peruvian armies. A prolific author, Lyautey reached the rank of marshall after successful service in Indochina, Madagascar, and Morocco. Although historians have emphasized the early exposure of the Peruvian military to discussions on guerrilla warfare and counterinsurgency through the teachings of French instructors, they often fail to consider Lyautey's influence on the development of ideas regarding the social and political role of the military.[45] Drawing on his colonial experience, Lyautey argued that the army was a paramount agent of culture, modernization, and nation building. As discussed by the historian Frederick Nunn, the ideas and prescriptions advocated by Lyautey had a long-lasting influence on the writings and thoughts of prominent Peruvian officers, including many who would later occupy key positions in the 1968–80 military government. Contemporary analyses of the French counterinsurgency campaigns in Algeria and Indochina also figured as important references in the Peruvian military literature of the 1960s.[46] Forecasting both the system of social and political control created by the military government of 1968–80 and the peasant patrols mobilized by the armed forces against the Sendero, Colonel Christian Sánchez stated in 1963 that a military-civilian alliance constituted the main agent of both development and national security. In another article, General Francisco Morales Bermúdez, who would serve as head of state during the "second phase" of the military government (1975–80), argued that the mission of the military was to "maintain the internal order of the republic" and to "contribute to national development." For Edgardo Mercado Jarrín, another prominent member of the 1968–80 military government, a main responsibility of the army was to act as an "agent of civilization" through the comprehensive vocational training and education of the predominantly indigenous and peasant recruits who could then act as a "vanguard of the modernized sector" when they returned to civilian life.[47] Thus, development, security, and nation building were to be attained in an orderly and nonparticipatory fashion under army supervision and without subverting the preordained class/ethnic hierarchies.

During its first brief military government in 1962–63, the armed forces abolished unpaid labor, and decreed a limited land reform in the valleys around Cuzco. But at the same time, they also carried out a massive dragnet against popular leaders and left-wing activists, sending fifteen hundred to two thousand individuals to prison. Prompted by military propaganda, and galvanized by ingrained urban creole fears of indigenous rural masses, the media launched an unrestrained campaign that fused anticommunist paranoia with race hysteria, demonizing peasant activists as both irrational and manipulated by Cuban agents, acting in complicity with local communists. As we have seen, however, Peru's volatile political situation not only predated the Cuban insurgency but, more important, also expressed the hegemonic crisis of oligarchic domination. From this perspective the "revolutionary situation" in the country was more a consequence of domestic mobilization and discontent, even as it corresponded to a broader global crisis of imperialist domination heralded by the Cuban Revolution and Vietnamese liberation struggle.

But the Cuban Revolution did galvanize the radical aspirations of the emerging New Left and justified its emphasis on direct action and support for the more militant manifestations of peasant and worker action. In this respect, the New Left stood in contrast to the more legalistic and evolutionary-reformist approach espoused by the Peruvian Communist Party—the dominant organization in the Left since the 1930s. Subordinated to the geopolitical interests of the USSR, the Communist Party after the Second World War espoused a strategy of support and collaboration with forces considered to represent antifeudal and anti-imperialist capitalist modernization. Despite the collaborationist stance of orthodox communism after 1948, the Peruvian Communist Party, along with many other communist parties in Latin America, was declared illegal. By the time it resurfaced in 1956, the labor federation that had been created with communist support was in disarray and its leadership infiltrated by APRA-backed organizers who had been trained in the AFL-CIO's principles of anticommunist "free-trade unionism."[48]

It was, however, among the armed forces that cold war anticommunism left its most pervasive and enduring imprint. After the Second World War, concerns with hemispheric stability, together with the containment of communism, emerged as top priorities in U.S. policy towards the region. The $38.2 million for direct military assistance allocated for Latin America in 1950—the year Truman approved new inter-American military collaboration—had climbed to $105 million by mid-1954.[49] In Peru, President Odría's anticommunism was rewarded with a substantial increase in U.S. military assistance, from a meager $100,000 in 1950 to over $9 million in 1956, his last year in office. Between 1950 and 1966 almost four thousand Peruvian military personal were trained either in the United States or in the Panama Canal Zone—slightly fewer than the number of Brazilian trainees during the same period. Between 1949 and 1969 more than eight hundred officers received additional specialized training in the infamous School of the Americas. Overall up to 20 percent of each graduating class from the Escuela Militar was estimated to have received training in the United States.[50] Drawing upon this experience, the Peruvian army established a specialized counterinsurgency unit whose training included study of the Vietnam War. Peru's own counterinsurgency campaign ran parallel to the escalation of the U.S. war in Southeast Asia. As the historian Daniel Masterson writes, the U.S. experience in Vietnam inspired and strengthened the Peruvian military resolve "to repress massively their own guerrilla threat and demonstrate their counterinsurgency expertise to their U.S. military mentors."[51]

As elsewhere in Latin America, the adoption of guerrilla warfare and insurrection by the emerging New Left in Peru was a direct response to the new corporatist-technocratic military regimes and increased U.S. military interventionism in the region against democratically elected left-wing and progressive regimes. These conditions for insurrection began to develop in the country during the 1962–63 institutionalized government of the armed forces, whose measures signaled the materialization of a mature cold war regime committed to the deterrence at all costs of the political aspirations of popular and left-wing forces. The most important of the armed groups of the 1960s was the Movimiento de Izquierda Revolucionaria (MIR). Formed of two guerrilla fronts strategically located in the proximity of the two epicenters of peasant insurgency in the central and southern Andes, the MIR, led by the lawyer Luis De la Puente, had its origins in APRA-Rebelde, a splinter fraction that had earlier broken with APRA over its growing conservatism.[52] Simultaneously operating on two fronts, MIR's campaign lasted from June 1965 to early January 1966, when members of its last column were summarily executed as they attempted to flee into the Amazon jungle. Not a single member of the MIR leadership who had engaged in the guerrilla campaign came out of it alive.

The counterinsurgency was based on tactics very similar to those used at the time in Vietnam: massive carpet bombings, creation of "strategic hamlets," targeting of civilian population, and large-scale population relocations. The military also engaged in acts of violence that would become the norm in its later campaign against Sendero, including mass rape, torture, summary executions, disappearances, and dropping individuals from planes or helicopters. As occurred in similar U.S.-backed counterinsurgent campaigns in Guatemala, Venezuela, and Colombia in the early to mid-1969s, the magnitude of the Peruvian military's response was in great disproportion to the nature of the threat. Although the guerrillas only engaged military personnel in combat situations—all told, fifty-six government soldiers were killed—and generally released prisoners after giving them a pep talk about the reasons of the armed struggle, it is estimated that the army killed eight thousand individuals, most of them indigenous.[53] The air force carried out massive napalm bombing raids in the areas surrounding the guerrilla bases in Pucuta (Junín) and Mesa Pelada (Cuzco); fourteen thousand hectares of crops were destroyed; ninety-three hamlets with approximately nineteen thousand inhabitants were forcibly relocated; and thirty-six hundred peasants were detained in hastily made concentration camps. An unknown number of detainees were also disappeared.

Although the military inflicted a crushing and definitive defeat on the guerrillas, the armed insurgency also left a deep impression—described by Villanueva as an institutional "psychic trauma"—that brought the high echelons of the armed forces to consider the feasibility of revolution. The guerrillas "rang the military's alarm bell," said one general who held a prominent political position in the 1968–80 military government, leading the military to the realization that structural change and not repression alone would be the best deterrent to a left-wing revolution.[54]

In 1963, the military had allowed a short-lived return to constitutional rule, which saw the election of Fernando Belaúnde to the presidency. But the crisis continued. Belaúnde's administration was marked by deepening political and economic polarization, rampant corruption of state functionaries, and unchecked favoritism toward U.S. economic and political interests, which prompted the military to once again step in. In early October 1968 they staged a second coup, this one with a much further-reaching agenda, aimed at "transforming the structure of the state and the social, economic, and cultural structures" of the country within the "principles of the Christian and Western tradition."[55] The military arrived to power at a crucial moment in the global reconfiguration of the imperialist order, as Peru's crisis of hegemony deepened under the burden of a politically weak and dependent bourgeoisie and a growing mass-democratic movement. The crisis was so deep that the new military government could act with a great margin of relative autonomy. Rather than creating a new revolutionary order, the military announced measures—including land reform, an expropriation of U.S.-owned oil and mining corporations, and the opening of trade and diplomatic relations with Eastern European countries—all aimed at modernizing and homogenizing capitalism in Peru, and at reconfiguring Peru's relationship to imperialism.[56]

Drawing on cold war security doctrine, the military government introduced the concept of "internal front" as a central aspect of its new legislation on "public order." Reflecting a military perspective that framed social problems as acts of war, the new legislation also established the concept of "preventive defense" of the national territory against real and potential enemies.[57] These new legislative and security initiatives created the conceptual and institutional framework for implementing regimes of exception.

Conclusion

Attempts to account for the extremely brutal nature of Peru's 1980–92 civil war must address the multiple historical and structural factors leading up to the conflict, including the way in which anticommunism, Maoist fundamentalism, and internal security doctrines coalesced to produce an unprecedented escalation of terror in a country whose history has been characterized by systemic class-based, racist, repressive violence. The experiment in authoritarian nationalist reform launched by the Peruvian military in 1968 did not solve the crisis of oligarchic legitimacy that began in the late 1950s but merely postponed its resolution. By the time it gave up power in 1980 and allowed a return to civilian rule, the country was in an even more volatile situation than it had been in the 1960s. Rather than reconciling themselves to the process of democratization that had taken place over the last two decades, economic and political elites deepened their defensive stance, taking refuge in a resuscitated exclusionary liberalism that rejected subaltern demands. They found themselves threatened in two directions, from a vibrant left-wing and popular mobilization that increasingly took the form of a movement against neoliberal restructuring, and by Sendero's growing "people's war." For its part, the military, having abandoned its developmentalist project, retained its counterinsurgent impulse, and with the return to democracy failing to bring with it political stability, it brought the lessons of the 1960s counterinsurgency and the U.S.-promoted internal security doctrine to impose order. Under pressure from the armed forces and with right-wing and APRA support, the 1979–80 Constitutional Assembly produced a new constitution that made it easy to call a state of exception. Meanwhile, the advance of economic liberalism was producing new waves of popular resistance, which were being met by an increased hardening of the Peruvian state. Unwilling to embrace a democratic and participatory solution to the unresolved crisis of hegemony, the elite instead opted to perpetuate the unstable social and political equilibrium that had characterized oligarchic domination. Sendero's armed insurgency provided an excuse for increased militarization and an increasing concentration of special powers in the executive branch during the civilian administrations of Fernando Belaúnde (1980–85) and Alan García (1985–90). By the time Alberto Fujimori became president, executive privilege served to bolster not only the counterinsurgency campaign but, more important, allowed Fujimori to avoid congressional oversight when implementing unpopular neoliberal restructuring and privatizations. The equally violent, arbitrary, and authoritarian actions of Sendero contributed to the pervasive atmosphere of fear and uncertainty that acted as a deterrent to popular mobilization.

The catastrophic conditions created by the war between Sendero and the Peruvian state joined with the dramatic scenario created by an extreme and highly authoritarian version of neoliberal restructuring to unleash "furies," which Mayer locates in local antagonisms, hatred of elite pretensions, desire for revenge, religious rivalries, and base interests and ambitions. [58] In the case of Peru, these furies had been put on hold by the tenuous political compact established by the 1968–80 military government, but returned with a vengeance in the wake of that compact's failure to solve the oligarchic crisis. For over a decade, the clash between the Peruvian armed forces and the armed insurgencies of Sendero and the Movimiento Revolucionario Tupac Amaru emerged as the immediate and most visible source of the terror and violence that threatened Peruvian society. What made this context unique, however, is that the usually bipolar field of forces pitting "revolution" against "counterrevolution" formed part of a more complex mix in which the state and its political elites were simultaneously challenged by an electoral Left and popular organizations whose goals and strategies were antagonistic to those espoused by Sendero.

Whereas the armed forces perceived Sendero combatants, Tupac Amaru militants, left-wing organizers, and grassroots activists as different manifestations of the same "communist threat," Sendero viewed other popular organizations not only as competitors, but as obstacles standing in the way of an all-out war that would lead to the realization of a "society of great harmony."[59] Deemed "enemies of the people," Sendero carried on selective assassinations of leaders of popular organizations, left-wing cadre, elected officials, and members of nongovernmental civil society organizations. At the same time, the armed forces carried out massacres and massive retaliations against civilians during the earlier stages of the conflict in an attempt to isolate Sendero from its alleged supporters. Although in Sendero's idiosyncratic version of Maoism, violence is considered paramount for attaining revolutionary purification, it was the escalation of the conflict itself and not ideology per se that constituted the motivation of their political struggle against the state, the Left, and popular organizations.

Close scrutiny of the conflict and its multiple determinants not only clarifies the reciprocal and uneven responsibilities of the state and the insurgency, but also counters the "obsessively monocausal," "overideologized and overpersonalized" explanations of the origins of political violence that pass as "explanation" in so many academic analyses of the war.[60] By privileging single-factor explanations, by ignoring the achievements of the Left in promoting participatory democracy and egalitarianism, and by denouncing the international (Cuban) support received by the Left as "insidious" while ignoring the international military aid and support received by the Peruvian state and armed forces, academic accounts of violence reproduce the blinkered assumptions of cold war anticommunism.[61] They also neglect the crucial role played by the Left and the popular movement in bringing about the demise of Peru's oligarchic state and the making of a popular democratic culture. More important, by downplaying the pivotal role of the internal security doctrine in forging the modern Peruvian state, these reinterpretations gloss over what otherwise has been aptly described as "a complex and tangled piece of intellectual history" that, in the aftermath of the Cuban Revolution, provided the equipment, training, and moral justification that "made mass killings permissible," in the name of national security.[62]

Despite being heavily influenced by cold war anticommunism in its assigning blame to left ideology as the cause of the 1980–92 war, the chronology put together by the Peruvian Truth and Reconciliation Commission clearly suggests that Sendero's escalation of violence was a direct consequence of the equally brutal retaliation of the armed forces against its combatants and prisoners; the increasing resistance of popular organizations to Sendero's political and military advances; and the state's recruitment and mobilization of armed peasants as counterinsurgent forces. During the final years of the conflict, as the army took a more administrative and less overtly violent approach to the cooptation and intimidation of the rural population, Sendero became even more inflexible and brutal in response to their weakening hold over the peasantry. In these conditions the force of circumstances prevailed over ideology as the motivating cause of violence and terror.

Sendero took Mao's Cultural Revolution as a model for political action, yet its military strategy was also informed by particular local experiences, including the shortcomings of Peru's 1960s guerrilla campaigns, the overthrow of the Chilean president Allende, and the defeat of Nicaragua's Frente Sandinista. Although developed within the traditions of the dogmatic and deterministic Marxist orthodoxy established by Comintern Stalinism and Maoism, Sendero ideology is also informed by a Kantian conception of real or exclusive oppositions that stands at odds with a more dialectical Marxist understanding of contradiction as a unity of opposites.[63] In fact, it could be argued that the violence perpetrated by Sendero against indigenous peasants drew less from Marxism or even Maoism than it did from cultural understandings of personalized authority, violence, and ethnic superiority common to highland gamonalismo that formed the shared social backdrop for many of the party's cadre and leaders. It was also shaped by deep-seated animosities, retaliation, and revenge between rural families, communities, and ethnic groups. These longstanding disputes become particularly contentious in communities that were sharply divided between those in favor of or against Sendero. Another important factor was the paternalistic and rationalist arrogance maintained by young urban-educated political cadres, who disdained uneducated, older peasants and the indigenous culture of the Andean countryside as ignorant and backward. These views resonated with longstanding traditions of cultural and racial prejudice in Peru.[64]

Starting in 1980, the Peruvian state's concurrent embrace of economic neoliberalism and resuscitation of counterinsurgency doctrine turned a volatile situation into a social catastrophe. Privatization and other structural reforms led to widespread immiseration, which fueled resistance to those reforms—either in the form of a democratic Left or Sendero—which the state increasingly responded to with counterinsurgent terror. In the 1960s, just at the moment that coastal creole racism had been driven into crisis by a powerful democratic grassroots peasant and workers movement, it was given a second life by cold war anticommunism, which allowed Peruvian elites to fuse their racial hatreds and fears onto the figure of the national security doctrine's "internal enemy." With the failure of the military's authoritarian developmentalist model—which had sought to incorporate dissent into new national institutions—the circle was complete: the coercive model of exclusionary state formation and economic development that defined Peruvian history from independence up to the mid-twentieth century was updated for modern times. Economic neoliberalization depended on counterinsurgent repression the same way that nineteenth-century liberalism depended on a range of extraeconomic coercion to maintain order. In this respect, the counterinsurgency launched against not just Sendero but also the broader Peruvian Left and popular movement not only enhanced the military capabilities of the state but, more important, expanded its ideological hold over the political and cultural imagination of a society in which the memory of war and the privatizations of neoliberal reforms have combined to undermine the appeals of collective organization and the critical stance of utopian thinking.

Notes

1. See Amnesty International, *Peru: Violations of Human Rights in the Emergency Zones* (New York: Amnesty International, 1988); Desco (Centro de Estudios y Promoción del Desarrollo), *Violencia política en el Perú, 1980–88*, 2 vols. (Lima: Desco, 1989); see also *Hatun Willakuy: versión abreviada del Informe Final de la Comisión de la Verdad y Reconciliación* (Lima: Comisión de la Verdad y Reconciliación, 2004).

2. The leader of the "Fracción Roja" within the Maoist Partido Comunista Peruano–Bandera Roja in 1970, Guzmán broke with the party to create the Partido Comunista Peruano–Sendero Luminoso as a clandestine organization advocating armed struggle as the only valid revolutionary strategy. For a discussion of this aspect of Sendero ideology, see Deborah Poole and Gerardo Rénique, *Peru: Time of Fear* (London: Latin America Bureau, 1992), 46–52. For histories of Sendero, see also Carlos I. Degregori, *Ayacucho, 1969–1979: el nacimiento de Sendero Luminoso* (Lima: Instituto de Estudios Peruanos, 1990); Gustavo Gorriti, *Sendero: historia de la guerra milenaria en el Perú*, vol. 1 (Lima: Editorial Apoyo, 1990); Lewis Taylor, *Maoism in the Andes: Sendero Luminoso and the Contemporary Guerrilla Movement* (Liverpool: Centre for Latin American Studies, 1981).

3. Izquierda Unida, "Programa y declaración de principios," in *Documentos fundamentales de Izquierda Unida* (Lima: Ediciones Patria Roja, 1983), 16–17. For history and assessment of the Izquierda Unida, see Nigel Haworth, "Radicalization and the Left in Peru, 1976–1991," in *The Latin American Left: From the Fall of Allende to Perestroika*, ed. B. Carr and S. Ellner (Boulder, Colo.: Westview Press, 1993), 41–60; and Lewis Taylor, "One Step Forward, Two Steps Back: The Peruvian Izquierda Unida, 1980–1990," *Journal of Communist Studies* 6 (1990): 108–19.

4. Abimael Guzmán, "Por la nueva bandera," in *Guerra popular en el Perú: el pensamiento Gonzalo*, ed. Luis Arce Borja (Brussels: Borja, 1989).

5. See Gabriela Tarazona-Sevillano with John B. Reuter, *Sendero Luminoso and the Threat of Narco-terrorism* (New York: Praeger, 1990).

6. Among others, see David Scott Palmer, "The Sendero Luminoso Rebellion in Peru," in *Latin American Insurgencies*, ed. G. Fauriol (Washington, D.C.: George Washington University, CSIS, and National Defense University, 1985), 67–88; David Scott Palmer, "Rebellion in Rural Peru: The Origins and Evolution of Sendero Luminoso," *Comparative Politics* 18, no. 1 (1986), 127–46; Cynthia McClintock, "Why Peasants Rebel: The Case of Peru's Sendero Luminoso," *World Politics* 37 (1984),

48–84. For a critical assessment of U.S. "Senderologists," see Deborah Poole and Gerardo Rénique, "The New Chroniclers of Peru: U.S. Scholars and Their "Shining Path" of Peasant Rebellion," *Bulletin of Latin American Research* 10, no. 2 (1991), 133–91.

7. For left-wing assessments of Sendero, see Raul Wiener, *Guerra e ideología: el debate entre Amauta y El Diario* (Lima: Ediciones Amauta, 1989); Confederacion Campesina del Perú, *Movilización campesina: respuesta democrática* (Lima: CCP, 1989). For racism and countersinsurgency, see Nelson Manrique and Alberto Flores Galindo, *Violencia y campesinado* (Lima: Instituto de Apoyo Agrario, 1986).

8. See, for example, Gorriti, *Sendero*, 158–69, where he attributes the creation of totalitarian politics and terror to Marx and Marxist traditions.

9. See, for example, Nelson Manrique, "Violencia e imaginario popular," in *Tiempos de ira y amor*, ed. Carlos I. Degregori et al. (Lima: Desco, 1990).

10. See Carlos Tapia, *Las fuerzas armadas y Sendero Luminoso* (Lima: IEP, 1997); also see Comisión de la Verdad y Reconciliación, *Informe Final*, vol. 2, *Los actores del conflicto*, http://www.cverdad.org.pe.

11. See, for example, Carlos Contreras and Marcos Cueto, *Historia del Peru contemporáneo*, 4th ed. (Lima: IEP, 2004). See also Tapia, *Las fuerzas armadas y Sendero Luminoso*; Comisión de la Verdad, *Informe Final*, vol. 2.

12. Marín Hopenhayn, *No Apocalypse, No Integration: Modernism and Postmodernism in Latin America* (Durham: Duke University Press, 2002).

13. Arno J. Mayer, *The Furies: Violence and Terror in the French and Russian Revolutions* (Princeton: Princeton University Press, 2000), 3.

14. The first quote is from ibid.; the second is by Gareth Stedman Jones, quoted in Jacob Stevenson, "Exorcising the Manifesto," *New Left Review* 28 (2004), 158–59. The third statement on the New Left is made by José Luis Rénique "De la 'traición aprista' al 'gesto heroico'—Luis de la Puente Uceda y la guerrilla del MIR-3," *Ciberayllu*, June 11, 2004, available at http://www.andes.missouri.edu/andes.

15. Nelson Manrique, *El tiempo del miedo: la violencia política en el Peru, 1980–1996* (Lima: Fondo Editorial del Congreso, 2002), 17; Rénique "De la 'traición aprista.'"

16. Kobena Mercer, "Welcome to the Jungle: Identity and Diversity in Post-Modern Politics," in *Welcome to the Jungle* (New York: Routledge, 1994), 267.

17. Rénique, "De la 'traición aprista.'"

18. See José Carlos Mariátegui, *Siete ensayos de interpretacion de la realidad peruana* (Lima: Minerva, 1980).

19. For gamonalismo, see Deborah Poole, ed., *Unruly Order: Violence, Power and Cultural Identity in the High Provinces of Southern Peru* (Boulder, Colo.: Westview

Press, 1994); Nelson Manrique, *Mercado interno y región: la Sierra central, 1820–1930* (Lima: Desco, 1989); Nils Jacobsen, *Mirages of Transition: The Peruvian Altiplano, 1780–1930* (Berkeley: University of California Press, 1993).

20. Aníbal Quijano, "Raza, etnia, nación en Mariátegui: cuestiones abiertas," in *José Carlos Mariátegui y Europa*, ed. Roland Forgues (Lima: Editorial Amauta, 1993), 167–88.

21. Alberto Flores Galindo and Manuel Burga, *Apogeo y crisis de la república aristocrática*, 4th ed. (Lima: Ediciones Rikchay Perú, 1987), 85.

22. Howard Handelman, *Struggle in the Andes: Peasant Mobilization in Peru* (Austin: Texas University Press, 1975); Hugo Blanco. *Land or Death: The Peasant Struggle in Peru* (New York: Pathfinder Press, 1972); Eric J. Hobsbawm, "Peasant Land Occupations," *Past and Present*, no. 62 (1974); and Hugo Neyra, *Cuzco: tierra y muerte* (Lima: Problemas de Hoy, 1964).

23. See Comité Interamericano de Desarrollo Agrícola, *Tenencia de la tierra y desarrollo socio-económico del sector agrícola en el Perú* (Washington, D.C.: Pan American Union, 1966). See also Virginia Guzmán and Virginia Vargas, *El campesinado en la historia: cronología de los movimientos campesinos, 1956–1974* (Lima: Ideas, 1981); also see Neyra, *Cuzco: tierra y muerte*, 64, 72–73.

24. Handelman, *Struggle in the Andes*, 102.

25. Founded in 1924 by Víctor Raúl Haya de la Torre, Acción Popular Revolucionaria Americana (APRA) became the most important popular nationalist and antioligarchic political party in Peru. By the 1950s, it had made a strategic shift and forged an alliance with the oligarchy's bourgeois faction.

26. Denis Sulmont, *Historia del movimiento obrero peruano, 1890–1977* (Lima: Tarea, 1977), 124–25, 209–13.

27. Originally established in 1929 as the Partido Socialista after the death of its founder, José Carlos Mariátegui, it became the Partido Comunista Peruano, affiliated with the Comintern (Communist International).

28. Alberto Flores Galindo, "Las sociedades andinas," in *Tiempo de plagas* (Lima: El Caballo Rojo, 1988), 169–79. See also Alberto Flores Galindo. *Buscando un Inca: identidad y utopía en los Andes* (Lima: Instituto de Apoyo Agrario, 1987), 301–18.

29. See Gustavo Riofrío, *Se busca terreno para próxima barriada* (Lima: Desco, 1978); Teresa Tovar, "Barrios, ciudades y democracia," in *Movimientos sociales y democracia: la fundación de un nuevo orden*, ed. Eduardo Ballon (Lima: Desco, 1986).

30. Handelman, *Struggle in the Andes*, 79–80; Neyra, *Cuzco: tierra y muerte*, 64; Sulmont, *Historia del movimiento obrero peruano*, 123–24.

31. In the mid-twentieth century, while other indigenous regions of Latin America saw the emergence of popular left-wing indigenous movements, in Peru the end of servile relations and massive rural emigration unleashed a complex process of

"de-Indianization" of a great part of the Indian population in both rural and urban areas. This "de-Indianized" population adopted and made positive the previously derogatory identities of "cholo" and/or "mestizo." See Aníbal Quijano, "The Challenge of the 'Indigenous Movement' in Latin America," *Socialism and Democracy* 19, no. 3 (2005): 55–78.

32. Neil Harvey. *The Chiapas Rebellion: The Struggle for Land and Democracy* (Durham: Duke University Press, 1998).

33. Mayer, *The Furies*; Antonio Gramsci, *Selections from the Prison Notebooks* (London: Lawrence and Wishart, 1986), 210, 275–76.

34. For a subtle analysis of the tensions and contradictions of the importance of the Cuban Revolution for Peru's New Left, see Alberto Flores Galindo, "La Nueva Izquierda: sin faros ni mapas," in *Tiempo de plagas*, 136–44; see also Ricardo Letts, *La izquierda peruana* (Lima: Mosca Azul, 1981).

"Foquismo" is a revolutionary theory delineated by Ernesto "Che" Guevara in his text "Guerrilla Warfare: A Method" (in *Che: Selected Works of Ernesto Guevara* [Cambridge, Mass.: MIT Press, 1969]), which was developed by Regis Debray in *Revolution in the Revolution* (New York: Grove Press, 1967). The theory claimed that in the underdeveloped countries a small rural guerrilla force could create the "subjective" conditions for a popular uprising and a socialist revolution.

35. Peter F. Klaren, *Peru: Society and Nationhood in the Andes* (New York: Oxford University Press, 1999), 333.

36. Tad Szulc. "Change Is Noted in Latin Church: Support Reported Growing for Social Revolution," *New York Times*, February 1, 1965; Andrés Gallego and Rolando Ames, eds., *Gustavo Gutiérrez: acordarse de los pobres. Textos esenciales* (Lima: Fondo Editorial del Congreso del Perú, 2004).

37. Víctor Villanueva, *El CAEM y la revolución de la Fuerza Armada* (Lima: IEP, 1972)

38. See Monika Ludescher, "Estado e indígenas en el Perú," *Law and Anthropology*, 10 (1999): 122–264.

39. Villanueva, *El CAEM y la revolución de la Fuerza Armada*, and *¿Nueva mentalidad militar en el Perú?* (Lima: Editorial Mejía Baca, 1969).

40. For "passive revolution," see Gramsci, *Selections from the Prison Notebooks*, 106–20.

41. APRA and the military maintained an animosity that had its origins in the killing of more than thirty officers and soldiers of the Peruvian armed forces by APRA rebels during the 1932 Trujillo insurrection and the ensuing summary death by firing squad of alleged hundreds of APRA militants.

42. The Alliance for Progress was the United States' broad assistance program for Latin America, started in 1961 by the Kennedy administration. The Alliance was

established with the explicit purpose to counter the influence of the Cuban Revolution. Along with initiatives to relieve poverty and social inequality, it also included programs of military and police assistance, and training in counterinsurgency methods.

43. Augusto Zimmerman, *El plan Inca: objetivo, revolución peruana* (Lima: El Peruano, 1970), 127, 135–36.

44. See Frederick Nunn, "Professional Militarism in Twentieth-Century Peru: Historical and Theoretical Background to the Golpe de Estado of 1968," *Hispanic American Historical Review* 59, no. 3 (1979): 391–417.

45. See Daniel Masterson, *Militarism and Politics in Latin America: Peru from Sánchez Cerro to Sendero Luminoso* (New York: Greenwood Press, 1991), 163.

46. Nunn, "Professional Militarism in Twentieth-Century Peru," 416.

47. Quoted by Nunn, in ibid., 398, 392, 407.

48. Sulmont, *Historia del movimiento obrero peruano*, 102–4.

49. Peter H. Smith, *Talons of the Eagle: Dynamics of U.S.-Latin American Relations* (New York: Oxford University Press, 2000), 126, 131.

50. Villanueva,. *El CAEM y la revolución de la Fuerza Armada,* 65–71; Masterson, *Militarism and Politics in Latin America,* 212–13.

51. Masterson, *Militarism and Politics in Latin America,* 217, Villanueva, *El CAEM y la revolución de la Fuerza Armada,* 73.

52. A second, short-lived guerrilla campaign was conducted by the Ejército de Liberación Nacional (National Liberation Army), made up of former members of the youth wing of the Partido Comunista Peruano in the highland department of Ayacucho.

53. Sara Beatriz Guardia, *Proceso a campesinos de la guerrilla Tupac Amaru* (Lima: n.p., 1972); Villanueva, ¿*Nueva mentalidad militar en el Perú*. The *New York Times* reported one hundred deaths as consequence of five hundred pounds of napalm dropped in bombing raids around the Satipo-Pucuta area; see "Peru Bombs Andean Jungle in Drive on Pro-Red Bands," *New York Times,* August 14, 1965. See also Henry Raymont, "Peru Reports Anti-Guerrilla Drive," *New York Times*, September 11, 1965; "Peru Said to Hit Rebels from Air, Bombings Are Reported," *New York Times*, September 20, 1965; and "U.S. Copters to Aid Peru's War on Reds," *New York Times*, September 30, 1965.

54. Villanueva, *El CAEM y la revolución de la Fuerza Armada*, 137; Masterson, *Militarism and Politics in Latin AmericaI*, 219.

55. *Manifiesto del Gobierno Revolucionario de las Fuerzas Armadas, 2 de Octubre de 1968*, quoted in Villanueva, ¿*Nueva mentalidad militar en el Perú?* 199–201.

56. Aníbal Quijano, *Nationalism and Capitalism in Peru: A Study in Neo-Imperialism* (New York: Monthly Review Press, 1971).

57. Monika Ludescher, "Estado e indígenas en el Perú."

58. Mayer, *The Furies*.

59. Arce Borja, *Guerra popular en el Perú.*

60. Mayer, *The Furies*, 17–18.

61. Manrique, "Violencia e imaginario," and Rénique, "De la traición aprista." See also Florencia Mallon, "Vanguardia Revolucionaria and Shining Omens in the Indigenous Communities of Andahuaylas," and Ivan Hinojosa, "On Poor Relations: The Nouveau Riche, Shining Path and the Radical Peruvian Left," both in *Shining and Other Paths: War and Society in Peru, 1980–1995*, ed. Steve Stern (Durham: Duke University Press, 1998). For a critical assessment of the Left and popular democratic culture in Peru, see Deborah Poole and Gerardo Rénique, "Popular Movements, the Legacy of the Left, and the Fall of Fujimori," *Socialism and Democracy* 14, no. 2 (2000): 53–74.

62. Mark Mazower, "Violence and the State in the Twentieth Century," *American Historical Review* (October 2002): 1171–72.

63. For Guzmán's adoption of Kant's conception of real or exclusive oppositions, see Poole and Rénique, *Peru: Time of Fear*, 50–51.

64. For *gamonal* forms of violence in Sendero, see Poole, *Unruly Order*, and Carlos I. Degregori, "Harvesting Storms: Peasant *Rondas* and the Defeat of Sendero Luminoso in Ayacucho," in Stern, *Shining and Other Paths*, 131–32.

The Cold War That Didn't End

Paramilitary Modernization in Medellín, Colombia

FORREST HYLTON

There is no revolution without counterrevolution.
—ALBERTO LLERAS CAMARGO

The cold war is not yet two decades over, yet what seemed to be its enduring resolution—the "Washington Consensus" of the 1990s—has already unraveled. In many Latin American countries, particularly along the
Andean corridor, a revived Left has emerged to fill the vacuum. In Colombia, though, a distinct form of state formation is being advanced, one that,
even as it seeks to break the impasse of a now five-decade-long civil war,
draws heavily from historic yet dynamic patterns of political repression,
regional configurations of capital accumulation, and patriarchial networks
of local power. Its showcase is Medellín, the most conservative city in the
continent's most conservative country. In the face of a string of leftist successes in the Andes, with radical populists elected in Venezuela, Bolivia,
Ecuador, and Paraguay, the Right in recent years can boast one spectacular
triumph. Medellín has been undergoing a dramatic boom for the past few
years. Even before the crash of the housing market in the United States,
levels of high-rise construction in Medellín surpassed those of Los Angeles
and New York combined. Since 2002, the profusion of apartment towers,
luxury hotels, supermarkets, and shopping malls has been breathtaking.
The country's largest conglomerates and over seventy foreign enterprises
now have their Colombian headquarters in Medellín, among them Philip
Morris, Kimberly Clark, Levi Strauss, Renault, Toyota, and Mitsubishi. A
thirty-thousand-square-foot convention center opened in 2005, and over

a dozen international business conferences have been held there annually, generating more than $100 million in investment and business deals annually. Medellín's fashion industry is at present second only to São Paulo's; its medical sector is a Latin American leader in organ transplants, AIDS research, and cancer research. An upscale museum-park complex in the city center, replacing the old outdoor market and red-light district, houses the work of the Medellín artist Fernando Botero—whose renderings of torture at Abu Ghraib earned worldwide recognition—with sculptures featured in an open-air setting.

In 2005 Colombian TV launched a local version of the U.S. program *Extreme Makeover*, in which contestants submit to the cosmetic surgeon's knife and emerge with a radically altered appearance. In Medellín, the show's popularity was emblematic of the city's own transformation over the last decade. Medellín is a media-saturated, image-conscious city, dominated by advertising and public relations; billboards abound, so it is impossible to avoid the message, projected by a small army of civic boosters, that Medellín is improving at breakneck speed. The emphasis on progress and modernization is relentless. Ruled by a live-and-let-live pact between right-wing narcoparamilitary forces, on the one hand, and a media-friendly center-left municipal government on the other, from 2002 to 2007, Medellín itself underwent a series of cosmetic operations quite as drastic as anything on TV.

During the 1980s the city had been notorious as the home of the narcobaron Pablo Escobar's Medellín Cartel. It ranked as the homicide capital of the world: between 1990 and 2002, fifty-five thousand people were murdered in Medellín, mainly young men.[1] The velocity of the change has been startling, even for cocaine capitalism: the city's homicide rate has now been reduced by a factor of six, and by 2005 was distinctly lower than those of Detroit, Baltimore, or Washington, D.C.[2] To cap it all, in 2006 Medellín's native son Álvaro Uribe Vélez succeeded in winning a historic second term as Colombia's president, having pushed through the necessary rewrite of the national constitution. What follows is an effort to understand the nature of the plastic surgery involved in Medellín's new look by analyzing the evolution of youth gangs, leftist guerrillas, and right-wing paramilitaries in the transition from an industrial to a FIRE (finance, insurance, and real estate) economy anchored in the production and export of cocaine.

From Gold to Coffee

The contemporary crisis needs to be placed in "overlapping long, medium, and short-term time frames," which, as Arno Mayer says in the interview in this volume, are needed to analyze the relationship of ideology to terror. Medellín's role as the capital of reaction in Latin America—and as the motor force in the politics of Uribe's Colombia—can only be explained in terms of its longer-term place in the country's history. Its contemporary particularities reflect patterns of class, racial, and regional formation inherited from the past two centuries. Medellín is situated in a broad upland valley, with mountain ranges to its east and west, in the cattle-ranching, banana, gold, and coffee country of Antioquia, where a deeply conservative Catholic Church has long been entrenched. Founded as a gold-mining town and trading center in 1675, Medellín emerged as the region's commercial capital by the late eighteenth century, its merchants profiting from the long-distance overland trade in cheap imported commodities. This period, when gold production exploded during the Bourbon reforms, provides the key to understanding ruling-class and regional formation. Gold mining took off in the second half of the eighteenth century in the lower Cauca River region, and then after 1780, in highland valleys, which were quickly settled in a widely dispersed network of towns.[3]

But it was through long-distance contraband trade in gold and British textiles that upwardly mobile, racially mixed entrepreneurs made room for themselves toward the top of a class hierarchy dominated by *criollos*. In the new highland commercial centers of Medellín and Rionegro, "black" became a synonym for "poor," reflecting the coexistence of race mixture and racism (one-third of the highland population was composed of slaves). Precisely because race mixture between "white" and "black" was so common in the nineteenth century (usually the result of informal unions between elite men and working women), these terms could be used to describe classes of "rich" and "poor" after slavery was abolished at mid-century. The language of class in Antioquia reflected the area's peculiar racial ideology, regional settlement patterns, and colonial legacy.[4]

Untouched by the Wars of Independence (1810–25), Antioquian elites became the country's leading merchant bankers but did not dominate export production, of which there was very little during the first three decades of the republic. That came later, in the last third of the nineteenth century and the beginning of the twentieth, when land-hungry *paisas* fanned out to the south to settle what became known as the "coffee axis" (*eje cafetero*), the center of national economic and cultural development through the 1960s. These *paisas*—"countrymen," the Antioquians' name for themselves—were united by a tenacious regional-chauvinist ideology: hard-working, light-skinned Catholic conservatives, identified against the "lazy" and undisciplined indigenous and Afro-Colombians in the south.[5] As mestizos, coffee smallholders shared with their rulers a sense of racial and cultural superiority. The church had strong, durable roots and institutional presence in schools and private lives throughout the country, nowhere more so than in Antioquia.

Rather than controlling land and labor, as they did in much of Antioquia, merchant-bankers controlled commercialization, credit, pricing, and transportation in the coffee axis to the south. In some cases they financed the settlement of new towns and incorporated a class of peasant smallholders into the clientelist networks of the Conservative and, to a lesser degree, the Liberal Party. Fin-de-siècle banking crashes prompted *antioqueño* coffee merchant-financiers to diversify from a single cash crop, vulnerable to price collapses on the international market, into light manufacturing. From the start, industrialization in Medellín developed out of local entrepreneurial initiatives and capital formation, rather than as a result of U.S. investment or franchises. At the beginning of the twentieth century, Antioquia—having emerged unscathed from the three-year civil conflict of 1899–1902, known as the War of a Thousand Days—moved to the center of national economic life, and Medellín became the key nexus for investment, speculation, and the accumulation of value.

The coffee boom, together with rapid industrial growth, spurred urban expansion: Medellín's population doubled to one hundred thousand in the first two decades of the twentieth century, and the organization and occupation of urban space changed dramatically as paisa elites adopted a self-consciously modernizing ideology. Urban planning was institutionalized in 1899 through the Sociedad de Mejoras Públicas (SMP), a "society for public improvements" run at the behest of the business lobby. The SMP allocated municipal contracts for parks, roads, and neighborhoods, and organized the paving of Santa Elena Canyon. An electricity plant was built in 1897, and street lighting installed in 1898. In 1889 an engineering school supplemented the city's first university, founded as early as 1871. Medellín had a regulated slaughterhouse in 1911, sewage treatment in 1913, and trolley cars by 1919.[6]

Catholic Corporatism

Most crucial for Medellín's subsequent development, however, was its burgeoning textile industry. Don Emilio Restrepo founded the region's first cotton mill in 1905, converting the nearby town of Bello into an industrial suburb. The initial workforce largely consisted of young women from the surrounding countryside. Textile factories offered a "respectable" occupation under the patriarchal protection of family firms and the Catholic Church. The Jesuits—following Leo XIII's *Rerum Novarum*—were an important influence on the first-generation working class, which enjoyed relatively good wages, benefits, and labor legislation. At the same time, migration from the coffee *municipios* of southern and southeastern Antioquia was crucial to the formation of Medellín's political culture, bringing a paternalist pattern of rural clientelism to the new industrial setting. This political culture and economy proved to be an inhospitable environment for independent class politics.

Led by the Restrepo and the Echeverría families, the city's industrialists exercised a personalized authority, as Catholic Social Action shaped the management of Don Jorge Echeverría's business empire—the two largest firms were Coltejer (founded in 1907) and Fabricato (1923)—emphasizing "absolute personal loyalty and obedience." This helped shape a working-class ethos of vertical ties to *patrones* and prompt, efficient execution of orders. Catholic elites and middle classes adopted an ideology of private charity and good works: the obligations of social betters to perceived inferiors. Where it emerged—as in a Communist-led strike wave in the mid-1930s—independent labor action was ruthlessly crushed, and did not survive the passage from one generation to the next.

The expanding city was largely managed through the SMP, which regulated urban space—prohibiting the carting of goods by mule train, for example, in order to make way for trams, cars, and bicycles; horses, cattle and donkeys were to be kept outside the city. The SMP oversaw the construction of middle- and working-class suburbs, and tore down historic sections of the center to make way for new buildings and office blocks. They also pressured landowners to convert rural areas of the city into the urban fabric. Avenida La Playa was readied for trams and cars, to carry workers and middle-class professionals to work from outlying neighborhoods during the 1920s and 1930s. Antioquia's regional development regime—industrialization, transport and communications networks, and urban restructuring—served as a model for the rest of the country after state elites translated economic clout into national political advantage between 1904 and 1920.

Import-substitution industrialization and production for the national market were the twin supports of this system in the postwar period. Light manufacturing—beverages, textiles (woolens and cotton), food, candy, cigarettes, coffee packing—was protected from competition by high tariffs on imported goods, and subsidized by generous government loans and credit as well as infrastructural development. Investment in industry was coordinated with state economic policy, especially after the mid-1940s. Cotton manufacturing in Medellín became "the crowning achievement" of the Colombian path to modernization.[7] The city's leaders were active forces in the formation of ANDI, the National Industrialists' Association, and Fedecafe, the Coffee Growers' Federation—powerful national lobbies that pushed their class interests. After the late 1940s, since ANDI succeeded in imposing protectionism over the objections of the *librecambistas* [free traders] in Fedecafe in the late 1940s, the two *gremios* [business lobbies] set much of the economic policy for the nation, with the central government acting as a transmission belt for its implementation.[8]

Industrial paternalism—initially as the self-proclaimed "protector" of the single working girl's virginity—was revamped in the 1940s and 1950s, as a second generation of industrialists took the reins of their family firms. The Restrepos and Echeverrías were convinced that the modern industrial factory could be made into a "mechanism for preventing the spread of communist agitation in Colombia" as well as "a model for society at large"; this would be the new idiom for oligarchic rule.[9] Women were as systematically removed from mill jobs as they had been recruited into them thirty years earlier, to be replaced by male "breadwinners" with "dependent" households. For male textile workers, who formed a small, relatively privileged minority of the Medellín proletariat, wage levels were high enough to permit consumption of domestic and imported goods; benefits included recreation, health, and schooling. Whereas Fordist production regimes deepened national markets through mass consumption throughout the North Atlantic, in Colombia, the industrial proletariat was a true "aristocracy of labor."

Unlike other industrial centers in Colombia—Barrancabermeja, Barranquilla, Cali, Santa Marta—organized labor in Medellín did not forge a distinctive tradition of independent class politics. Outside the Jesuit-led Unión de Trabajadores Colombianos, founded in 1946, the working class was fragmented. This was the golden age for Medellín's merchant-industrialist elite. In 1947 *Life* magazine tagged the city a "capitalist paradise." The "Manchester of Colombia" had skyscrapers, cinemas and theaters, wide avenues, parks and monuments, schools and universities, commercial boulevards for pedestrians, and a local railroad system, as well as innumerable well-endowed churches, their edifices bulking over every neighborhood. The city's equatorial-mountain climate, hovering at 18° centigrade, promised an "eternal spring."

The Cold War

The assassination of the populist Liberal leader Jorge Eliécer Gaitán in 1948, an overlooked event of the early cold war, helped plunge most of Colombia into the murderous civil conflict of La Violencia, and wiped out any hopes of an opening for left reformism within the state-sanctioned political arena.[10] Medellín remained untouched by the general carnage. In terms of profit rates and class collaboration, the city's economy continued to run smoothly—indeed, in 1947 and 1949, industrial production surpassed previous records. Though supporters of the Conservative president Mariano Ospina and, after 1950, the hard-right Laureano Gómez, paisa industrialists prohibited partisan propaganda in their factories during La Violencia, even if elites gave tacit sanction to killings in the peripheral municipalities.[11] Migrants who found jobs in the mills during this period continued to come from the central and southwest Antioquian coffee zones, where La Violencia was less intense than on the periphery, and Liberal supporters were not barred from jobs. Led by the Echeverrías and ANDI, the Medellín elite consciously promoted an image of the city as an "oasis" of peaceful capitalist productivity, beneficial to the nation, thanks to the social responsibility of its major industrialists. They gave full backing to the power-sharing deal known as the National Front Accord that was sealed between the parties, Liberal and Conservative, in 1957.

Yet the limits of the Antioquian model were already apparent. Each sector—textiles, cigarettes, beer, chocolates—remained subject to a family monopoly, and manufacturing never developed from light consumer goods into heavy goods and machinery. Capital investment was ultimately dependent on coffee remittances, recycled as subsidies for industry through the state's national-development fund. Any trickle-down remained tightly restricted, barely percolating beyond the upper layers of the textile employees when it came to turning workers into consumers. Once coffee prices entered the long decline of the 1960s and 1970s, and economies of the Far East—Taiwan, Hong Kong—became unbeatably competitive in terms of cheap clothing and light consumer goods, Medellín's days as a capitalist paradise were numbered.

At the same time, subdivision of inherited peasant plots, combined with population growth and the above-mentioned secular decline in coffee prices, contributed to worsening poverty in the countryside. The numbers streaming into the city in search of work increased after the mid-1960s. Squatter neighborhoods sprouted up the green hillsides on either side of the Medellín River, especially in the northern Aburrá Valley: warrens of hand-built dwellings constructed from cheap brick, wood, cinder blocks or *bareque*, and interconnected by steep flights of steps. Their expansion was guaranteed by the elite's stubborn blocking of agrarian reform. Within a few decades these fast-growing slums would house half the city's population of 2.2 million. Meager state resources were funneled through neighborhood committees, the Juntas de Acción Comunal. But the fact that police and army units were sent in to demolish hillside settlements was a symptom of the crisis of authority on the city's new frontiers.

Meanwhile, as industrial employment stagnated, a burgeoning layer of lower-middle- and working-class urban youth faced a jobless future; a larger public university system helped produce a new generation of the middle-class with higher education but lacking prospects of professional security.[12] The hopes raised by the expanding manufacturing economy of the postwar decades, for social mobility and improved housing, education, health, and working conditions, were dashed for succeeding generations by the crisis of the antioqueño model. As Medellín's new barrios organized, protested, and petitioned to obtain public services in the 1970s, a young, jobless, reasonably well-educated proletariat added an insurgent edge to the mobilizations. Rural guerrillas had been a permanent feature of the Colombian political landscape since the 1950s, remnants of a marginalized but resilient and deep-rooted Left; by the 1960s these were chiefly constituted in the FARC (Fuerzas Armadas Revolucionarias de Colombia) and ELN (Ejército de Liberación Nacional).

By the late 1970s a broader urban Left was becoming visible, as worker, student, and guerrilla networks began to converge with the new neighborhood movements on the hillsides. This nascent coalition was met with severe repression by state forces—trade unionists, students, professors, and left-wing community leaders were detained, beaten, or killed. The bipartisan National Front accords functioned to exclude left forces from official political representation. Popular initiative increasingly took the form of radical insurrectionism, aiming to overthrow the failed social model. But in Medellín, and eventually the country as a whole, it was the Right that took the offensive and forged a new order.

From el contrabando *to* la cocaína

The single most dynamic force contesting the Antioquian model's replacement in Medellín over the next two decades was the rising class of traffickers and import-export men, bred by the informal economy. Cheap goods—clothing, cars, cigarettes—smuggled in from the duty-free zone of Colón, Panama, in order to beat high import tariffs, would prove a lucrative alternative to domestic production, and an effective means of laundering money. Growing up in Rionegro and Envigado, conservative suburbs outside of Medellín, Pablo Escobar, son of a peasant-farmer and a schoolteacher mother, was dabbling in contraband and criminal activities from an early age. He cut his teeth as a young thug in the "Marlboro Wars" of the early 1970s, in which rival gangs fought over the contraband cigarette trade, and began to use hired killers against each other.[13]

Many leading cocaine capos of the second generation, including Escobar, got their start in the late 1960s as underlings in networks of contraband imports of U.S. manufactured goods run by older *contrabandistas*. These networks linked Miami and Colón to Turbo, Antioquia's Caribbean port in Urabá, as well as the string of towns in the Antioquian lowlands leading out to it—Frontino, Dabeiba, Mutatá, Chigorodó, Apartadó. In keeping with regional tradition, Escobar and his generation were ambitious contraband entrepreneurs: each had his own labor networks based on kinship and friendship, and collectively, they quickly displaced or killed the old men who had trained them. The level of violence they brought to the business was not inevitable, but may have been the condition of possibility for supplanting their elders.

Though portrayed as the leader of a "cartel," in reality by the end of the 1970s Escobar had established a monopoly on protection, making him the first among equals in a cocaine export consortium that included one traditional ruling-class family and many people of relatively "low birth," men of mixed racial backgrounds from undistinguished families—"blacks." With his monopoly on protection, Escobar was more *mafioso* than trafficker. Others were better at exporting cocaine, but they had to pay him for each kilo shipped. Coca paste purchased in Bolivia and Peru was flown to Colombia and refined into cocaine in clandestine laboratories. Through Escobar, "blacks became rich."[14]

In the 1970s and 1980s, the cocaine export business was far more dynamic than traditional manufacturing industries at the height of their expansion in the 1940s and 1950s, and created more jobs in the licit as well as illicit economy. More wealth was redistributed through patronage, clientelism, and corruption than had ever been redistributed during the previous era's oligarchic model of industrial development, in which each sector was monopolized by one or two family firms. And the generalized economic crisis of the 1970s meant that the new narcoentrepreneurs, with Escobar at the top, could tap into a vast pool of skilled and semiskilled labor in a city with industrial rhythms and infrastructure. Many people from these working-, middle-, and upper-middle-class layers became part of Escobar's retinue, earning far more than their counterparts in the licit economy.

Unprecedented amounts of illegally obtained cash had to be laundered through front businesses—car dealerships, hotels, auto shops, urban real estate companies, interior decorating and graphic design firms, modeling agencies, retail stores, restaurants, and upscale *discotecas*—and bogus accounting practices. For many of these jobs, only well-educated men from decent families (*doctores*) would do. Owned by traffickers through intermediaries, Colombian banks in Panama, Miami, and Medellín sprang up to meet the new demand for laundering. This helped the shift toward an economic model in which construction, real estate, insurance, and financial services were primary, while industry, excepting cocaine, was secondary.

Escobar and company faced little state repression, or even rhetorical sanction, and certainly none who could resist the offer of *plata o plomo*—silver or lead. This group established the various interlocking networks of the coca trade—purchase, processing, credit lines, transportation—that became known as the Medellín Cartel, and whose long tentacles linked the coffee heartlands to eastern tropical frontiers and the northern Atlantic coast. Escobar and others helped finance infrastructural projects, including roads and airports, to facilitate the development of the new industry. The glitzy tastes and brazen violence of this *clase emergente* were in dramatic contrast to the penny-pinching piety and conservatism of Medellín's traditional oligarchs. Of the city's ruling families, initially only the Ochoas—under the patriarchal leadership of Don Fabio, alias "El Gordo," the Fat One—bridged the gulf between old money and new. Land deals were the preferred method of laundering the truckloads of narcodollars. Escobar and others bought up vast tracts of impoverished cattle country in the tropical lowlands of northern Antioquia and the Magdalena Medio Valley, where land values were low as ranchers fled the threat of FARC kidnapping and extortion. Alberto Uribe Sierra, father of the current president of Colombia, married a poor relation of the Ochoas, was a key intermediary in these real-estate transactions, and soon became a major ranch owner himself. As cocaine money helped fuel a real estate and construction boom in which local capital, freed from industrial development, could make more lucrative investments, and with the central government encouraging the growth of business and financial services, the economic and political clout of the cartel was bolstered by a broader alliance with the old oligarchy.

Helicoptering in to their new domains, Medellín's narcobarons and their entourages found themselves prey to kidnapping and extortion by the local guerrillas. Their response was to recruit their own private armies and death squads, as well as agitating for stepped-up state-level counterinsurgency policies. In 1981 Escobar and other traffickers joined with army officers, police, and party bosses to organize MAS (Death to Kidnappers). They also turned their hired killers against FARC supporters and other leftists in Medellín itself, plunging the city into a murderous downward spiral. The narcoelite would impose its own solution to the social crisis of Medellín, at a terrible price. Narcocapital would be the bridge from the industrial model to the "new economy" makeover, based on finance, insurance, real estate, and services—though Escobar would have to be sacrificed in the process.

The rise of the contrabandistas to political influence in Medellín, and the country as a whole, did not go unopposed. The early career of President Uribe is instructive in this regard. Although he boasts a management diploma from Harvard, acquired in 1993, the eighteen-year-old Uribe passed out of Medellín's Jorge Robledo high school in 1970 with "special exemption" from the final examinations. As his father's income swelled through land deals, the young Uribe was fast-tracked through the municipal authority structures: he became head of the real estate office of Medellín's Public Works Department in 1976, at the age of twenty-four. After stints at the Labor Ministry and the Department of Civil Aviation—where pilots' licenses were distributed for the fleet of planes working for Escobar—Uribe was ushered in as mayor of Medellín in 1982, as quid pro quo for his father's contributions to Belisario Betancur's presidential campaign. But this proved unacceptable to some of Antioquia's traditional politicians. After five months, Uribe, who would openly avail himself of Escobar's organization when his father was killed on his ranch by the FARC in 1983, was removed from the mayor's office.

Wholesale Slaughter

The vector of multiplying murder and mayhem, one that turned the city into a war zone on par with Beirut, was not the cocaine business itself. It was the determination of a reformist wing of the Liberal Party, on the one hand, and the Reagan administration, on the other, to drive Escobar out of politics and extradite him and his business partners to the United States. In 1982, not long before Uribe was appointed mayor of Medellín—by then, the city had become known to traffickers as "the sanctuary"—Escobar became an alternate deputy for one of the Liberal Party's consummate political bosses (caciques) after being publicly expelled from the "New Liberalism" by two rising young stars within the Liberal Party, Luis Carlos Galán and Rodrigo Lara Bonilla. Through his cacique and an intermediary, Escobar tried to expose Lara Bonilla's alleged ties to drug money in Congress, but Lara Bonilla retaliated, depriving Escobar of parliamentary immunity and seeking to extradite him. In March 1984, Lara Bonilla also oversaw an operation that seized fifteen tons of cocaine at the cartel's Tranquilandia laboratory complex.

This was tantamount to a declaration of war. In April 1984 Escobar had Lara Bonilla killed by a young assassin on a motorcycle (a type of violence Escobar had personally helped pioneer ten years earlier in Medellín), and then fled to Noriega's Panama. Escobar and his associates, who now called themselves "the Extraditable Ones"—the Castaños, Galeanos, Moncadas, Ochoas, and Gonzalo Rodríguez Gacha, alias "El Mejicano"—offered to turn themselves in and dismantle their export business if the government refused to implement the extradition treaty signed with the United

States. Under pressure from domestic public opinion as well as the U.S. government, the administration of Belisario Betancur declined. In July 1984, the judge investigating Lara Bonilla's assassination was murdered; the following November, Escobar's men set off a car bomb outside the U.S. Embassy in Bogotá. Escobar was soon to became the "true *empresario* of the car bomb in the Western Hemisphere."[15]

In its war against Colombia's numerous incorruptible politicians, civil servants, police, and journalists, the region's cocaine export mafia turned select groups of young men from Medellín's *comunas*, particularly in the northeast (Comunas 1–4), into a private army of snipers and hit men. U.S. Drug Enforcement Agency operatives as far away as Miami feared them. This "armed wing" (*brazo armado*) of the mafia operated through a series of front businesses (*oficinas*) that managed relations between Escobar and gangs like Los Priscos, Los de Rigo, and La Germania in the northeast, "Tyson" and "Kika" Múñoz Mosquera in the northwest, and La Ramada in Bello (the industrial suburb just across the northern border of Medellín). The army and police, in turn, targeted young men in the comunas and Bello for massacre.

Continued urban warfare spurred the specialization, concentration, and professionalization of youth gangs—the cell forms of organized crime in Medellín. A 1987 government-commissioned study concluded that it was impossible to speak of *la violencia* in Colombia; one now had to consider *las violencias*, especially in Medellín. Though Escobar had close ties to the M-19 guerrilla group, which began operations in the mid-1970s, his anticommunist associates—Fidel Castaño, el Negro Galeano, "el Mejicano"—had opposed the peace process between the government and rural insurgencies initiated by President Belisario Betancur, himself from Antioquia. Following the precedent set in the Middle Magdalena region (where Antioquia, Santander, Cundinamarca, and Boyacá meet the Magdalena River), which had been "cleansed" of communists, trade unionists, and peasant radicals, the counterinsurgent bloc of traffickers announced its determination to rid the country of "subversion" by exterminating the Unión Patriótica (the UP, a broad left political party founded by the FARC) and the Partido Comunista Colombiano, or PCC, in 1985 as part of negotiations with the Bentancur administration.[16]

Though not as strong in Medellín as elsewhere, the UP offered the hope of a concerted resistance against both the old oligarchy and the new gangster class. But by organizing in the open, it also exposed its supporters to

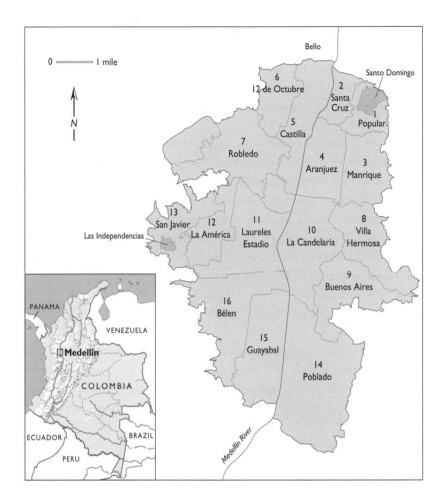

Map of Medellín, showing comunas.
Originally published in "Medellín's Makeover," *New Left Review* 44
(March–April 2007). Courtesy: *New Left Review*.

violent repression by the Right. In Antioquia as elsewhere, students, teachers, journalists, lawyers, and especially trade unionists and peasant activists associated with the alliance were subject to assassination. The UP was destroyed not as a result of internal failings, real as these were, but because it could not withstand the sustained right-wing terror directed against it.[17] The peace process between Betancur and the insurgencies unraveled in 1985–86 after the M-19 seized the Palace of Justice, and in Medellín death squads hit factories, universities, and high schools where the insurgencies and the UP recruited most heavily. Around the country, some five hundred UP militants and candidates—including the popular presidential candidate Jaime Pardo Leal—were murdered. In 1989, when the Antioquian governor Antonio Roldán Betancourt publicly condemned massacres carried out by right-wing death squads against UP supporters, Escobar and associates killed him with a car bomb.

Soon after, they car-bombed the Bogotá offices of *El Espectador*—which stubbornly supported extradition after "the Extraditables" assassinated its distinguished editor, Guillermo Cano, in 1986—and, in August 1989, assassinated Luis Carlos Galán, Escobar's bête noire, an unusually popular politician sure to have won the Liberal Party nomination. Galán would likely have reopened negotiations with left insurgents, and prospects for peace receded in the wake of his death as armed left militias multiplied throughout Comunas 1 and 2 in the northeast.

Armies of the Left

Though there had been gangs in the city since the 1960s, their activities had never impinged directly on everyday life. Now they put a brake on processes of community self-organization—education, public services, and better employment—making many of the hillside neighborhoods all but unlivable. The late 1980s therefore witnessed the spread of nominally independent *milicias populares*—"popular militias"—initially under the supervision of left community activists and guerrilla leaders from the Ejército de Liberación Nacional (ELN) and M-19. United by a broadly left-insurrectionary outlook, they aimed to root out gangs and crime from their neighborhoods through force of arms, and institute their own form of self-government.

The negotiations initiated with the rural guerrilla forces by the Betancur government in the early 1980s had allowed for the establishment of safe havens, euphemistically called "campos de paz," which played an important role in educating and training the popular militias. Building on preexisting, yet loose and shape-shifting youth gang structures at the local level, the ELN in the northeast, and the FARC in Comuna 13 and other western districts, endeavored to fashion urban militias in preparation for armed insurrection.[18] Before the state intervened against them, popular militias, most of them linked in one way or another to the ELN, succeeded in defeating small and medium-sized criminal gangs. Militias were dedicated, at least in theory, to community empowerment, and their activities included improvement projects such as clean-up, paving, painting, sports and recreation, as well as night patrols and the resolution of domestic and neighborly disputes.[19]

The immediate outcome of state repression was to strengthen the armed groupings of the Left. Responding to the deteriorating political and security situation, the growth of popular militias accelerated in the late 1980s; many of their commanders enjoyed popular support and legitimacy.[20] If the former governor Gilberto Echeverry's fear of a communist takeover of the city, expressed in a letter to the Liberal president César Gaviria, seems comically exaggerated—especially in light of global shifts then unfolding—the spread of microsovereignties, exercised in the name of "the people," was real.[21]

Given the overall balance of power, however, the provisional victories of popular militias against the smaller gangs could only give rise to more violent, professional criminal groupings with closer ties to narcotrafficking and, ipso facto, elements within the state security agencies. For Escobar's networks, war with the left militias served as a laboratory for gang mutation toward concentration, centralization, and fusion with the most authoritarian elements of the state. Under siege, the left militias now began to reproduce the authoritarian state and gangster practices against which they had organized themselves. This was an evolution comparable—*mutatis mutandis*—to that of ETA elements in the Basque country or Provos in Northern Ireland. Ultimately, the armed urban Left would be undermined not only due to state repression and growing gangster terror but also because it lacked the political resources to combat those tendencies within its own ranks.[22]

Law and Disorder

A besieged President Barco invited greater U.S. military and Drug Enforcement Agency involvement in fighting the Extraditable Ones, and U.S. anti-drug aid to the Colombian military and police would jump from $300 million to $700 million between 1989 and 1991. With the Medellín and Cali organizations at war with one another in 1989, a U.S.-trained and -funded elite joint task force of out-of-towners—the Bloque de Búsqueda, or Search Bloc—was formed to hunt Escobar and the young men who worked for him. In response, Escobar put a price on the head of each policeman not working for him. Often coordinating with local National Police loyal to Escobar, hired killers from *las oficinas* eliminated the out-of-towners in rapid succession. In the first fifteen days, thirty were killed.

In November 1989, one of Escobar's lieutenants blew up a passenger plane in mid-flight, killing 110 people, in a botched effort to kill César Gaviria, Galán's successor in the Liberal Party (and future president). The following month, a truck bomb exploded in front of the headquarters of Colombia's secret police—at that time, the largest ever detonated outside the Middle East—creating a crater that damaged twenty-three city blocks and killed fifty-nine people, injured a thousand, and damaged more than fifteen hundred buildings. In return, the Bloque de Búsqueda massacred young people by the hundreds. There were four thousand homicides that year in Medellín.

Escobar hired a veritable army from the northeastern and northwestern Medellín comunas to wage war against the state.[23] Some five hundred policemen were assassinated in Medellín in 1990–91, and Escobar's minions set off 150 car bombs. In 1991, the new constitution drafted by President Gaviria's Constituent Assembly barred the extradition of Colombian nationals to the United States, and Escobar finally "turned himself in" to the prison he had built and staffed with handpicked police and bodyguards. Once Escobar had negotiated the terms of his surrender with the Gaviria government in July 1991—he would be jailed in a palatial "prison" of his own construction, staffed by his own guards—Colombian military, police, and intelligence agencies led a ferocious wave of repression against comuna dwellers: twenty to forty young men were found dead each weekend.[24] By 1992 Escobar had "escaped" and was at war with the government again; for the second consecutive year, there were more than six thousand homicides in Medellín.

Under renewed pressure from Washington, the Gaviria administration and U.S. agencies now forged an alliance with the Cali cartel and, crucially, Escobar's former associates in the Medellín Cartel, that came to be known as Los Pepes—an acronym for "Those Persecuted by Pablo Escobar." The group was founded by the brothers Carlos and Fidel Castaño, the Ochoas, what remained of the Galeanos and the Moncadas, and a retired military official known as "Rodrigo 00" (Doble Cero), who had led antiguerrilla death squads in the countryside with the Castaños. Throughout 1993 Carlos Castaño, a former Escobar employee, led the campaign against his ex-boss, using hit squads composed of gang youths from Medellín. Castaño went after Escobar's gangs and white-collar associates, but also targeted his own primordial enemies: "communist subversives."[25] An ally in this pursuit was Diego Fernando Murillo, known as Don Berna, head of security for one of Escobar's lieutenants, "el Negro" Galeano, before turning against the *capo di tutti capi*.

Unlike Escobar, Los Pepes wanted to work for the establishment, and their alliance with it was informal in name only. Their "local knowledge" consisted in fighting fire with fire: using money and intelligence from the Cali cartel, Los Pepes' kidnappers, torturers, killers, arsonists, and car bombers eliminated the legal infrastructure of Escobar's organization, the remaining oficinas of criminals and hired killers loyal to Escobar, and either destroyed or took over businesses and properties owned by intermediaries. They fed intelligence and information to the Bloque de Búsqueda (who also received it from the CIA and U.S. Army Intelligence), and vice versa. Don Berna met with the Bloque commander in front of Delta Force and DEA agents; the latter used Don Berna's men—who lived down the street from them—as bodyguards when going on missions off the military base to which they were theoretically confined.[26] Los Pepes had been given a license to massacre, and the carnage was epic, on the scale of La Violencia of the 1950s. In 1993, the homicide rate was 311 per 100,000, nearly ten times higher than it would be in 2006. Five thousand five hundred Medellín residents were murdered in total, with Los Pepes killing as many as six of Escobar's people per day. Victims would appear in public, with signs around their neck containing messages signed by Los Pepes, who took advantage of the climate of terror they had created in order to take over organized crime in the city.

Soon after Escobar was murdered in December 1993, several dozen trade unionists were slaughtered throughout the Valle de Aburrá—a signal that despite Escobar's death, Carlos Castaño, Rodrigo oo, and Don Berna had arrived to stay. Don Berna's job was to take care of high finance and investment in the city, as well as to manage gangs of hit men, oficinas, and, not least, politicians, from the neighborhood level all the way up to congressional representatives and senators. In the early Clinton years, no one in Washington was concerned about former U.S. allies in Antioquia. With the network of contacts developed during the Los Pepes period, Don Berna and La Terraza, a gang of gangs based in Manrique (Comuna 3), became the principal conduit through which cocaine from the emergent "cartel" from the northern part of the department of Valle del Cauca—where Don Berna was born—flowed toward U.S. consumer markets through Urabá. Escobar's death therefore signaled not the end of narcocapital's influence in Medellín, but its coming of age.

From the Governor's Mansion to the "Casa de Nari"

By 1995, the influence of the *clase emergente* was apparent at three different levels. First, the links forged through Los Pepes had strengthened the ties between state-security organs, narcoparamilitaries and Medellín's gangs. Second, cocaine capital laundered through real estate, finance, insurance, and construction had now captured the state government of Antioquia, in the person of Álvaro Uribe.[27] After serving as a Medellín city councilor in the mid-1980s, Uribe had been a senator representing Antioquia from 1986 to 1994 and in 1995 was elected governor of the state. Together with his consigliere, Pedro Juan Moreno Villa—later named by the DEA for his suspiciously large potassium permanganate imports—Uribe now moved to bind the paramilitary forces of the cocaine industry into Colombia's state security system. The mechanism for this was the Defense Ministry's new *Convivir* structure—designed to give government backing to local "security and vigilance" units grouped alongside Colombia's military and police. Financed by private enterprise but, with Uribe in the governor's mansion, operating with "the support and legal sanction of the state," these heavily armed death squads enjoyed near-total impunity; killings of human-rights activists and labor leaders duly accelerated.[28] In Antioquia and Córdoba, the Convivir were largely coextensive with Castaño's ACCU paramilitaries (Autodefensas Campesinas de Córdoba y Urabá). Seven Convivir units functioned in Medellín alone.[29]

From the mid-1990s, a third development helped to cement the new order at street level. Don Berna had inherited the "Envigado Office"—a network of specialist killers—after Escobar's death. Gang leaders now negotiated formal arrangements with Medellín's municipal government through the newly created "Office of Peace and Coexistence."[30] For many, this simply meant joining the Convivir. In the late 1990s, publicly sanctioned security forces incorporated into Don Berna's growing network "cleansed"—*limpiaron*—a large area of the city center, dominated by a red-light district and open-air market on the north side and a street of gay salons to the west. Hired thugs in the pay of Don Berna threatened, displaced, or murdered the district's "disposable" inhabitants—drug sellers, addicts, prostitutes, street kids, petty thieves, called *desechables*—to make it safe for urban redevelopment. After 2000, this city-wide "pacification" campaign was supported by state security forces, businessmen, politicians of both parties, and the Catholic Church.

The alliance between Don Berna and Carlos Castaño, which began to incorporate more and more of the city's gang structure, constituted a near monopoly of violence. That made it a state unto itself. Don Berna's *muchachos* were organized into the Bloque Cacique Nutibara; Castaño's forces worked under the local commander Rodrigo 00—another veteran of Los Pepes—in a unit called the Bloque Metro. Making offers that local gang leaders could not refuse, the two groups had conquered 70 percent of the city by 2002, according to the state's intelligence agencies. Gangs that tried to hold out were either forced to pay tribute or disappeared altogether by the time the paramilitaries demobilized in late 2003.

Nevertheless, leftist militias continued to control substantial redoubts in the slums of the northeast and west of Medellín. Comuna 13 remained an unbreachable stronghold. In May 2002, after the mayor and his entourage were repelled by gunfire, state forces launched a military offensive code-named Operation Mariscal on Comuna 13; the troops withdrew after intensive house-to-house fighting failed to break the militias. Following Uribe's election as president in 2002, however, further massive assaults were launched. In late 2002 and early 2003, the army's Operation Orión against Comuna 13 was allegedly coordinated with Bloque Metro and Bloque Cacique Nutibara paramilitaries, who remained behind to occupy the conquered territories. By the end of 2003, Don Berna had taken over the city's independent gangs and, with the help of his network in state security agencies, vanquished the last of the remaining militias, as well as Bloque Metro, which had become a liability; an assassin in the employ of the Bloque Cacique Nutibara killed Doble Cero in May 2004.[31]

A new order had been established in Medellín, one that would outlive its chief narcoparamilitary architect. Don Berna's trajectory from hired gun to mafia don to "pacifier" of Medellín epitomizes the refeudalization of power in Colombia's neoliberalized economy, underwritten by cocaine profits as the former, industrial model was based on coffee. This fusion of politics, property, and organized crime, reflected in the paramilitary grip over security for capital investment, links the city's bad old days to its good new ones, and largely determines the present and future shape of the built environment.

By the time he demobilized the Bloque Cacique Nutibara in November 2003, Don Berna had become the undisputed don of dons in Medellín, accomplishing what Escobar could not: the unification of organized crime with the establishment. Following Don Berna's victory over rivals, homicide and violent-crime rates fell precipitously, even as the city's first mass graves for the uncounted dead were uncovered in the central west and northeast. When Don Berna was arrested in mid-2005, his control of the transport sector allowed him to direct a two-day general strike in protest. Unlike other strikes in Uribe's Colombia, this one did not meet with military or police violence.

While continuing to manage extortion, contract killing, gambling, drug sales, and so on, from prison, Don Berna also had an important hand in construction, transport, wholesale and retail, finance, fashion, private security, real-estate development, and cable television. In the 2004 elections, thirty of Don Berna's candidates won posts as heads of neighborhood associations, the Juntas de Acción Comunal. They campaigned through an nongovernmental organization called Corporación Democracia, led by Giovanni Marín, alias Comandante R, a butcher-turned-ideologue who ran for Congress in 2006, but failed to make the jump from crime to official politics. Regarding his past, Marín declared, "My conscience is clear. People should know that we collaborated in pacifying the city; that we handed over a city at peace."[32] Once he had been extradited to the United States in June 2008, Don Berna preferred to declare himself guilty than to respond publicly about his political-military actions, or to name names of generals, businessmen, and public officials. The region's ruling class should have been grateful indeed.

Parcelized Sovereignty

Don Berna's pacification process coincided with the landslide election victory of Mayor Sergio Fajardo in October 2003. Superficially, the *modus operandi* of each pole of power and authority could hardly be more different. Fajardo is U.S.-educated (a doctoral thesis in mathematics from the University of Wisconsin–Madison), a jeans-wearing newspaper columnist and media personality, an "independent" of the Center Left, untarnished by identification with either of Colombia's political parties. Support for him was strongest amongst the middle class, but was astonishingly high overall—around 90 percent at one point, compared to President Uribe's estimated 70 percent. Boosters liked to point to Fajardo's relative lack of corruption: accounting processes were transparent, budgeting participatory. This needs some qualification: Fajardo's family owns one of Colombia's largest construction and cement firms, which allegedly benefited from

King Juan Carlos of Spain Library, Santo Domingo, Comuna 1.
Photo by Lina Britto. Courtesy: Lina Britto.

noncompetitive contracts to build luxury housing in El Poblado, the city's
wealthiest neighborhood.

Fajardo undertook a program of showpiece public works, many aimed at
the hillside slums where the state has either been absent, or manifest only
as a heavy fist. An ambitious project called Medellín, the Most Educated involved the construction of six public park and library complexes in areas like
the northeastern and western comunas, to go along with ten new schools
that will serve twenty thousand students, at a total cost of $1.6 billion. As
the map of schools and park-library complexes demonstrates, for the first
time city government is establishing a nonrepressive presence in comunas
long disputed by gangs, militias, and narcoparamilitaries. The library in
Santo Domingo, in the northeast, is to sit on the other side of a high wall
from the neighborhood's houses. Composed of two black pod-like structures, it looks like a military research installation (similar to a branch office
of U.C. Berkeley's Livermore Laboratory). This is the classic architecture of
pacification, with security functions built into the design.[33] "Pacification" is
the condition of possibility for the much-touted improvements in tourism,

investment, and security. Taking the credit for it, Don Berna explained that his troops understood the need to create the "necessary climate so that investment returns, particularly foreign investment, which is fundamental if we do not want to be left behind by the engine of globalization."[34]

The chief political aim of the narcoparamilitaries has long been negotiated demobilization—"going legit"—and the Medellín municipal government offered demobilizing paramilitaries the best terms in the country, which included job skills training, another point of convergence of the agendas advanced by City Hall and Don Berna. By 2006, close to four thousand demobilized paramilitaries flocked to the city. But the major area of agreement remains the necessity of adapting the city to the needs and security of foreign capital. Don Berna's concern to create a favorable climate for overseas investors has been noted; Fajardo echoes the need to "project" the image of a "vibrant city, once again taking its place as a business hub and tourist destination."[35]

Andean Paradigm?

For over half a century, Medellín has been an exemplar for national development far beyond Colombia's borders; a "capitalist paradise" of the cold war. The city appears ready to assume the role once more. When Medellín's native son and Antioquia's former governor Álvaro Uribe was inaugurated as president of Colombia, the outlaws became the establishment, a development predicted by the brilliant comedian and peace activist Jaime Garzón, who was murdered on the orders of Carlos Castaño in August 1999. Following the crisis of the 1970s and early 1980s and the shift away from protected manufacturing toward banking, real estate, and financial services, a new class of narcoentrepreneurs, whose influence radiated outward to those above and below them, precluded the emergence of a national popular bloc, the seeds of which were decimated by state and paramilitary violence.

Medellín's model of a dynamic, narcotics-based, finance, insurance, real estate and service-sector economy—its slums now gilded with the occasional showpiece project—has become nationalized. If neoliberalism can generally be understood to represent a restoration of ruling-class power, in Medellín it has been infinitely bloodier, and more tinged by a cold war history of counterinsurgency than elsewhere in the hemisphere.[36] Unable to continue converting their power into official political representation, narcoparamilitary bosses like Don Berna have seen their authority wane since the "para-gate" scandal began in late 2006, but narcoparamilitarism continues to rule Medellín, and much of Colombia. It is a form of neoliberalism in extremis, in which private economic-political power supplants the state in the form of a parastate, one that performs state functions but is opposed to democratic accountability *in principle*.

Paramilitary organization depends largely on the unquestioning loyalty and obedience of subalterns to superiors, and is not responsive to the needs of its foot soldiers, much less the citizenry of *barrios populares*. Organized along mafia lines, the parastate of neoliberalism was deepened through political terror, extraeconomic coercion, and rent extraction backed by threats, intimidation, and violence. The popular economy of the slums has been incorporated into paramilitary rackets—protection, drugs and guns, public works, transportation, labor markets, licit commerce, rental housing— while the city center has been made safe for banking and financial services, tourism, "culture," business conferences, real estate speculation, and local as well as foreign capital investment. Private security firms, many of them paramilitary-owned, guard downtown, as well as the showpiece projects in the slums. More than half of Medellín's population lives in poverty; three-quarters of people in the hillside comunas earn less than the minimum wage; nearly half a million lack basic services—water, sewage, electricity.

Despite its progressive, democratic facade, the new order is antidemocratic to the core, and not only accepts appalling levels of inequality, injustice, impunity, and political murder, but clouds the issues with endless public relations offensives. As the twenty-first century began, the ruling right-wing alliance—of neoliberal elites, paramilitary death squads, narcotraffickers, and politicians looking for a way out of the impasse of civil war—generated a perverse form of paramilitary modernization that deepened neoliberalism through the parcelization of sovereignty: a new pole of power, the parastate, that emerged alongside the state. Although Don Berna no longer runs organized crime in Medellín, neither his sudden departure from the local scene nor the Fajardo-Salazar demobilization program has cast enough light to wipe out the long narcoparamilitary shadow cast over the city's working-class majority in the comunas, and its valuable real estate in the city center and suburbs.

After three generations of cocaine-fueled urban warfare, Medellín is positioned to become the leading edge of economic integration with the

United States, by linking the coffee axis of the Andean interior to the Pacific and Atlantic coasts. Since 1990, Antioquia has been planned as "the best corner of America" for large-scale capital investment in mining, transport infrastructure, megaprojects like dams and canals, hardwood logging, and palm plantations. Regional elites appear close to achieving their dream, first expressed during the coffee export boom more than a century ago, to integrate their highland capital with the lowlands of the Caribbean and Pacific littorals, against the backdrop of American free-trade projects for the hemisphere.[37]

Thus tectonic shifts in Medellín's political geomorphology can only be understood against the larger national context and interstate system in which the city and its hinterlands are embedded. In the 1980s and 1990s, Colombia's longstanding "organic crisis" turned into a deadlocked civil war, with the United States backing the Colombian military-paramilitary Right, and the FARC helping to shape the global narcotics industry at the point of production. Recent neoliberal modernization under Uribe appeared to break the deadlock, nowhere more so than in Medellín. In retrospect it is therefore clear that, to quote Mayer again, as in Europe in the early twentieth century, in Medellín and Colombia in the early twenty-first century, whatever the "extent and intensity of crisis, it [didn't take] the form of pre-revolution rooted in popular discontent and protest. In fact, the essence of the crisis was the opposite: a drive by aggressive ultra-conservatives to harden the established order."[38]

Yet if the region's ruling class has overcome its qualms in turning to narcocapital and paramilitaries to secure investment, property rights, and profitability, such a basis provides little grounds for the new order's legitimacy. Though paramilitary chiefs did well from Uribe's demobilization program—until fourteen were extradited in May 2008 because some of them had begun "to sing" (*cantar*)—paramilitary grunts have either found themselves returned to the bleak social conditions they sought to escape, or have continued fighting for new, "emergent [paramilitary] groups"—which are in reality a mix of new and old—in the wake of demobilization.

After being extradited to the United States in June 2008, Don Berna pleaded guilty to charges of trafficking cocaine and laundering money, preempting any discussion of connections to politicians, businessmen, bankers, military and police officials, and landlords. In 2008–9, however, disgruntled paramilitaries led by Salvatore Mancuso and Éver Veloza, alias

H.H., considering themselves short-changed by the outcome of Uribe's demobilization initiatives, began to talk about dealings with generals, politicians, business leaders, and U.S. multinationals, and were promptly extradited to the United States along with a dozen other top military chiefs. Mancuso has begun to discuss massacres committed under his orders in Antioquia when Uribe was governor. For his part, Don Berna wrote an open letter, from his prison cell in the Metropolitan Detention Center in Brooklyn, to Colombian authorities confirming his support for the current mayor Alonso Salazar's campaign.

In late March 2007 a CIA operative leaked documents to the *Los Angeles Times* showing that Colombia's army chief, General Mario Montoya, who commanded the 2002 Operation Orión assault on the slums of Medellín's Comuna 13, had signed an accord with one of Don Berna's henchmen and a local police commander on the joint planning and implementation of the offensive, which had left at least fourteen dead and dozens more "missing."[39] At the end of 2006 the congressional opposition led by the Polo Democrático Alternativo sparked a Colombian supreme court investigation into alleged rigging of regional elections by Uribe's allies, with narco-paramilitary collusion. Since then more than sixty legislators, including the president's cousin, Senator Mario Uribe, have been arrested or are under investigation. Uribe's former intelligence chief, Jorge Noguera—answerable only to President Uribe—and the minister of justice and interior's brother, Guillermo Valencia Cossio, who was head of the Fiscalía in Medellín until the time of his detention in September 2008, have also been arrested. "Para-gate" continues to unravel, coming ever closer to Uribe himself, which has made the executive increasingly dangerous in its attacks on perceived enemies, the country's judicial branch, and indigenous peoples chief among them.[40]

The beacon of neoconservatism in Latin America sheds a noxious glare, a grim reminder that Medellín's makeover rests on the graves of tens of thousands of its citizens. One can only hope that Medellín's homicide rate continues to drop, but intensified competition for control of narcotics exports, organized crime, and urban neighborhoods, especially on the city's periphery, appears to be leading to yet another round of warfare. Indeed, Daniel Rendón, alias Don Mario, brother of the demobilized paramilitary lord of Urabá, has been disputing the monopoly hitherto exercised by Don Berna's Envigado Office, whose power has waned since Don Berna began negotiating a reduced sentence in the United States. In the first half of 2008, Medellín's homicide rate was up by more than 15 percent over the same period in 2007, which suggests that the city's much-touted peace is partial at best, and highly unstable, despite its superficial *brillo*.[41] Resistance to the new model, and not only of the armed variety, has been formidable, hence the *sangre y fuego*—blood and fire—expended to overcome it.

Notes

Portions of this essay were published in *New Left Review* and *NACLA Report on the Americas* and are reprinted with permission. The author wishes to thank the editors of this volume for their helpful suggestions for revision.

1. Marleny Cardona et al., "Escenarios de homicidios en Medellín (Colombia) entre 1990–2002," *Revista Cubana de Salud Pública* 31, no. 3 (July–September 2005). For annual homicide figures for 1981–96, see Ana Jaramillo et al., *En la encrucijada: conflicto y cultura política en los noventa* (Medellín: Corporación Región, 1998), 110–11.

2. Homicide rates in 2005, per 100,000: Washington, D.C.: 45; Baltimore: 42; Detroit: 42; Medellín: 32.5.

3. Ann Twinam, *Miners, Merchants, and Farmers in Colonial Colombia* (Austin: University of Texas Press, 1982).

4. Mario Arango Jaramillo, *Impacto del narcotráfico en Antioquia* (Medellín: Tercer Mundo Editores, 1987), 11–12.

5. See Nancy Appelbaum, *Muddied Waters: Race, Religion and Local History in Colombia, 1848–1946* (Durham: Duke University Press, 2003), 31–51.

6. Fernando Botero Herrera, *Medellín, 1890–1950: historia urbana y juego de intereses* (Medellín: Universidad de Antioquia, 1996), 30–63.

7. Ann Farnsworth-Alvear, *Dulcinea in the Factory: Myths, Morals, Men, and Women in Colombia's Industrial Experiment, 1905–1960* (Durham: Duke University Press, 2000), 14.

8. Eduardo Sáenz Rovner, *La ofensiva empresarial: industriales, políticos, y violencia en los años 40 en Colombia* (Bogotá: Editorial J. M. Arango, 1992).

9. Farnsworth-Alvear, *Dulcinea in the Factory*, 14, 53.

10. U.S. Secretary of State George Marshall was in Bogotá for the Ninth Pan-American Congress, which led to the formation of the Organization of American States, when Gaitán was murdered. It was commented on extensively by British, French, and U.S. government consular officials. See Gonzalo Sánchez, ed., *Grandes potencias, el 9 de abril y la Violencia* (Bogotá: Planeta, 2000).

11. See Mary Roldán, *Blood and Fire: La Violencia in Antioquia, 1946–53* (Durham: Duke University Press, 2003).

12. Marco Palacios, *Entre la legitimidad y la violencia: Colombia, 1875–1994* (Bogotá: Norma, 1995), 298.

13. Interview with Pablo Escobar, in German Castro Caycedo, *En Secreto* (Bogotá: Planeta, 1996), 283–84.

14. Arango Jaramillo, *Impacto del narcotráfico en Antioquia*, 13–20.

15. Mike Davis, *Buda's Wagon: A Brief History of the Car Bomb* (London: Verso, 2007), 109.

16. Carlos Medina Gallego, *Autodefensas, paramilitares, y narcotráfico en Colombia* (Bogotá: Editorial Documentos Periodísticos, 1990), 166–242.

17. This assertion runs counter to Steven Dudley's argument in *Walking Ghosts: Murder and Guerrilla Politics in Colombia* (New York: Routledge, 2004), but relies in part on Dudley's own evidence, as well as arguments and evidence from Mauricio Romero, *Paramilitares y autodefensas, 1982–2003* (Bogotá: Editorial Planeta–IEPRI, 2003).

18. Ramiro Ceballos Melguizo, "The Evolution of Armed Conflict in Medellín: An Analysis of Major Actors," *Latin American Perspectives* 28, no. 1 (2000): 113; William Estrada and Adriana Gómez, eds, *Somos historia: Comuna nororiental* (Medellín: SPI, n.d.), 65–88, 106–7, 128–33; Alonso Salazar, *No nacimos pa' semilla* (Bogotá: CINEP, 1990), 86–87.

19. The most empirically rich, intimately detailed journalistic portrait of militia developments in the northeast is Gilberto Medina Franco, *Una historia de las milicias en Medellín* (Medellín: Instituto de Capacitación Popular, 2006). It confirms the preponderance of the ELN in the formation of nominally "independent" militias.

20. Mary Roldán, "Cocaine and the 'Miracle' of Modernity in Medellín," in *Cocaine: Global Histories*, ed. Paul Gootenberg (London: Routledge, 1999), 165–83.

21. Cited in Ana Jaramillo et al., *En la encrucijada: conflicto y cultura política en los noventa* (Medellín: Corporación Región, 1998), 65, n. 9.

22. Interviews with lawyers, journalists, community activists, and former militia commanders, Medellín, June 1999; May 2000; July 2002.

23. Interview with former members of La Ramada, Medellín, May 2000.

24. Roldán, "Cocaine and the 'Miracle' of Modernity," 175.

25. Alonso Salazar, *La parábola de Pablo* (Bogotá: Planeta, 2002), 307–14. Castaño was the founder of ACCU (Peasant Self-Defense Forces of Córdoba and Urabá), a paramilitary network that aimed to recapture FARC territory in the corridor leading to the Gulf of Turbo in the Caribbean.

26. The best account of the relationship between U.S. government forces and Don Berna's men, as well as the latter's role in Los Pepes, is by an investigative journalist, Mark Bowden, *Killing Pablo: The Hunt for the World's Greatest Outlaw* (New York: Penguin, 2001), 165–200. Bowden obtained access to U.S. and Colombian government officials involved (including General Colin Powell), as well as secret cable traffic between the U.S. embassy in Bogotá and Washington.

27. The Presidential Palace in Bogotá is called the Casa de Nariño. The late demobilized paramilitary Antontio López, alias Job, one of Don Berna's negotiators, referred to it as the Casa de Nari in a recorded telephone conversation with another paramilitary, which was released in August 2008. "Job" discussed the meetings he attended there with government officials. The phrase has been widely circulated in Colombian media and popular culture, and is frequently employed as shorthand for encapsulating the casual, easy access of paramilitary representatives to President Uribe's closest circle.

28. Roldán, "Cocaine and the 'Miracle' of Modernity," 178. See also Joseph Contreras, *Biografía no autorizada de Álvaro Uribe Vélez: el señor de las sombras* (Bogotá: Editorial Oveja Negra, 2002), 120–46.

29. Astrid Mireya Téllez Ardilla, *Milicias populares: otra expresión de la violencia social en Colombia* (Bogotá: Rodríguez Quito Editores, 1995), 107. See also Fernando Cubides, "From Private to Public Violence: The Paramilitaries," and Gonzalo Sánchez, "Introduction: Problems of Violence, Prospects for Peace," both in *Violence in Colombia, 1990–2000: Waging War and Negotiating Peace*, ed. Charles Bergquist et al. (Wilmington, Del.: Scholarly Resources, 2001), 11, 131.

30. In 1994 some eight hundred militias—not aligned with the FARC or ELN—agreed to an accord with the Gaviria government, in which the former militia leaders were recognized as security chiefs in their own neighborhoods, within a structure known as Coosercom. FARC and ELN-linked militias in the city then united to occupy the demobilized territory, killing several hundred Coosercom members. In 1996, the government moved to dissolve Coosercom itself, on the grounds of its gangsterish behavior. Despite this poor record, the same "peace process" was attempted with the criminal gangs through the Office of Peace and Coexistence. See Sánchez, "Introduction," 11. It is worth noting that the current mayor, Alonso Salazar, began his political career designing these accords.

31. Adam Isacson, "Plan Colombia: Six Years Later," Center for International Policy, Washington D. C., November 2006, available at http://www.cipcol.org/.

32. Quoted in Javier Sulé, "Medellín orgulloso," *El País* (Madrid), May 2006.

33. Mike Davis, *City of Quartz* (New York: Verso, 1990), 228, 240, 256–57.

34. Quoted in Amnesty International, "The Paramilitaries in Medellín: Demobilization or Legalization?," September 2005, 35, available at http://www.amnesty.org.

35. Quoted in *El Colombiano*, August 20, 2005.

36. David Harvey, *Spaces of Global Capitalism* (New York: Verso, 2006), 7–68.

37. James Parsons, *Antioquia's Corridor to the Sea: An Historical Geography of the Settlement of Urabá* (Berkeley: University of California Press, 1967).

38. Arno Mayer, "Internal Crisis and War since 1870," in *Revolutionary Situations in Europe , 1917–1922,* ed. Charles Betrand (Montreal: International Centre for European Studies, 1977), 201. The author wishes to thank Greg Grandin for the quotation and citation.

39. "Colombia army chief linked to outlaw militias," *LA Times*, March 25, 2007. See also "Colombian rebels threaten to expose political links," *Financial Times*, March 1, 2007.

40. "Cousin Mario," *The Economist*, April 26, 2008. For a scholarly account of the prehistory of the parapolitics scandal, see Mauricio Romero, ed., *Parapolítica: la ruta de la expansión paramilitar y los acuerdos políticos* (Bogotá: Corporación Nuevo Arco IRIS–CEREC–ASDI, 2007).

41. Comisión Colombiana de Juristas, "Neoparamilitarismo y nuevas masacres," *Boletín No 29: serie sobre los derechos de las víctimas y la aplicación de la Ley 975,* September 3, 2008.

Reflections

You Say You Want a Counterrevolution

Well, You Know, We All Want to Change the World

COREY ROBIN

If we want things to stay as they are, things will have to change.
—GUISEPPE DI LAMPEDUSA, *The Leopard*

The idea that the United States is a conservative power, an agent of containment and counterrevolution, will not come as news to scholars (or the peoples) of Latin America. Yet U.S. officials and elites have consistently donned the mantle of radicalism and reform in their conduct of U.S. foreign policy. At times, they have embraced actual revolutions, from the French to the Russian to the Chinese: even the *New York Times* hailed Castro's overthrow of Batista.[1] More typically, they have couched traditional power politics and reason of state in the rhetoric of progress and change, applying to the instruments of Metternich a generous coat of Mazzini and Marx. It is tempting to dismiss this talk as hypocrisy. But that only begs the question: if hypocrisy is the homage vice pays to virtue, why does a conservative power like the United States deem revolution the better part of virtue and reaction the emblem of vice?

Even that formulation may be misleading, however, for it assumes that conservatism is opposed to change, that it stands for stasis and the status quo. Yet conservatism has always been a forward movement; its call for a defense or restoration of the old regime is inevitably a cry for a transformation of that regime. Edmund Burke, archfoe of the French Revolution, yearned for the return of the monarchy. But even he understood that whatever was rebuilt in France after the restoration would, as he put it in a letter to an émigré, "be in some measure a new thing."[2] At its most sophisticated—in the hands of a Maistre, Nietzsche, or Hayek—conservatism blazes a visionary path to a new world, in which the old regime is so completely reconfigured and reimagined that it literally qualifies as the future. Once we understand these dynamic and creative elements of conservatism, we will see how and why it is that the United States can so easily navigate—indeed, command—the reactionary currents of Latin American history.

Despite its gauzy traditionalism, conservatism was born in angry and agonistic revolt against the French Revolution and has not lost that spirit since. To make a revolution against revolution—not just against a revolution but against revolution as such—is no easy task, however. "Whoever fights monsters should see to it that in the process he does not become a monster," wrote Nietzsche.[3] Conservatives have never become the monster they imagine the Left to be, but they have managed to absorb the manners and mores, style and sensibility, of the Left. Without abandoning their core belief—that society is and must remain a hierarchy of personal rule, in which the best men command the bodies and minds of their inferiors—conservatives have learned from the Left how to make feudalism fashionable and privilege palatable.

While conservatives are hostile to the goals of the Left, particularly the empowerment of society's lower castes and classes, they often are its best students. Sometimes, their studies are self-conscious and strategic, as they look to the Left for ways to bend new vernaculars—or new media—to their suddenly delegitimated aims.[4] Fearful that progressive *philosophes* had taken control of popular opinion in France, reactionary theologians in the middle of the eighteenth century looked to the example of their enemies. They stopped writing abstruse disquisitions for each other and began to produce Catholic agitprop, which would be distributed through the very networks that brought enlightenment to the French people. They spent vast sums funding essay contests, like those in which Rousseau made his name, to reward writers who wrote accessible and popular defenses of religion. Previous treatises of faith, declared Charles-Louis Richard, were "useless to the multitude who, without arms and without defenses, succumbs rapidly to *Philosophie*." His work, by contrast, was written "with the design of putting in the hands of all those who know how to read a victorious weapon against the assaults of this turbulent *Philosophie*."[5]

Pioneers of the Southern Strategy in the Nixon Administration, to cite a different kind of example, understood that after the rights revolutions of the sixties they could no longer make simple appeals to white racism. From now on, they would have to speak in code, preferably one palatable to the new dispensation of color-blindness. As the White House chief of staff H. R. Haldeman noted in his diary, Nixon "emphasized that you have to face the fact that the whole problem is really the blacks. The key is to devise a system that recognized this while not appearing to."[6] Looking back on this strategy in 1981, the Republican strategist Lee Atwater spelled out its elements more clearly: "You start out in 1954 by saying, 'Nigger, nigger, nigger.' By 1968 you can't say 'nigger'—that hurts you. Backfires. So you say stuff like forced busing, states' rights and all that stuff. You're getting so abstract now you're talking about cutting taxes, and all these things you're talking about are totally economic things and a byproduct of them is blacks get hurt worse than whites. And subconsciously maybe that is part of it."[7] More recently, David Horowitz has encouraged conservative students "to use the language that the left has deployed so effectively in behalf of its own agendas. Radical professors have created a 'hostile learning environment' for conservative students. There is a lack of 'intellectual diversity' on college faculties and in academic classrooms. The conservative viewpoint is 'under-represented' in the curriculum and on its reading lists. The university should be an 'inclusive' and intellectually 'diverse' community."[8]

At other times, the education of conservatives is unknowing, happening, as it were, behind their backs. By resisting and thus engaging with the pro-gressive argument day after day, they come to be influenced, often in spite of themselves, by the very movement they oppose. Setting out to bend a vernacular to their will, they find their will bent by the vernacular. At least that is what Atwater claims has occurred within the Republican Party. After stating (above) that "subconsciously maybe that is part of it," Atwater adds: "I'm not saying that. But I'm saying that if it is getting that abstract, and that coded, that we are doing away with the racial problem one way or the other. You follow me—because obviously sitting around saying, 'We want to cut this,' is much more abstract than even the busing thing, and a hell of a lot more abstract than 'Nigger, nigger.'"[9] Republicans have learned to dis-guise their intentions so well, Atwater suggests, that the disguise has seeped into and transformed the intention. Assuming such a transformation has indeed occurred, we might well ask whether conservatives have ceased to be what they set out to be, but that is a question for another day.

Even without directly engaging the progressive argument, the conserva-tive may absorb, by some elusive osmosis yet to be identified, the deeper categories and idioms of the Left, even when those idioms run directly counter to the official conservative stance. When Phyllis Schlafly took up her pen against the women's movement, she seemed unable to conjure the prefeminist view of women as deferential wives and mothers. Instead, she celebrated the activist "power of the positive woman." And then, as if borrowing a page from *The Feminine Mystique*, she railed against the meaninglessness and lack of fulfillment among modern women, though she blamed that on feminism rather than sexism.[10] One also can detect a certain sexual frankness—even feminist concern—in the early conversations of the Christian Right that would have been unthinkable prior to the women's movement. In 1976, Beverly and Tim LaHaye wrote a book, *The Act of Marriage*, which Susan Faludi has rightly called "the evangelical equivalent of *The Joy of Sex*." There, the LaHayes claimed that "women are much too passive in lovemaking." God, the LaHayes told their female readers, "placed [your clitoris] there for your enjoyment." They also complained that "some husbands are carryovers from the Dark Ages, like the one who told his frustrated wife, 'Nice girls aren't supposed to climax.' Today's wife knows better."[11]

Whether gifted mimics or unwitting apprentices, conservatives glean from the Left and the world it creates nothing less than a recipe for making a new old regime. They develop a taste and talent for the masses, mobilizing the street for spectacular displays of power while making sure that power is never shared or redistributed. (The famous frontispiece of Hobbes's *Leviathan* offers a vivid illustration of what a mobilization for a display, as opposed to redistribution, of power, looks like.) When speaking to large audiences, Nazi officials used the informal *du* rather than the stuffier *Sie*; they also discouraged the use of *Frau* and *Herr* as forms of address. They urged teachers to treat their students as comrades and described Kant's categorical imperative as "the only conceivable basis for collective life" because it enjoined "a spirit of mutual assistance" among the German people.[12]

Far from being an innovation of the twentieth-century radical Right, reactionary populism runs like a red—or brown—thread throughout conservative discourse from the beginning. Even Maistre, archmonarchist and avowed opponent of popular sovereignty, could not resist the populist tug of his time. "Monarchy is," he wrote, "without contradiction, the form of government that gives the most distinction to the greatest number of persons." Ordinary people "share" in its "brilliance" and glow, though not in its decisions and deliberations, because "man is honoured not as an agent but as a *portion* of sovereignty."[13]

From the Left, conservatives learn that men and women, whether through willed acts of force or some other exercise of human agency, can order social relationships and political time. "Citizens!" exclaimed Maistre. "This is how counter-revolutions are made."[14] (It would be difficult to imagine a Loyseau or Bossuet declaring, "Men"—much less "Citizens"—"this is how a monarchy is made.") The Left declares the Year 1, the Right the Year Negative 1. Both sides, however, share a belief in the power of men to create history, to propel it forward or backward, and by virtue of that belief, adopt the future as their preferred tense. Ronald Reagan, septuagenarian of the American morning, offered the perfect distillation of this phenomenon when he invoked, repeatedly, Thomas Paine's "We have it in our power to begin the world over again"—much to the embarrassment of George Will, who sniffed that Reagan was "painfully fond of the least conservative sentiment conceivable."[15]

Unlike the Left, however, conservatives are resolutely hostile to equality and the redistribution of power. As democratic arguments gathered greater force during the long nineteenth century, we see conservatives turning increasingly to racism, imperialism, and war as a way of reconciling their animus toward equality with their embrace of the mass.[16] To be successful, conservatives must appeal to the mass without disrupting the power of elites, or, to be more precise, they must harness the energy of the mass to reinforce or restore the power of elites. That is what racism and empire do: they take the wind out of the revolution's sails by turning the majority or the nation into a lordly class, ruling over a minority or another nation through a form of politics Marx called "the imperialism of the peasant class"[17] and we might call democratic feudalism. Though the members of this new ruling class know that they are not equal to each other, they are compensated by the illusion of superiority—and, often, the reality of rule—over others. As the U.S. slaveholder James Henry Hammond put it, "In a slave country every *freeman* is an aristocrat."[18]

Because conservatives can never settle for stagnant forms of rule or benign assertions of supremacy—their vision is too dynamic and volatile for that—they often turn to war as their preferred way of life. It was Maistre who first noted that "human blood must flow without interruption somewhere or other on the globe, and that for every nation, peace is only a respite."[19] More than a century later, Mussolini would write, "War is to men as maternity is to women."[20] (Modern warfare has the added benefit, as Lukács noted, of making history a "mass [though not a democratic] experience": where Frederick II declared "that war should be waged in such a manner that the civilian population simply would not notice it," Napoleon made war part of "the inner life of a nation."[21]) In a universe where nothing stands still, war becomes the way of the world and history a permanent register of violent struggle—a bloody business, to be sure, but how else to be an aristocrat when all that's solid melts into air?

Condorcet says somewhere that a counterrevolution is a revolution in reverse, to which Maistre angrily replied, "What they call the counterrevolution, will not be a *contrary revolution*, but the *contrary of revolution*."[22] For Condorcet, at least as Maistre seems to be interpreting him, counterrevolution is like an angry younger brother: no matter how hard he tries to distinguish himself, he is always trailing after his elder sibling. Maistre wouldn't have it: counterrevolution, he insisted, is no younger brother; it's not even a member of the family. In a sense, they're both right. Counterrevolutions are intimately related to revolutions: they come into being as a reaction to redistributive challenges from below and much of what they know they only know because they've learned it from the revolution. But counterrevolutions also have their own independent identities. Neither nostalgic throwbacks nor simple reactions, they are syncretic and hybridic movements, borrowing from a mishmash of sources to create a unique pastiche of contradictory effects: the vitality of popular culture and the stuffiness of elite rule; the wild anarchy of violence and the iron law of oligarchy; a democratic openness to new recruits and an unyielding defense of antique privilege. This pastiche is essential, for what counterrevolutions are trying to do is nothing less than square the circle: to make elitism popular, to remake a regime that claims never to have been made in the first place (the old regime was, is, and will be; it is not made)—tasks no other political movement has had to undertake. It is no wonder that Habermas, David Harvey, and others have claimed that postmodernism contains a reactionary, even counterrevolutionary, current.[23] With its willful embrace of high and low, irony and faith, counterrevolution may well have been the first—and certainly remains to this day the quintessential—postmodern political form.

So it is with conservatism (though there are counterrevolutions that are not conservative, it is difficult to imagine a conservatism that is not counterrevolutionary). Which brings us back to the United States and Latin America. As Greg Grandin argues in the introduction to this volume and as the succeeding essays amply demonstrate, revolution—and its containment—has been at the center of U.S.-Latin American relations for over a century. From the preemption of a Cuban revolution against Spain in 1898 to the intervention in the Mexican Revolution to the proxy wars in Central America in the 1970s and 1980s, the United States has conducted a counterrevolution of hemispheric proportions. And it has defended that counterrevolution in the language of the Left. Woodrow Wilson claimed that his intervention in Mexico would turn peasants into citizens.[24] John F. Kennedy claimed that his goal was to "complete the revolution of the Americas." Ronald Reagan invoked everyone from Paine to Sandino as antecedents for the Contras. Like its European counterpart, the American counterrevolution walks right and talks left.[25]

Two centuries ago, Alexis de Tocqueville wrote that North Americans "love change, but they are afraid of revolutions."[26] Since then, his argument has been elaborated (most famously by Louis Hartz)[27] as an explanation for the retrograde policies the United States so often adopts abroad. The United States, the argument goes, is a nation born equal. Not equal in a material sense but in an ideological sense. Thanks to an absent feudalism and quicksilver social metabolism, the United States has acquired a democratic political culture without having to undergo a revolution like the French or the Russian. Its egalitarianism is an easy inheritance, not a strenuous achievement. While the people of such a country may be liberal and democratic—in a "go along to get along" sort of way—they can never be radical. They just don't get revolution, and what they get, they don't like. Faced with a revolution, at home or (more likely) abroad, they grow angry and hostile; uninflected liberalism mutates into snarling illiberalism, blithe indifference into manic antipathy.

Tocqueville's account is suggestive but it gets the mutation backward. In the face of a revolutionary challenge, American counterrevolutionaries don't move from left to right. They move from right to left. Though opposed to the project of political egalitarianism, of using state power to create a more just society, they advance their opposition through the tropes of liberal democracy. They adopt and adapt its culture and discourse, wielding the language of rights and reform for the sake of regress and reaction. The representative figure here is the American slaveholder: preparing to found a feudal republic on the eve of the Civil War, he invokes Galileo and Bacon. Refusing the identity of the staid traditionalist, he prefers the title of the heretic and the scientist, that fugitive intelligence who marches to his own drummer and thereby advances the cause of progress.[28]

Far from being an American exception, the southern slaveholder would prove to be the conservative rule—a harbinger of a century when right-wing exorcisms of the Left would be carried out in the name of modernity and holy violence would sport the emblem of enlightenment. For conservatives, this would entail no profession of bad faith: the containment of multitudes is the essence of their self-declared position. As Michael Oakeshott would write, "It is not at all inconsistent to be conservative in respect of government and radical in respect of almost every other activity."[29] Again, hardly news to the peoples of Latin America but a useful reminder nonetheless.

Notes

1. David Brion Davis, *Revolutions: Reflections on American Equality and Foreign Liberations* (Cambridge, Mass.: Harvard University Press, 1990), 60–77.

2. Cited in J. C. D. Clark's introduction to Edmund Burke, *Reflections on the Revolution in France*, ed. J. C. D. Clark (Stanford: Stanford University Press, 2001), 104.

3. Friedrich Nietzsche, *Beyond Good and Evil*, trans. Walter Kaufmann (New York: Vintage, 1966), 89.

4. Cf. Karl Mannheim, "Conservative Thought," in *Essays on Sociology and Social Psychology*, ed. Paul Kecskemeti (London: Routledge and Kegan Paul, 1953), 106; Albert Hirschman, *The Rhetoric of Reaction: Perversity, Futility, Jeopardy* (Cambridge, Mass.: Harvard University Press, 1991), 11, 81, 84; Darrin M. McMahon, *Enemies of the Enlightenment: The French Counter-Enlightenment and the Making of Modernity* (New York: Oxford University Press, 2001), 27–28.

5. McMahon, *Enemies of the Enlightenment*, 27–28.

6. Quoted in Robert Perkinson, *Texas Tough: The Rise of America's Prison Empire* (New York: Metropolitan Books, 2010), 297.

7. Quoted in Ibid., 303.

8. David Horowitz, "The Campus Blacklist," *FrontPage* (April 18, 2003), at http://www.studentsforacademicfreedom.org/.

9. Perkinson, *Texas Tough*, 303.

10. Phyllis Schlafly, *The Power of the Positive Woman* (New York: Harcourt Brace Jovanovich, 1977), 7–8.

11. Susan Faludi, *Backlash: The Undeclared War against American Women* (New York: Doubleday, 1991), 251.

12. Claudia Koonz, *The Nazi Conscience* (Cambridge, Mass.: Harvard University Press, 2003), 114, 146, 153, 158.

13. Joseph de Maistre, *Considerations on France*, trans. and ed. Richard A. Lebrun (1974; New York: Cambridge University Press, 1994), 89.

14. Ibid., 79.

15. Gary Wills, *Reagan's America* (New York: Penguin, 1988), 355.

16. Cf. Barrington Moore Jr., *Social Origins of Dictatorship and Democracy: Lord and Peasant in the Making of the Modern World* (Boston: Beacon Press, 1966), 436, 442, 447.

17. Karl Marx, "The Eighteenth Brumaire of Louis Bonaparte," in *The Marx-Engels Reader*, ed. Robert C. Tucker (1972; New York: Norton, 1978), 609–10.

18. Quoted in Peter Kolchin, *American Slavery, 1619–1877* (1993; New York: Hill and Wang, 2003), 195.

19. Maistre, *Considerations on France*, 23.

20. Quoted in Robert O. Paxton, *The Anatomy of Fascism* (New York: Knopf, 2004), 156.

21. Georg Lukács, *The Historical Novel*, trans. Hannah and Stanley Mitchell (Boston: Beacon Press, 1962), 23–24.

22. Maistre, *Considerations on France*, 105; Hannah Arendt, *On Revolution* (New York: Penguin, 1963), 18; Arno J. Mayer, *Dynamics of Counterrevolution in Europe, 1870–1956: An Analytic Framework* (New York: Harper and Row, 1971), 37–38.

23. Jürgen Habermas, "Modernity versus Post-Modernity," *New German Critique* 22 (1981): 3–22; Habermas, *The Philosophical Discourse of Modernity: Twelve Lectures*, trans. Frederick Lawrence (Cambridge, Mass.: MIT Press, 1987), 3–5, 120; *Habermas and Modernity*, ed. Richard J. Bernstein (Cambridge, Mass.: MIT Press, 1985), 25, 30–31, 87–88, 90–91, 134–35, 161–75, 196 , 229; David Harvey, *The Condition of Postmodernity* (Oxford: Blackwell, 1990), 41–42; Terry Eagleton, *The Illusions of Postmodernity* (Oxford: Blackwell, 1996).

24. In regard to Mexico, Wilson famously said that he was "going to teach the South American Republics to elect good men." Quoted in Burton J. Hendrick, *The Life and Letters of Walter H. Page*, vol. 1 (New York: Doubleday, 1922), 204. One of the anonymous readers of this volume points out that, of Wilson's three U.S. interventions in Mexico—the coup against Madero, the occupation of Veracruz, and the expedition sent against Pancho Villa—the first was "clearly counterrevolutionary," the second and third more debatable.

25. See Greg Grandin's *Empire's Workshop: Latin America, the United States, and the Rise of the New Imperialism* (New York: Metropolitan Books, 2006), chaps. 1 and 2.

26. Alexis de Tocqueville, *Democracy in America*, trans. George Lawrence, ed. J. P. Mayer (New York: HarperCollins, 1969), 638.

27. Louis Hartz, *The Liberal Tradition in America* (New York: Harcourt Brace, 1955).

28. Cf. John C. Calhoun, "Speech on the Force Bill" and "Speech on the Reception of Abolitionist Petitions," in *Union and Liberty: The Political Philosophy of John C. Calhoun*, ed. Ross M. Lence (Indianapolis: Liberty Fund, 1992), 434, 467–68; Alexander Stephens, "The Cornerstone Speech," and Josiah Nott, "Instincts of Races," in *Defending Slavery: Proslavery Thought in the Old South*, ed. Paul Finkelman (Boston: Bedford/St. Martin's, 2003), 90–92, 208; Thomas Roderick Dew, "Abolition of Negro Slavery," in *The Ideology of Slavery: Proslavery Thought in the Antebellum South, 1830–1860*, ed. Drew Gilpin Faust (Baton Rouge: Louisiana State Press, 1981), 27, 51, 53.

29. Michael Oakeshott, "On Being Conservative," *Rationalism in Politics and Other Essays* (1962; Indianapolis: Liberty Press, 1992), 435.

Thoughts on Violence and Modernity in Latin America

NEIL LARSEN

1

A history without violence would, for us at least, be unrecognizable *as* history. Yet violence as phenomenon appears, paradoxically, to exist apart from the history in which it is omnipresent. Violence seems, almost unconsciously, to found the historical imagination itself and at the same time to exist apart from it, as a moral or metaphysical absolute. In the final analysis this no doubt has to do with the impossibility of disassociating the idea of violence from that of death as physical annihilation. Taken to its extreme, violence could end history by destroying virtually all historical agents. Indeed, it must rank as one of the great historical feats of modernity that it has actualized what was before this merely theoretical possibility and even learned to make us accommodate ourselves to it in our daily lives. Alongside the abstract repugnance it universally merits in the language of official "values," violence as means and as sheer adaptation advances at a sure and accelerating pace. Whatever they may convey on the level of official historical sanctions, the stories and images of catastrophic violence—whether of Auschwitz or Hiroshima, of the Escuela de Mecánica[1] or El Mozote,[2] or for that matter of Columbine High, 9/11, Guantánamo, or Abu Ghraib—inform us just as predictably of the adaptive cost that lived history can be relied upon to exact from its subjects: it *is* this bad, it will continue, and it will get worse. The real likelihood of violent annihilation becomes for many something to be factored into the equations of contemporary life, as one would a marriage or a retirement, while for the rest its specter becomes a permanent part of the domestic landscape.

Thus the forbiddingly difficult task of *historicizing* violence, political or otherwise—a task now, in the age of preemptive wars and suicide bombings, rendered more difficult and more urgent than ever. This if nothing else is what so emphatically commends the work of the historian Arno Mayer, which in part occasions this essay and the volume to which it seeks to contribute. In works such as *The Persistence of the Old Regime*, *Why Did the Heavens Not Darken?*, and *The Furies*, Mayer has effectively withstood the nearly universal tendency that, by allowing the abstract and formal repudiation of violence to become the ideology of a real, daily adaptation to its regimes, absolves modern political history of its inherently violent foundations. Mayer marshals an impeccably objective historiography to prove, in *The Furies*, that by reducing the violence unleashed by the revolutions of 1789 and 1917 to a generic phenomenon understood either to vitiate their emancipatory content or to be completely external to them, one simply cannot explain them as events. Revolutionary and counterrevolutionary violence and terror do not, as Mayer shows, cancel each other out, much less validate the Burkean conservatism that abjures them both. Their mutual determination, rather, traces a specific form of historical motion, that of the modern social revolution in its full scope. Up to a point at least, Mayer successfully historicizes violence by methodically refusing to remove it from the historical context of revolution itself as both an objective social process and as an event in real time about which it is still impossible to think except, however minimally, in a historical spirit. In the end, the guillotine delivers a violent death just like any other instrument, and can dispatch a Robespierre as readily as a Louis XVI. But the history that gave us the guillotine cannot be detached from the history of the political movements and ideologies that initially legitimate its use against some and not others.

That is, violence itself, for Mayer, remains, essentially, an *event*, inseparable from the larger chain of events that lead into and flow out of it. Hence the remarkable impact of a work such as *Why Did the Heavens Not Darken?*, which ties the decision of the German National Socialist regime to implement the Final Solution, whatever its ideological predispositions, to the political fall-out from events on the battlefields of the Eastern Front, specifically the fall of the siege of Moscow in 1941. However controversial Mayer's historical theory of the Holocaust may in fact be, it forces us to reflect on Auschwitz as, on one level at least, a terrible historical contingency. That the violence of the death camps has more than a contingent quality is in no sense disputed by Mayer here. But by arguing, indeed seeking to prove to us that this violence was, as event, initially inseparable from the violence of the anti-Soviet war, the flight into the metaphysics of violence, into its combined existential abstraction and rationalization, is prevented.

II

Are Mayer's methodically historical account of violence as event, and, more pointedly, his insistence on the often underestimated historical role of counterrevolutionary violence and terror in shaping the violence and terror of revolution, illuminating or especially pertinent to the modern history of Latin America? In the most general sense, obviously, yes—as they are for history generally. But in a certain narrower sense, the answer is, ironically, no, if only because political and state violence in Latin America have, especially since 1945, been so notoriously and self-evidently the practice of the Latin American counterrevolution (in league with U.S. imperialism) that the correction is almost superfluous. While revolutionary violence and terror are obviously not unknown in modern Latin American history, they cannot be compared to the Jacobin and Soviet experiences in the latters' obsessive, ideologically overdetermined interest for historiography, especially cold war liberal historiography. If anything, the postwar Latin American experience of political violence is what stands in a position to illuminate and buttress Mayer's historical argument even further—an argument that, not unlike surrealism according to the theory of the "real maravilloso,"[3] would make immediate sense to the Latin American man on the street.

But this in turn points to a more basic question than the above, and one to which a work such as *The Furies* can no doubt help to supply answers: what is the structural relationship of revolution and counterrevolution to the process of capitalist modernization itself in Latin America, as compared to this relationship in Western Europe and even in Imperial and Soviet Russia? In both of the latter cases, violent revolution is the prelude to far-reaching social and political processes of modernization. Despite their obvious differences vis à vis each other, and the fact that, in the wake of its effective collapse in 1991, the Soviet model begins to look in certain ways more "Latin American," 1789 and 1917 really have no precise historical analogues in Latin America. Where is so determinate and strict a succession of such elemental historical processes as political revolution and social and economic modernization to be observed in Latin American history?

In a more punctual sense, perhaps the cases of Mexico and Cuba might be cited here. The Mexican Revolution, curiously, approximately shares the chronology of the Soviet experience: from revolutionary inception in the second decade of the twentieth century to economic crisis and political implosion or near implosion in the 1980s and 1990s. Cuba's revolutionary modernization, uniquely configured by the geopolitics and the chronology of the cold war, probably parallels more closely than any other Latin American revolution the orthodox sequence of a 1917, in which the direct seizure of power is followed by a sweeping social and economic transformation together with a largely successful monopolization of violence as legitimate force on the part of the revolutionary state. But with the end of the cold war, Cuba, even more than Mexico, has had to trade off the political integrity of its revolutionary institutions in exchange for conceding many if not most of the economic and social reforms for which these institutions once stood. Their shared, close proximity to the dominating power to their north—a power that, for all its counterrevolutionary fervor and propensity to violence can, ironically, ill afford significant social upheavals just across its borders—probably explains more about the formal, institutional longevity of these modernizing revolutions (ironically coupled to their effective social reversal) than could any deeper homology with the historical syntax of 1789 or 1917.

As a rule, however, revolutions are more frequent if also more sporadic, short-lived and fragmented events—that is, much more *volatile*—in Latin America than in the European and North American theaters of modernity. This has given rise to a widely broadcast caricature of Latin America as the land of the eternal coup d'état, complete with the inevitable medal-strewn *miles gloriosus* and menacing men with guns—a caricature in which the political difference between those against the wall and those manning the firing squad soon disappears. But behind the caricature lies what is nevertheless an important historical qualification, perhaps so obvious as to be in danger of being set aside: that, because capitalist modernization is itself such a violent and volatile affair in Latin America, the revolutions and counterrevolutions that are its "birth pangs" are likewise so. Latin American revolutions occupy a place more transverse, so to speak, to the history of economic modernization, a less punctual place than in the case of their epoch-creating models in 1789 and 1917.

The reasons for this are, in a sense, the central problem of modern Latin American political and economic history and long a stock-in-trade of Latin

American historians. But it is, for all that, rare that anyone thinks in a very sustained way about the general, structural relation of revolutionary and counterrevolutionary violence to modernization and modernity in Latin America, even if, on a local level, one often thinks about little else. (Rare, that is, that one thinks through this relation and still thinks *historically* rather than veering off into the realms of liberal morality and metaphysics.) In this sense, Mayer's magisterially comparative account of 1789 and 1917—one in which the crucial factors not only of chronological disparity but also (even more crucially for Latin Americanists) of unequal capitalist development are plainly determinant—can serve as a fundamental point of orientation.

III

Has, then—to proceed in this analogous mode—the counterrevolution definitively triumphed in Latin America? Has the old regime survived, in the end, or come back to overturn all efforts to effect revolutionary change? In the plainest sense, yes. With the heavily qualified exceptions of Cuba and Venezuela—and the frankly even more circumscribed and adventitious exceptions of the regime changes in Brazil or Bolivia—the class elites that dominated Latin American states and societies at the outset of the cold war retain their dominant position. But to further sustain this viewpoint, one would have immediately to qualify and relativize its terms. "Counterrevolution" and "old regime" in precisely what sense? For Mayer the old regime of landowning aristocrats is associated with a feudal or at best transitionally capitalist mode of production. It is at the very least a matter of debate as to whether such a class has ever existed in Latin America. While landed wealth in Latin America remains a crucial political power, its own relationship to the uneven and fraught process of economic and social modernization invites little comparison, it seems to me, to the class positionings of money-wise English baronets, Prussian Junkers, or Russian boyars. Rural elites in Latin America are typically not the grudging accommodators and sly survivors of modernizing liberal bourgeoisies but themselves principal agents of modernization and liberalization. They are less the junior partners of a local than of an absentee, ultramarine "foreign" bourgeoisie whose banks are practically as powerful as states. While the cities in Latin America have been the sites of the "middle-class" revolts that have forced retreats and (when in league with rural uprisings) land reforms on the "old regime," these cities themselves were and remain in many ways the mere extension of traditional class power, the portuary nodes of a network of class relations centered outside both country and city.

All of this, of course, points to the structural fact of colonial and neo-colonial domination of Latin America and that domination's determinant role in forcing and, in the wake of the "neoliberal" Thermidor, reinforcing an export-led, extroverted path of modernization, one in which both rural and industrial products in the form of commodities enter a world market, so to speak, as equals. In Latin America the countryside does not, by feeding the cities, perform its historic role of potentiating capitalism's phase of "primitive accumulation." Both countryside and city must be fed by the world market, dominated in its turn by always-already accumulated masses of capital that set the limits to any local process of modernization, and for which the politics of "old" and "new" regimes in, say, Argentina or Honduras are effectively a matter of indifference.

Here, that is to say, Mayer's painstaking insistence on the violence of modern revolution as the latter's active constituent but at the same time as irreducibly political and event-driven, apposite as this is to his critical objective as a historian, begins to fail us. The working premise of *The Furies* is, like Marx's in his political writings, that revolutions are the nodal flash points and the semiconscious instruments of a kind of capitalist (or "socialist") modernization from within. They are thresholds of the modern. The "old regime" can "persist" because that to which it will eventually give way is moving against it on the same social and national plane. But the revolutions and counterrevolutions of modern Latin America, especially in the cold war and post–cold war periods, take place within a framework of modernization that is a given of both colonial and neocolonial social formations—a modernization in this sense "from without"—and, paradoxically, also a constitutive absence. The modern in Latin America is perpetually unfinished business, a success that breeds its own failure as a very part of its development; it is not a threshold but the single doorway leading into and out of—what else?—a labyrinth. Because both are arrayed alongside and at the same time against the abstract plane of a protean modernity that is inseparable from the social itself, the friction of "old" and "new" regimes, of revolution and counterrevolution, becomes chronic rather than punctual and generates a violence that seems circular and irrational.

This is, in fact, the violent irrationality latent—and nowadays more and more manifest—in all modes of capitalist modernity, but one that it has, so far, been the function of peripheral zones like Latin America to have displaced onto themselves and to absorb, whether by enduring the unilateral, directly violent batterings of imperialist domination and subjugation or through the medium of social and economic "policy." (Think, to cite a timely and stark analogy here, of the transition in Iraq from the regime of indirectly murderous U.N.-approved sanctions to that of direct, overtly and massively violent U.S. invasion and occupation.) But one may reasonably speculate whether the coming phase in the history of the capitalist modernity once ushered in through the "strait gate" leading from the guillotine to the voting booth and the stock exchange may now have become the roosting place for a rather different species of "furies," on their way "home," so to speak, from places like Latin America. In that sense, it is perhaps Latin America's seemingly irrational form of violence as a political relation of means to end that might prompt us to rethink the history of violence set forth in works like *The Furies*.

IV

I want at this point to expound, however briefly, one such rethinking, likely, for linguistic reasons, to be unfamiliar to most readers in Latin America and the United States. This is the work of a group of radical critical theorists centered around the contemporary German journals *Krisis*[4] and *Exit!*,[5] the most prominent of whom is Robert Kurz, author of works such as *Der Kollaps der Modernisierung*,[6] *Schwarzbuch Kapitalismus*[7] (a monumental historical study of capitalism from the standpoint of a radically revised, post–cold war Marxism), and *Weltordnungskrieg*.[8] Kurz's fundamental thesis, an intensely controversial one to be sure, is that, in the wake of the post-Fordist "third" industrial revolution ushered in by microelectronics, vastly increased levels of productivity and the corresponding rise in the organic composition of capital are pushing all social formations subordinate to the law of value—that is, *all* social formations—to the brink of a terminal crisis of reproduction. Because the continued self-valorization of capital now, at currently attained levels of productivity, requires a vastly diminished quantity of abstract labor power, enormous pools of that labor power become effectively "unexploitable," permanently superfluous to the needs of self-valorization. Those familiar with Marx's classical exposition of the law of the rising organic composition of capital—and the subsequent "law of the tendency of the rate of profit to fall"—will be able to fill in the last blank here: absolute declines in the capacity to valorize labor power mean absolute declines in the capacity to extract surplus value. Expressed in terms of the commodity and commodity form: as labor power more and more ceases to be a saleable commodity, the commodity form itself loses its content, becoming an increasingly "fictional" social form. It is actualized only through ever more desperate "flights forward" into financial speculation and the resort to what Kurz and others refer to as outright "economies of plunder"—that is, throwing onto the market whatever pools of money or directly saleable commodities there are that can be looted for short-term gain or to stave off eventual collapse, whether these are gathered in the savings accounts of pensioners, the fraudulently overvalued portfolios of Enron and Worldcom stockholders, or in the subsoil of Iraq. The "Great Recession" that began with the subprime mortgage crisis of 2007 and nearly produced a worldwide collapse of the financial sector in 2008 has since, at least in the view of this writer, added considerable plausibility to Kurz's analysis.

According to Kurz, the economies of the third and former second world were the first to succumb to this crisis. The attempt, common to both, at competing successfully on the world market through an accelerated, or "re-cuperative" (*nachholend*) modernization has, in this view, effectively failed. Economies from the former Soviet Union to Argentina simply could not undertake the immense capital investment required to achieve levels of productivity commensurate with those of the United States or the European Union and Japan and, in some cases (e.g., the former East Germany, or German Democratic Republic) experience the devalorization of an entire national-industrial base virtually overnight. India, China, and Brazil may prove to be the only (temporary?) exceptions to this rule—but for how long, and at what social cost to their own populations? Meanwhile, the societies of sub-Saharan Africa, of much of Central and Southeast Asia, and of a significant swath of Latin America virtually fall off the map, becoming little more than immense, stagnant reservoirs of "unexploitable" labor power crowded into gargantuan, unlivable cities, "monetary subjects without money" forced to compete in the most violent fashion for the crumbs of globalization. This is reality *now* for the majority of the planet, a reality recently described in chilling fashion by the urbanist Mike Davis in his book *Planet of Slums*.[9]

That such a crisis must and does lead to catastrophic increases in and the constant proliferation of new forms of violence is self-evident. Perhaps, after all, much the same could be said, *mutatis mutandis*, of the crises of the old regime that led successively to 1789, 1917, and even, in Mayer's argument, the "second Thirty Years War" of 1914–45. But the structural relation of violence to the total process of social formation and reproduction has surely changed. The violence of ethnic cleansing, of death squads and paramilitarism, of suicide bombings and preemptive wars—of, to paraphrase in English the title of Kurz's *Weltordnungskrieg*, "world civil war"—has ceased to be punctual and "foundational" and become both chronic and corrosive. Violence more and more leaks out of politics and the state, calling forth ever more violent state reprisals and policing measures in its turn. In Kurz's view, violence becomes the *ultima ratio* not merely of the state, but of strained market relations themselves, of the commodity logic that the modern state was erected to institute and regulate.[10] Violence now enters the market directly as a kind of apocalyptic form of reproduction, no longer buying in order to sell (Marx's famously succinct formula for the capital relation) but *looting* in order to sell. As it once did in its early youth, capitalism again writes its history in the "annals of blood and fire." But this time it is a primitive accumulation in reverse.

Ernst Lohoff, a frequent contributor to *Krisis* and the author of an important critical study of the civil-cum-international war that produced the break-up of Yugoslavia in the 1990s,[11] has recently synthesized this historical rethinking of violence in rigorously theoretical and systematic terms. In his article "Gewaltordnung und Vernichtungslogik"[12] ("Violent Order and the Logic of Annihilation") Lohoff traces what he terms the "violent core" ("Gewaltkern") of the social subject of commodity society to the historical foundations of modernity itself. Hobbes's defense of the absolutist state as the only bulwark against "bellum omnia contra omnes," reread by Lohoff in light of the contemporary rise in "poststate" violence, reveals violence itself to be a constitutive ideological element of the civic values of freedom and equality to which it is officially anathema. "Men are equal," for Hobbes, "insofar as they all share a mutual capacity to kill one another."[13] "Hobbes's construct brings into view the fundamental relationship in which men are displaced by their own unsocial sociality [*ungesellschaftliche Gesellschaftlichkeit*]. Contract and right are not the precipitates of human cooperation but rather grow out of a sublimated praxis of violence [*Gewalttätgkeit*], a praxis that is not abandoned in a fully normalized commodity-producing society, but that is presupposed in it."[14]

The state as the generalized, universalized, and externalized form of a violence inherent in the social logic of alienated, commodity relations goes on to perfect its social base of market subjects by claiming the exclusive, "sovereign" right to wage war.[15] And, by warring against other states and evolving standing armies of conscript citizens "a certain regimentation of violence [*Gewaltregime*] evolves, without which the modern, monadic subjects of market competition and work could simply not have arisen. The fraternity of the national 'we,' the self-induction into militarized corps of fellow countrymen, prepares the ground for the market 'I.'"[16]

When, however, commodity relations themselves enter into the purportedly terminal crisis described in the paragraphs immediately above, the resulting weakening of the state monopoly on violence, the "leakage" of violence from the political onto the directly social and economic planes, forces the submerged "Gewaltkern" of modern, "monetary" subjectivity back out of its sublimated, political forms and into the open, making society and economy themselves into virtual battlefields. In "poststate" war, writes Lohoff, "the separation between war as end and warlike means breaks down; the path becomes the goal. The economics of war [now] function as an economics of plunder, as the form of reproduction peculiar to a business of war, from which the appearance of abstract universality has fallen away. In ways quite reminiscent of the battles of early modernity, it is now increasingly up to war to supply the means of war."[17]

V

A Latin Americanist who reads Kurz and Lohoff will, however skeptically, likely experience something like a shock of recognition. Until much of the rest of the world caught up to it in the 1990s, seemingly disproportionate and irrational outbreaks of violence—from the overthrow of Arbenz in the 1950s to the mass torture and killings carried out by military dictatorships in Brazil and the Southern Cone in the 1960s and 1970s to the counterrevolutionary terror in Central America in the 1980s—made Latin America into the grisly poster child of wanton, "civil" blood-letting. That one of history's greatest and bloodiest monopolists of violence, the United States, played a decisive role in virtually all of this cruel history must never for a moment be forgotten, but Dulles, Kissinger, and Elliot Abrams found ready collaborators among the ranks of the Latin American praetorians and "lumpenbourgeoisies." Consolidated and, if such a thing is possible, routinized and normalized on the social and economic rack of neoliberalism, the horrific mass murders of, say, the Argentine "Proceso" or the Reagan-sponsored

Nicaraguan "Contra" terror nevertheless continue to pose a terrible, Sphinx-like question to survivors and historians alike. Bluntly phrased: were all these deaths in vain? Here and there a few generals or police captains and other egregious cases go to jail, but the reforms, radical and modest, for which so many died now seem almost beyond recall, much less imaginable in the present. Can such catastrophic violence and injustice really have had built into it no redemptive denouement?

Perhaps history will eventually surrender up an answer, but in the meantime one must consider whether this redemption tends still, in fundamentally Enlightenment fashion, to be imagined as the missing final act of the drama of progressive, liberal modernization. Those who die for "liberty, fraternity and equality" are, so it is said, redeemed by the fact that these ideals become enshrined in the institutions of the state and civil society. But what of those who die at the hands of these very ideals and institutions themselves, ideals and institutions which, having now outlived themselves and grown violent and nihilistic with the progressive crumbling of their commodity-structured, modernized economic and social underpinning, turn on their subjects because, like unsaleable commodities, the latter paradoxically now stand in the way of the social automaton that liberates and equalizes them only in the abstract? Indeed, what of those who die at the hands of such ideals and institutions, while still believing in them? For that matter, what of those who, in wreaking such violence, become the agents of a retro-Hobbesian modernity while imagining themselves to be the champions of tradition and the knights of the old regime? It is only against the violent backdrops of 1789 and 1917, no doubt, that these historical actors (among whom we must also be included) could recognize themselves. But in modern Latin America, as, increasingly now, in the rest of the world, the stage may already have been set for something else.

Notes

1. The Escuela de Mecánica, "School of Mechanics," operated by the Argentine military, became notorious as a center for secret detention and torture during that country's "dirty war" in the 1970s and early 1980s.

2. El Mozote was the site where, in 1981, the U.S.-backed Salvadoran military massacred upwards of nine hundred civilians in the worst atrocity of that country's 1980s civil war.

3. In his famed preface to the first edition of his novel *El reino de este mundo* (1949), Alejo Carpentier turned the tables of iconoclasm against surrealism itself, suggesting that what, in Paris, could only be a private, intellectualized experience induced by drugs became, once inserted into the new historical context of Latin America's mythically inflected popular culture, the stuff of everyday life: the *"real* maravilloso."

4. See http://www.krisis.org/.

5. See http://www.exit-online.org/.

6. Robert Kurz, *Der Kollaps der Modernisierung: Vom Zusammenbruch des Kasernsozialismus zur Krise de Weltökonomie* (Frankfurt Am Main: Eichborn Verlag, 1991). A Portuguese translation, *O colapso da modernização* (São Paulo: Editorial Paz e Terra) was published in 1992.

7. Robert Kurz, *Schwarzbuch Kapitalismus* (Frankfurt am Main: Eichborn Verlag, 1999).

8. Robert Kurz, *Weltordnungskrieg* (Horlemann: Bad Honnef, 2003).

9. Mike Davis, *Planet of Slums* (London: Verso, 2006).

10. See, especially, Robert Kurz, "Die Realen Gespenster der Weltkrise," in *Weltordnungskrieg*, 45–74.

11. Ernst Lohoff, *Der Dritte Weg in den Bürgerkrieg: Jugoslavien und das Ende der nachholenden Modernisierung* (Horlemann: Bad Honnef, 1996).

12. Ernst Lohoff, "Gewaltordnung und Vernichtungslogik," *Krisis: Beiträge zur Kritik der Warengesellschaft*, no. 27 (2003): 17–63. Available online at http://www.krisis.org/.

13. Lohoff, "Gewaltordnung und Vernichtungslogik," 20. My translation. German original: "Die Menschen sind insofern gleich," for Hobbes "als sie sich allesamt gegenseitig umbringen können."

14. Ibid., 21. My translation. German original: "Macht Hobbes' Konstrukt das Gründverhältnis sichtbar, in das ungesellschaftliche Gesellschaftlichkeit Menschen versetzt. Vertrag und der Recht sind kein Niederschlag menschlicher Kooperation, sonder erwachsen aus sublimierter Gewalttätigkeit, Gewalttätigkeit, die im warengesellschaftlichen Normalvollzug nicht zugelassen, ihm aber vorausgesetzt ist."

15. "The dominance of the principle of sovereignty as it concerns the intercourse between states, merges, in the final analysis, with the *ius ad bellum.*" Ibid., 31, my translation. German original: "Für den zwischenstaatlichen Verkehr fällt die Herrschaft des Souveränitätsprinzips dagegen letztinstanzlich mit dem ius ad bellum zusammen."

16. Ibid., 29. My translation. German original: "Hat sich jenes Gewaltregime herausgebildet, ohne das sich die Moderne Konkurrenz- und Arbeitsmonade letztlich gar nicht hätte entwickeln können. Die Brüderlichkeit des nationalen WIR, das Sich-Einfügen in den wehrhaften Volkskörper, bereitete dem Waren-ICH."

17. Ibid., 49. My translation. German original: "Die Trennung von Kriegsziel und kriegerischen Mittel ist hinfällig; der Weg ist zum Ziel geworden. . . . Kriegsökonomie . . . funktioniert als Plünderungsökonomie, als die besondere Reproduktionsform der Kriegsbetrieber, die aufgehört haben, als abstrakte Allgemeinheit aufzutreten. Ganz ähnlich wie in den frühzeitlichen Konflikten ist es zunehmend am Krieg, den Krieg zu ernähren" (49).

Conclusions

Latin America's Long Cold War

A Century of Revolutionary Process and U.S. Power

GILBERT M. JOSEPH

This collection has sought to provide a new agenda for the study of revolutionary change and political violence in twentieth-century Latin America. In the process it also helps to redefine notions of cold war in Latin America.[1]

Socially Embedding Political Violence

Inspired by Arno Mayer's provocative comparative treatment of violence and terror in the French and Russian Revolutions—and by Greg Grandin's introductory essay that applies (and qualifies) Mayer's "furies" for twentieth-century Latin America—the volume's essays have provided a timely critique of triumphalist, post–cold war revisions of modern social revolutions, which effectively have sought to disconnect the category of political violence from socially embedded historical struggles. Whereas these revisionist historians (abetted by currents in postmodern cultural criticism and semiotics) typically portray revolutionary violence as the "meaningless spawn of modern politics," or the product of arrogant and uncompromising radicals whose left utopian projects have run amok, the present contributors, applying fine-grained historical and ethnographic analysis to episodes of revolutionary and counterrevolutionary violence in Latin America, interpret these episodes as the very birth pangs of the region's modernity. That birth was delayed and fiercely contested over the course of the twentieth century: it was embedded in an often ferocious dialectic that involved diverse reformist and revolutionary midwives for social change and national development, and their antagonists, who were willing to exercise all manner of counterforce to abort projects for structural change. This dialectic played out in overlapping and interdependent domestic and international fields of political and social power. It reverberated through local contests over land, labor, political office, the control of markets and natural resources, and the shape that ethnic and gender relations, and citizenship itself, would take— all of which became imbricated in projects of nation and state formation, and the imperatives of interstate relations. Initially this dialectic shaped regional life in the turbulent decades following the Mexican and Soviet Revolutions, which we refer to as the first cold war. It then intensified in the years following the Second World War (the cold war proper), especially in the wake of the Cuban Revolution and its revolutionary promotion within (and beyond) the hemisphere, which triggered particularly excessive counterrevolutionary responses in the region's Southern Cone and its final Central American killing fields. This volume illuminates several of the signature episodes that epitomized Latin America's "century of revolution," from its onset in Mexico in 1910, seven years before the Bolshevik Revolution, through the 1990s peace accords that brought an (often partial and uneasy) resolution to decades of revolutionary and counterrevolutionary violence in Central America. Moreover, in sharply framing questions of what violence meant in twentieth-century Latin America and from whence it sprang, this collection also has implications for the role that violence is likely to play in the region's present and future politics (of which more later).

As we know, post–cold war triumphalism proved to be of rather brief duration. The stunningly rapid demise of the Washington Consensus in Latin America and elsewhere (even before 9/11 and war in the Middle East, largely owing to self-inflicted wounds), powerfully revealed the end of a very brief "end of history." Such real world developments must prove unsettling for the triumphant liberalism that drives hard revisionist scholarship on revolutionary movements and political violence. In such renditions, political violence is often rendered unfathomable, senseless, a mirror onto the dark side of the human soul (and thereby largely ahistorical), typical of the contests that have always pitted true-believing, often ruthless revolutionaries against their similarly unrestrained antagonists. In such accounts, revolutionary violence and terror become the inverse—and serve to preempt— liberal democracy in the West or its peripheries.[2] And yet, twentieth-century Latin American history belies such tropes. As Grandin argues and as many of the collection's essays bear out, rather than serving as the rhetorical opposite of liberalism in Latin America, violence and terror served first to prop up exclusionary, authoritarian landed regimes that were firmly allied with the United States, and later, in many countries, severed the relationship between "individual dignity and social solidarity," thus "destroying the more capacious, social understanding of democracy that had prevailed in the region after World War II and laying the foundation for neoliberalism."[3] Thus, this volume contends, the history of political violence in twentieth-century Latin America affords "a sociologically nuanced view of the chronological unfolding of the [region's] ideological hardening and polarization, one that refuses a tautological positing of ideological radicalism as the cause of radicalization. It forces an appreciation of the catalytic power of political reaction to breed ever more accelerating rhythms of frustration, fear, and extremism."[4]

Far from being "unfathomable," political violence in twentieth-century Latin America has been so identifiable as a factor in buttressing class and ethnic exploitation, restricting channels of political involvement, and perpetuating models of exclusionary nationalism and dependent development, on the one hand, and in advancing projects to challenge these ills, on the other, that the region's historians have often taken political violence for granted. In the process, they have ceded the examination of critical questions regarding violence and terror's practice and meaning to practitioners of other disciplines. The contributions to *A Century of Revolution* help to redress this imbalance, fleshing out the elite and popular dynamics of—and the complex interrelations between—revolutionary and counterrevolutionary violence.

Grandin's introductory essay concludes with several programmatic suggestions. Among them are: (1) *The need to construct precise chronologies of revolutionary/counterrevolutionary engagement*. Such chronologies allow us to distinguish actors' post hoc claims of historical inevitability from the actual indeterminacy and contingency of revolutionary scenarios, which not only restores agency to an array of participants, but enables us to scrutinize the distinct ways in which "red" and "white" violence feed off each other, most notably when left and right forces vie to fill the vacuum of sovereignty that emerges in contests for state power. (2) *The necessity of acknowledging the dynamism and adaptability of counterrevolution*. Here, particular attention should be given to the Right's capacity to recruit new allies and refashion its worldview in the face of revolutionary challenges, occasionally mimicking discourses and organizational practices of the Left, while harnessing and projecting local fears and sentiments into an anticommunist ideology with global reach. (For this mimicking, see Corey Robin's contribution to this volume.) (3) Finally, there is *the related need to examine how Latin America's diverse, socially embedded conflicts played out in international fields of power*, and thereby constitute important problems in the international and transnational history of U.S. empire and global cold war.

Related to this last theme is the suggestive point on which Grandin concludes: that we define Latin America's revolutionary twentieth century as a "distinct historical period." The point here, in keeping with the central dialectic the volume poses, is that from the Mexican Revolution through the Central American insurgencies, the progress of both Latin America's efforts to overcome its inequitable and stunted development *and* the United States' rise, first to hemispheric and then to global hegemony, "proceeded on parallel tracks, with each greatly informing the shape the other took."[5] In other words, Latin America's century of revolution proceeded in the context of a long cold war. This attempt to examine the intricacies of political violence that attended revolutionary and counterrevolutionary movements *and* the imperial dynamics of cold war, *within the same conceptual frame*, makes this volume rather unique. *A Century of Revolution* thus attempts to provide a coherent interpretation of Latin America's twentieth-century political history, suggesting broader regional conclusions based on the histories of individual countries that are typically viewed alone.

The Long Cold War

Obviously such a task requires a rather different understanding of what we mean by the term "cold war," and how we might periodize it. For most historians and social scientists of Latin America the term has been reserved for the period that began with the hardening of relations between the United States and the Soviet Union around 1947 and ended with the implosion of the Soviet Union sometime between 1989 and 1991. "Cold war" has served as a kind of "shorthand to describe either direct U.S. or Cuban [or Soviet] intervention in Latin American politics, or the collateral damage from super-power conflict."[6] With some notable exceptions prior to the present volume, what has been lacking is a framework for understanding the *grassroots* dynamics and meanings of the Latin American cold war, one that would better integrate the conflict's domestic and foreign dimensions.[7] Studies have proceeded largely in the conventional channels of diplomatic history, focusing on discrete U.S. policy objectives and high-profile leaders and events (e.g., the Cuban Missile Crisis) and drawing disproportionately on U.S. government documents. And because there has been so little cross-talk between foreign relations scholars and historians of Latin American politics and society, relatively little attention has focused on how evolving U.S. interests and patterns of international conflict (of which the postwar superpower rivalry constituted only a part) factored into transforming the region's political, social, and cultural life over medium and longer durations.

Newer work, such as that represented in the essays here, contends that conventional assumptions about the Latin American cold war are in need of revision, beginning with notions of chronology. On a variety of fronts throughout the course of the twentieth century, Latin American elites and popular classes participated in local and national political struggles that rarely escaped the powerful undertow of international conflicts. At certain junctures—in the wake of the Mexican Revolution of 1910, or after the Cuban Revolution launched its strategy of international armed struggle in the 1960s and 1970s, or during the transnationalized anticommunist crusade of the 1970s and 1980s—these contests and the leftist and rightist ideologies that fueled them transcended national borders and influenced relationships among the world's great powers.[8] As we see in one contribution after another in this volume, it was common practice for Latin American ruling elites to utilize anticommunist/cold war rationales and racialized "civilizing" discourses, which were frequently imported from outside the region and then refashioned to meet local needs. Such doctrines and tropes buttressed the creation of legitimation of authoritarian regimes, and enabled elites to repress, wage war against, and thereby discipline their citizens—to "maintain the weight of the night," as Chilean state-builder Diego Portales rather candidly expressed the elite project of hegemony. As local contests throughout Latin America were subsumed in broader, polarizing ideological conflicts whose logic was at least as much North-South as East-West (even during the cold war proper), opposition movements, like the states they opposed, received inspiration and material support from abroad. Nevertheless, this volume's case studies go a long way to counter right-wing interpretations of leftist insurgencies and states as principally inspired or directed by Moscow, which (apart from its decades-long support of revolutionary Cuba) more often than not neglected and underestimated them. (Witness particularly the essays by Gould, Winn, and McAllister on Central America and Chile, which demonstrate a lack of external support and firepower, which, along with compelling internal factors, sealed the fate of revolutionary movements and projects in the face of a fierce U.S.-supported reaction.) Indeed, the new research showcased here and elsewhere typically depicts Latin America's Lefts as *sui generis* and autonomous, firmly attached to deeply rooted traditions of popular liberalism and to radical, communally driven forms of social democracy and populism—even when their programs and communiqués were articulated in more standard Marxist-Leninist discourse.[9]

By extending the cold war back to the Mexican Revolution, the twentieth-century's first great social revolution, this collection redefines the notion of cold war in rather bold fashion. Here it is not a fight among proxies of post–Second World War superpowers, but an attempt by the United States (and its local clients) to contain insurgencies that challenged post-(or neo-)colonial social formations predicated on dependent economies and class, ethnic, and gender inequality. To be sure, there had been challenges to the United States's ascendant hegemony even before the Mexican (and Bolshevik) Revolutions: marines had been landing on Caribbean and Central American beaches to defuse modernizing nationalist challenges for the better part of two decades (for example, when they toppled the Nicaraguan liberal modernizer José Santos Zelaya in 1909). Seen in the context of North-South imperial dynamics, one could make the case that the Latin American cold war began in 1898 and has not yet ended. Over a century ago, in his famous corollary to the Monroe Doctrine, President Theodore Roosevelt told the U.S. Congress that "chronic wrongdoing or an impotence which results in a general loosening of the ties of civilized society may, in America as elsewhere, ultimately require intervention by some civilized nation," namely, "however reluctantly," the United States. It is hard to refute the fact that over the course of the past century, the United States has repeatedly intervened to protect its southern neighbors from foreign and evil empires and ensure that the "ties of civilized society"—as Washington defined them—remained firm. With talk so pronounced in the first years of the new millennium about the "benevolent hegemony" and "benevolent empire" of the United States, with the Bush administration having demonstrated its preemptive resolve to contend globally to guarantee not only U.S. interests but its prescriptions for global civilization as well (defined in terms of Washington's notions of international security and markets), and with the new Obama administration showing a surprising degree of diplomatic continuity with its predecessor, are we not embarked on another dichotomizing rendition of cold war? In this incarnation, there is a new "axis of evil," composed of narcotraffickers, terrorists, rogue regimes and movements, and failed states. The members of this network (which include some holdovers from the last conflict, such as Fidel Castro and the Nicaraguan Sandinistas) can be constructed as broadly or narrowly as circumstances dictate—just as communism was.[10] Indeed, as Forrest Hylton demonstrates in his essay, yesterday's Colombian narcoterrorist paramilitaries have been reinvented and embraced as the movers and shakers behind Medellín's new glittering model of globalization.

At certain moments, as when Vladimir Putin sends arms to Hugo Chávez's Bolivarian Socialist regime in Venezuela, or the United States faces off with Russia over the latter's intervention in Georgia, we experience an eerie sense of déjà vu, which has led scholars, mainstream journalists, and novelists alike to speak of a "new cold war" (or at least a "big chill").[11] The question remains, however, whether we are experiencing something really new or witnessing the latest stage of a broader pattern of continuity. Reflecting on the longue durée of U.S. imperialism and its continuities in North-South relations, one maverick diplomatic historian quipped, "Maybe there was no cold war in Latin America at all, at least in the conventional sense of explaining all important events through the prism of U.S.-Soviet rivalry."[12]

For our purposes, there seems to be a good case for locating the onset of Latin America's long cold war with the tumultuous upheaval in Mexico at the end of the twentieth century's first decade. Mexican and international historians have long and robustly debated the character of the revolution, and the consensus is that its causation owed more to endogamous than exogenous factors.[13] Still, the revolution's internal and external dimensions must be related—and historicized by period and region—as Friedrich Katz's scholarship here and elsewhere persuasively demonstrates.[14] The outbreak of hostilities in November 1910 quickly ushered in the demise of Mexico's thirty-four-year Porfirian dictatorship, the longest-running liberal-positivist, oligarchical regime in Latin American history. And although the revolution rather quickly moved to the center and turned inward under the winning Constitutionalist faction (as its leadership displayed little inclination to exercise a "world historical" role in the manner of the Soviets or, later, the Chinese and Cubans), it had profound hemispheric consequences. Not only did agrarian activists affiliated with the losing radical and populist factions fan out to other regions of Mexico, there to create intriguing social laboratories of revolutionary reform (e.g., Felipe Carrillo Puerto in

Yucatán); others, including internationalists like the Nicaraguan Augusto César Sandino, traveled to Central America to organize on large estates and oppose oligarchic rule. One internationalist sojourner, India's M. N. Roy, traveled to revolutionary Mexico after being exiled from the United States by President Woodrow Wilson; there he helped found the Mexican Communist Party before moving on to Europe and Asia to work with the Third Communist International. Still other radical intellectuals and cultural workers extended Mexico's revolutionary impulse across borders: probably best known is the Mexican muralist Diego Rivera, who pioneered expressive forms of public and plastic art that would galvanize later generations of popular and revolutionary mobilization far beyond Mexico (including in the United States itself).[15]

Although the ideology of Mexico's early institutional revolutionary state (the so-called Sonoran Dynasty of Alvaro Obregón and Plutarco Calles, from 1920 to 1934) was rather moderate, "the Revolution"—epitomized by its first decade of violent popular struggle, which was immediately codified in the highly nationalist constitution of 1917 that loomed like a sword of Damocles over the heads of foreign investors—quickly riveted the United States' attention. As Katz shows, Washington's response to Mexico in the 1920s and 1930s alternated between threat and accommodation, which played a significant role in tempering the nature and pace of reform of Mexico's "revolution from above." At the same time, however latent, the Mexican Revolution's social, agrarian, and nationalist promise made it impossible for the United States to adhere to the political and economic assumptions and practices that had previously guided nearly half a century of unrestrained dollar and gunboat diplomacy in Latin America.

Of course, Mexico's revolution played out against the backdrop of the institutionalization of the Bolshevik regime, and the onset of Comintern activity in the Western hemisphere.[16] In the 1920s and early 1930s, the anticommunist hysteria that had such violent consequences in the United States and for the popular domestic movements that Olcott, Gould, and Klubock document (a harbinger of more elaborate "dirty wars" that would follow), also played out internationally in U.S. hostility toward the Calles regime. Despite wooing foreign capital, bringing the revolution's agrarian reform to a screeching halt, and repressing independent unions, Calles was consistently cast as a Bolshevik proxy (much as Cuba would be decades later), not least when Washington occupied Nicaragua in the late 1920s to eradicate the Sandino rebellion and "quarantine Mexican revolutionary contagion."

However, the onset of the Great Depression and, later, the ascendance of Franklin D. Roosevelt's New Deal administration at home and the rise of the Axis powers abroad, would serve to moderate U.S. policy toward the Mexican Revolution, which now manifested itself in the form of populist President Lázaro Cárdenas's radically nationalist reforms, such as the 1938 oil expropriation. Indeed, throughout the region as whole the United States now took a more multilateralist ("Panamerican" or "Good Neighbor") stance towards populist and popular front regimes and movements, several of which were significantly influenced by Mexican precedents to extend social rights and forge a more inclusive national-popular identity.

This good neighborliness would be short-lived, as the essays in parts 2 and 3 bear out. Recent work by social and labor historians has begun to flesh out Latin America's brief but tumultuous "democratic spring" in the years immediately following the Second World War. The war had spurred economic growth and facilitated the politicization of Latin American societies led by labor and the Left. Large numbers of working- and middle-class Latin Americans had also been inspired by the democratic rhetoric generated in the fight against fascism, not least by the massive transnational propaganda effort mounted in collaboration with local elites by Nelson Rockefeller's Office of the Coordinator of Inter-American Affairs. Initially, the United States lent support to this democratic effervescence, which prompted Latin American oligarchic and military elites temporarily to acquiesce to popular demands for greater political and economic participation in their societies. By the late 1940s, however, with bipolar conflict hardening, Washington's experiment with multilateralism and social democracy was quickly shut down.[17] By 1958, the Eisenhower administration was pouring $100 million a year into the region's militaries, primarily to maintain "internal security." In the decades that followed, every Latin American military establishment except Cuba's received assistance from the United States, with the most repressive among them receiving the largest allocations. Washington's "Public Safety Program" provided weapons and training for foreign police and security forces. Ostensibly the program was meant to underwrite both the inculcation of democracy and the suppression of communism; yet there never was much doubt which principle had priority. Consider the role-playing exercise that was staged during these years at the International Police Academy in Washington, D.C., where foreign trainees pretended to run a police command center during a simulated crisis of urban unrest. Trainees were charged with suppressing a subversive group called "the

National Committee for Agrarian Reform," which was supported from across the border with a mythical country known as "Maoland." At the end of the training course, the foreign policemen were each given a copy of FBI director J. Edgar Hoover's book about communist infiltration of the United States, *Masters of Deceit*. They were also told that their nations' militaries should stay out of politics. Which discourse would prove more compelling was easy to predict. All told, during the cold war proper, the United States would train over two hundred thousand Latin American security personnel, thirty-five thousand of them at the School of the Americas, which became known popularly within the region as the "School of Coups," because so many Latin American coup leaders figured as its alumni. These programs, as well as others sponsored by U.S. surrogates such as Israel, South Africa, France, and Argentina, schooled Latin American enforcement personnel in various aspects of anticommunist dogma, high-tech surveillance, interrogation, and terror—the linchpin for all of which was the doctrine of internal security. It is hardly surprising, therefore, that they came to see subversion and infiltration everywhere, particularly in movements and initiatives for social reform.[18]

Of course the hemispheric containment of communism during the cold war proper was not limited to the training and financing of brutal security states (which McAllister examines in the case of Guatemala), or the orchestration of coups, destabilizing "psy ops," and "low-intensity conflict" (tactics analyzed in relation to Chile and Central America in the essays by Winn and Gould). In Cuba and Nicaragua, the United States organized invading "Contra" forces; and when circumstances required or low-cost opportunities beckoned, Washington itself invaded (in the Dominican Republic, Panama and Grenada).

Yet even as the contributors provide accounts of U.S-supported counter-revolution, the agents who implemented it on the ground, and the consequences it wrought, they do so dialectically: imperial intervention both responded to the immanent threat of postwar structural change and, in turn, provided the impetus for new revolutionary movements and initiatives. In this sense, the Cuban Revolution may be seen as an important fulcrum in Latin America's century of revolution: the frustration and anger engendered by Latin America's failed democratic spring, which in Guatemala included the overthrow of Jacobo Arbenz's popular social democratic regime in 1954 and, later, the virtual liquidation of the Old Left that was attempting to rekindle it, produced a radicalization of the Left's political agenda in one nation after another—and a resolve to avoid the fate of Guatemala. In this sense, the Cuban case served "both [to crystallize] decades of regional experience and [to link] that experience to a broader, global crisis of legitimacy that by 1968 had threatened to overwhelm both West and East alike."[19] It is hard to argue with Lillian Guerra's contention that perhaps no other revolution since Haiti's, led by slaves at the end of the eighteenth century, has so directly threatened the hemispheric or larger world order: symbolically and materially undermining U.S. power and structures of capital, and shredding the myth of the imperial hegemon's "'democratic' intentions toward Latin American nations whose internal political processes it strove to manipulate for over two hundred years (despite official proclamations of respect for national sovereignty)."[20]

This stripping away of the veneer of U.S. innocence and exceptionalism is brought out effectively by Michelle Chase in her discussion of the Latin American voices that rose to defend the newly triumphant Cuban Revolution against American indictments of its revolutionary tribunals. These writers contrasted the measured and judicious violence of the tribunals with the United States' legacy of "imperialist violence," not only throughout the region in support of tyrants like Fulgencio Batista, but also against people of color at home. Thus, while Washington and *Time* magazine cast the trials as a "bath of blood," rooted in the "Latin capacity for brooding revenge," Mexican critics conjured images of America's own "furies"—its tradition of lynchings and other episodes of class and race violence that endured long after the Civil War and the abolition of slavery.

Yet, as the essays by McAllister, Gould, Rénique, and Hylton illustrate, while the Cuban Revolution was indeed epochal, mass movements and insurgencies empowering campesinos, workers, and middle sectors were queuing up simultaneously throughout the region—in Guatemala, Nicaragua, Peru, and Colombia. Rénique's contribution, for example, recovers an impressive movement of Peruvian peasants and workers in the late 1950s and 1960s—a movement that recent "end of history" interpretations following the cold war have either elided or discounted.

As with Haiti, Cuba's Fidelista revolution prompted a rethinking of everything the world's ruling elites took for granted; and as with Haiti (and Mexico), these elites, led by Washington, sought to paint Cuba as a pariah, a rogue nation. Cuba's broader understanding of its revolutionary mission and (unlike Haiti) its capacity to project that vision within and outside Latin America (most notably in Africa), served to fuel imperial elites' characterization of Cuba. But it also spawned imitators in the Andes, Central America, and the Southern Cone. What makes the Cuban conjuncture particularly consequential is the revolution's capacity to fracture schlerotic Old Left groupings and inspire New Left activists even after the limitations of its *foco* strategy became painfully obvious. As the essays by Winn, McAllister, Gould, and Rénique suggest, the revolutionary initiatives in Chile, Guatemala, Nicaragua, and Peru, which were predicated on New Left political identities and the merits of *concientización* ("consciousness-raising"), were as much reactions to the Cuban model as they were products of it. The *vía chilena*'s experiment with political pluralism; the attempt by Guatemala's Ejército Guerrillero de los Pobres to incorporate entire indigenous communities into its insurgency; the Sandinistas' efforts to harness radical Christian currents with an undogmatic Marxism in Nicaragua—and more recently, the attempts of Venezuelan Bolivarian Socialism and Bolivian radical *indigenismo* to forge new political paths—all reflect some level of engagement (positive and negative) with the Cuban experience. Significantly, Fidel Castro has consistently counseled allies such as Daniel Ortega and Hugo Chávez to learn from the Cuban Revolution's mistakes as well as its successes.

The success of the Right against revolutionary movements in the final stages of the cold war can be attributed to a number of factors. No doubt, at least in part, it owed to the capacity of the Right to address—and coopt—some of the frustrated popular demands that had driven so many reformers and revolutionaries in the first place. But in the final analysis, most accounts suggest that it was the fusion of imported, high-tech, "best counterinsurgent practice" with a ferocious brand of local repression and terror that enabled right-wing regimes in Central America and much of South America's Southern Cone to destroy the New Left's ideological and political challenge in the period that ran from the 1960s to the mid-1990s.[21]

The legacies of those brutal decades are with us still. Certainly the cold war is still palpable in Central America and the Southern Cone, the Andean nations, and even Mexico, as relatives of the victims of terror continue to protest past atrocities, exhume graves, and actively press legal claims against the perpetrators—thus far, with mixed results. Nor has the violence entirely subsided: lynchings and other episodes of extrajudicial violence continue to bubble up in countries like Guatemala, Nicaragua, Honduras, El Salvador, and Mexico. Such local violence frequently maps onto the fault lines and frustrations of recent cold war pasts, and in some cases intersects with newer manifestations of *bandidaje*, gang violence, and drugs and arms smuggling.

At the regional level, Grandin provocatively argues that the cold war's furies laid the groundwork for neoliberalism by preempting alternative development strategies. Thus, especially in Central America and the Southern Cone, cold war terror silenced demands for economic justice, hollowed out the egalitarian content from postwar democracy, severed alliances between reforming elites and popular classes, and used repression to reduce powerful collective movements to individual survival strategies. In his view, Latin America's "transition to democracy" did not come with the eclipse of the cold war's counterinsurgent military regimes; rather, they themselves brokered the transition, and their brutal "success" made the region's subsequent radical free-market policies possible.[22]

In the essays by Hylton and Larsen, the new neoliberal landscape that has emerged following the cold war is a bleak one. It is characterized by weak states, endemic violence, judicial impunity, and the perpetuation of counterrevolutionary and paramilitary elites. Such self-avowed "modernizing elites" are now even better positioned to profit in today's globalized, crony-ridden "economies of plunder," where the distinctions between licit and illicit spheres have even less meaning than during the cold war proper. Meantime, the gap between rich and poor continues to widen: 221 million Latin Americans, virtually half of the region's total population, live in poverty—165 million of them on less than two dollars a day.[23] In Mexico, the poster nation for Washington "free trade" doctrines (and also for narcotics and arms smuggling), two-thirds of the country's economically active population survives on informal activities (as street vendors and the like); more than 30 percent is unemployed or underemployed; and hundreds of thousands are driven annually to migrate without documents. In short, although the cold war witnessed in one nation after another the formation of new political subjectivities and a lifting of the weight of the night, the material burdens that the day confers remain onerous indeed.

And yet, an assessment of the legacies of the cold war proper or of Latin America's century of revolution should not end on such a bleak note. As this volume suggests, decades of revolutionary process have served (especially in Central America) as a battering ram to crack the unity of the old landed order, eradicate outdated, coercive rural labor regimes, and pave the way for more modernized labor relations (if only the euphemistic "flexibilization" of labor that underwrites the current neoliberal model). And while social and criminal violence and judicial impunity reflect the blowback of the cold war and are indicators of the shrunken state that is meant to serve the needs of ruling elites, they have not gone unchallenged. Local defense initiatives and mass movements for truth telling and forensic accountability throughout the region have not only registered some tangible gains; in the process they have significantly altered the cultural fabric of societies and the manner in which the past is collectively remembered.

Finally, while hopes among the more self-critical groups of the Left have begun to fade regarding the possibilities for structural change in post–cold war Latin America, there is also cause for some optimism, based in part on the essays collected here. Initially, it was hoped that, with the onus of communism lifted, the promotion of social justice issues might rise to the top of the agenda for inter-American relations. It immediately became clear (among other things, in the Bush administration's signing-off on a coup attempt against Chávez in Venezuela), that Washington would not foment projects for structural change, and was too preoccupied elsewhere to engage much with Latin America anyway. In the meantime, however, the failure of Washington Consensus policies to narrow the income gap either within nations or between North and South (preponderant evidence suggests these gaps have widened), coupled with popular dissatisfaction with traditional political parties and corporatist labor arrangements, have produced a resurgence of the Left in many countries in the region (the so-called Pink Tide since about 2005). This watershed must be read against the changes in political subjectivity that occurred during Latin America's century of revolution, particularly since the 1960s. Winn, McAllister, and Gould, in particular, relate the violence of revolutionary and counterrevolutionary process to movements of communal and especially personal liberation. Elsewhere, the political scientist Elisabeth Wood contends that in El Salvador men and women committed themselves to the insurgency of the 1970s and 1980s not because the nation's violent and exploitative order left them no other option, but because of the dignity and self-fulfillment that such commitments conferred.[24] This kind of participation, whatever the eventual outcome of a specific insurgency or revolution, was particularly disruptive for societies structured around rigid social roles and ethnic, class, and gender hierarchies.[25] Despite the terror and repression visited upon them, the popular classes often emerged from these struggles with new expectations and expanded notions of their rights. McAllister's ethnography revealed Chupolenses' recollections of the pleasures of agency, "pride in their own ingenuity and courage in the face of the enemy," even in the bleakest moments of the scorched-earth years. No doubt many individuals have drawn on these memories and experiences in their fight to ameliorate life under the neo-liberal order. In most societies they now contend on a different rhetorical plane, with a language of legal proceduralism and human, ethnic/cultural, and gender rights replacing that of social transformation. In Venezuela and Bolivia, and other parts of South America, social transformation remains very much on the agenda, and is intimately tied to state-driven initiatives that include South-South alliances for economic development. Still, it remains to be seen how these national projects will ultimately adapt to imperial challenges posed by the United States, and how the revolutionary state will use foreign antagonisms and the fear of counterrevolution to shape political culture and discipline expressions of dissent at home.

Notes

1. For a companion volume that also contributes to this latter endeavor, see Gilbert M. Joseph and Daniela Spenser, eds., *In from the Cold: Latin America's New Encounter with the Cold War* (Durham: Duke University Press, 2008).

2. See Grandin's introduction to this volume, "Living in Revolutionary Time," and his book *The Last Colonial Massacre: Latin America in the Cold War* (Chicago: University of Chicago Press, 2004).

3. Grandin, *The Last Colonial Massacre*, xv.

4. Grandin, introduction to this volume, "Living in Revolutionary Time," 1.

5. Ibid.

6. Greg Grandin, "Off the Beach: The United States, Latin America, and the Cold War," in *A Companion to Post-1945 America*, ed. Jean-Christophe Agnew and Roy Rosenzweig (New York: Blackwell, 2002), 426–45, quotation on 430.

7. Such exceptions would include Grandin, *The Last Colonial Massacre*; Joseph and Spenser, *In from the Cold;* Daniela Spenser, ed., *Espejos de la guerra fría: México, América Central y el Caribe* (Mexico City: Miguel Angel Porrúa, 2004); Odd Arne Westad, *The Global Cold War, Third World Interventions and the Making of Our Times* (New York: Cambridge University Press, 2005); and Richard Saull, *Rethinking Theory and History in the Cold War: The State, Military Power and Social Revolution* (London: Frank Cass, 2001).

8. See, for example, Friedrich Katz, *The Secret War in Mexico: Europe, the United States, and the Mexican Revolution* (Chicago: University of Chicago Press, 1981); the

essays by Piero Gleijeses and Ariel Armony on Cuba's and Argentina's transnationalization of the cold war, in Joseph and Spenser, *In from the Cold*; and Gleijeses's *Conflicting Missions: Havana, Washington, and Africa, 1959–1976* (Chapel Hill: University of North Carolina Press, 2002).

9. See, for example, the discussion and works cited in Gilbert Joseph, "What We Now Know and Should Know: Bringing Latin America More Meaningfully into Cold War Studies," in Joseph and Spenser, *In from the Cold*, 3–46, esp. 29 and nn. 117–18.

10. This discussion draws on ibid., 6 and nn. 11–12.

11. Ibid., 6–7 and n. 15; also see Steven F. Cohen, "The New American Cold War," *Nation*, July 17, 2006; Steven Lee Myers, "No Cold War, but Big Chill," *New York Times*, August 16, 2008; and Edward Lucas, *The New Cold War: Putin's Russia and the Threat to the West* (New York: Palgrave Macmillan, 2008).

12. Max Paul Friedman, personal communication, May 1, 2008.

13. See, for example, the spirited debate between Alan Knight and John Hart in *Rural Revolt in Mexico and U.S. Intervention*, ed. Daniel Nugent (San Diego: Center for U.S.-Mexican Studies, 1988).

14. Katz, *The Secret War* and *The Life and Times of Pancho Villa* (Stanford: Stanford University Press, 1998); for a historiographical discussion, see Gilbert Joseph and Daniel Nugent, eds., *Everyday Forms of State Formation: Revolution and the Negotiation of Rule in Mexico* (Durham: Duke University Press, 1994), esp. 5–23.

15. See, for example, John Dwyer, *Agrarian Dispute: The Expropriation of American-Owned Rural Land in Postrevolutionary Mexico* (Durham: Duke University Press, 2008).

16. Daniela Spenser, *La Internacional Comunista en México: los primeros tropiezos* (Mexico City: CIESAS, 2006).

17. For the coming and demise of Latin America's "democratic spring," see Grandin, *The Last Colonial Massacre*; Leslie Bethell and Ian Roxborough, eds., *Latin America between the Second World War and the Cold War* (Cambridge: Cambridge University Press, 1992); and Leslie Bethell and Ian Roxborough, "The Impact of the Cold War on Latin America," in *Origins of the Cold War: An International History*, ed. Melvyn Leffler and David Painter (New York: Routledge, 1994), 293–316.

18. Martha Huggins, *Political Policing: The United States and Latin America* (Durham: Duke University Press, 1998); and Leslie Gill, *The School of the Americas: Military Training and Political Violence in the Americas* (Durham: Duke University Press, 2004). I am grateful to Max Friedman for bringing the international training course to my attention.

19. Grandin, "Living in Revolutionary Time."

20. Lillian Guerra, "Beyond Paradox: Counterrevolution and the Origins of Political Culture in the Cuban Revolution, 1959–2009," in this volume.

21. For a discussion and relevant citations, see Grandin, *The Last Colonial Massacre*, esp. 169–98; also see Joseph, "What We Now Know," 24–27. Of course, the capacity of New Left challenges varied significantly throughout the hemisphere. In Argentina, Brazil, and Uruguay, the left groups and organizations that were targeted by right-wing terror regimes were far less formidable and cohesive than mass movements such as Allende's Popular Unity or the Nicaraguan Frente Sandinista de Liberación Nacional (FSLN), or the guerrilla fronts in El Salvador and Guatemala.

22. See Grandin, *The Last Colonial Massacre* and "Living in Revolutionary Time"; for a discussion of this argument, see Joseph. "What We Now Know," 27–28.

23. Donald Huddle, "Post-1982 Effects of Neoliberalism on Latin American Development and Poverty: Two Conflicting Views," in *Economic Development and Cultural Change* 45, no. 4 (July 1997): 881–97, esp. 889; and Juan Forero, "Free Trade Proposal Splits Bolivian City," *New York Times*, March 9, 2005.

24. Elisabeth Wood, *Insurgent Collective Action and Civil War in El Salvador* (Cambridge: Cambridge University Press, 2003).

25. Recently, several Latin Americanist historians have argued for a "revisionist framework" for New Left studies that more explicitly draws attention to the "non-armed aspects of radical challenges to political and social norms." Their work draws our attention to transgressive, largely urban countercultural practices: "new aesthetic sensibilities, trends in film, literature, theater, music, the arts, as well as the impact of Liberation Theology." For a discussion of this proposal, and of the influences on it by new cultural histories of the U.S. New Left, see Eric Zolov, "Expanding Our Conceptual Horizons: The Shift from an Old to a New Left in Latin America," *A Contracorriente* (an online journal of Latin American social history and literature, http://www.ncsu.edu/acontracorriente/) (Winter 2008): 47–73, esp. 51–52, 73. Zolov and others link these countercultural forms and aesthetic sensibilities to transnational processes, "without disaggregating them from the discourses and proximity of violent revolutionary movements." Thus, although Latin America's emerging counterculture was "in many respects emulative of foreign models, at the same time intrinsic to its popularity among youth—and what made it anathema to the conservative press—was its posture of defiance of traditional hierarchies that formed the core principal of the new youth style" (73). Reminiscing about his own sixties activism against imperialism, the Mexican anthropologist and cultural critic Roger Bartra observes: "Marijuana was linked to Marxism, unconventional forms of eroticism went along with [support for] the guerrillas. In my house, beatniks and aspiring revolutionaries would get together, those searching for artificial paradises along with those who wanted to destroy systems of oppression." Roger Bartra, "Memorias de la

contracultura," *Letras Libres* (November 2007): 35; also cited in Zolov, "Expanding Our Cultural Horizons," 47–48. Later, in the mould of Che Guevara, Bartra would join the Communist Party and consciously suppress his bohemianism in the interest of furthering mass revolutionary action, with checkered results. Zolov's call to explore the congruence and fluidity of transgressive cultural practices and political ideology, as well as the transnational underpinnings of this dynamic, deserves more attention than this collection can provide. For more discussion of the cultural and transnational dimensions of the Latin American cold war, see Joseph and Spenser, *In from the Cold*.

History as Containment

An Interview with Arno J. Mayer

GREG GRANDIN

GREG GRANDIN: Your work in the early 1960s focused on the emergence of a "new diplomacy" after the First World War, locating its origins in the struggles between "the forces of order and the forces of movement" in Europe and the United States over how best to respond to a number of challenges and threats. Those included the rise of mass politics at home and Leninism abroad, as well as nationalist movements contesting imperial and colonial rule. Your comparative approach was certainly ahead of its time, considering that "transnationalism" is very fashionable in diplomatic history circles today. But what seems truly innovative is the close attention you paid to the relationship between domestic and international factors in generating interstate tensions and conflicts.

ARNO J. MAYER: I'm not sure what I was doing was that new. It was informed by a commitment to comparative history. Most diplomatic historians will tell the story of the foreign policy and diplomacy either of one country or between two countries, but it seemed to me that the world which emerged from the First World War could no longer be dealt with in that way. It makes no sense to look at just France and Germany, for example, because both were embedded in larger configurations—social, economic, cultural, political, and so forth. And there was also my attention to, as you say, the relationship between domestic and foreign considerations.

GG: It was the road-not-taken by subsequent diplomatic historians, who tend to focus their debates on whether politics, economics, or, more recently, culture, have primacy in driving international relations. Yet by placing those determinants within a comparative framework you largely steered clear of tricky "first cause" arguments—though "comparative," or "transnational," for that matter, doesn't seem like the right word to describe your method, which stresses the need to situate "crisis politics" within interdependent and mutually reinforcing fields of power and to analyze their evolution in multiple, overlapping time frames.

AJM: Systematic attention to the relationship between foreign and domestic policy was certainly both a conceptual and historical concern I've had through the years. It came naturally to someone who got his Ph.D. in international relations and then wrote his dissertation in history. I left political science because I didn't want to be trapped in conceptual abstractions. We all do taxonomies, typologies, and so forth. But rather than coming out of thin air, they ought to be constructed from the historical circumstances and materials you are dealing with. In retrospect, the weakness of my earlier work was that in analyzing the domestic sources of foreign policy, I was too fixed on politics and short-changed other factors—social, economic, and above all cultural—which I did not address until *The Persistence of the Old Regime* [1988].

GG: Latin Americanists would certainly recognize the argument of that book, which takes many of the assumptions of modernization theory that at the time were used to explain underdevelopment and violence in the third world and applies them to Europe. In particular, it looks at how, in the world's most advanced capitalist countries, rapid economic and technological changes ran headlong into "premodern," or feudal, political structures, class relations, and ideological and cultural sentiments, leading to total war.

AJM: I did try to apply those arguments to Europe. This seems to me self-evident, that you have a gap between the old and the new, which creates tensions and explosions. But it wasn't just modernization theory. [Joseph] Schumpeter described it as the interpenetration of feudal and bourgeois sectors. Marxists were concerned with this as well, with what Ernst Bloch called the "the simultaneity of the nonsimultaneous," or "the synchronicity of the nonsynchronous." We are living through this today in the United States.

GG: You place great importance on the power of political reaction, and in many ways history as you write it could be considered "history as containment," not of communism but of mass democracy.

AJM: I don't think I deserve any credit for something that is so obvious. When you have a frontal challenge to an established order, with not just a political or economic dimension but cultural and religious ones as well, be it in the domestic sphere or at the interstate level, there would have to be a reaction. It goes without saying that those invested in it would try to mount a defense. When I got on to this issue, when I made up that typology "conservative," "reactionary," "counterrevolutionary" for the *Dynamics of Counter-Revolution* [1971], I was moved to go both to Princeton's library and to the Bibliothèque Nationale in Paris. It was back when they still used card catalogues, and there were plenty of entries under the heading "conservatives." But when it came to "counterrevolution," the label didn't exist. There were lots of references to "reaction," but they were all in the natural sciences—mathematical, physical, and chemical reactions. That shook me up a bit, because those who make up the catalogue and subject categories after all read the books we write and are part of the scholarly community. Yet even in France, which lived through the French Revolution, there was nothing. It just struck me as transparent that there would be reaction and attempts to contain the revolutionary threat.

GG: Yet you emphasize not only reaction but also the dynamic nature of reaction, how it transforms in relation to the threat it seeks to contain, and how during moments of stress the dialectic between reaction and counter-reaction takes on a life of its own.

AJM: That's right. It's not so much the containment of mass politics, but of democratic mass politics. The one thing that is clear today is the threat of right-wing populism, the mobilization of the masses for the purposes of containing not just revolutionary but reformist elements.

GG: This follows your concern with the relationship between ideology and interests, and your critique of a strain of Marxism that sees too tight a relationship between the two and doesn't appreciate how the latter can escape the bounds of the former. In your work, mobilizations launched by elites to defend their positions often slip from their control, taking on a momentum and an ideology that ultimately prove destructive for all. This is partly how you explain the insanity of the First World War, provoked and escalated by those who sought to contain the threat of mass democracy long after that threat had subsided.

AJM: This is the old question of economic determinism, and what Marxists used to call the relative autonomy of politics. There is autonomy of the political realm, and at some moments there can be a complete detachment of ideology from interests. E. H. Carr was an influence on me. He came out way ahead in the debate he had with Isaiah Berlin over free will and historical determinism. But I do have some reservations now, which I didn't have earlier, in the way Carr, in *What Is History?*, deals with the question of historical possibilities. In my recent work[1] on the Middle East, on Israel in particular, it seems to me there were some other possibilities, and one needs to explore their intellectual, social, and political bases and carriers. In my case, I had to rethink what I believe to be Carr's somewhat exaggerated criticism of Berlin for calling for close attention to historical possibilities at critical crossroads.

GG: And you deal with the question of contingency, of the openness of history, in *The Furies* [2000], particularly as it relates to the chronological unfolding of political violence, in a way that many of the contributors to this volume seem to have appreciated.

AJM: If anything drove me out of political science, it was that political scientists do not take chronology seriously. It makes a difference whether something happened on February 4th or February 5th. To completely expunge the chronological dimension from political thinking, as it was taught, is to make light of the succession of events, and as a consequence you get a totally different reading. Take the problem of how Nazism is studied, the debate between the intentionalists and the functionalists. The intentionalists give nearly complete primacy to ideology and *Mein Kampf*—I'm greatly oversimplifying of course—while the functionalists look at very, very complicated situations in which ideology emerged, crystallized, and became operative at critical turning points. In *Why Did the Heavens Not Darken?* [1988], I argued that there is no coming to grips with the radicalization of the Nazi regime without taking close account of both the text and the context of ideology.

GG: Your work is more conceptually driven than most historians. What are some of the influences?

AJM: Immediately after I got my Ph.D., in the fall of 1953, I spent four months in Southeast Asia, primarily in India. Before that, in 1949 or 1950,

I spent a summer in Israel on a program organized by the Foundation for World Government, headed by Stringfellow Barr.[2] The idea was to see how the collectives, the kibbutzim, might offer a useful development model for the third world, although it wasn't then called the third world. After that, when Barr decided to visit India, he asked me to join him. It was there that I began to rub up against a different world, and learned to look at Europe from the outside. In Travancore-Cochin (Kerala), I joined Ram Lohia, the socialist leader, as he campaigned for election, and heard many debates about competing development strategies. I witnessed from close up the depth of poverty in a state that had India's highest literacy rate, but where the life expectancy of rickshaw drivers, who start spitting blood at eighteen, was in the low twenties.

That gave me, an émigré, a radically new perspective on Western discussions of these issues, which further complicated my vision of the world. When you are born and raised in the Grand Duchy of Luxembourg, you can only laugh at the notion of national history. The dialect I grew up with is not even a written language. So from the beginning I had a wider view of Europe, bordered as we were by Belgium, France, and Germany. No matter what subject I would think about, it made no sense to think in Luxembourgian terms. There are a number of historians who come from small countries who have developed a pan-European vision. There's the Belgian [Henri] Pirenne (1862–1935), the Swiss [Jacob] Burckhardt (1818–97), and the Dutchman [Pieter] Geyl (1887–1966).

Even though I am a refugee from political science, I benefited from its commitment to conceptualization, which historians tend to resist instinctively. When you write conceptual history you leave yourself open to the charge that you are forcing your data to fit a preconceived conceptual frame. François Furet kept telling me that my concept of *ancien régime* fitted every country in Europe but France. Needless to say, practitioners of conceptually formed history must control their temptation to round off the corners. Given your own work I should ask, are there major debates in Latin American history?

GG: There are in colonial Latin American history, which still thinks in terms of broad epochs and still considers the rise and demise of Spanish colonialism, and the emergence of nationalism, as world-historical events. But twentieth-century Latin American historiography largely focuses on individual countries, and as you say, historians don't like to conceptualize. The demise of dependency theory—not so much the assumptions behind it, which many historians most likely share, but as a generative framework of debate—has led to a kind of provincialism and fragmentation. There's been a turn to regional history, microhistory, social history, and now cultural history. Most Latin Americanists are sympathetic to thinking about larger transformations, but they focus on narrower topics that tend to preclude the possibility of debate, and of comparison.

AJM: One of the things I was reminded of by your introduction to this volume is the evolution of historiography. First there was the turn toward quantification. Now we have social and cultural history as well as the history of mentalities and ideologies. Throughout there is a tacit reaction against economic determinism. If you ask me, that's what Braudel and the boys in France were all about.[3] So you have quantification, you have social history, you have cultural history, you have everything except politics and economics. But—and this is a question that has become clear to me after participating in the discussions leading to this book—how could you make sense of Latin America without politics and economics, and, at the same time, without a comparative reading of the different national experiences? It must come back to politics and economics. But your introduction also reminded me of a definition offered by a German sociologist, I forget his name, of crisis: whatever else it is, crisis is not *Dauerzustand*—a permanent condition.

GG: What's episodic in the West is enduring in the rest. But in Latin America, there is also a strong emphasis on analyzing particular *coyunturas*, or conjunctures.

AJM: It must be the continuing influence of structuralism. In any case, working through conjunctures is much better than thinking of history as perpetual crisis. It provides more of a sense of alignments and possibilities.

—Princeton, N.J., September 15, 2008

Notes

1. Arno J. Mayer, *Plowshares into Swords: From Zionism to Israel* (London: Verso, 2008).

2. Stringfellow Barr was a classicist, historian, and mid-century internationalist, as well as president of St. John's College in Annapolis, Maryland. With Scott Buchanan he founded the Foundation for World Government in 1948.

3. In *Why Did the Heavens Not Darken?* Mayer criticizes Fernand Braudel and the Annales school for reducing historical events like the Holocaust to mere "dust"; viii.

Contributors

Michelle Chase received her doctorate from the history department of New York University. Her dissertation, "A Conflicted Liberation: The Gender Politics of the Cuban Revolution, 1952–1962," explores the role of women and gender in the insurrection, revolution, and counterrevolution.

Jeffrey L. Gould is the James H. Rudy Professor of History at Indiana University, Bloomington, and the author of *To Lead as Equals: Rural Protest and Peasant Consciousness in Chinandega, Nicaragua, 1912–1979* (1990), *To Die in This Way: Nicaraguan Indians and the Myth of Mestizaje, 1880–1965* (1998), and with Aldo Lauria-Santiago, *To Rise in Darkness: Revolution, Repression, and Memory in El Salvador, 1920–1932* (2008).

Greg Grandin is a professor of history at New York University. He is the author and editor of a number of books, including *The Last Colonial Massacre: Latin America in the Cold War* (2004) and *The Blood of Guatemala: A History of Race and Nation* (2000), which won the Latin American Studies Bryce Wood Award. His most recent book, *Fordlandia: The Rise and Fall of Henry Ford's Forgotten Jungle City* (2009) was a finalist for a National Book Award, National Book Critics Circle Award, and Pulitzer Prize. He is a member of the American Academy of Arts and Sciences.

Lillian Guerra is an associate professor of Caribbean history at the University of Florida, Gainesville. She is the author of two books, *Popular Expression and National Identity in Puerto Rico* (1998) and *The Myth of José Martí: Conflicting Nationalisms in Early Twentieth-Century Cuba* (2005).

Forrest Hylton is an associate professor of history at the Universidad de los Andes (Bogotá), and is the author of *Evil Hour in Colombia* (2006), and with Sinclair Thomson, *Revolutionary Horizons: Past and Present in Bolivian Politics* (2007).

Gilbert M. Joseph is the Farnam Professor of History and International Studies at Yale University. His most recent book is *In from the Cold: Latin America's New Encounter with the Cold War*, coedited with Daniela Spenser (2008). He is currently completing a popular history of the Mexican revolution and its legacy (with Jurgen Buchenau), and working on a project that examines transnational lives, politics, and cultural encounters in the twentieth century.

Friedrich Katz is the Morton D. Hull Distinguished Service Professor Emeritus of Latin American History at the University of Chicago and the author and editor of a number of books, including *The Secret War in Mexico: Europe, the United States, and the Mexican Revolution* (1981), *The Life and Times of Pancho Villa* (1998), and *Hitler sobre América Latina: el fascismo alemán en Latinoamérica, 1933–1943* (1968).

Thomas Miller Klubock is an associate professor of history at the University of Virginia. He is the author of *Contested Communities: Class, Gender, and Politics in Chile's El Teniente Copper Mine, 1904–1951* (1998). His current research focuses on the history of land, labor, and ecological change in Chile's southern temperate rain forests.

Neil Larsen teaches comparative literature and critical theory at the University of California, Davis. He publishes, in equal measure, on Latin American literature and culture and on Marxian social and cultural theory. His most recent book is *Determinations* (2001).

Arno J. Mayer is emeritus professor of history at Princeton University and the author of numerous books, including *Political Origins of the New Diplomacy, 1917–1918* (1959), *Politics and Diplomacy of Peacemaking: Containment and Counter-Revolution at Versailles, 1918–19* (1968), *Dynamics of Counter-Revolution in Europe, 1870–1956: An Analytical Framework* (1971), *The Persistence of the Old Regime: Europe to the Great War* (1981), *Why Did the Heavens Not Darken? The "Final Solution" in History* (1988), *The Furies: Vio-*

lence and Terror in the French and Russian Revolutions (2000), and *Plowshares into Swords: From Zionism to Israel* (2008). He is currently working on his memoirs.

Carlota McAllister is an assistant professor of anthropology at York University in Toronto, Canada. Her book on Chupol, *The Good Road: Conscience and Consciousness in a Postrevolutionary Village*, will be published by Duke University Press. She is currently conducting research on environmental activism in Chilean Patagonia.

Jocelyn Olcott, an associate professor of history at Duke University, is the author of *Revolutionary Women in Postrevolutionary Mexico* (2005) and coeditor of *Sex in Revolution: Gender, Politics, and Power in Modern Mexico* (2006). She is currently working on two book projects: "The Greatest Consciousness-Raising Event in History: International Women's Year and the Challenge of Transnational Feminism" and "Sing What the People Sing: Concha Michel and the Cultural Politics of Mexican Maternalism."

Gerardo Rénique is an associate professor at the City University of New York and the Latin America editor for *The International Encyclopedia of Revolution and Protest* (2009). He is a contributor to and editor of a special issue of *Socialism and Democracy* titled "Latin America: The New Neoliberalism and Popular Mobilization" (2009) and coproducer (with Tami Gold) of the documentary *Land, Rain and Fire: Report from Oaxaca* (2006).

Corey Robin is an associate professor of political science at Brooklyn College and the City University of New York Graduate Center. A frequent contributor to the *London Review of Books* and *The Nation*, he is the author of *Fear: The History of a Political Idea* (2004). He is currently working on a book about conservatism and counterrevolution.

Peter Winn is a professor of history and international relations at Tufts University. He is the author of *Weavers of Revolution: The Yarur Workers and Chile's Road to Socialism* (1989) and *Americas: The Changing Face of Latin America and the Caribbean* (1992).

Index

Communist Party of Chile, 121, 122–23; in Chile's Revolution of 1970–1973, 242, 244–45, 253; support for Mapuche self-determination by, 146–50; support of activism in Lonquimay by, 128, 136, 143–45, 157n97. *See also* Chilean Revolution

Communist Party of Colombia (PCC), 350

Communist Party of Cuba (PSP), 185, 190n21, 190n23, 209, 220–24

Communist Party of El Salvador (PCS), 19–20, 89, 92–106; central leadership of, 95–98, 117n18; electoral strategies of, 93–94, 101, 107; grassroots movement of, 94–96; registration lists of, 106. *See also* La Matanza of 1932

Communist Party of Mexico (CPM), 62–64; in Comarca Lagunera, 65–66, 67, 77–78; Matamoros massacre, 68–77; memorialization of June 29 by, 77–82, 85n64; women's activism in, 79–81

Communist Party of Peru, 316, 318–19, 323, 325, 334n25. *See also* Sendero Luminoso

Communist Party of the Soviet Union (CPSU), 56

Concha, Malaquias, 125, 141

Condenados de Conado (Fuentes), 209–10

Condorcet, Marie-Jean Caritat, 375

Confederación Campesina del Perú, 318–19

Confederación de Trabajadores de Cuba, 185

Confederación Regional Obrera Mexicana, 56

Conrad, Joseph, 36n28

Consejo de Oficios Varios (Chile), 142

Consejo Nacional de Cultura (Cuba), 223–24

conservatism, 17, 24–26, 371–78. *See also* neoliberalism

Contras (Nicaragua), 28, 90, 114–16, 129n49, 205, 391

Contreras, Manuel, 273n19

Contreras Labarca, Carlos, 144, 157n97

Corporación Democracia (Colombia), 358

Corral, Enrique, 283, 299

Cortez, Álvaro, 104

Cossio, Guillermo Valencia, 363

Cristeros (Mexico), 55

Cuba, 4, 330, 385; anti-imperialist nationalism in, 179–83, 187–88, 201, 206, 219–20; Batista regime in, 163–64, 167–77, 179, 188, 190n23, 193n42; Bay of Pigs invasion in, 203, 207–8; coup of 1952 in, 172, 190n23; insurrection against Machado in, 21, 177–78, 188; opposition movements in, 167, 171–72, 175, 194n44; revolutionaries of 1868 in, 42n82; Shell Petroleum in, 177; Soviet missiles in, 2; Ten Years' War in, 180; U.S. policies toward, 27–28, 201–5, 218, 322; War of Independence of, 173, 187

Cuba: Paradox Found, 201

Cuban American National Foundation, 219

Cuban Revolution, 31, 384, 398, 401, 406–8; Alliance for Progress program, 335n42; Code of Social Defense of, 216; Committees for the Defense of, 217; counterrevolutionary violence in, 168–71, 187–88, 190n21, 190–91nn23–27, 193n39, 193nn41–43; economic reforms of, 188, 198n105; in El Escambray, 23, 205, 207–15; escalation of

Huenchullán, Arturo, 128, 154n23
Huerta, Victoriano, 49–50, 52, 55
Huggins, Martha, 3, 37n36
Hungarian Uprising, 187
Huntington, Samuel, 311
Hylton, Forrest, 30, 403, 407, 409

Ibáñez, Carlos, 130–32, 136–38, 151
Ignatieff, Michael, 9
Ilianova, Olga, 145
industrial *tomas,* 249–50
Insurgent Cuba (Ferrer), 42n82
International Police Academy (U.S.), 406
International Telephone and Telegraph
     Corporation (ITT), 242
Izquierda Unida (Peru), 310–11

James, C. L. R., 15
James, Daniel, 108
Jara, Víctor, 264, 269
Jiménez, José Antonio, 178
Johnson, Lyman, 87n78
Juárez, Benito, 55, 66

Kamenev, Lev Borisovich, 59
Kant, Immanuel, 330–31, 374
Katz, Friedrich, 19, 26
Kellogg, Frank, 54
Kennedy, Edward, 265
Kennedy, John F., 323, 335n42, 377
Kirchner, Néstor, 37n35
Kissinger, Henry, 270–71, 390
Klubock, Thomas, 5, 19–20, 22, 26, 404
Der Kollaps der Modernisierung (Kurz),
     387
Koreman, Megan, 175–76
Krisis (journal), 387
Kurz, Robert, 387–90

labor systems, 408–9; Chile's resident
     estate labor (*inquilinaje*) system, 122,
     127–31, 133; Colombia's organized

labor, 343–44; Peru's *gamonalismo*
     system, 315–16, 318, 319–20
LaFeber, Walter, 12
Lafertte, Elías, 140, 158n102
LaHaye, Beverly, 374
LaHaye, Tim, 374
land ownership and use, 385; in Chile's
     reducción policy, 122, 123–27, 131–45,
     150–51; in Chile's socialist revolution,
     240–41, 246–50; in Chile's squatter
     movements, 132–38, 246–47; in El
     Salvador's coffee industry, 90–92,
     116n1; in Mexican land reforms, 47,
     52, 58, 60, 66–67, 82; municipal ar-
     chives of, 109; in Nicaragua's Sand-
     inista movement, 111–12, 116, 120n49;
     in Peru's peasant land occupations,
     317–19; registration and titles for, 126–
     27, 129–30, 132, 136–37, 149; removal
     of common lands, 5. *See also* labor
     systems
Lara Bonilla, Rodrigo, 349
Larsen, Neil, 409
Laugerud, Kjell, 282
League of Agrarian Communities, 66
Leiva, Sebastián, 145, 158n102
Leiva Tapia, Juan Segundo, 135–38, 140
Lenin, Vladimir, 51, 56
León de la Barra, Francisco, 49
Leo XIII, Pope, 342
Levenson, Deborah, 11
liberation theology: in Guatemala, 283,
     285; of Nicaragua's Sandinistas, 21, 31,
     90, 111; in Peru, 321–22
Lohia, Ram, 419
Lohoff, Ernst, 389–90
Longan, John, 34n12
Lonquimay (Chile). *See* Mapuche rebel-
     lion of 1934
López, Antonio, 365n27

Mexico (*cont.*)
government of, 51–53, 54, 59–60, 64; Porfirian dictatorship in, 48, 49, 66, 403
Mintz, Sidney, 38n41
MIR (Chile). *See* Revolutionary Left Movement
Mojica, Julia, 118n28
Moncada family (Colombia), 354–55
Monroe Doctrine, 60
Montes, César, 280, 299–300
Montoya, Mario, 363
Moraga, Juan de Dios, 141
Morales, Domingo, 286
Morales Bermúdez, Francisco, 324
Morán, Rolando, 280
Morejón Valdés, Pedro, 191n27
Morones, Luis, 56
Morrow, Dwight, 55
Morse, Wayne, 165–66
El Movimiento Contra Bandidos (Cuba), 205, 207–15
Movimiento de Izquierda Revolucinaria (MIR) (Peru), 326
Movimiento de Liberación Nacional (MLN) (Guatemala), 25
Movimiento Revolucionario Tupac Amaru (MRTA) (Peru), 311, 329
Múgica, Francisco, 60
Murillo, Diego Fernando (Don Berna), 354–58, 360–64, 366n26
Mussolini, Benito, 375

National Industrialists' Association (ANDI) (Colombia), 342, 344
Naumov, Oleg, 57
Nazism, 60–61; French collaboration with, 175; scholarship on, 36n26, 382–83, 418–19
Negrete, Manuel, 74, 76

neoliberalism, 30, 311, 314, 409; in Colombia, 360–64; in Peru, 328–29, 331–32; role of old regimes in, 386–87; Washington Consensus on, 30, 338, 398–99, 409–11
Neruda, Pablo, 269
New Empire, The (LaFeber), 12
Nicaragua, 3, 4; Contra counterrevolution in, 28, 90, 111–16, 120n49, 205; cotton economy of, 116; El Porvenir cooperative in, 115–16; labor strikes in, 110; liberation theology in, 21, 31, 90, 111; Mexican support in, 55; OPEN 3 barrio in, 112–13; Sandinista revolution in, 89–90, 111–16, 408, 413n21; Somoza era of, 3, 111–12, 116; U.S. intervention in, 27–28, 114–16, 402, 404–5; Zelaya regime of, 402. *See also* Sandinistas
Nicholas I (czar of Russia), 48
Las Niochas estate (Chile), 135
Nixon, Richard, 270, 372–73
Noguera, Jorge, 363
Noriega, Manuel, 222
Nos impusieron la violencia (Fuentes), 208–10
Nun, José, 12–13, 23–24, 28
Nunca más, 37n35
Núñez, Andrés, 79
Nunn, Frederick, 323

Oakeshott, Michael, 378
Obregón, Álvaro, 51–53, 54, 59–60, 64
Ochoa, Arnaldo, 222–23
Ochoa family (Colombia), 348, 349, 354–55
O'Donnell, Guillermo, 6, 24
Office of the Coordinator for Inter-American Affairs, 405
Oglesby, Elizabeth, 42n80

Stalin, Joseph, 19, 46, 53, 56–59
Steiner, George, 1–2
Stern, Steve, 11, 21
El Sur (newspaper), 144–45

Taussig, Michael, 6, 9, 38n41
Taylor, William, 108
Terrones Benítez, Adalberto, 84n19
Teruggi, Frank, 264
Thompson, E. P., 107
Tigres de Masferrer (Cuba), 190n23
Tilly, Charles, 30
Timmerman, Jacobo, 6
To Lead as Equals (Gould), 110
Toltén estate (Chile), 135, 139, 140–41
tomas de fundos (Chile), 246, 248–50
tomas de sitio (Chile), 246–47
Toqueville, Alexis de, 377
Trade Unionists against Terror
    (Levenson), 11
tribunals of the Cuban Revolution,
    21–22, 163–88; anti-imperialist rheto-
    ric of, 179–83; context of violence of,
    167–71, 187–88, 194n51; exections re-
    sulting from, 165, 176–77, 182–83, 186,
    198n101; goals of, 165–67; legal pro-
    cedures of, 181–83, 184, 196nn81–82,
    197n84; on legitimate versus ille-
    gitimate violence, 171–77; political
    function of, 176–78, 195n68; public
    support for, 166–67, 183–86, 197nn94–
    95; Sosa Blanco trial of, 166–67, 170–71,
    186; U.S. denunciations of, 164, 165–
    66, 172, 176, 179–83, 185, 196nn76–77
Tri-Continental Conference of 1944, 4
Trotsky, Leon, 53, 56, 59
Truman, Harry, 325
Tupac Amaru (MRTA) (Peru), 311, 329
26th of July Movement (M-26). *See*
    M-26

"two demons" narratives, 37n35, 276–78,
    302–4

U.N. Truth Commission on Guatemala,
    10
Unión de Trabajadores Colombianos,
    344
Union of Artists and Writers of Cuba
    (UNEAC) (Cuba), 223–24
Unión Patriótica (UP) (Columbia),
    350–52
United States: anti-communist focus
    of, 25, 325, 406; ascendant hegemony
    of, 29, 400, 402–3; Bucareli Treaty
    with Mexico of, 54; Civil War of, 29;
    Cuban exiles in, 27–28, 165, 189n9,
    200–205, 214, 218–19; Cuban policies
    of, 27–28, 201–5, 322; denunciations
    of Cuban tribunals by, 164, 165–66,
    172, 176, 179–83, 185, 196nn76–77;
    extradition treaties with Colombia
    of, 349–50, 353, 358, 362–63; imperial
    anticolonialism of, 39n50; invasion
    of Iraq by, 387; National Security
    Doctrine of, 270; neoliberal Washing-
    ton Consensus of, 30, 338, 398–99,
    409–11; School of the Americas in,
    325; trade embargo of Cuba, 228
Uribe, Mario, 363
Uribe Sierra, Alberto, 348–49
Uribe Vélez, Álvaro, 30, 339–40, 348–49,
    356, 362–63, 365n27
Urrutia, Manuel, 165
Uruguay, 3, 205; New Left in, 413n21;
    U.S. intervention in, 27, 33n8
U.S. Drug Enforcement Agency, 350,
    353–55, 356
U.S. intervention, 2–5, 18, 26–30, 33n8,
    205, 390–411; Alliance for Progress
    program in, 323, 335n42; in Chile's

Library of Congress Cataloging-in-Publication Data

A century of revolution : insurgent and counter-
insurgent violence during Latin America's long cold
war / Greg Grandin and Gilbert M. Joseph, eds.
p. cm. — (American encounters/global interactions)
Includes bibliographical references and index.
ISBN 978-0-8223-4720-0 (cloth : alk. paper)
ISBN 978-0-8223-4737-8 (pbk. : alk. paper)
1. Revolutions—Latin America—History—20th
century. 2. Political violence—Latin America—
History—20th century. 3. Terrorism—Latin
America—History—20th century. 4. Latin
America—Politics and government—20th century.
I. Grandin, Greg, 1962– II. Joseph, G. M.
(Gilbert Michael), 1947– III. Series: American
encounters/global interactions.
F1414.C425 2010
980.03'3—dc22   2010016648